Women Beware Women

Continuum Renaissance Drama

Series Editors: Andrew Hiscock, Bangor University, UK, and Lisa Hopkins, Sheffield Hallam University, UK

Continuum Renaissance Drama offers practical and accessible introductions to the critical and performative contexts of key Elizabethan and Jacobean plays. Each guide introduces the text's critical and performance history but also provides students with an invaluable insight into the landscape of current scholarly research through a keynote essay on the state of the art and newly commissioned essays of fresh research from different critical perspectives.

Doctor Faustus Edited by Sarah Munson Deats

A Midsummer Night's Dream Edited by Regina Buccola

Volpone Edited by Matthew Steggle

1 Henry IV Edited by Stephen Longstaffe

The Duchess of Malfi Edited by Christina Luckyj

Forthcoming titles:

King Lear Edited by Andrew Hiscock and Lisa Hopkins

The Jew of Malta Edited by Robert A. Logan

WOMEN BEWARE WOMEN

A Critical Guide

Edited by Andrew Hiscock

continuum

Continuum International Publishing Group
The Tower Building   80 Maiden Lane, Suite 704
11 York Road   New York
London SE1 7NX   NY 10038

www.continuumbooks.com

© Andrew Hiscock 2011

All rights reserved. No part of this publication may be reproduced or transmitted in any form or by any means, electronic or mechanical, including photocopying, recording, or any information storage or retrieval system, without prior permission in writing from the publishers.

British Library Cataloguing-in-Publication Data
A catalogue record for this book is available from the British Library.

ISBN: 978-1-8470-6093-8 (Paperback)
      978-1-8470-6092-1 (Hardback)

Library of Congress Cataloguing-in-Publication Data
Women beware women: a critical guide/[edited by] Andrew Hiscock.
   p. cm. – (Continuum Renaissance drama)
   Includes bibliographical references and index.
   ISBN 978-1-84706-093-8 (pbk.) – ISBN 978-1-84706-092-1 (hardback)
   1. Middleton, Thomas, d. 1627. Women beware women. I. Hiscock, Andrew, 1962–

   PR2714.W66W663 2011
   822'.3–dc22

2010029087

Typeset by BookEns, Royston, Herts.

Contents

	Acknowledgements	viii
	Series Introduction	ix
	List of Illustrations	x
	Timeline	xi
	Introduction *Andrew Hiscock*	1
Chapter 1	The Critical Backstory *Robert C. Evans*	18
Chapter 2	Out of the Repertoire: *Women Beware Women* and Performance History *Paul Innes*	43
Chapter 3	In the Repertoire: *Women Beware Women* on Stage *Annaliese Connolly*	59
Chapter 4	The State of the Art *Joost Daalder*	77
Chapter 5	New Directions: *Women Beware Women* and Jacobean Cultural Narratives *Anne McLaren*	99
Chapter 6	New Directions: *Women Beware Women* and the Arts of Looking and Listening *Helen Wilcox*	121
Chapter 7	New Directions: *Women Beware Women* and Genre Theory *Edward Gieskes*	139
Chapter 8	New Directions: 'Two kings on one throne': Lust, Love, and Marriage in *Women Beware Women* *Coppélia Kahn*	156

Chapter 9 Learning and Teaching Resources: Mapping
Texts, Spaces and Bodies 171
Liz Oakley-Brown

Bibliography 189

Notes on Contributors 201

Index 203

For Siân, with love

Acknowledgements

This volume has had a relatively long gestation period, but it has been a pleasure to work with so many dedicated scholars in a sustained manner from whom I have learned so much about Middleton's tragedy and his cultural, theoretical and critical contexts. I would like to take this opportunity to thank all of the contributors for their commitment to and enthusiasm for this volume from the very beginning. Lisa Hopkins, my series co-editor, and the editorial team at Continuum, notably Anna Fleming and Colleen Coalter, have been unfailing in offering advice and support throughout the evolution of this collection. This volume would not have been possible without the sustained and careful attention which Linda Jones, research administrator at Bangor University, devoted to the preparation of the manuscript. She performed an invaluable service and I offer to her and all of my abovementioned colleagues my sincere thanks. This volume has also been enriched by the helpful advice and assistance offered by library staff at Bangor University and the British Library. I would also like to express my appreciation of the enthusiasm for Middleton studies and the History of the Book in general expressed by my colleagues in the School of English at Bangor, especially Tom Corns, Stephen Colclough, Ceri Sullivan and Helen Wilcox. Most of all, my thanks go to my invariably supportive family, Siân, Bronwen and Huw.

Andrew Hiscock
Bangor, July 2010

Series Introduction

The drama of Shakespeare and his contemporaries has remained at the very heart of English curricula internationally and the pedagogic needs surrounding this body of literature have grown increasingly complex as more sophisticated resources become available to scholars, tutors and students. This series aims to offer a clear picture of the critical and performative contexts of a range of chosen texts. In addition, each volume furnishes readers with invaluable insights into the landscape of current scholarly research as well as including new pieces of research by leading critics.

This series is designed to respond to the clearly identified needs of scholars, tutors and students for volumes which will bridge the gap between accounts of previous critical developments and performance history and an acquaintance with new research initiatives related to the chosen plays. Thus, our ambition is to offer innovative and challenging Guides which will provide practical, accessible and thought-provoking analyses of Renaissance drama. Each volume is organized according to a progressive reading strategy involving introductory discussion, critical review and cutting-edge scholarly debate. It has been an enormous pleasure to work with so many dedicated scholars of Renaissance drama and we are sure that this series will encourage to you read 400-year old playtexts with fresh eyes.

Andrew Hiscock and Lisa Hopkins

List of Illustrations

1 *Two new playes [...] written by Thomas Middleton* (1657) [halftitle page]. This image is reproduced by kind permission of the Master and Fellows of Trinity College, Cambridge.   xiv

2 *Two new playes [...] written by Thomas Middleton* (1657) [frontispiece]. This item is reproduced by permission of The Huntington Library, San Marino, California.   15

3 Robert Fludd's depiction of the relationship between man's body and the created world (Tract. I. Sect. I. Lib. V, *Utriusque Cosmi, Maioris scilicet et Minoris, metaphysica, physica, atque technica Historia* (1617–1619), p. 105). This image is reproduced by kind permission of The Bancroft Library.   99

4 'Gedekte tafel' [Laid table] by an unknown artist of the Flemish or Dutch school, c. 1615. This image is reproduced by kind permission of the Museum Boijmans van Beuningen, Rotterdam.   125

5 Pieter de Grebber, 'Musicerend gezelschap' ['Music-making group'], c. 1623. This image is reproduced by kind permission of the Museo de Bellas Artes de Bilbao.   136

Middleton, *Women Beware Women* and its Contexts

Selective Timeline

1580	Middleton born in London
1598	Enters University of Oxford
1601	Reports of connections with London players
1602	Marries Mary Marbeck
c. 1603	*The Phoenix*
c. 1608	*The Roaring Girl*
c. 1611	*A Chaste Maid in Cheapside*
c. 1615	*The Witch, More Dissemblers Besides Women*
1620	Invested as City Chronologer for London
c. 1621?	*Women Beware Women*
1622	*The Changeling*
1624	*A Game at Chess*
1627	Middleton dies
1657	Publication of *Two New Playes. Viz. More Dissemblers besides Women. Viz. Women, beware Women*
1691	Gerard Langbaine, *An Account of the English dramatick poets*
1808	Charles Lamb (ed.), *Specimens of English Dramatic Poets who lived about the Time of Shakespeare. With notes*
1815	Charles Wentworth Dilke (ed.), Old English Plays
1840	Rev. Alexander Dyce (ed.), *The Works of Thomas Middleton*
1885–86	Arthur Henry Bullen (ed.), *The Works of Thomas Middleton*
1886	A. C. Swinburne, 'Thomas Middleton' in *The Nineteenth Century*
1927	T. S. Eliot, 'Thomas Middleton' in *The Times Literary Supplement*
1955	Samuel Schoenbaum, *Middleton's Tragedies: A Critical Study*. First full-length critical study wholly devoted to Middleton
1968	Roma Gill's edition of *Women Beware Women* (Ernest Benn)
1975	J. R. Mulryne's edition of *Women Beware Women* (Methuen)
1980	Margot Heinemann, *Puritanism and Theatre: Thomas Middleton and Opposition Drama under the Early Stuarts*
1994	William C. Carroll's edition of *Women Beware Women* (A. C. Black/ Norton)
1999	Richard Dutton's edited collection, '*Women Beware Women*' and *Other Plays* (Oxford University Press)

2007 *Thomas Middleton: The Collected Works*. General editors: Gary Taylor and John Lavagnino (Oxford: Clarendon Press). *Women Beware Women* edited by John Jowett

TWO NEW PLAYES.

VIZ.
- More DISSEMBLERS besides WOMEN.
- WOMEN beware WOMEN.

WRITTEN
By *Tho. Middleton*, Gent.

London, Printed for *Humphrey Moseley* and are to be sold at his Shop at the Prince's Arms in St. *Pauls* Churchyard. 1657.

1 *Two new playes [...] written by Thomas Middleton* (1657)
This image is reproduced by kind permission of the Master and Fellows of Trinity College, Cambridge

Introduction

Andrew Hiscock

It was inevitable that the eagerly-awaited publication of *Thomas Middleton: The Collected Works* in 2007, by the general editors Gary Taylor and John Lavagnino, would excite even more scholarly interest in the enormous textual output of this major dramatist and contemporary of Shakespeare. And it is, indeed, John Jowett's edition of *Women Beware Women* in that *Collected Works* which is the standard reference text for all of the scholarship collected in this present volume.[1] Discussions of critical and theatrical neglect figure prominently throughout the chapters which follow concerning the reception of Middleton's tragedy in times past. Nonetheless, we should perhaps remain mindful that earlier generations of readers were similarly attracted with renewed vigour to Middleton with the advent of a newly published edition of his works. The Victorian poet Swinburne, for example, hailed the 1885–86 publication of Arthur Henry Bullen's lightly re-edited eight-volume series of *The Works of Thomas Middleton* (the texts being originally edited by the Reverend Alexander Dyce and published in 1840) in the following manner:

> [...] since Charles Lamb threw open its gates to all comers in the ninth year of the nineteenth century, it cannot but seem strange that comparatively so few should have availed themselves of the entry to so rich and royal an estate [of early modern drama]. The subsequent labours of Mr. Dyce have made the rough ways plain and the devious paths straight for all serious and worthy students. And now again Mr. Bullen has taken up a task than which none more arduous and important, none worthier of thanks and praise, can be undertaken by an English scholar.[2]

Charles Lamb's *Specimens of English Dramatic Poets who lived about the Time of Shakespeare. With notes* first appeared in 1808 and was clearly very influential in the relatively brief encounters it offered for its readers to often hitherto unknown or neglected dramatic texts. In the case of *Women Beware Women*, Lamb treated the reader to edited highlights from chosen speeches with 'helpful' signal titles, such as 'Lover's Chidings' and 'Wedlock'. On occasions, he also provided more extended insights into the selected texts leavened with a

2 WOMEN BEWARE WOMEN

judicious comment here and there: he re-presented the celebrated 'chess scene' between Livia and the Widow from Middleton's tragedy, for example, unexpectedly proposing that 'This is one of those scenes which has the air of being an immediate transcript from life. Livia the "good neighbour" is as real a creature as one of Chaucer's characters. She is such another jolly Housewife as the Wife of Bath.'[3]

Furthermore, it is evident that this anthology circulated a little more widely among intellectual society of the early nineteenth society than Swinburne suspected. Wordsworth appears to have begun reading the *Specimens* in the first year of publication and Keats also owned his own copy. In his 'Lectures on the Dramatic Literature of the Age of Elizabeth' (1817), William Hazlitt praised 'the flowing vein of Middleton'. He devoted himself most particularly to a sustained comparison between *Macbeth* and Middleton's *The Witch* (1616), adding, 'I will conclude this account with Mr. Lamb's observations on the distinctive characters of these extraordinary and formidable personages.'[4] Mary Shelley also seems to have relied on Lamb's collection for an epigraph which was selected from Middleton's *No Wit, No Help like a Woman's* (1611) for her novel *Lodore* (1835).[5] Indeed, if T. S. Eliot is to be believed, this collection went on to shape reading habits for well over a century:

> The accepted attitude toward Elizabethan drama was established on the publication of Charles Lamb's *Specimens*. By publishing these selections, Lamb set in motion the enthusiasm for poetic drama which still persists, and at the same time encouraged the formation of a distinction which is, I believe, the ruin of modern drama – the distinction between drama and literature. For the *Specimens* made it possible to read the plays as poetry while neglecting their function on the stage. It is for this reason that all modern opinion of the Elizabethans seems to spring from Lamb [...][6]

As Swinburne points out, Lamb's *Specimens* was succeeded notably in 1840 by the Reverend Alexander Dyce's *Works of Thomas Middleton. Now first collected with some account of the Author and Notes [...] in five volumes*, and then by the eight volumes of Arthur Henry Bullen's *The Works of Thomas Middleton* (1885–86).[7] It is, however, becoming apparent from the increasingly documented reading practices of those who have turned to the dramas of Middleton (and other early modern playwrights) across the centuries that patterns of textual appetite and response do recur. An abiding interest among critics and editors alike in the sometimes shadowy writer behind these plays has remained unabated. We are frequently invited to ponder the cultural conditions which may have fostered the critical and performative neglect of his dramatic writing. There is also much concern with theatrical questions of discontinuity, propriety and authorial collaboration. And, of course, where access has been made possible through print to (at least a selection of) Middleton's drama, attention is returned to the challenges of an early modern dramatist whose output is of such a prolific and generically diverse nature that it is rivalled only by Shakespeare himself in the period.

In addition, there are particular scholarly anxieties with respect to *Women Beware Women* itself. Although the tragedy is thought to have been written and

INTRODUCTION 3

performed around 1621, it was not published until 1657 (over a quarter of a century after the dramatist's death) in *TWO NEW PLAYES. VIZ.* More DISSEMBLERS besides WOMEN. *VIZ.* WOMEN beware WOMEN. WRITTEN By *Tho. Middleton,* Gent.⁸ Thus, the asynchronicity in the theatrical and material production, circulation and consumption of this tragedy (as we move from the late Jacobean period to that of the final months of Cromwell's life in the Interregnum) presents a thorny subject for critical enquiry and speculation. Nonetheless, while Middleton's dramatic output was still being accounted for in early modern print culture, the prefatory text ('To the Reader') in this 1657 publication affirmed that the cultural capital of the writer's name still had considerable currency. Indeed, the printer submitted that he

> was not a little confident but that [Middleton's] name would prove as great an Inducement for thee to Read, as me to Print them: Since those Issues of his Brain that have already seen the Sun, have by their worth gained themselves a free entertainment among all that are ingenious: And I am most certain, that these will no way lessen his Reputation, nor hinder his Admission to any Noble and Recreative Spirits.⁹

Considerable scholarly energies have been devoted in the last fifty years to dispelling the belief that early modern dramatists must remain mysterious figures who left no traces behind them for succeeding generations. T. S. Eliot, for example, recommended that we approach this enigmatic playwright by way of the *via negativa*: 'It is difficult to imagine his "personality" [...] Middleton, who collaborated shamelessly, who is hardly separated from Rowley [...] He remains merely a name, a voice [...] He has no real message; he is merely a great recorder.'¹⁰ However, in the post-war period, there emerged a widespread critical commitment to recuperate early modern dramatists from these shadows. With reference to Middleton, Mark Eccles argued categorically in 1957 that 'A great many documents concerning Middleton have come to light at the Public Record Office and at the Guildhall of London. They tell little about his plays, but much about his life and family.'¹¹ More recently, if Gary Taylor's discussion 'Thomas Middleton: Lives and Afterlives'¹² has certainly been warmly welcomed for uncovering a more tangible figure than had hitherto been encountered in earlier generations of criticism, we are reminded even here at several reprises of what we *do not possess* in the surviving documents concerning the life of *a great recorder*. Most notably, as Taylor highlights, unlike contemporaries such as Sidney, Jonson, Shakespeare, Donne, Bacon, Beaumont and Fletcher, the freelancing Middleton left no one fund of his work to be tapped easily by later communities of printers and readers. As a result, we may often find ourselves locked in a game of hints and guesses in order to ascertain the nature of the cultural status attributed to Thomas Middleton in Jacobean society, and what was the depth of the acquaintance with his dramas among London theatre-going society and beyond in his own lifetime.

Eliot had assured his inter-war readership that Middleton 'was not very highly thought of in his own time',¹³ and it is certainly true that in the account of Ben Jonson's conversations north of the border with the Scottish poet William Drummond of Hawthornden (related by the latter) that Middleton was *just* worthy of reference in the Londoner's considered judgements upon the contemporary (Jacobean) poetic scene. Indeed, on this occasion, Jonson seems to have been noticeably sparing in his praise: '[Gervase] Markham [...] was not of the / number of the Faithfull .j. [i.e.] Poets and but a base fellow / that such were Day and Midleton.'[14] Moreover, in Jonson's play, *The Staple of News* (1626), Middleton's polemical anti-Spanish drama *A Game at Chess* is dismissed as 'the poore *English-play*'.[15] Later readers may savour the irony that in 'the Water Poet', John Taylor's *The Praise of Hempseed* (1620), Drummond's guest finds himself rubbing shoulders with a throng of distinguished Jacobean poets rather more snugly than he would have wished:

> And many there are liuing at this day,
> Which doe in *paper* their true worth display:
> As *Dauis*, *Drayton*, and the learned *Dun*,
> *Ionson*, and *Chapman*, *Marston*, *Middleton*,
> With *Rowlye*, *Fletcher*, *Withers*, and *Massinger*,
> *Heywood*, and all the rest where e're they are,
> Must say their lines, but for the paper sheet,
> Had scarcely ground whereon to set their feet.[16]

Elsewhere, the poet-playwright William Heminges, the son of Shakespeare's fellow actor John Heminges, is credited with one of the first contemporary tributes to the dramatist in a 1632 poem in which he celebrates the textual pyrotechnics of 'squoblinge Middleton';[17] and another early modern dramatist, Thomas Heywood, informs us that the author of *Women Beware Women* liked to be known just as 'Tom'.[18] More generally, of course, much knowledge of his work could indeed have been hampered by the facts that: not all of the published plays in which he had a hand bore an attribution to him (even in his own lifetime); some of his works may have been difficult to obtain in print; and some plays clearly never made it into print at all, and are lost as a consequence.[19]

When *Women Beware Women* was first published in 1657 it was accompanied with a commendatory sonnet ('UPON The Tragedy of My Familiar Acquaintance, THO. MIDDLETON') penned by Nathanael Richards, himself a poet and playwright. Here, 'this worthy *Tragedy*' is celebrated as one of the productions from 'among the best / Of *Poets* in his time'. This naturally builds upon the claims made by the printer in the prefatory address cited above. Much more tantalizing for those pondering the question of the tragedy's stage history, Richards contends that 'I that have seen't, can say, having just cause, / Never came *Tragedy* off with more applause.'[20] Unfortunately, more revealing records of ovations from theatre audiences in this period have yet to be uncovered, if they have survived at all. During the Restoration, the eminent figure of John Dryden regularly drew attention in his prefaces and critical essays to the theatrical legacies of Shakespeare, Jonson, Beaumont and Fletcher, but there are slim pickings more generally in the period when it comes to Middleton. Nonetheless, it is apparent that print copies of *Women Beware Women* were circulating for purchase, if an interested reader were so inclined. At the close of *Nicomede a tragi-comedy translated out of the French of Monsieur Corneille by John Dancer as it was acted at the Theatre-Royal, Dublin; together with an exact*

INTRODUCTION 5

catalogue of all the English stage plays printed till this present year 1671, 'Tho. Midleton Women Beware Women' is numbered among the entries for 'A True, perfect, and exact Catalogue of all the Comedies, Tragedies, Tragi-Comedies, Pastorals, Masques and Interludes, that were ever yet Printed and Published [...] all which you may either buy or sell, at the Shop of Francis Kirkman, in Thames-street, over-against the Custom House, London' – and the title reappears in a similar manner in *An exact catalogue of all the comedies, tragedies, tragi-comedies, opera's [sic], masks, pastorals and interludes that were ever yet printed and published till this present year 1680*.[21] Milton's nephew, Edward Phillips, was rather more reticent in his account of Middleton in his *Theatrum Poetarum* (1675) than he had been for Marlowe or Shakespeare, but nevertheless signalled for his readers, '*a copious Writer for the English Stage, Contemporary with* Johnson *and* Fletcher, *though not of equal repute, and yet on the other side not altogether contemptible, especially in many of his Plays*'.[22] Some ten years later, William Winstanley's *The lives of the most famous English poets, or, The honour of Parnassus in a brief essay of the works and writings of above two hundred of them, from the time of K. William the Conqueror to the reign of His present Majesty, King James II* (1687) rehearsed almost exactly the same formulas with reference to Middleton; however, unlike Phillips, Winstanley did cite *Women Beware Women* as being among the dramatist's most notable productions.

The recurring fascination in seventeenth-century critical discussions with the application of rankings to Shakespeare and his contemporaries was to establish a model which remained in place for centuries to come. In the closing years of the century, Gerard Langbaine's *An account of the English dramatick poets, or, Some observations and remarks on the lives and writings of all those that have publish'd either comedies, tragedies, tragi-comedies, pastorals, masques, interludes, farces or opera's in the English tongue* (1691) again drew upon Heminges's poetic narrative and invited readers to compare 'The squibbing Middleton' against 'Heywood Sage'. Yet in a subsequent discussion devoted wholly to Middleton, the prolific dramatist was hailed as

> an Author of good Esteem [...] He was Contemporary with those Famous Poets *Johnson*, *Fletcher*, *Massinger* and *Rowley*, in whose Friendship he had a large Share; and tho' he came short of the two former in parts, yet like the *Ivy* by the Assistance of the *Oak*, (being joyn'd with them in several Plays) he clim'd up to some considerable height of Reputation. He joyn'd with *Fletcher* and *Johnson*, in a Play called *The Widow* [...] in the Account of *Johnson*; and certainly most Men will allow, That he that was thought fit to be receiv'd into a *Triumvirate*, by two such Great Men, was no common Poet.[23]

In Robert Shiells's *The lives of the poets of Great Britain and Ireland, to the time of Dean Swift. Compiled from ample materials scattered in a variety of books* (1753) these claims are once again rehearsed, but in a foreshortened format; yet Sheills does submit for the reader's edification that 'We have not been able to find any particulars of this man's life, further than his friendship and connection already mentioned, owing to his obscurity, as he was never considered as a genius, concerning which the world thought themselves interested to preserve any particulars.'[24] Robert Dodsley's twelve volume *A Select Collection of Old Plays* (1744) did not offer *Women Beware Women* up for scrutiny, but in the later 1780 reprinting with critical notes, readers were informed solemnly that 'Thomas Middleton [...] Though an Author of considerable reputation, the memory of him is almost lost. No contemporary writer hath transmitted any circumstances concerning him.'[25]

As has been indicated above, Lamb's *Specimens of English Dramatic Poets* (1st pub. 1808) excited a sustained interest in a wide variety of dramatic texts from the early modern period (even if they only appeared in excerpted form). Interestingly, Lamb chose to establish his own parenthetical liaison in the collection between Rowley's *A New Wonder: A Woman Neer Vext* and Middleton's *Women Beware Women* with the following interjection:

> The old play-writers are distinguished by an honest boldness of exhibition, they shew every thing without being ashamed. If a reverse in fortune be the thing to be personified, they fairly bring us to the prison-gate and the alms-basket. A poor man on our stage is always a gentleman, he may be known by a peculiar neatness of apparel, and by wearing black. Our delicacy, in fact, forbids the dramatizing of Distress at all. It is never shewn in its essential properties; it appears but as the adjunct to some virtue, as something which is to be relieved, from the approbation of which relief the spectators are to derive a certain soothing of self-referred satisfaction. We turn away from the real essences of things to hunt after their relative shadows, moral duties: whereas, if the truth of things were fairly represented, the relative duties might be safely trusted to themselves, and moral philosophy lose the name of a science.[26]

Such pressing concerns with the possible moral (and generic) 'proprieties' or otherwise of the dramaturgy of Middleton and his contemporaries have often remained uppermost in critics' minds when they have responded to a play such as *Women Beware Women*. In this instance, Lamb is deftly inviting his readers to ponder the nature of their own appetites for dramatic narrative and, indeed, the wider pressures of received thinking at work in their society. Whatever T. S. Eliot's reservations in the next century (cited above) regarding the legacy of Lamb's collection in shaping critical responses for generations to come, the 1808 publication clearly did spur some readers on to seek a more satisfying acquaintance with the complete playtexts from which Lamb had lifted excerpts. Certainly, Charles Wentworth Dilke was a great admirer of Lamb's collection, and indeed was prompted to publish his own six-volume collection *Old English Plays* (1815), with a full text of *Women Beware Women* appearing in volume five. In general, the plays anthologized in this collection were accompanied with very few annotations, but a perplexed Dilke did note after the violation of Bianca in Act 2, that '[although] the resistance of [Bianca] seems to have been sincere, it cannot but seem strange that her opposition should not be such as to alarm her mother-in-law; but our poet, like many of his contemporaries, has crowded too many material incidents into his piece to render all of them probable and consistent.'[27] It is at such points that the sometimes contrary motions of the reading and theatrical experience are perhaps most clearly highlighted – an analogue which springs to mind is that of attempting to describe the complexity of Velásquez's haunting painting *Las Meninas* (1656), and being endlessly visually stimulated by the *mise-en-abîme* of surveillance as you stand before the canvas itself. Whereas Dilke struggled to remember in his mind's eye all the various narratives being played out simultaneously during the game of chess, such stresses are mostly foreign to audiences in the theatre: indeed, we are invariably (and richly) exercised by the fine texture of visual and aural spectacle of such scenes on stage.

While Dilke's contemporary, William Hazlitt, seems to have deeply admired the 'chess scene', he also expressed anxieties in his account of *Women Beware Women*, most particularly with reference to the apparent lack of a controlling authorial presence:

> Middleton's style was not marked by any peculiar quality of his own, but was made up, in equal proportions, of the faults and excellences common to his contemporaries. In his *Women Beware Women*, there is a rich marrowy vein of internal sentiment, with fine occasional insight into human nature, and cool cutting irony of expression. He is lamentably deficient in the plot and denouement of the story. It is like the rough draught of a tragedy, with a number of fine things thrown in, and the best made use of the first; but it tends to no fixed goal, and the interest decreases, instead of increasing, as we read on, for want of previous arrangement and an eye to the whole [...] The author's power is *in* the subject, not over it; or he is in possession of excellent materials, which he husbands very ill. This character, though it applies more particularly to Middleton, might be applied generally to the age. Shakespear alone seemed to stand over his work, and to do what he pleased with it [...] The characters of Livia, of Bianca, of Leantio and his Mother, in the play of which I am speaking, are all admirably drawn. [And the chess scene] is a master-piece of dramatic skill.28

In direct comparison with so many critical discussions of Middleton down the centuries, Hazlitt signals here his frustration at his inability to secure a clear textual identity for this eminent dramatist in stylistic, narrative, or any other terms. Hazlitt recognizes the substantial nature of the dramatist's achievement (even if it was not, he felt, always fully realized in artistic terms), but clearly shares Dilke's discomfort at the multifariousness of the tragedy's intrigue. Nonetheless, whatever the persisting nature of the structural and moral concerns highlighted by readers and critics of his plays, it soon became clear that Middleton's dramatic craft and poetic achievement could no longer pass unremarked. When Coleridge prepared for his 1818 'Lectures on European Literature', he had some clear (if rather brief) notes on the most important points to be addressed about the age of Elizabeth I's successor: '1603 – King Solomon Stuart – & the Parliament in compliment repealed Elizabeth in order to enact a more merciless one –. The consequences as might be expected – *Honor to Shakespear* – Middleton/Ben Jonson, flattered.'29

In the following decade Sir Walter Scott found himself at a loose end at home in Abbotsford, and resolved to pick his way through some 'old' playtexts which included Middleton's *Michaelmas Term* (1607) – as we discover from his journal entry for 1 August 1826:

> Yesterday evening did nothing for the idlesse of the morning. I was hungry, ate and drank and became drowsy. Then I took to arranging the old plays of which Terry had brought me about a dozen and dipping into them scrambled through two – One calld *Michaelmas Term* full of traits of manners and another a sort of bouncing tragedy called *The Hector of Germany or The Palsgrave*. [by Wentworth Smith (1615)]. The last, worthless in the extreme, is like many of the plays in the beginning of the 17th Century written to a good tune. The dramatic poets of that time seem to have possessed as joint stock a highly poetical and abstract tone of language so that the worst of them often remind you of the very best. The audience must have had a much stronger sense of poetry in those days than now since language was received and applauded at the Fortune or the Red Bull which could not now be understood by any general audience in Great Britain. This leads far.[30]

How far it did lead becomes evident when we consider the proliferation in the nineteenth century of newly edited collections of a wide range of early modern writers. In terms of Middleton studies, the importance of Dyce's publication in 1840 of *The Works of Thomas Middleton* has already been indicated. Interestingly, in his prefatory discussion, Dyce clearly acknowledged that the reading habits of the general public would have been shaped by the format adopted by Lamb's *Specimens* and similar collections: 'All the surviving works of Middleton are comprehended in the present volumes; and though, perhaps, to a certain class of readers, a selection from his writings might have been more acceptable, I am confident that the entire series is requisite to satisfy the lovers of our early literature.'[31] This discussion is also notable for the ways in which it addresses many, if not all, of the *leitmotiven* which characterize critical engagements in any period with Middleton's writing. How were discomforted readers to decipher the moral undertaking and structural complexity of his dramatic art? By way of response, Dyce submitted reassuringly that *Women Beware Women* was 'indeed remarkable for the masterly conception and delineation of the chief characters, and for the life and reality infused into many of the scenes; though the dramatis personae are almost all repulsive from their extreme depravity, and the catastrophe is rather forced and unnatural'.[32] Now that those troublesome hurdles had been negotiated, we could return to the rankings. At no point was anyone to lose sight of the fact that this contemporary of Shakespeare was worthy of serious consideration: 'The dramatists with whom, in my opinion, Middleton ought properly to be classed – though superior to him in some respects and inferior in others – are Dekker, Heywood, Marston, and Chapman: nor perhaps does William Rowley fall so much below them that he should be excluded from the list.'[33]

Swinburne's willingness to submit Shakespeare and his competitors and collaborators to much more nuanced and sustained scrutiny clearly placed him in the vanguard of a new mode of critical response to early modern literature which emerged in the later decades of the nineteenth century; and his vigorous response to Bullen's edition in a review article for the periodical *The Nineteenth Century* remained his most substantial contribution to a re-evaluation of Middleton's drama.[34] Unsurprisingly, given his own poetic vocation, Swinburne returned attention to the rich variety and arresting innovations of Middleton's dramatic language. He found *Women Beware Women* 'full to overflowing of noble eloquence, of inventive resource and suggestive effect, of rhetorical affluence and theatrical ability', and thus rediscovered for the late nineteenth century a *squoblinge Middleton* who had first been identified in the 1630s. Nevertheless, for all the incisiveness of his studies of Middleton and his contemporaries, there were clear continuities in evidence between Swinburne's critical emphases and those which had been published in earlier decades. In Swinburne's opinion, Middleton had surely erred in expending his energies on such a convoluted intrigue, and in thus turning away from 'the admirable subject of his main action': if only he had concentrated squarely upon the plight of Bianca, we are assured, 'he might have given us a simple and unimpeachable masterpiece'.[35] One wonders what shape such a masterpiece might have taken: would this tragic narrative of a fallen woman respond more closely to the needs of a society which had already encountered the challenges of Elizabeth Gaskell's *Ruth* (1853), George Eliot's *Adam Bede* (1859), or (perhaps, more strikingly, for Swinburne) the plaintive depictions of the adulteress Guinevere in scenes from the pre-Raphaelites?

Moreover, it appears that Middleton's failure to equip the reader with a secure moral compass remained a source of grave misgiving: 'It is true that the irredeemable infamy of the leading characters degrades and deforms the nature of the interest excited: the good and gentle old mother drops out of the list of actors just when some redeeming figure is most needed to assuage the dreariness of disgust with which we follow the fortunes of so meanly criminal a crew' – in such a chaotic environment, we are thus left to look to our own moral well-being in the company of 'so subordinate and inactive a character as the Cardinal'![36] In Swinburne's account there is a familiar eulogy of the dramatic craft of the 'chess scene', but here (once again) we are asked to bear witness to the legacy of the *Specimens of English Dramatic Poets* and to renew our acquaintance with the Wife of Bath, as Lamb had directed: 'the high comedy of the scene between Livia and the Widow is as fine as the best work in that kind left us by the best poets and humourists of the Shakespearean age; it is not indeed unworthy of the comparison with Chaucer's which it suggested to the all but impeccable judgement of Charles Lamb'.[37] However, Swinburne remained implacable regarding the gross improprieties of 'the upshot of the play' ('the dragnet of murder') and, most importantly, of the 'underplot' centring upon Isabella: 'The lower comedy of the play is identical in motive with that which defaces the master-work of Ford: more stupid and offensive it hardly could be.'[38]

Exactly contemporary with Swinburne's animadversions on Middleton's drama was the publication of George Saintsbury's *A History of Elizabethan Literature* (1887). Before anything of substance could be communicated on the Jacobean's writing career, it appeared once again that we would have to address ourselves to the league table: 'It has not been usual to put Thomas Middleton in the front rank among the dramatists immediately second to Shakespere; but I have myself no hesitation in doing so.'[39] If this particular record had now been set to rights, Saintsbury (like Swinburne) could not find it in himself to equivocate about what he identified as evidence of ethical failure widely apparent across the length and the breadth of the collected works: 'in striking contrast to Shakespere and to others, Middleton has no kind of poetical morality in the sense in which the term poetical justice is better known [...] he is, in short, though never brutal, like the post-Restoration school, never very delicate'.[40] Here, and throughout his discussions of early modern dramatic literature, Saintsbury duly surveyed the size and the shape of the achievements of the chosen playwright against those of the Bard in order to establish the degree to which the former was to be found wanting. Conversely, as might be witnessed in his account of *Women Beware Women*, when praise was to be dished out, it was Shakespearean praise: we are thus assured that this tragedy 'is one of Middleton's finest works, inferior only to *The Changeling* in parts, and far superior to it as a whole [...] [Here,] Middleton's Shakesperian verisimilitude and certainty of touch appears.'[41]

In many ways, T. S. Eliot's essay 'Thomas Middleton', published in 1927 in the *Times Literary Supplement* and reprinted in his collection *Elizabethan Essays* (1934), has come to be viewed as a watershed moment in the history of critical engagement with Middleton's drama, and the modern period of scholarship devoted to the Jacobean playwright can be seen to have its roots in the critical discussions unfolding in these inter-war years. However, we should not be overhasty in seeking to establish too many discontinuities in the critical discourse adopted in the second quarter of the twentieth century with that which had preceded it. Like so many of his predecessors, Eliot often urged readers to approve here, disapprove there and to keep in reserve some misgivings – and then there were those rankings... If, as we witnessed at the beginning of this introductory discussion, Eliot remained convinced that Middleton was 'not very highly thought of in his own time', it had nevertheless to be acknowledged that 'He was one of the most voluminous, and one of the best, dramatic writers of his time.'[42] Chiming in again with the sentiments of earlier generations, Eliot found the figure of the dramatist always eluded his grasp – and, equally interestingly, for the modernist poet and dramatist this realization was articulated in terms of aesthetic discomfort, rather than tantalising enquiry: 'He has no point of view, is neither sentimental nor cynical; he is neither resigned, nor disillusioned, nor romantic; he has no message. He is merely the name which associates six or seven great plays.'[43]

More generally, *The Changeling* constituted Middleton's crowning achievement in tragedy for Eliot – even if *Women Beware Women* was 'less disfigured by ribaldry or clowning, [it remained] more tedious'. The reasons for this state of affairs would seem to lie in the play's sustained investment in the 'conventional moralizing of the epoch; so that, if we are impatient, we decide that he gives merely a document of Elizabethan humbug – and then suddenly a personage will blaze out in genuine fire of vituperation'.[44] Eliot's ongoing critical interests in, what he perceived as, tragedy's generic dependency upon dramatic modes familiarly associated with melodrama clearly informed his insights into

Middleton in this essay; and he marvels that a dramatist who offers up 'what appears on the surface a conventional picture-palace Italian melodrama of the time', is nevertheless able to strike gold by unexpectedly accessing 'permanent human feelings'. Indeed, this particular Jacobean strikes gold again and again: 'Middleton understood women in tragedy better than any of the Elizabethans – better than the creator of the Duchess of Malfy, better than Marlowe, better than Tourneur, or Shirley, or Fletcher, better than any of them except Shakespeare alone'.[45]

The critical environment surrounding *Women Beware Women* in the modern period is mapped out and developed further in innovative ways in the chapters which follow. Robert C. Evans's discussion of the reception of Middleton's tragedy is understandably focused predominantly upon the modern period when *Women Beware Women* has enjoyed the most sustained and detailed attention from critics and theatre companies. Evans invites us to reflect upon the ways in which twentieth-century scholarship in particular engaged with critical discourses of character, dramatic structure, recurring motifs of figurative language, and generic hybridity – and in more recent decades there has clearly emerged a lively interest in the possible sources, the gender politics, and the oblique moralism of Middleton's tragedy. As this chapter unfolds, it becomes increasingly evident that the successive currents of Middleton scholarship have in many ways shadowed the steps taken by Shakespearean critics in the same period.

In the next two chapters, sustained attention is devoted to the challenges which performance and performance history pose for those studying the tragedy. Paul Innes obliges us to ponder anew the enduring narratives of critical neglect and to re-encounter *Women Beware Women* through the lens of Robert Weimann's critical theorizings on Shakespearean stagecraft. Concentrating especially upon questions of textual, dramatic and audience authority, Innes focuses upon the discrepancy between theatrical and textual consumption of this play. In its sensitive exploration of the violent sexual politics in *Women Beware Women*, this provocative and ambitious discussion points up the enormous diversity of possible audience experiences of this text as well as detailing the manner in which theatre companies have chosen to realize the tragedy on stage. In the next, equally wide-ranging chapter by Annaliese Connolly, we are asked to attend to the challenges which Middleton's tragedy has posed for acting companies on both sides of the Atlantic since the 1960s, when it entered the repertoire. Connolly demonstrates not only the ways in which successive productions have sought to negotiate Jacobean theatre conventions in their stagings for modern audiences, she also persuasively highlights how the play has been seen to engage with the *zeitgeist* of recent decades. Indeed, it seems that audiences and critics alike have turned repeatedly to *Women Beware Women* in order to explicate the brutalizing conditions of life in late capitalist society. In his discussion of 'The State of the Art', Joost Daalder completes the consideration of the tragedy's reception by focusing squarely upon the rapidly expanding landscapes of contemporary Middleton scholarship. He explores the editorial and narrative practices which have been performed latterly upon *Women Beware Women*, paying particular attention to the ever-increasing critical appreciations of Middleton's sophisticated dramatic language. Reviewing the critically changeful responses to the figure and status of Middleton himself, Daalder goes on to stress the ways in which recent studies have shown themselves determined to identify the dramatist as *a great recorder* of early modern appetites – political, theological and erotic. He concludes by urging us to reflect upon the pressing question of Middleton's 'relevance' – has he simply become a convenient glass with which to reflect the flaws of a broken society, or does this great contemporary of Shakespeare demand a more ambitious response from audiences in the twenty-first century?

As will soon become apparent, Daalder's discussion is intimately linked to the subsequent *New Directions* section which maps out, with four new critical discussions, a wide range of innovative and thought-provoking fields of enquiry. In '*Women Beware Women* and Jacobean Cultural Narratives', Anne McLaren (like Paul Innes) urges us to consider the ways in which Middleton's tragedy interrogates a whole host of expectations surrounding cultural and textual authority. However, whereas Innes unveils possibilities of agency in dramatic production, McLaren highlights how *Women Beware Women* may be seen to engage directly with the vicissitudes of Jacobean political life. Drawing widely upon examples from early modern print culture, she dissects the thoroughgoing interrogation of received thinking on cultural order (in terms of kingship, imbalanced gender relations, religious confession, moral hierarchy, and political/ erotic subjectivity) which was being undertaken in Early Stuart England. Indeed, as this discussion progresses, it becomes all too persuasive that the spectacular reversals experienced in the course of Middleton's dramatic narrative link closely with the cultural stresses and strains of the crisis-ridden years which brought James VI/I's reign to a close. Gary Taylor has been highly successful in convincing twenty-first century readers that 'The artists of Middleton's own time provide [...] parallels for his life and work', most notably Frans Hals and Caravaggio.[46] And in '*Women Beware Women* and the Arts of Looking and Listening' Helen Wilcox develops this enquiry more comprehensively by attending in detail to this 'deeply sensual play'. Introducing us to a dramatic world in which sight and taste and smell excite and disorient one character after the next, she then concentrates upon the even more dynamic drama of seeing and hearing in which Middleton's audiences are also compelled to participate. In this decadent Italianate society racked by political and erotic misgovernment, characters like Leantio, Livia and the Duke seek to regain control of their volatile environment with the resources of violence and subterfuge, and thus come to resemble increasingly the arresting images from seventeenth-century visual culture familiar at that time in collections assembled by royal, patrician and religious patrons throughout Europe. Equally interestingly, in the final phase of her discussion, Wilcox encourages us to attend to the vibrant and unexpectedly diverse aural culture of Middleton's dramatic world – a world in which 'music bids the soul of man to a feast'.

In '*Women Beware Women* and Genre Theory', Ed Gieskes locates the Jacobean tragedy in a theoretical debate dating back to antiquity and which meditated the nature of creativity, textual consumption and literary taxonomies. This was a debate which exercised the *literati* of early modern Europe as much as it has generations of critics in more recent decades. In this discussion, Middleton is seen to exploit the possibilities of generic *brassage* with a vigour equal to that of any of his fellow dramatists in Jacobean England. Unpicking critical judgements made by the likes of Sidney, Lyly and Jonson and allowing them to compete for our attention with the submissions of eminent literary and cultural theorists (such as Rosalie Colie, Fredric Jameson, Mikhail Bakhtin, and Pierre Bourdieu), Gieskes carefully organizes a stimulating enquiry not only into the generic undertakings of *Women Beware Women*, but also more generally into the creative ways in which we may engage with 'the historical resources of kind'. In the final contribution to this section, ' "Two kings on one throne": Lust, Love, and Marriage in *Women Beware Women*', Coppélia Kahn explores Middleton's tragedy in terms of early modern cultural understandings of marriage and, indeed, of the ramifications surrounding the dissolution of wedlock. Performing a close reading of the intrigue's changeful accounts of coupledom, Kahn demonstrates the ways in which Middleton forces us to reflect upon the political and erotic collapse of husbandry in this dramatized society, and how this in turn leads to a spectacular re-evaluation of female agency and a sequence of 'compromised' unions. Drawing attention to a whole host of early modern theorists of marriage, this discussion progressively unmasks the complex gendering of power politics in *Women Beware Women*. Moreover, Kahn also discloses how the tragedy compels audiences to acknowledge that those seeking transformation in a highly disciplinary culture often take recourse to a stunted vocabulary of sexual and political violence.

In the final section of this volume, Liz Oakley-Brown explores the creative ways in which *Women Beware Women* may be studied in the university classroom and offers in her select bibliography an insight into the enormously diverse and vibrant scholarship which is now being devoted to the hitherto neglected tragedy. Returning attention initially to the seventeenth-century sites of the play's production on stage and in print, Oakley-Brown then reflects upon the ways in which the analysis of early modern documents and ongoing critical debates may enrich student engagements with the text.

The present introductory discussion began with a notably enthusiastic response to Middleton's works – that of Swinburne to the 1885–86 edition by Bullen. And, in turn, it is thus perhaps fitting to return to the reception of that particular publication by way of conclusion. Whereas Swinburne greeted this new multi-volume series with considerable pleasure, on examining the wider responses in the 1880s to this publication it quickly becomes evident that the reception was not universally that of unalloyed joy. The anonymous reviewer for *The Pall Mall Gazette* in June 1885 swiftly identified the *magnum opus* as 'a piece of hasty work', and confessed to the readership that 'There really was really very little to say about Middleton, and Mr. Bullen should have resisted the temptation of saying it in ninety-three pages.' It was then time to refer back once again to the league table:

> Fletcher, Webster and Ford are followers of Shakespeare, who from every conceivable point of view deserve the title of great dramatists better than Middleton. Massinger, if a worse poet, is obviously a better dramatist, Dekker, by his superior humanity and his priority in the same field of humour, is no less certainly before him. It is not until honourable places

2 *Two new playes* [...] written by Thomas Middleton (1657) [frontispiece]
This item is reproduced by permission of *The Huntington Library, San Marino, California*

for these five men have been found that Middleton can be admitted to struggle for precedence with Heywood. What does Mr. Bullen think that he gains by these preposterous claims for his favourite?[47]

Having now witnessed order returned to the perverse literary narrative which Bullen was seeking to promote, the *Gazette*'s readership could be soothed by the knowledge that there were nonetheless some treasures to be discovered among the dramatist's work; and the reviewer acknowledged grandiloquently that 'Having protested against these little things, we proceed to thank the editor for these handsome and useful volumes.' Furthermore, one tragedy was reserved for comparatively fulsome praise: 'It is perhaps, in *Women beware Women* that we can be most sure of coming upon Middleton at his best, and Middleton alone.' This Jacobean dramatist, who would be branded by T. S. Eliot as a *shameless collaborator* some 40 years later, appears here in a more seductive light, and we are asked to attend once again to the figure who looks out at us from the engraving in the 1657 publication. Now that Middleton had been ranked, faulted and pondered as a victim of neglect, there was nothing more to be done than to consign this vexing *uomo misterioso* to the shadows whence he had come.

There is a pleasant portrait of him, of which the present editor gives an etching, a grave dark man with melancholy eyes, and a chaplet of laurel in his hair; if this portrait was a true one, Middleton had a certain likeness to Edgar Poe.[48]

Notes

1 Thomas Middleton, *Thomas Middleton: The Collected Works*, gen. ed. by Gary Taylor and John Lavagnino (Oxford: Oxford University Press, 2007).
2 'Thomas Middleton', in Algernon Charles Swinburne, *The Complete Works of Algernon Charles Swinburne*, ed. by Edmund Gosse and Thomas James Wise, 20 vols (London: William Heinemann; New York: Gabriel Wells, 1926), vol. XI of Bonchurch edition ('Prose Works', I), p. 382.
3 Charles Lamb, *Specimens of English Dramatic Poets who lived about the Time of Shakespeare. With Notes, A new edition in two volumes* (London: Edward Moxon, 1835, 1st pub. 1808), I, p. 167. Interestingly, this would be an analogy that would be endorsed by Swinburne some eighty years later. See 'Thomas Middleton', in Swinburne, *The Complete Works of Algernon Charles Swinburne*, vol. XI, p. 401.
4 'Lectures on the Dramatic Literature of the Age of Elizabeth' (1817), in William Hazlitt, *The Complete Works of William Hazlitt*, ed. by P. P. Howe after edition of A. R. Waller and Arnold Glover (London and Toronto: J. M. Dent & Sons, 1931), vol. VI, pp. 181, 222.
5 *Lodore*, II, ch. XV. See Mary Shelley, *The Novels and Selected Works of Mary Shelley*, ed. by Fiona Stafford, vol. VI (London: William Pickering, 1996), p. 195.
6 'Four Elizabethan Dramatists', in T. S. Eliot, *Elizabethan Essays* (London: Faber & Faber, 1934), p. 8.
7 See respectively: Thomas Middleton, *Works of Thomas Middleton. Now first collected with some account of the Author and Notes [...] in five volumes*, ed. by Rev. A. Dyce (London: Edward Lumley, 1840); Thomas Middleton, *The Works of Thomas Middleton*, ed. by A. H. Bullen (London: J. C. Nimmo, 1885–86).
8 London, Printed for Humphrey Moseley and are to be sold at his Shop at the Prince's Arms in St. Pauls Churchyard. 1657. For discussion concerning the critical debate surrounding the date of composition for *Women Beware Women*, see Gary Taylor, 'Introduction: The Middleton Canon', in Middleton, *The Collected Works*, pp. 415–16.

16 WOMEN BEWARE WOMEN

9   Thomas Middleton, *Two New Playes. Viz. More DISSEMBLERS besides WOMEN. VIZ. WOMEN beware WOMEN* (London, 1657), sig. A3r.
10 'Thomas Middleton', in Eliot, *Elizabethan Essays*, pp. 87, 89, 99.
11 Mark Eccles, 'Thomas Middleton A Poett', *Studies in Philology*, 54 (1957), 516–36 (p. 516).
12 Gary Taylor, 'Thomas Middleton: Lives and Afterlives', in Middleton, *The Collected Works*, pp. 25–58.
13 'Thomas Middleton', in Eliot, *Elizabethan Essays*, p. 87.
14 See 'Conversations with Drummond', sect. 11, lines 166–70, in Ben Jonson, *Ben Jonson*, ed. by C. H. Herford and Percy Simpson (Oxford: Clarendon Press, 1925), vol. I, p. 137. In the lines which follow, we also learn from Drummond 'That Chapman and Fletcher were loved of him / Overbury was first his friend. Then turn'd his mortall enimie.'
15 See *The Staple of News*, III.ii.210, in Ben Jonson, *Ben Jonson*, ed. by C. H. Herford and Percy and Evelyn Simpson (Oxford: Clarendon Press, 1938), vol. VI, p. 334; and for Wotton reference, see Logan Pearsall Smith, *Life and Letters of Sir Henry Wotton*, 2 vols (Oxford: Clarendon Press, 1907, rep. 1966), I, p. 201, a scandalous anti-Spanish play which is also recorded as having been viewed by Jonson's compatriot, Sir Henry Wotton.
16 John Taylor, *The praise of hemp-seed With the voyage of Mr. Roger Bird and the writer hereof in a boat of brown-paper, from London to Quinborough in Kent. As also, a farewell to the matchlesse deceased Mr. Thomas Coriat. Concluding with the commendations of the famous riuer of Thames* (London, 1623), p. 27.
17 Cited in Taylor, 'Lives and Afterlives', p. 50. The reference to 'squibbing Middleton' is excerpted anonymously in a later publication with the new title 'On the Time-Poets': see *Choyce drollery, songs & sonnets being a collection of divers excellent pieces of poetry, of severall eminent authors, never before printed* (London, 1656), p. 6.
18 In this diminutive, he seems to have shared company in Heywood's mind at least with Dekker and Nashe. See Thomas Heywood, *The hierarchie of the blessed angells Their names and offices the fall of Lucifer with his angells* (London, 1635), p. 206.
19 For further discussion here, see Taylor, 'Lives and Afterlives', pp. 51–52.
20 Middleton, *Two New Playes*, sig. A4r. However, it appears that any memory of such ovations must have disappeared within a generation and certainly before the close of the century. Gerard Langbaine notes that 'This Drama, if we give Credit to Mr. Richards, a Poet of that Age, was acted with extraordinary applause'. See entry 'Thomas Middleton', in Gerard Langbaine, *An Account of the English Dramatick Poets, or, Some observations and Remarks on the Lives and Writings of all those that have publish'd either comedies, tragedies, tragi-comedies, pastorals, masques, interludes, farces or opera's in the English tongue* (Oxford, 1691), p. 374.
21 See respectively: Pierre Corneille, *Nicomede a tragi-comedy translated out of the French of Monsieur Corneille by John Dancer as it was acted as the Theatre-Royal, Dublin; together with an exact catalogue of all the English stage plays printed till this present year 1671* (London, 1671), p. 15; Nicholas Cox (attr. Gerard Langbaine), *An exact catalogue of all the comedies, tragedies, tragi-comedies, opera's, masks, pastorals and interludes that were ever yet printed and published till this present year 1680* (Oxford, 1680), p. 15.
22 Edward Phillips, *Theatrum Poetarum, or, A compleat collection of the poets especially the most eminent, of all ages [...] together with a prefatory discourse of the poets and poetry in generall* (London, 1675), p. 180.
23 Langbaine, *An Account of the English Dramatick Poets*, p. 370.
24 Robert Shiells, *The Lives of the Poets of Great Britain and Ireland, to the time of Dean Swift. Compiled from ample materials scattered in a variety of books [...]*, 5 vols (London, 1753), vol. I, p. 352.
25 *A select collection of old plays, in twelve volumes. The second edition, corrected and collated with the old copies, with notes critical and explanatory* (London, 1780), vol. V, p. 309.
26 Lamb, *Specimens of English Dramatic Poets*, I, p. 163.
27 C. W. Dilke (ed.), *Old English Plays; being a Selection from the Early Dramatic*

INTRODUCTION 17

    Writers, 6 vols (London: Whittingham and Rowland, 1815), p. 51. A similar sentiment is expressed with regard to the tragedy's finale at p. 127.
28 Hazlitt, *Complete Works of William Hazlitt*, vol. 6 includes 'Lectures on the Dramatic Literature of the Age of Elizabeth', pp. 214–15.
29 Notes for lecture 12 (March 1818) from the series 'Lectures on European Literature' (1818). See Samuel Taylor Coleridge, *The Collected Works of Samuel Taylor Coleridge*, ed. by R. A. Foakes (London: Routledge & Kegan Paul; Princeton: Princeton University Press, 1987), vol. II: Lectures 1808–19 'On Literature', p. 206.
30 Sir Walter Scott, *The Journal of Sir Walter Scott*, ed. by W. E. K. Anderson (Oxford: Clarendon Press, 1972), pp. 179–80.
31 'Preface', in Middleton, *Works of Thomas Middleton*, ed. by Dyce, I, p. vii.
32 'Preface', in Middleton, *Works of Thomas Middleton*, ed. by Dyce, I, p. lv.
33 'Preface', in Middleton, *Works of Thomas Middleton*, ed. by Dyce, I, p. lvii.
34 Algernon Charles Swinburne, 'Thomas Middleton', *The Nineteenth Century*, 19.107 (January 1886), 138–53. Hereafter, textual quotations taken from this article are taken from Swinburne, *The Complete Works of Algernon Charles Swinburne*.
35 'Thomas Middleton', in Swinburne, *The Complete Works of Algernon Charles Swinburne*, XI, p. 400.
36 'Thomas Middleton', in Swinburne, *The Complete Works of Algernon Charles Swinburne*, XI, pp. 400–1.
37 'Thomas Middleton', in Swinburne, *The Complete Works of Algernon Charles Swinburne*, XI, p. 401.
38 'Thomas Middleton', in Swinburne, *The Complete Works of Algernon Charles Swinburne*, XI, pp. 400–1.
39 George Saintsbury, *A History of Elizabethan Literature* (London: Macmillan, 1887), p. 266.
40 Saintsbury, *A History of Elizabethan Literature*, p. 268.
41 Saintsbury, *A History of Elizabethan Literature*, p. 272.
42 'Thomas Middleton', in Eliot, *Elizabethan Essays*, p. 87.
43 'Thomas Middleton', in Eliot, *Elizabethan Essays*, p. 89.
44 'Thomas Middleton', in Eliot, *Elizabethan Essays*, pp. 93–94.
45 'Thomas Middleton', in Eliot, *Elizabethan Essays*, p. 95.
46 Taylor, 'Lives and Afterlives', p. 25.
47 The Pall Mall Gazette, Wednesday, 24 June 1885, issue 6326, p. 6.
48 The Pall Mall Gazette, p. 6.

CHAPTER ONE

The Critical Backstory

Robert C. Evans*

The earliest recorded commentary on Thomas Middleton's *Women Beware Women* appeared in 1657 in the first edition of the play, where it was printed alongside his tragicomedy titled *More Dissemblers Besides Women*. The publisher, Humphrey Moseley, extolled both texts as 'Excellent Poems', while the author Nathanael Richards, in a commendatory verse, praised the tragedy as a memorable work and notably asserted that 'I that have seen't, can say, having just cause, / Never came *Tragedy* off with more applause'.[1] These earliest references, and indeed the fullest treatment of critical responses to Middleton's writing down the centuries (such as passing references to *Women Beware Women* by William Winstanley in 1687 and Gerald Langbaine in 1691[2]) may be found in Sara Jayne Steen's invaluable study, *Ambrosia in an Earthern Vessel: Three Centuries of Audience and Reader Response to the Works of Thomas Middleton*. In addition, J. R. Mulryne's landmark critical edition of the tragedy also draws attention to annotations found in various early copies of the first publication of *Women Beware Women*. These include a list of recollected lines, attempts to decipher stage action, and possible memories of a seventeenth-century performance.[3] However, it was not until the nineteenth century that commentary on the tragedy began to appear in any extended form. Like many other works by early modern playwrights (other than those by Shakespeare), *Women Beware Women* was treated in the eighteenth and nineteenth centuries as a text to be read rather than as a script to be performed. In general, critics in this period often concentrated on ranking Middleton's play, especially in comparison with works by Shakespeare – but sometimes also in comparison with works by other early modern dramatists. Responses to the play in the nineteenth century reflect many of the recurring critical concerns of the Romantic and Victorian periods, including an interest in realistic characterization, a preoccupation with artistic unity, and a focus on the didactic potential of literature.

The Nineteenth Century

In 1808 Charles Lamb applauded *Women Beware Women* for its realism, even singling out Livia for seeming 'as real a creature as one of Chaucer's characters. She is such another jolly Housewife as the Wife of Bath'.[4] However, it was William Hazlitt who offered the earliest extended assessment of this play, praising it for its 'rich marrowy vein of internal sentiment, with fine occasional insight into human nature, and cool cutting irony of expression'. Nevertheless, he found Middleton 'lamentably deficient in the plot and denouement', arguing that the play resembled a rough draft, 'with a number of fine things thrown in, and the best made use of first; but it tends to no fixed goal, and the interest decreases [...] for want of previous arrangement and an eye to the whole'. Hazlitt added that he found Livia, Bianca, Leantio, and the Mother were 'all admirably drawn', and he was merely the first of many subsequent readers to praise the chess scene as 'a master-piece'. Furthermore, like many later critics, Hazlitt detected an early 'proneness' in Bianca toward hedonism, but he is unusual in praising Leantio's 'manly, independent character' in the first act.

Hazlitt's reservations about Bianca foreshadowed an anonymous opinion (perhaps by C. W. Dilke) from 1823 which saw her as typical of Middleton's women, who rarely possess 'real virtue, or any share of gentle affection. They are almost all lascivious, faithless, or cruel', and thus Bianca stands as just one among a host of Middleton's female characters 'who rebel against the conjugal duties, and conspire against their husbands' lives'.[5] Yet this unnamed author also considered the work 'Middleton's finest play', and praised it for being 'as full of incident as any play in the English language'. He found the change in Bianca's character after her seduction 'admirably managed', praised Leantio's 'beautiful eulogy upon marriage', and felt that although the Cardinal's criticism of the Duke was 'on the whole a little tedious', it was nonetheless 'impressive'.[6] In contrast, Henry Hallam, writing in 1839, agreed that the play was 'full of action', but he found the characters 'all too vicious to be interesting' and claimed that 'the language [did] not rise much above mediocrity'.[7] However, in 1840, introducing his important edition of Middleton, Alexander Dyce managed to agree both with Hallam and with the anonymous writer of 1823, arguing that the play 'is indeed remarkable for the masterly conception and delineation of the chief characters, and for the life and reality infused into many of the scenes', while also asserting that 'the dramatis personae are almost all repulsive from their extreme depravity'. He added that 'the catastrophe is rather forced and unnatural' and that the play became less and less interesting as it went along.[8] Interestingly, such dissatisfaction with the dénouement of *Women Beware Women* would remain as one of the most recurring sources of debate among critics down the ages.

Anthony Trollope, annotating his personal copy of Dyce's edition in the mid-1870s, expressed decidedly mixed reactions about *Women Beware Women*. He found the 'execution of the last portion [...] as bad as the plot', but nevertheless praised much of the first three acts – acts which suggested that Middleton, with more practice, 'might have excelled all the Elizabethan dramatists except Shakespeare'. The eminent novelist found Bianca, Livia, and Isabella 'abominable', and submitted that 'the plot [was] so detestable, there being not a single part which is not abhorrent' that Middleton 'could never have become a great poet'.[9] Similar ambivalence appeared in an 1875 assessment by Adolphus

William Ward, who praised some of Middleton's 'fire' and 'vivacity', but objected that he 'fails to show himself capable of true tragic dignity; and though his aim is undoubtedly moral, he is unable to furnish any relief of lofty sentiment to the grossness of the situations; while the humorous characters are revoltingly coarse'.[10]

While much of the nineteenth-century criticism discussed thus far often concentrated upon perceived failures in plotting and tragic grandeur and upon the repulsiveness of many of the characters, Arthur Henry Bullen, in introducing his edition of *The Works* in 1885–86, praised *Women Beware Women* as 'among the highest achievements of the English drama'. He hailed it as 'a pitiful, thrice-pitiful story, worked out with relentless skill to a ghastly catastrophe'. He contended that the 'passionate energy and concentrated bitterness of the language is as remarkable as in *The Changeling*' and considered the play as one of several achievements that justified 'Middleton's claims to be considered a great dramatist'.[11] Moreover, an anonymous reviewer of Bullen's edition in 1886 in fact praised the play as 'Middleton's masterpiece', calling it 'as a whole [...] much superior' even to *The Changeling*, which the reviewer also admired.[12] It was Algernon Charles Swinburne, however, who set the tone for much subsequent commentary in a lengthy essay published in 1886, and it is hard to overstate the significance of his essay. Swinburne offered one of the longest and most considered of the nineteenth-century assessments, praising 'the facility and fluency and equable promptitude' of the play's style and celebrating the work as 'full to overflowing of noble eloquence, of inventive resource and suggestive effect, of rhetorical affluence and theatrical ability'. He found the opening 'quite masterly', and asserted that 'the scene in which the forsaken husband is seduced into consolation by the temptress of his wife is worthy of all praise for the straightforward ingenuity and the serious delicacy by which the action is rendered credible and the situation endurable'. However, Swinburne was unwavering in his condemnation of the subplot and the conclusion: 'one is repulsive beyond redemption by elegance of style, the other is preposterous beyond extenuation on the score of logic of poetical justice'.[13] If Swinburne still considered the play 'noble' and 'memorable', he did not fail to underline for his readers that 'the irredeemable infamy of the leading characters degrades and deforms the nature of the interest excited'. He regretted the eventual disappearance of 'the good and gentle old mother whose affectionate simplicity is so gracefully and attractively painted', claiming that 'the splendid eloquence of the only other respectable person in the play is not of itself sufficient to make a living figure, rather than a mere mouthpiece for indignant emotion, of so subordinate and inactive a character as the Cardinal.' In his concluding remarks he returned to the familiar question of genre: the play's 'lower comedy' was deemed particularly 'stupid and offensive', but he praised the 'the high comedy of the scene between Livia and the Widow' as being 'as fine as the best work' of that sort from the whole era.[14] In his judicious assessment of both the strengths and the weaknesses of the tragedy, Swinburne helped bring critical commentary on Middleton's play to a new level of maturity.

As the nineteenth century neared its end, Middleton began to receive more – and more extensive – attention, and *Women Beware Women* was often singled out for praise among his known works. Thus, an anonymous reviewer in 1886 thought the play could 'stand side by side with any non-Shakespearean work of the epoch'. Although he found it characteristically 'deficient [...] in tenderness', he praised it for its powerful plot, life-like characterization, poetic dialogue, and romantic opening scenes, and argued that 'the whole has a grim irony that lifts it into the highest regions of the drama'. There were found to be 'many passages of exquisite poetry' and, like many earlier (and indeed later) critics, he praised the chess scene and the subsequent intrigue, but censured the closing masque.[15] One of the lengthiest commentaries on the play to be published in the nineteenth century appeared once again anonymously in December 1886. Although most of this commentary consisted of plot summary and quotation, that fact alone implies the growing respect the play was now receiving: it merited detailed acquaintance from the wider reading public. This writer saw *Women Beware Women* as evidence of the 'maturity' of Middleton's 'genius' and praised specific moments highly: the reader was particularly directed to Act 4, scene 1 as an example of Middleton's 'superior imaginative power'. Most intriguing, however, was a quite exceptional admiration for the masque: its tone is here described as dark and 'the catastrophe melancholy, and as pitiful as that of Hamlet [sic]'. This was high praise indeed and it reflects the persistent tendency in the nineteenth century to compare and contrast Middleton with Shakespeare.[16]

By the time one reaches the commentary of George Saintsbury, published in 1887, comparisons with Shakespeare were becoming more and more frequent. Saintsbury called *Women Beware Women* a 'remarkable' play – 'one of Middleton's finest works, inferior only to *The Changeling* in parts, and far superior to it as a whole'. He praised Middleton's 'Shakesperian verisimilitude and certainty of touch' in depicting the 'temptation of Bianca' and concluded by asserting that, with a little more work, Middleton could have made this play and several other works 'worthy to rank with all but Shakespeare's very masterpieces'.[17] Similarly strong commendation came from Charles Harold Herford in 1894. Herford thought the tragedy undoubtedly Middleton's 'most powerful single play' and praised the masterful main plot and the vivid, if unattractive, leading characters.[18] However, a comment by one of his contemporaries, the eminent scholar Edmund Gosse, was far more equivocal. Gosse wrote that although some scholars considered *Women Beware Women* 'the finest of Middleton's plays', to agree with this assessment 'would be to excuse too much of what we may call the ethical tastelessness' of Middleton's era. Gosse felt that the plot was 'so excessively disagreeable, and the play close[d] in a manner so odious, that the reader's sympathy is hopelessly alienated'. Even so, by way of conclusion, he submitted that this 'radical fault may perhaps disturb, but can scarcely destroy[,] our appreciation of the beauty and invention of the style'.[19]

The Twentieth Century, 1900–45

Thus, by the end of the nineteenth century, many of the main tendencies of subsequent critical responses to *Women Beware Women* had already been sketched out. These include: praise for the play's realism; the vivid characterization of Livia; and the expert rendering of the chess scene. Disagreement persisted, however, concerning the initial moral status of Bianca, and the closing masque. Later critics would return to many of these topics repeatedly while also, of course, approaching the play with all the various critical methodologies that have characterized twentieth-century criticism. Nonetheless, in the first two decades of the new century, extended commentary on the play was fairly rare, and much of it resembles commentary published during the preceding decades. In 1902, for instance, Moody and Lovett's *A History of English Literature* dismissed the play as 'unpleasant in plot, and marred by the obtrusion of crude horrors',[20] although brief complimentary references also abounded. In 1912 Mable Buland detailed the work's chronological organization,[21] while in 1919 Arthur Symons concluded that 'rarely has better material been more callously left to spoil'. Like practically every other commentator, Symons praised the chess scene and, in general, extolled Middleton's powers of characterization.[22] More sympathetic was Gamaliel Bradford's response in 1921. He found the play not 'agreeable', but nevertheless a work of 'tremendous tragic power' – even though Bianca emerged as 'a shallow, witless fool': 'No remorse stirs in her, no pity, no tenderness for the husband whom she has wronged'. Indeed, Leantio was 'far more touching and truly tragic' than his wife. In this critical discussion, the masque was thought to represent 'indiscriminate butchery' and thus, brought the play 'rather clumsily' to an end.[23] In 1922 Janet Spens found the 'young couple [...] utterly selfish', but suggested that the 'girl's complete lack of any moral principle [was] drawn with great skill'. By way of additional comment, Spens submitted that the 'unpleasant underplot' seemed 'to be there merely to give the impression of a thoroughly corrupt society'.[24] In the opening decades, little in the writings of these early twentieth-century commentators staked out any radically new directions for the critical understanding of *Women Beware Women*.

Without a doubt, however, the most influential commentary on the tragedy from the 1920s came from T. S. Eliot, whose essay was originally printed in the *TLS* in 1927. Ultimately, the fact that Eliot directed international critical attention to this hitherto relatively neglected tragedy proved more significant than any new interpretations he offered in this essay. His apparently unassailable status in this period as a pre-eminent author and critic ensured that his assessments of early modern dramatists warranted immediate attention. Eliot declared *Women Beware Women* to be inferior to *The Changeling*, but did find much to admire, especially in the characterization. Middleton had depicted 'real human passions' and 'permanent human feelings' and showed an interest – 'more than any of his contemporaries – in innuendo and double meanings'. In the chess scene, the 'irony could not be improved upon', and there was 'hardly anything truer in Elizabethan drama than Bianca's gradual self-will and self-importance' after the Duke seduces her. Despite some flaws in the ways she is depicted, Bianca was for Eliot 'a real woman; as real, indeed, as any woman in Elizabethan tragedy': in fact, 'Middleton understood women in tragedy better than any of the Elizabethans [...] except Shakespeare alone'.[25] This high – and highly influential – praise shaped the responses of many of the generations of readers and critics that followed. The impact of Eliot's comments on the works of Middleton (and

THE CRITICAL BACKSTORY   23

other early modern authors) continues to offer interesting evidence of the ways in which literary canons are both formed and transformed within critical and cultural debate.

Also significant was the growth, at this time, of Middleton's reputation among critics who taught literature in colleges and universities. Before this period, much commentary on non-classical writers had been produced by amateurs (in the best sense of that term). Now, with the development of academic interest in the so-called 'modern languages' and with the establishment of more and more departments of 'English', the study of Middleton and many other British writers became increasingly professionalized. One of the first sustained academic discussions of *Women Beware Women* came in 1935 from M. C. Bradbrook. She found the work 'slighter' than *The Changeling* and thought its themes 'nearer to a thesis': 'a study in the progressive deterioration of character', its first part 'much more natural than the latter half'.[26] Bradbrook was the first of many to compare the play with Middleton's comedies. She drew attention to the structure of contrasting plot and subplot, and emphasized the growth of irony and even comedy as the work developed (pp. 225–29). In keeping with her scholarly interest in the organization of early modern dramatic narrative, Bradbrook often chose to highlight specific formal features: thus, Leantio's 'two soliloquies are exactly parallel'; and 'more than a third' of Act 3, scene 2 'is taken up by asides.' She explored the effectiveness of the minor characters, imagery, and subplot, commenting that not one scene 'is really superfluous': everything contributed to 'the conflict between love and mercenary selling of love, with self-destruction envisaged as the inevitable result of the spiritual suicide of lust and ambition' (p. 234). Reflecting developments occurring at this time in Shakespearean scholarship, Bradbrook highlighted the many examples of food imagery in the tragedy, but reported that other key images were principally 'drawn from plagues and diseases, from treasure and jewels, and from light and darkness' – and, most importantly, that the 'metaphors of disease [were] nearly always applied to lust, reinforcing the connection between spiritual and physical death'. Given these concerns in her discussion, it remains noteworthy that she felt that Middleton stressed imagery and theme less emphatically than other playwrights of his era; rather, she argued, Middleton relied 'upon action and characterization in a way which no one else did (except Shakespeare)'. His language, unusually among his contemporaries, was found to depend on implication and 'pregnant simplicity' (pp. 238–29). In short, Bradbrook had devoted to the play the kind of probing attention which had been lacking in many preceding assessments.

From now on, academic attention to the play became increasingly frequent. In 1936 Una Ellis-Fermor praised Middleton's depiction of Livia as credible and skilled, extolled his blending of comedy and tragedy, and commended his 'knowledge of the hardening of the spirit under certain forms of shock and misery' – a knowledge she considered 'his peculiar province in tragedy' and one unequalled even by Shakespeare.[27] Notably, she claimed that although Bianca progressively hardens, her 'love for the Duke redeems her at the end' (p. 143) – and this remains a much-debated contention among critics. On the eve of the Second World War, Henry W. Wells also published a commentary on the tragedy, noting (as typical of Middleton) the work's leisurely opening, but perhaps over-hasty conclusion. Summarizing many (by this stage) familiar critical points of interest, Wells defended the masque from charges of total failure, admired Middleton's depiction of the Mother and Cardinal, praised his characterization and style ('homely in imagery, abrupt in rhythm'), highlighted the play's frequent use of satire, and extolled the union of major and minor intrigues.[28]

The first modern academic study to be devoted solely to Middleton – by Richard Hindry Barker – may have been written around 1943, but it was not published until 1958. In the interim, however, other studies appeared. In 1946, for instance, Frederick S. Boas praised the opening scene of the tragedy for its 'charming picture of domestic bliss', extolled the chess scene as 'a masterpiece of high comedy', admired the opening scene of Act 3, but found the concluding melodrama 'unequal to the [earlier] brilliant workmanship'. In general, Boas valued the play more for its 'lighter and more genial scenes', than for its 'catastrophic close'.[29] Two years later, Daniel Dodson hailed the play as 'one of the finest of the whole Jacobean period' and called it 'the apex of Middleton's unassisted, serious, dramatic efforts'.[30] He admired its total effect and its effective characterization, arguing that in depicting Livia, Middleton reversed his usual procedure by showing a 'realist passing into a state of unreality'. Most intriguingly, Dodson suggested that Livia was incestuously attracted to Hippolito, but he also thought her 'one of the most consummately artistic bawds in the history of literature'. Like so many of his predecessors, he drew attention to the chess scene as 'a masterpiece of irony and double-entendre', but Dodson's main contribution lay in seeing Livia as a truly tragic character (pp. 377–80).

The Twentieth Century: 1945–60

In the years following the end of the Second World War, the academic study of English literature grew from strength to strength, and Middleton – like many other early modern authors – was a prime beneficiary. In fact, by the mid-1950s, interest in Middleton's tragedies finally resulted in an entire book-length study by Samuel Schoenbaum.[31] Schoenbaum focused principally upon the theme of lust in *Women Beware Women* and its tone of 'pitiless detachment and irony', yet he also pointed to various flaws, including a 'tedious, almost irrelevant' subplot, imperfect pacing, and a final breakdown in structure. Schoenbaum contended that the play's verse was 'the most relaxed and luxuriant that Middleton ever permitted himself' and interestingly discussed Middleton's treatment of the play's main source at length. Controversially, he claimed that Bianca was 'able to lose her virtue only because she never really possessed it' and alleged that Middleton failed 'to see the romance of Bianca's elopement from Venice, nor [could] he regard her affair with the Duke with sympathy' (a much-disputed claim). For Middleton (Schoenbaum argued), 'the entire story has an unrelieved sordidness, and all the participants are base' (pp. 103–12). More generally, Schoenbaum considered the tragedy as a whole 'perhaps the most unpleasant of Middleton's serious plays'. The characters were debased, the atmosphere was full of 'cynical materialism', and the marriage of Leantio and Bianca was 'based on physical appetite alone' (pp. 115–18). Thus, Middleton is found to depict in Schoenbaum's discussion a collection of 'moral idiots whose utter inability to comprehend the sinfulness of their careers makes them ultimately repulsive': the characters generally 'fail to understand that the universe is governed by an inexorable moral order' and 'that someday they will be called to judgment' (pp. 124–26). Despite the fact that *Women Beware Women* is set in Italy, its atmosphere remained for Schoenbaum English, bourgeois, domestic, and often, brutally comic. Indeed, irony was used with special effectiveness, allowing our access to the dramatic world to remain objective rather than sympathetic. However, the last act was 'a failure, and with it the play collapses' (pp. 128–32).

In an article from 1956, A. Bronson Feldman branded Leantio a contemptuous 'slave of lust' who is 'properly punished' for eloping with Bianca. In addition, Feldman faulted Middleton himself for 'abrupt transitions', inappropriate humour and blank verse of a sometimes 'greasy velocity'. He found Leantio's jealousy disgusting, and the 'sniggering vulgarity' of the Ward led Feldman to detect the presence of 'the perspiring authorship of William Rowley', Middleton's frequent collaborator. If Feldman did praise the 'vital talk' of various characters, he felt that with this tragedy Middleton had 'failed dismally' and seemed to care 'as little for art as he cared for morality'.[32] In the following year G. R. Hibbard used the tragedy to help illustrate the alleged decadence of Jacobean drama.[33] He thought that the play lacked any political dimension and considered the last two acts superfluously didactic. Hibbard chose to stress the ordinary, unheroic nature of the Duke and Cardinal and argued that Middleton seemed uninterested in issues of human dignity. Interestingly, he hailed the tragedy as 'surely the most powerful criticism of the education of women and of the *marriage de convenance* in Elizabethan drama', focusing upon a pitiable Isabella who sought, from Hippolito, the affection denied her by her father. The play was Middleton's indignant protest against the 'brutalizing and degrading' tendency to treat other people as things, a tendency Hibbard considered the work's chief theme. If Livia emerged a Machiavellian, devilish symbol of this sort of evil, she was also 'the most interesting figure' (pp. 42–48). Returning to a favourite critical interest in genre, Hibbard saw the first half of the play as presenting a new kind of tragedy, but he argued that ultimately Middleton betrayed 'his own art' by turning a 'naturalistic, psychological drama' into 'a melodramatic revenge play' full of unsubtle preaching (pp. 52–53).

Hibbard's article would provoke much later discussion, and in fact it is interesting to note that by this point in the twentieth century it had become increasingly possible – thanks to the development of bibliographical scholarship, the growth of college libraries and academic presses, and a growing emphasis on professionalism and specialization – for academic contributions and debates to proliferate and to be read by a wider, interested public around the world. The many responses to Hibbard's piece were just one reflection of this growing trend. However, in the context of this particular discussion, the most important immediate event of 1958 was the publication of Richard Hindry Barker's

Thomas Middleton (which had been written around 1943).³⁴ Barker began by contrasting the structure of *Women Beware Women* with that of *The Changeling*, arguing that the play resembled *The Revenger's Tragedy* since it had 'no central figure'. He found the characters complex (motivated by lust and greed but exhibiting 'twinges of conscience'), but Leantio struck him as a weak, lustful thief who was sometimes 'so mean as to be utterly contemptible'. Meanwhile, Bianca was 'difficult to analyze because she seems different at different times': at first, she feels physical passion for Leantio but later she seems motivated mainly by 'greed or ambition or pride' (pp. 131–36). Barker afforded less attention to Isabella and Hippolito (the latter is 'a rather conventional figure' who seems 'colorless' and 'inconsistent'), but he extolled Livia as especially memorable while disputing Dodson's assertion that she has incestuous feelings for her brother. Comparing the play as a whole to 'modern naturalistic drama', he concluded that it was 'really a tragicomedy': 'a play in which serious and comic action are set side by side' to show 'the variety and the multiplicity of life'. If the characters were ranked from most serious (the Cardinal and Isabella) to the least (the Ward), Barker argued that the contrasts between the characters could create the kind of 'contrapuntal effects so common in modern plays and novels' (pp. 138–45).

The Twentieth Century: 1960–70

In 1960 Robert Ornstein was far less encouraging.³⁵ He considered *Women Beware Women* 'less mature' than *The Changeling*, finding it lacking in 'economy' and in 'intensity of tragic effect'. There were too many major figures, too much time was wasted on Sordido and the Ward, and there was a 'collapse of tone, plotting, and characterization in the last act' which resulted in sensational and melodramatic representation. From Ornstein's perspective, the major characters 'were not born to play tragic roles', and so Middleton 'had to slaughter them wholesale to create a superficial impression of tragic doom'. The play remained 'a drama of reaction rather than action' and was 'concerned not so much with the consequences of immoral decision' as with its psychological nature (pp. 190–92). Ultimately, all the characters were 'doomed by Middleton's dramatic thesis', rather than by their individual personalities. Thus, the playwright's moralism itself emerged as shallow, and the impression of underlying cynicism seemed 'the result of Middleton's unsuccessful attempt to create tragedy out of the materials and conventions of satiric comedy' (pp. 197–98). In the same year R. B. Parker chose to stress the importance of comedy in *Women Beware Women*, arguing that Middleton used 'comic inflation' in a world 'now shown to be frighteningly vulnerable' – a world in which Leantio, Bianca, and Isabella were weak characters 'at the mercy of their degenerate environment' (p. 192).³⁶ Like many critics of the 1960s and 70s, Parker focused on the questions of recurring imagery and key themes, including images of gluttony, rankness, disease and poison, and themes of lust, materialism and untrustworthiness (the latter emphasized by the key word 'stranger' [pp. 193–94]). He asserted that the recurring 'devices of coincidence and irony [were] [...] exploited in ways which expose the stupidity and powerlessness of the characters and deprive them of the dignity of free-will and self-determination', so that they become 'moral idiots' from whom 'the spectator's sympathies are alienated'. By the end of the play, according to Parker, the comedy had diminished and was replaced not by tragedy, but by satire and even absurd (and unsuccessful) farce (pp. 196–99).

Parker's concern with key words and images – a focus that reflects the rise of the so-called 'New Criticism', with its close attention to textual details – was also taken up in a 1961 article by Christopher Ricks.[37] For Ricks, the tragedy was 'about the corruption of life and love by money', and subtle word-play emphasized this theme. Key words included 'business' and 'employ', as well as 'work', 'labour', 'idle', 'leisure', 'use', 'abuse', 'service', 'husbandry', 'game', 'sport', 'expenses', 'pride', 'tumbling', 'monuments', 'tender', 'gentlewoman', 'wench', 'reward', 'debt', 'pay', 'flesh', 'bear double', and 'provide'. Meanwhile, in 1962,[38] Edward Engelberg emphasized the 'dominant metaphor of sight – or the lack of it', arguing that often in the play perception it 'is partial and distorted, and so reality is tragically misapprehended'. Eye-imagery was pervasive, contributing to plot development and even infiltrating the comedy (pp. 21–25). Ultimately, however, Middleton 'opposes no real clarity of sight to blindness [...] to offset the optical illusions of his blinded characters' (p. 28). In the same year, Irving Ribner defended the play from the common charges of its sordid characterization and clumsy conclusion.[39] Viewing the work as a 'dramatic symbol of the damnation of all mankind', he extolled the ways the two plots 'shape an ethical statement', and contrasted the Cardinal and Livia as representatives of opposed moral choices: 'All the others are moral equivocators, and moral equivocation sets the dominant tone', so that the final 'mass murder is necessary and proper' and symbolizes 'the inevitable collapse' of a corrupt society (p. 138). From Ribner's perspective, Middleton combined realism and symbolism, 'ritualistic parody' (as in the chess scene), and skilful 'poetic imagery'. Although few characters in Jacobean drama 'exhibit the illusion of reality so fully as Leantio and Bianca', in this critical discussion the play's unity was rooted more in theme than in consistent characterization (p. 151). In this concern with the underlying 'unity' of Middleton's tragedy in terms of theme and symbolism, Ribner may be seen as representative in this instance of a whole generation of 'formalist' critics at work in this period.

Like Ribner, T. B. Tomlinson in 1964 also felt that *Women Beware Women* merited some high praise.[40] He thought the play revealed the promise of a domestic tragedy-in-the-making, and argued that it deserved more stagings than it had so far received (p. 166). He emphasized the text's comic aspects, noted Leantio's flawed personality and argued strikingly that the 'aggressively flat' verse reinforced the characters' 'bourgeois values' and the tragedy's 'uncompromisingly naturalistic' tone (pp. 167–69). Like Tomlinson and many other critics in this post-war period, George Core in 1968 also stressed the importance of imagery.[41] In addition, Core found the play 'remarkably modern in its depiction of vice – and the ennui and despair vice inevitably brings in its wake': indeed, it had to be seen as transcending its roots in the conventions of revenge tragedy (pp. 66–68). Core considered the play's dominant image to be 'the canker'. However, more generally, if he was unable to stifle his disappointment regarding the presentation of the masque, he nonetheless praised the play's poetry and ingenious design (pp. 68–74).

The same year in which Core's article was published – 1968 – was also significant in that it witnessed the publication of Roma Gill's important edition of the play.[42] The preparation of such editions – designed for the college and university classroom – was an indication not only of the growing professionalization of literary study at this time, but also of Middleton's growing presence on the syllabus for students of literature. Gill attended to the familiar critical concerns of a scholarly edition (authorship, date, sources, variants), but also (like many editors of the time influenced by the New Criticism) offered an extensive discussion of the play's figurative language. She supported a composition date of roughly 1621, arguing that the play's quality suggested a mature author (pp. xiv–xv). She stressed greed as a central theme, defended the subplot (the Ward was *intended* to 'be tedious'), emphasized how Middleton departed from his sources in creating Leantio and the Duke, and saw the Mother as the most conventional female character (pp. xvi–xx). More generally, she asserted that Middleton 'enters an area of female experience untouched by Shakespeare' by showing 'the slow awakening to sin and reality as gentle, impetuous girls change into ruthless, scheming women'. Unlike some other commentators, Gill is notable in viewing Bianca as genuinely innocent at first (only in this way 'can her subsequent cruelty have its full impact'), although she found some flaws in the way that character was finally presented (pp. xxi–xii). If Livia's growth as a central figure deserved praise, Gill nevertheless argued that there were 'only two characters – Sordido and the Cardinal – who do not call for a complex response'. Like many of her predecessors, Gill was forced to conclude that we react to the work 'intellectually and not emotionally', and so the play was 'cruel but oddly unmoving': 'There is no time for deep emotional involvement. [...] The verse too has a swift economy, most remarkable in the frequent asides.' In the final phases of the intrigue, speeches 'lengthen and images are extended as Middleton makes a misguided grab for the emotions'. Thus, the vigorous attempts at moralization ultimately weakened the work: the conclusion was 'unashamedly theatrical', but the masque was so ingeniously conducted that it did not seem uninspired (pp. xxiv–xxv).

Another sign of growing critical interest appeared with Charles Barber's 1969 edition of Middleton's tragedy.[43] Barber suggested that 'the whole question' of the play's date 'must still be considered wide open', briefly discussed sources and Middleton's departures from them, suggested that the work's main theme was male domination, and argued that Bianca was not inconsistent but slowly revealed latent qualities of 'wilfulness, pertness, irresponsibility, quickness of wit, and a certain hardness' (pp. 1–4). Importantly, Barber underlined that 'Middleton's attitude to his characters is one of complete detachment [...] we are never invited to identify with them'. For him, the play's conclusion evoked 'pity rather than terror [...] but it does this with considerable intensity'. Barber's introduction ended with a brief listing of stagings, including three (one televised) from the 1960s (pp. 7–9). The fact that the play had now begun to be revived for performance would open a whole new dimension for later commentators, and indeed the 1960s saw a real growth of interest in the study of early modern plays *as* plays.

THE CRITICAL BACKSTORY 29

In the same year in which Barber's edition was published, an essay by Inga-Stina Ewbank also appeared.[44] Ewbank explored the unity of Middleton's tragedy by comparing its interests in realism and morality to those of a nineteenth-century social novel, such as *Vanity Fair*. The play's themes were deemed to be 'love, money and class', and the structure depended less on plot than on 'interlinked groups of characters' (p. 58). The characters mostly lacked 'ethical insight into their own actions', but Middleton provided 'reminders of an inexorable moral order'. Ultimately, the milieu was found to be densely realistic, with an 'almost documentary use of objects' and phrasing rooted in 'as if' and 'as when' constructions. Paradoxically, however, Leantio, who soliloquized more than anyone else, 'gives far less sense of an inner life' (pp. 59–65). Most interestingly, Ewbank defended the masque ('it shows Middleton's peculiar power of combining the ordinary with the horrible'), and praised Middleton's 'unique power of constructing group scenes' for dramatic representation (pp. 69–70). Dorothea Krook's generic study (also published in 1969) began by focusing on 'the problem of the dividing line between tragedy and satire or satiric comedy'.[45] She argued that the play *was* mainly tragic, but emphasized the 'profoundly, incurably commonplace' nature of Leantio and Bianca, who 'are typical products of their bourgeois setting and ethos' (pp. 146–49). Both characters were innocent at first and had to be viewed as such if the play were to be considered truly tragic, yet each could be coarse. Meanwhile, Livia was depicted with a skill that rivaled Shakespeare's; she was 'a complete original', whose immorality was paradoxically grounded in affection (pp. 150–66). Krook asserted by way of conclusion that the play succeeded as a 'very good tragedy of the low mimetic kind' whose bare language 'exactly matches' the play's 'prevailing moral atmosphere' (pp. 173–81).

The Twentieth Century: 1970–80

By the early 1970s, the body of Middleton scholarship was growing apace – much of it still obviously influenced by the fundamentally 'formalist' (or 'New Critical') orientation that had remained so important in the post-war period. In 1970 David M. Holmes argued that most of the major characters show a 'defective conception of love', and he demonstrated that Middleton emphasized this idea through the often derisory language employed in his dialogues to refer to 'love' and attraction (p. 165).[46] Holmes' discussion is especially notable for comparing *Women Beware Women* to other plays by Middleton, and in the following year, Leonora Leet Brodwin developed this enquiry further by viewing the play as a 'tragedy of Worldly Love' (p. 320).[47] For Brodwin, both Leantio and Bianca appeared essentially innocent at first, and Bianca's fall resulted less from greed than from a desire for protection. Yet the quick transformation of both young lovers suggested the shallowness of their initial affection (pp. 320–25). Perhaps the most intriguing aspect of Brodwin's discussion was her claim that the Duke seemed to grow in moral stature and came close to achieving an almost noble love for Bianca (p. 332).

In 1972 Norman A. Brittin discussed the ways Middleton departed from his sources (by reducing the characters, for instance, 'from seventeen to eleven' and by shortening the narrative's chronological organization from 25 years to a few months). He also emphasized such themes as lust and contrasting early modern views of marriage (pp. 119, 127).[48] Interestingly, Brittin considered Leantio the play's most sympathetic figure, but found the masque marred by too formal a style. This year also saw the publication of two major articles.[49] J. B. Batchelor began by arguing that the sources 'tend to be much more sympathetic to Bianca than is Middleton' (p. 79). He claimed that 'Middleton reorganizes the structure of events so that they accord, to some extent, with the Cardinal's morality' – 'only with the Cardinal's intervention' does the story come into focus (p. 80). Batchelor suggested that the 'opening scene, presenting as it does an anonymous lower-class family (none of the characters are named) can seem dull in the theatre', but he also noted how that scene is echoed in Act 1, scene 2 and how the absence of Leantio's father is a significant change from the source (pp. 80–81). Interestingly, Batchelor stressed the 'five spectacles' that endow each act with 'a piece of pageantry': indeed, he saw the play as largely 'a series of formal scenes, mirroring each other, in which the two girls are seen as duplicate victims of society' who cope in contrasting ways (pp. 84–85). In the masque, Livia, as Juno Pronuba, is found to be 'a diabolical parody of the Cardinal', and the masque itself is seen to accelerate the play's pace and increase its moral complexity. Ultimately, Batchelor concluded, Middleton sought 'to act upon the unwary auditor' so as 'to seduce him, to bring him to extreme moral perplexity, and then to betray him' (pp. 85–88). Finally in this year, Charles A. Hallett argued that in the tragedy Middleton traced 'the psychological stages in the growth of a cynic. Livia, representing the accomplished cynic, was a key to what Bianca will become'. The play thus does not map out 'as is usually believed, a journey into greater and greater sin but rather the series of rationalizations that lead to the erection of a barrier against self-knowledge', so that the work 'cannot be classified as tragedy' (p. 375). For Hallett, Bianca seemed imbued 'with more actuality than perhaps any other previous character in Elizabethan or Jacobean drama', since she was 'a thoroughly mediocre person, one who makes no effort to translate her experiences in life into knowledge about life' (p. 381). Thus, *Women Beware Women* represented 'a new type of drama for the Jacobean stage, a drama whose primary interest is not in the great but in the common man, the man we would today call the anti-hero' (p. 387).

The next year, 1973, witnessed the publication of three Middleton studies – by Dorothy Farr, by Barbara Joan Baines, and by Caroline Lockett Cherry.[50] Farr praised the plotting and characterization in the first four acts but then objected to the 'staginess' of Act 5 (p. 72). On the whole, Farr found the play to be a successful dramatic experiment, with Leantio especially as an innovative central figure (p. 94). Baines's monograph, meanwhile, argued that *Women Beware Women* presented 'an entire society of the damned' in which weak characters became 'entangled in a great social evil' (p. 126). Bianca's progressive decline was tragic, but mainly because it resulted in the fall of her husband. His 'moral sensibility' was finer than hers, and 'his capacity for suffering' makes him tragic (pp. 131–38). Of the three publications in this year, Cherry's monograph offered the most substantial discussion of *Women Beware Women* (pp. 178–207) – a discussion which emphasized the play's realism (p. 178) and stressed its implicit moralism. Most of the female characters' problems in the play (Cherry contended) 'stem from women's subservient, sub-human position'; the women 'are first presented as the victims of a selfish commercial society whose perverted values form the necessary breeding ground for all the evil that invests the play'. The women were treated as objects and almost as slaves, especially through the practice of enforced marriage (pp. 184, 187–88). Yet the women themselves became corrupted by their own mistreatment – a fact that helped render Bianca an especially complex character (pp. 190, 195). Clearly responding to the growing emphasis on feminist criticism at this time, Cherry explored the tragedy predominantly in terms of the representation of female experience, arguing that by the end of the play Bianca came to feel a real and attractive affection for the Duke – she had 'grown into a genuine love of heroic proportions, however immoral she is' (pp. 199–200). Turning to other female characters, Cherry argued that Isabella's incest was 'perhaps the most shocking sin of the play'. Livia should be viewed as 'totally amoral although not usually malicious', and ultimately emerged as 'a comic figure endowed with tragic functions' (pp. 200–3).

The next landmark in critical engagements with the tragedy was the publication of J. R. Mulryne's enormously influential Revels Plays edition in 1975.[51] Mulryne dealt at length with matters of text, date, sources, analogues, lineation, and press variants. He not only offered a thorough critical assessment, but also gave a lengthy consideration of various stagings. He suggested that 'the few years before 1624 offer a more probable date [of composition] than those after', discussed Middleton's adaptation of his sources (pp. xxxvii–li), briefly surveyed early criticism, and then discussed matters of morality, dramatic idiom (pp. li–lxii), and characterization (pp. lxiii–lxxvi). Mulryne argued that despite the play's Italian setting, the work 'comes across with little glamour and little fervour'; 'anatomizes lust and hypocrisy and moral blindness but does not indulge them' (p. liii). Its language was mostly 'spare and undecorated' (p. lvii), and in terms of characterization 'Middleton's touch is surest in the portrait of Leantio' (p. lxiii). Mulryne's edition typified the growing interest at this time in producing reliable scholarly texts for the works of Shakespeare's contemporaries. Shakespeare himself had long benefited from the production of such editions, but now his fellow early modern dramatists had begun to profit in this way, too.

Meanwhile, in the following year, Roger Stilling endorsed the conclusions of many earlier critics, finding that Women Beware Women was less vital than The Changeling and that even its strengths were mostly dark, destructive, and 'chilly' (pp. 256–57).[52] He noted how Middleton demolished the play's romantic situations, called Livia 'a Jacobean high priestess of the id' (p. 258), thought the transformations of Isabella and Bianca too extreme, and suggested that Bianca saw 'in her sexual betrayal something about her own nature that shocks her deeply' (p. 259). Although Stilling considered Middleton's tragedy to be a 'gloomy, at times perfunctory play', he thought it revealed Middleton as a 'great dramatist' for his 'unfailing ability to reveal the psychological torments of the fallen condition' (p. 262). Also in 1976, Huston D. Hallahan tried to defend Middleton's concluding masque by arguing that the play as a whole juxtaposed 'the unrealistic and extraordinary with the realistic and ordinary so that the former qualifies and informs the latter' (p. 67).[53] Hallahan reproduced many examples from the visual arts of the early modern period (especially emblem books) in order to demonstrate that this practice was commonplace. In 1976 A. L. and M. K. Kistner also published a substantial discussion, addressing the victim status of the female characters, the theme of individual responsibility, and the play's unity (p. 17).[54] More generally, they argued that most of the characters are more ethically aware – and thus morally responsible – than had sometimes been assumed (pp. 23–24). Intriguingly, the Kistners suggested that Livia, like a vice figure, symbolized the evil inherent in both Bianca and Isabella, so that 'in following her, they follow their own wills'. The selfishness of the main characters made conflict inevitable, and an 'atmosphere of bleak amorality [...] pervades the play' (pp. 24–30).

In 1977 Larry S. Champion not only provided his own assessment of *Women Beware Women* but also offered a detailed overview of earlier criticism.[55] The fact that such a panoramic perspective could now be undertaken was itself a clear indication of just how much had been published on the play in the preceding decades. Champion emphasized such themes as passion, social decadence, and sexual depravity in Middleton's tragedy, and paid particular attention to the mixed moral natures of Bianca and Isabella (pp. 153–55). He found Leantio the most fully developed character, and argued that the final act 'provides a frightening culmination of the numerous strands of passion [...] leaving a sense of utter exhaustion' as Middleton 'undermines the spectators' easy confidence in the efficacy of Christian morality' (pp. 155–61). Equally illuminating was Champion's assertion that, far more than in other tragedies of the time, Middleton's characters seem confined to their own perspectives, so that spectators must supply most of the moral judgment (pp. 162–63). In the same year Marjorie S. Lancaster's discussion began by arguing that although the 'artistic quality' of *Women Beware Women* might seem debatable, 'its theatricality cannot be seriously questioned' (p. 69).[56] She thought the play deliberately echoed *Romeo and Juliet*, compared the Mother to Juliet's nurse, and contrasted the uses of the upper stage in 1.3 and 2.2 (pp. 76–80). Lancaster's article was one of the first to attend to the play critically as a piece for theatrical *performance*.[57]

By the end of the 1970s *Women Beware Women* had become a subject of frequent critical discussion. The play was touched on briefly by Paula S. Berggren in 1978,[58] who argued (rather oddly) that Bianca 'manages to sin yet emerge morally intact' since she 'seems redeemed by the exploration of her own possibilities' through adultery with the Duke (p. 358). More persuasive were four commentaries from 1979.[59] George E. Rowe asserted that the play 'reproduces Middleton's comic world more closely than do his two other tragedies', and he saw the play's society as one of insubstantial game-playing and cynical hedonism (pp. 194–95). Similarly, Nicholas Brooke began by arguing that the play developed from 'apparent naturalism' to 'extreme stylization'. Among many interesting comments, Brooke noted that it is mainly the Ward who speaks in prose, that Leantio's materialism is apparent at once, and that the play moves up the social scale with each new act (pp. 90–97). Verna Ann Foster saw an effective dramatic tension between Middleton's skilful psychological characterization and the work's implied moral judgments (pp. 508–9). Thus, Bianca learns to love the Duke almost as a father, and the Duke succeeds 'as a lover in every respect in which Leantio fails as a husband'. Furthermore, 'the relationship between Isabella and Hippolito illuminates that between Bianca and the Duke, and a portion of the sympathy earned by the lovers in the subplot redounds to those in the main plot' (p. 510). Instead of merely degenerating, Bianca finally emerges as 'a fully tragic heroine' who 'gains greater powers of discrimination and more extensive sympathies, self-assurance, and self-knowledge, and, indeed, a love more profound and enduring than the early romantic attachment it displaces' (pp. 516–17). Finally, in this year of burgeoning Middleton scholarship, John F. McElroy reassured his readers that from the very start of the play, the audience possessed 'a clear, straightforward, unwavering relationship with the characters, and with it a fixed perspective, not only superior to theirs, but virtually omniscient. As a result, we are never in doubt about how to assess what they do or say' (p. 299).

The Twentieth Century: 1980–85

By the end of the 1970s the kind of formalism associated with the so-called 'New Criticism' had begun to strike many critics as distinctly old-fashioned, and so the new decade brought an increasing emphasis on different kinds of study, especially a scholarship that sought to approach literature with a more insistently historicized (or even 'new historicist') methodology. Earlier approaches did not die out altogether, but there was a growing appetite to see Middleton and his tragedy from new perspectives. The year 1980, for instance, brought the publication of Margot Heinemann's landmark study of Middleton.[60] Her treatment of *Women Beware Women* stressed distinctions of class and the play's relevance to late-Jacobean social tensions. She praised the characters' unusual psychological consistency, emphasized Leantio's bourgeois values and background, and stressed the contrasting background of Bianca. In her desire to embed Middleton firmly in a Jacobean historical moment, Heinemann highlighted how the aristocratic decadence depicted onstage might be contrasted with the solid middle-class values of Middleton's audience (pp. 181–85). Indeed, in treating women, sex, and marriage, 'Middleton [was] very much a modern of his time', and his depiction of court corruption was highly topical, so that the Duke may even have reminded some auditors of the corrupt Duke of Buckingham. Heinemann stressed that Middleton adapted his source to emphasize a Christian and even fairly democratic viewpoint, and that the final masque seemed deliberately designed to mock the characters for violating Christian morality (pp. 189–97).

In the next year, Kenneth Muir began by asserting that *Women Beware Women* was 'surely better' than *The Changeling*, but then focused on Livia, who crucially united the main plot and subplot.[61] He also endorsed the view that Livia felt incestuous passion for her own brother (pp. 76–77). If Muir found the appearance of the Cardinal as a spokesman for traditional morality an asset, he also argued that what was 'less satisfactory [was] that Middleton makes no attempt to explain how the Cardinal has become reconciled to the marriage he has passionately denounced' (p. 82). Another article on the tragedy at the same time was published by Jennifer Strauss, who made a connection between the play and the medieval traditions of theatre and morality, pondering a range of negative views of dancing in the period, and the rapid changes in character development occasioned by a first exposure to sin.[62] Maintaining this emphasis upon an historicized performative approach, John Potter argued that Middleton 'used public festivals as the essential organizing principle' in *Women Beware Women*, and identified this as being 'the most original and striking aspect of his dramatic art' (pp. 368–69).[63] From his perspective, as the play develops, Bianca's loss of innocence 'is displayed through an increasing disjunction between gestures and their significance', so that 'what is ostensibly a game, a feast, a marriage masque is revealed as rape, prostitution, murder' (p. 370). In this context, hitherto 'innocent' images of eating, music, and dancing become symbols of 'coarse sexuality', and the marriage banquet not only develops themes from the chess scene but foreshadows the final masque. Potter unusually argued that 'the Cardinal's moral attitudes are suspect from his first speech', since he 'repeats moral commonplaces that he neither believes nor understands', and he intriguingly noted that the final masque both opens and closes with a kiss (pp. 373–79).

An important critical collection from 1983 contained two essays devoted to Middleton's tragedy.[64] Stephen Wigler's discussion began by focusing on varieties of real or symbolic incest in the play. In each of the three romantic liaisons in the work, the partners differ substantially in age, and the older partners resemble parents (pp. 183–84). Bianca seems, at first, an 'isolated and frightened girl' who is 'emotionally needy' and seeking 'reassurance and protective love'. This is the reason why the Duke 'succeeds in seducing her so readily', and it helps to explain why, after the seduction, she 'behaves like a spoiled, willful child' and 'becomes increasingly child-like as the affair progresses' (pp. 184–89). From Wigler's point of view, 'Isabella's choice of her uncle expresses a neurotic need' for fatherly protection and love, and in fact 'Middleton characterizes Hippolito's relation to Isabella as comfortingly oral rather than disturbingly genital, as in the case of the Ward'. Finally, to complete his discussion, Wigler affirms that 'Livia's relationships with Leantio and Hippolito are essentially maternal and nurturing', and the same is true of her relationship with Isabella (pp. 192–96). Michael McCanles's essay in the same volume returned debate to the familiar question of Middleton's moralism, arguing that the 'main purpose of the play is to illumine the causal relation between human moral qualities and motivations defined as mutually exclusive of each other'. Characters were sometimes actors and sometimes acted upon, and relations among them and their actions can be graphically charted using abbreviations and pointing arrows. Paradoxically, characters could 'be motivated by ethical imperatives to commit murder', since 'human good and evil both exclude and imply each other' (pp. 203–6).

In the following year, 1984, Neil Taylor and Bryan Loughrey explored the complicated implications of the chess scene by relating it not only to the moves of an actual chess game but also to Middleton's play *A Game at Chess*.[65] By thoroughly discussing chess both as a literal game and as a metaphorical device, Taylor and Loughrey dealt with such matters as the nature of existence, relations between the sexes, methods of characterization, social hierarchy, the use of puns, and other aspects of language used in the plays. Published in the same year, J. A. Cole's critical discussion added new insights to a much-discussed topic: the use of food imagery in the play.[66] Cole stressed that much of the food imagery contained 'reference to specific kinds of food, specific days or times of day when food is taken, and specific social or class relationships between providers and consumers' (p. 86).

Particularly suggestive also was a 1985 article by G. B. Shand on the stagecraft of the work – an article that reflected a growing interest generally in the literally *dramatic* aspects of early modern drama.[67] Shand compared Middleton to Marlowe, arguing that both playwrights show little affection for their characters, and indeed deliberately alienate audiences from their creations. Thus, in *Women Beware Women*, the 'major effect' of Middleton's stagecraft 'is to break down all sense of community, both among the characters and between those characters and their theatrical audience. This breakdown is achieved by 'multiple staging (where one element of a split stage picture comments on another), by isolation blocking (where characters stand apart to speak judgmentally about others, or to be spoken about), by intensive use of the aside, [...] and by virtually slapstick business which goes far beyond simple irony into the realm of the outrageous practical joke' (p. 29). Shand discussed all these theatrical devices in detail and also highlighted how modern productions have often ignored the effects Middleton's dramatic art generated. Shand's discussion of the concluding masque – 'arguably the most scornful finale in Jacobean tragedy, and one of the most daring as well' – sought particularly to solve the problem of how and why Guardiano dies (pp. 33–35).

The Twentieth Century: 1985–95

In 1986 Rowland Wymer dealt in passing with the theme of suicide in the play,[68] but more substantial discussions were published in that same year by Laura Severt King, A. A. Bromham, and T. McAlindon.[69] King argued that 'by rapidly and credibly turning sympathetic, quite ordinary characters base and even violent, Middleton stressed the danger of aristocratic depravity to the rest of society. Images of disease and contagion reinforce the point that the corruption of society's elite endangers everyone' (p. 44). A. A. Bromham, meanwhile, began by calling *Women Beware Women* 'the pinnacle' of Middleton's 'dramatic achievement' (p. 309) and then proceeded to claim that 'the play makes a contribution to the contemporary debate about James I's peaceful foreign policy which was intense in the early 1620s' (p. 310). He noted that the word 'peace' is often repeated in the play, and contended that the 'source of the moral deadness of society in *Women Beware Women* is shown to be the morally irresponsible pursuit of security, of false peace in the sphere of personal relations, which is ultimately destructive of honor and integrity' (pp. 314–15). For Bromham, 'The peace sought by characters [...] is a false peace based on a desire for quiet and the avoidance of difficult moral decisions, and to many people in contemporary

England such seemed the peace which James I was actually pursuing in his response to events in Europe' (p. 325). At the outset of his own discussion McAlindon confessed that he found *Women Beware Women* to be 'a less thrilling play' than *The Changeling*, but ultimately 'a more subtle and satisfying one' (p. 209). He argued that Middleton's mixture of comedy, tragedy, and satire puts 'the stamp of ordinariness on evil' and created 'in the audience a mood of ironic detachment from the misfortunes of the principle characters'. Most interestingly, he stressed that nearly every scene in the play 'dramatises a welcoming or a farewell, so that the rituals of hospitality invade language itself, providing metaphors for all forms of human interaction and every psychological posture' (p. 210).

In the following year, Laura Bromley argued that 'an examination of the subtext of the play reveals more topical and specific causes of human tragedy than original sin and social corruption'. Her argument developed with the contention that 'It is not free choice but insecurity – economic, social, and psychological insecurity – that finally attaches Bianca to the Duke, Isabella to Hippolito, and Livia to Leantio. Middleton locates the sources of this insecurity in the breakdown of traditional social hierarchies and in the loss of authority in the family, state, and church'.[70] Bromley showed great sympathy for Leantio, but also saw most of the younger characters as lacking 'nurturing families' to guide them (pp. 311–14). Also publishing that year, Anthony B. Dawson dissented from most previous criticism by claiming that the Duke does not merely seduce Bianca but actually rapes her (pp. 303–4).[71] Thus, Bianca had good reasons to feel insecure in Florence (p. 304), and there is little to distinguish her original marriage from her eventual rape (p. 310). Dawson's article, like a growing number of studies from the 1980s, responded in a focused and lively manner to the concerns of an increasing body of feminist scholarship devoted to early modern drama in this period.

Commentary on *Women Beware Women* published in 1988 tended to be brief.[72] Alexander Leggatt emphasized not only the satire and irony of the work but also its cynicism, and proposed that the 'closest the play takes us to tragic recognition is the wry, sad awareness' that Livia and Leantio show 'of the smallness of their own satisfactions' (pp. 147–49). In a memorable line, Leggatt submits that 'Middleton's characters even at their most religious cannot get beyond Christianity as a superior form of fire insurance' (p. 150). Meanwhile, David Farley-Hills contended that Bianca was 'doomed from the beginning by an ineluctable fate' and that in the concluding masque, 'Middleton's propensity for the absurd finally gets the better of him' (pp. 130–31). Even more briefly, Bryan Loughrey and Neil Taylor suggested that by 'trading her body for her freedom, Bianca recommits herself to the commercial ethos' first voiced by Leantio (p. xix). In 1989 Michael Cameron Andrews published short commentaries on the play, while a lengthier piece came from Albert H. Tricomi.[73] Andrews argued that Bianca's especially impressive death 'brings her closer to being a tragic figure than one would have imagined possible' (p. 98). Meanwhile, Tricomi's discussion insisted that the play deserved 'to be recognized as a major political tragedy and, particularly, as a powerfully conceived "popular" anticourt drama'. Indeed, for Tricomi, 'Middleton sought to deconstruct the symbolism of power and privilege' in ways that would reflect on Jacobean corruption. In his opinion, the five different courtly spectacles – 'the Duke's triumphal entry, the chess match and seduction, the banquet celebration, the engagement ceremony, and the nuptials masque' – were presented ironically (pp. 65–66), and in many other ways Middleton satirized Renaissance courts, including the subplot's emphasis on wardships and enforced marriages (pp. 68–72). As Tricomi's use of the verb 'deconstruct' suggests, his scholarship was clearly sensitive to many of the methodologies prominent in literary criticism of the 1980s, including not only 'deconstruction' itself but also a growing focus on Renaissance court culture and on the issues of political subversion.

The year 1990 saw the publication of a particularly valuable casebook edited by R. V. Holdsworth.[74] In this volume, Holdsworth offered an especially thorough discussion of stagecraft and stagings – one of the most distinctive features of the study of early modern drama in the closing decades of the twentieth century. He claimed the work to be 'by far [Middleton's] most theatrically ambitious and demanding play', noting that it had 'four sharply differentiated women' and that it was 'nearly a third as long again as the Middleton average'. Thus, it required a fast paced performance in order to prevent extensive cuts (p. 249). In an illuminating manner, Holdsworth drew attention to the play's emphasis on the key words 'strange' and 'stranger' and also to its habit of leaving characters unnamed for much of the action, even though settings were often explicitly labelled (pp. 252–54). This technique was found to contribute to a sense of distance, both among the characters themselves and in our own responses to them – an effect also produced by the frequent use of asides (p. 254). In the next year both Joan Lord Hall and Ingrid Hotz-Davies offered discussions of the tragedy.[75] While Hotz-Davies found that the play revealed a Middleton who was neither a feminist nor an anti-feminist (p. 37), Hall asserted that 'for the most part the forces driving the characters are social or economic, not spiritual' (p. 72). Interestingly, the latter also claimed that in the masque, the characters, having agreed to play parts 'that initially seemed alien or were imposed on them, [...] now become caricatures of these adopted personae' (p. 73).

In 1992 a short discussion of the tragedy in a book by Bruce Boehrer and also a brief article by Charlotte Spivack were published.[76] Boehrer argued that *Women Beware Women* combined 'a conservative suspicion of affection in marriage with a more radical sense of the family as an institution that *promotes* affection', so that the play promoted 'a devaluation of kinship ties both through its rhetoric and through its action' (pp. 108–9). Spivack, also concerned with family relations, saw marriage as a central theme of the play and thus the final masque as more inevitable and defensible than has often been assumed (p. 49). Ultimately, the concluding masque for Spivack 'is probably one of the most successfully integrated examples of the "fatal revels" in the entire period' and is highly relevant to the pervasive marriage theme (p. 53).

Richard A. McCabe's *Incest, Drama and Nature's Law* (1993) offered a number of intriguing comments on Middleton's tragedy, emphasizing the play's atheistic ethos, stressing the mostly unnatural affections the work presents, noting that Hippolito is only two years older than his niece, and suggesting that sexual jealousy may play a part in Hippolito's murder of Leantio (pp. 222–26).[77] Zara Bruzzi and A. A. Bromham examined the Italian setting of *Women Beware Women*, viewing the play as an admonition about sin, a reflection on the Jacobean court, and a vehicle for 'oblique political comment'.[78] The original model for the play's Duke allegedly resembled King James in various unattractive ways, while the Cardinal spoke as if he were a Calvinist, voicing views of which Middleton's city audience would likely have approved (pp. 252–56). Bruzzi and Bromham also asserted that the tragedy (ironically) echoed two masques by Ben Jonson in order to remind the audience of the scandals surrounding Frances Howard, and these echoes reflect negatively on James (pp. 260–61).

It was in 1994, however, that a signal event in scholarship on the play occurred: the publication of a new edition by William C. Carroll.[79] Carroll agreed (but not confidently) with the usually suggested date of c. 1621, and noted (after examining the sources) that the best scenes and most memorable character (Livia) are Middleton's own innovations. He endorsed the play's high ranking by critics and connected the work to contemporary early modern debates about women (pp. xvii–xxi). Addressing growing critical concerns with performative issues, Carroll also offered some analysis of the work's stagecraft and stage history, rendering his edition as indispensable to all readers of the tragedy as that of J. R. Mulryne. By the mid-1990s interest in Middleton's *Women Beware Women* showed no signs of flagging, as may be evidenced by the publication in 1995 of an article by Ann C. Christensen and discussion in a book by Ilse Born-Lechleitner.[80] Christensen detailed the importance of literal and symbolic houses and households in the play, arguing that just as 'household structures and activities frame the action, so architectural metaphors dominate the verbal text, with domestic situations standing for the moral state of their inhabitants' (p. 494). Thus, Leantio's failures as a householder were just the first of many such failures in this work. Born-Lechleitner's discussion, on the other hand, tended to summarize both the play and many previous opinions about it and thus provides a fitting final item for the present survey.

In well over three hundred years since the first publication of *Women Beware Women*, Middleton's play has become the subject of ever-increasing critical attention and admiration, and, as the present discussion has indicated, scholarship on the play has grown considerably in its thoughtfulness and variety, most especially in the twentieth century. However, it should be noted that the commentaries on *Women Beware Women* down the centuries continue to offer valuable insights into the circulation, consumption and interpretation of this often perplexing text – and this knowledge must remain a source of comfort for those who are convinced that much critical work still remains to be performed on this remarkable tragedy.

Notes

*   For assistance in tracking down and obtaining much of the material in this chapter, I wish to thank five superb interlibrary loan librarians: Belinda Jackson, Beth Parrish, Judy Shepard, Angelina Smith, and Karen Williams.

1   Sara Jayne Steen, *Ambrosia in an Earthern Vessel: Three Centuries of Audience and*

Reader Response to the Works of Thomas Middleton (New York: AMS Press, 1991), pp. 59–60. Steen's anthology culls material from the seventeenth century to the end of the nineteenth, while her equally valuable annotated bibliography – *Thomas Middleton: A Reference Guide* (Boston: G. K. Hall, 1984) – offers a comprehensive survey of commentary published from the seventeenth century to the end of the 1970s. Both books have proven indispensable to the present survey, which covers major commentary published between 1657 and 1995. Anyone seriously interested in Thomas Middleton is automatically indebted to Steen.
2   Steen, *Ambrosia*, pp. 65 and 67.
3   J. R. Mulryne, 'Annotations in some copies of *Two New Plays by Thomas Middleton, 1657*', *The Library*, 5th series, 30 (1975), 217–21.
4   Steen, *Ambrosia*, p. 82. For a passing comment by Nathan Drake, see p. 83.
5   Steen, *Ambrosia*, p. 93. This view was explicitly echoed by an anonymous author writing in 1840. See Steen, *Ambrosia*, p. 106.
6   Steen, *Ambrosia*, pp. 94–96.
7   Steen, *Ambrosia*, pp. 99–100.
8   Steen, *Ambrosia*, p. 100. For a similarly mixed assessment of the play by E. P. Whipple in 1859, see Steen, *Ambrosia*, p. 122. Whipple praised the work for showing 'a deep study of the sources of human frailty' and 'considerable skill in exhibiting the passions', but he felt that it lacked 'pathos, tenderness, and humanity' (ibid.). Similar opinions were expressed by an anonymous author in 1840, who praised the work's 'fine poetry', 'elegant expression', 'just reflections and sentiments', 'good versification' and 'variety of characters and passion', but who faulted the hurried, ham-handed, and catastrophic ending. Steen, *Ambrosia*, p. 107. See praise of the play's 'graceful and delicate' language in 1843 by James Russell Lowell (ibid., pp. 117–18).
9   Steen, *Ambrosia*, p. 125.
10 Steen, *Ambrosia*, p. 135. It might also be noted in this context that William Minto in 1874 objected to the uniformly 'vile' characters and to the undignified ending, and he echoed many of the same ideas in 1885, although he then added that 'in the expression of incidental moments of passion, Middleton often rises to a sublime pitch of energy' (ibid., p. 141).
11 Steen, *Ambrosia*, pp. 144 and 147–48.
12 Steen, *Ambrosia*, p. 154; see also p. 149.
13 Steen, *Ambrosia*, pp. 172–73.
14 Steen, *Ambrosia*, p. 173.
15 Steen, *Ambrosia*, pp. 179–80. Similar criticism of the ending can be found in another anonymous review of 1886, but here the reviewer's censure is balanced by his praise of Livia, who is considered to be among 'the most shrewd and intelligent of all [Middleton's] female characters', despite her moral failings (ibid., pp. 184 and 186–87).
16 Steen, *Ambrosia*, pp. 194, 196, 197–98.
17 Steen, *Ambrosia*, pp. 204–5.
18 Steen, *Ambrosia*, p. 207.
19 Steen, *Ambrosia*, p. 209.
20 William Vaughan Moody and Robert Morss Lovett, *A History of English Literature* (New York: Scribner's, 1902), p. 131.
21 Mable Buland, *The Presentation of Time in the Elizabethan Drama* (New York: Holt, 1912), pp. 170–71.
22 Arthur Symons, *Studies in the Elizabethan Drama* (New York: Dutton, 1919), p. 256.
23 Gamaliel Bradford, 'The Women of Middleton and Webster', *Sewanee Review*, 29 (1921), 14–29.
24 Janet Spens, *Elizabethan Drama* (London: Methuen, 1922), pp. 136–37.
25 T. S. Eliot, *Essays on Elizabethan Drama* (New York: Harcourt, Brace and World, 1956), pp. 89–90.
26 M. C. Bradbrook, *Themes and Conventions of Elizabethan Tragedy* (Cambridge: Cambridge University Press, 1935), pp. 224–39; for the quotations, see pp. 224–25.
27 U. M. Ellis-Fermor, *The Jacobean Drama: An Interpretation* (London: Methuen, 1936), pp. 140–42.

28 Henry W. Wells, *Elizabethan and Jacobean Playwrights* (New York: Columbia University Press, 1939), pp. 38–44.
29 Frederick S. Boas, *An Introduction to Stuart Drama* (London: Oxford University Press, 1946), pp. 233–37.
30 Daniel Dodson, 'Middleton's Livia', *Philological Quarterly*, 27 (1948), 376–81; see p. 376.
31 Samuel Schoenbaum, *Middleton's Tragedies: A Critical Study* (New York: Columbia University Press, 1955).
32 A. Bronson Feldman, 'The Yellow Malady: Short studies of five tragedies of jealousy', *Literature and Psychology*, 6 (1956), 38–52; see esp. pp. 44–46.
33 G. R. Hibbard, 'The tragedies of Thomas Middleton and the decadence of the drama', *Renaissance and Modern Studies*, 1 (1957), 35–64.
34 Richard Hindry Barker, *Thomas Middleton* (New York: Columbia University Press, 1958).
35 Robert Ornstein, *The Moral Vision of Jacobean Tragedy* (Madison: University of Wisconsin Press, 1960).
36 R. B. Parker, 'Middleton's Experiments with Comedy and Judgement', in *Jacobean Theatre*, ed. by John Russell Brown and Bernard Harris (London: Edward Arnold, 1960), pp. 178–99.
37 Christopher Ricks, 'Word-Play in *Women Beware Women*', *Review of English Studies*, 12 (1961), 238–50.
38 Edward Engelberg, 'Tragic Blindness in *The Changeling* and *Women Beware Women*', *Modern Language Quarterly*, 23 (1962), 20–28.
39 Irving Ribner, *Jacobean Tragedy: The Quest for Moral Order* (London: Methuen, 1962).
40 T. B. Tomlinson, *A Study of Elizabethan and Jacobean Tragedy* (Cambridge: Cambridge University Press, 1964).
41 George Core, 'The Canker and the Muse: Imagery in *Women Beware Women*', *Renaissance Papers* (1968), 65–76.
42 Thomas Middleton, *Women Beware Women*, ed. by Roma Gill (London: Ernest Benn, 1968).
43 Thomas Middleton, *Women Beware Women*, ed. by Charles Barber (Berkeley: University of California Press, 1969).
44 Inga-Stina Ewbank, 'Realism and Morality in "Women Beware Women"', *Essays and Studies* (1969), 57–70.
45 Dorothea Krook, *Elements of Tragedy* (New Haven: Yale University Press, 1969).
46 David M. Holmes, *The Art of Thomas Middleton* (Oxford: Clarendon Press, 1970).
47 Leonora Leet Brodwin, *Elizabethan Love Tragedy 1587–1625* (New York: New York University Press, 1971).
48 Norman A. Brittin, *Thomas Middleton* (New York: Twayne, 1972).
49 J. B. Batchelor, 'The Pattern of *Women Beware Women*', *Yearbook of English Studies*, 2 (1972), 78–88; Charles A. Hallett, 'The Psychological Drama of *Women Beware Women*', *Studies in English Literature, 1500–1900*, 12.2 (1972), 375–89. Another discussion from 1972 is also of note: François André Camoin, *The Revenge Convention in Tourneur, Webster, and Middleton* (Salzburg: Institut für Englische Sprache und Literatur, 1972), pp. 103–11.
50 Dorothy M. Farr, *Thomas Middleton and the Drama of Realism: A Study of Some Representative Plays* (New York: Barnes & Noble, 1973); Barbara Joan Baines, *The Lust Motif in the Plays of Thomas Middleton* (Salzburg: Institut für Englische Sprache und Literatur, 1973); Caroline Lockett Cherry, *The Most Unvaluedst Purchase: Women in the Plays of Thomas Middleton* (Salzburg: Institut für Englische Sprache und Literatur, 1973). See also, from the following year, Joseph Henry Stodder, *Satire in Jacobean Tragedy* (Salzburg: Institut für Englische Sprache und Literatur, 1974), pp. 133–38.
51 Thomas Middleton, *Women Beware Women*, ed. by J. R. Mulryne (London: Methuen, 1975).
52 Roger Stilling, *Love and Death in Renaissance Tragedy* (Baton Rouge: Louisiana State University Press, 1976).

53 Huston D. Hallahan, 'The Thematic Juxtaposition of the Representational and the Sensational in Middleton's *Women Beware Women*', *Studies in Iconography*, 2 (1976), 66–84.
54 A. L. Kistner and M. K. Kistner, 'Will, fate, and the social order in *Women Beware Women*', *Essays in Literature*, 3 (1976), 17–31.
55 Larry S. Champion, *Tragic Patterns in Jacobean and Caroline Drama* (Knoxville: University of Tennessee Press, 1977).
56 Marjorie S. Lancaster, 'Middleton's use of the upper stage in *Women Beware Women*', *Tulane Studies in English*, 22 (1977), 69–85.
57 For a more schematic discussion of the work, see Bruno Nauer, *Thomas Middleton: A Study of the Narrative Structures* (Zürich: Juris Druck & Verlag Zürich, 1977), pp. 51–67.
58 Paula S. Berggren, '"Womanish Mankind": Four Jacobean Heroines', *International Journal of Women's Studies*, 1 (1978), 349–62.
59 See George E. Rowe, *Thomas Middleton and the New Comedy Tradition* (Lincoln: University of Nebraska Press, 1977); Nicholas Brooke, *Horrid Laughter in Jacobean Tragedy* (New York: Barnes & Noble, 1979); Verna Ann Foster, 'The Deed's Creature: The Tragedy of Bianca in *Women Beware Women*', *Journal of English and Germanic Philology*, 78 (1979), 508–21; and John F. McElroy, '*The White Devil, Women Beware Women*, and the Limitations of Rationalist Criticism', *Studies in English Literature, 1500–1900*, 19 (1979), 295–312.
60 Margot Heinemann, *Puritanism and Theatre: Thomas Middleton and Opposition Drama under the Early Stuarts* (Cambridge: Cambridge University Press, 1980).
61 Kenneth Muir, 'The Role of Livia in "Women Beware Women"', in *Poetry and Drama 1570–1700*, ed. by Antony Coleman and Antony Hammond (London: Methuen, 1981), pp. 76–89.
62 Jennifer Strauss, 'Dance in Thomas Middleton's *Women Beware Women*', *Parergon*, 29 (1981), 37–43.
63 John Potter, '"In Time of Sports": Masques and Masking in Middleton's *Women Beware Women*', *Papers on Language and Literature*, 18.4 (1982), 368–83.
64 Kenneth Friedenreich, ed., *'Accompaninge the players': Essays Celebrating Thomas Middleton, 1580–1980* (New York: AMS Press, 1983). See, on pp. 183–201, Stephen Wigler, 'Parent and Child: The Pattern of Love in *Women Beware Women*' and also, on pp. 203–18, Michael McCanles, 'The Moral Dialectic of Middleton's *Women Beware Women*'.
65 Neil Taylor and Bryan Loughrey, 'Middleton's Chess Strategies in *Women Beware Women*', *Studies in English Literature, 1500–1900*, 24 (1984), 341–54.
66 J. A. Cole, 'Sunday dinners and Thursday suppers: Social and moral contexts of the food imagery in *Women Beware Women*', in *Jacobean Drama Studies: Jacobean Miscellany 4*, ed. James Hogg (Salzburg: Institut für Englische Sprache und Literatur, 1984), pp. 86–98.
67 G. B. Shand, 'The stagecraft of *Women Beware Women*', *Research Opportunities in Renaissance Drama*, 28 (1985), 29–36.
68 Rowland Wymer, *Suicide and Despair in the Jacobean Drama* (New York: St Martin's Press, 1986), pp. 51–54.
69 Laura Severt King, 'Violence and the masque: A ritual sabotaged in Middleton's *Women Beware Women*', *Pacific Coast Philology*, 21.1–2 (1986), 42–47; A. A. Bromham, 'The Tragedy of Peace: Political meaning in *Women Beware Women*', *Studies in English Literature, 1500–1900*, 26 (1986), 309–29; and T. McAlindon, *English Renaissance Tragedy* (Vancouver: University of British Columbia Press, 1986), pp. 209–35.
70 Laura Bromley, 'Men and Women Beware: Social, political, and sexual anarchy in *Women Beware Women*', *Iowa State Journal of Research*, 61.3 (1987), 311–21.
71 Anthony B. Dawson, '*Women Beware Women* and the Economy of Rape', *Studies in English Literature*, 27 (1987), 303–20.
72 See, for instance, Alexander Leggatt, *English Drama: Shakespeare to the Restoration 1590–1660* (London: Longman, 1988), pp. 147–51; David Farley-Hills, *Jacobean Drama: A Critical Study of the Professional Drama, 1600–25* (London: Macmillan,

1988), pp. 129–31; and Thomas Middleton, *Five Plays*, ed. by Bryan Loughrey and Neil Taylor (London: Penguin, 1988), p. xix.

73   Michael Cameron Andrews, *This Action of Our Death: The Performance of Death in English Renaissance Drama* (Newark: University of Delaware Press, 1989), pp. 95–98; Albert H. Tricomi, 'Middleton's *Women Beware Women* as Anticourt Drama', *Modern Language Studies*, 19.2 (1989), 65–77.

74   R. V. Holdsworth, ed., *Three Jacobean Revenge Tragedies*, Casebook series (Basingstoke: Macmillan, 1990). For Stachniewski's essay ('Calvinist Psychology in Middleton's Tragedies'), see pp. 226–47; for Holdsworth's article ('*Women Beware Women* and *The Changeling* on the Stage'), see pp. 247–74.

75   Joan Lord Hall, *The Dynamics of Role-Playing in Jacobean Tragedy* (New York: St Martin's Press, 1991), pp. 72–82; Ingrid Hotz-Davies, 'A *Chaste Maid in Cheapside* and *Women Beware Women*: Feminism, anti-feminism and the limitations of satire', *Cahiers Elisabéthains*, 39 (1991), 29–39.

76   Bruce Boehrer, *Monarchy and Incest in Renaissance England: Literature, Culture, Kinship, and Kingship* (Philadelphia: University of Pennsylvania Press, 1992), pp. 106–10; Charlotte Spivack, 'Marriage and Masque in Middleton's *Women Beware Women*', *Cahiers Elisabéthains*, 42 (1992), 49–55.

77   Richard A. McCabe, *Incest, Drama and Nature's Law 1550–1700* (Cambridge: Cambridge University Press, 1993), pp. 222–28.

78   Zara Bruzzi and A. A. Bromham, '"The soil alters; Y'are in another country": Multiple Perspectives and Political Resonances in Middleton's *Women Beware Women*', in *Shakespeare's Italy: Functions of Italian Locations in Renaissance Drama*, ed. by Michele Marrapodi et al. (Manchester: Manchester University Press, 1993; rev. edn 1997), pp. 251–71.

79   Thomas Middleton, *Women Beware Women*, ed. by William C. Carroll (New York: Norton, 1994).

80   Ann C. Christensen, 'Settling House in Middleton's *Women Beware Women*', *Comparative Drama*, 29.4 (1995–96), 493–518; Ilse Born-Lechleitner, *The Motif of Adultery in Elizabethan, Jacobean, and Caroline Tragedy* (Lewiston: Mellen, 1995), pp. 249–62.

CHAPTER TWO

Out of the Repertoire: *Women Beware Women* and Performance History

Paul Innes

The performance history of Middleton's *Women Beware Women* is peculiar, in both senses of the word. The play's relationship with the stage is strange because of the paucity of references to performances in the period for which it was written. The tragedy also has a very specific performance record which begs many questions, not least of which is: what is this play precisely about that appears to have rendered it unplayable for most of its existence.

The sordid world of the play, with its intermixing of sexual and political power, may well be the reason why *Women Beware Women* has often suffered such neglect. It is relatively easy to envisage why the play should disappear from sight at the Restoration, despite that period's own fascination with erotic representation on stage: the difficulty lies in the nature of sexual relations as they are presented by Middleton. Rapid changes in modes of characterization and the spectacular finale may also have deterred theatre companies. The eighteenth century's neo-classical literary culture and veneration for polite society would also have marked it as less than sympathetic to the excesses of Middleton's dramatic culture, in much the same way that Shakespeare is 'cleaned up' (or 'refined') for presentation on the post-Restoration stage.[1] And in the Romantic period, with its profound literary concern with the imaginative life of the individual, readers were for the most part similarly unreceptive to Middleton's art.[2]

Such historicizing comments provide a possible context for the neglect from which *Women Beware Women* has suffered. However, more detailed examination is required to determine what it is about *Women Beware Women* in particular that caused its absence from the repertoire for centuries, only to be rehabilitated in a spectacular fashion in the modern period.

Theorizing Early Modern Stage Culture

Since the 1980s there has been a significant and long overdue renewal of interest in the circumstances of writing and acting in the Tudor and Stuart playhouses.[3]

Unsurprisingly, given the relative infancy of this area when compared with textual history, the lion's share of the scholarship has been devoted to Shakespearean theatre, although a great deal of the commentary that has resulted can also usefully inform a discussion of Middleton's tragedy. The criticism of Robert Weimann in this area is particularly important here in delineating the popular roots of Renaissance drama and revealing their influence upon early modern dramaturgical practice.[4] Weimann also takes into account the necessary contexts of the Reformation and an evolving print culture as the overarching conditions in which shifting conceptions of authority impinged upon various areas of early modern cultural production, including English Renaissance drama.[5] More recently, he has developed his work with specific reference to the structural logic of Shakespeare's stagecraft:

> what would it mean to situate Shakespeare's text in the environment of a culture in which the new learning and writing had not fully supplanted the vitality in the oral communication of the unlettered, particularly when the transaction of that text on a stage – theatrical performance – was itself an oral-aural process?[6]

In this way Weimann interrogates Shakespeare's plays with the intention of recovering (as far as is possible) the dramatic indices that underpin the logic of Renaissance dramaturgy. It should be stressed that such a project goes against the grain of many well-mined textual readings, but it does not reject this more established form of engagement with the plays. Rather, in Weimann's words,

> My suggestion is that Elizabethan performance practice cannot be subsumed under any one purpose of playing; it must be viewed as plural, serving a number of diverse functions, as – far from being unified or unifying – a contested field in which early modern literary meanings can be constructed but also intercepted.[7]

Drawing attention to what he calls 'doubleness' (a given play's use of both literary and dramatic qualities),[8] Weimann investigates the different possibilities raised by the various texts of *Hamlet*, noting that there are dramaturgical as well as semantic conclusions to be drawn from them.[9] Weimann argues that 'the agency of playwriting is reconstructed as an important component of a larger nexus of socio-cultural and economic relations'[10] and, equally importantly, quotes Stephen Greenblatt's observation that 'It is impossible to take the "text itself" as the perfect, unsubstitutable, freestanding container of all its meanings'.[11] This enables him to elaborate a space for theorizing the practically unattainable recovery of Renaissance acting techniques on their own stages.[12]

Accordingly, we need not endorse the superior position traditionally accorded the dramatic text over and above that of a concern with the conditions of performance. Indeed, Weimann urges readers and audiences to consider a form of theatre study which points 'beyond any binary opposition between performance and text'.[13] In this context, it is important to note how dynamic is the exchange between the play as text and the play in performance, such that an easy opposition between the two is unsustainable. Indeed, the gap between these two poles itself inflects, or affects, the written text as well as the performance. This is a particularly critical observation, because it allows us to envisage how the practices of the theatre as an institution prefigure the written play as well as the play in performance.

The Dramaturgy of *Women Beware Women*

This brief conversation with Weimann can assist us enormously in contextualizing a performance study of Middleton's tragedy.[14] In his critical discussions, Weimann does gesture towards other dramatists in a way that allows wider possibilities of application to be inscribed in the processes he describes. Names such as Jonson and Marston reverberate throughout his discussions but, interestingly, Middleton is the one major figure missing from Weimann's account. The issue at stake, at least as far as *Women Beware Women* is concerned, is just how much this play's dramaturgy does indeed fit Weimann's model. What follows will be a necessarily schematic overview of the play's development, an attempt to highlight and bring together the various elements of stagecraft that occur in the play, and indeed that structure it in dramatic terms. The play will be discussed more or less a scene at a time, initially with the intention of bringing out the structuring stage techniques, up to and including the important chess scene (2.2). After that, the analysis will move to the second crucial area of character in performance, to be followed, finally, by some commentary on the conditions of playing before contemporary audiences. All three stages will be used to divide the text up into manageable sections, with a view, ultimately, to establishing what each of the three elements can tell us about the play's relationship with performance history. As an exercise, such a procedure has the added advantage of making us re-read the play afresh in the order in which it occurs on stage.[15]

In a sense two questions are at work in this analysis. First, just what is the relation of this particular play to the expectations of its own performance culture? And, secondly, what does this enable us to say about the resulting performance history? To reiterate: what is it about this play in particular that causes it to disappear from performance for so long, before returning to the stage with such startling vigour?

Like *Hamlet*, the initial scene of *Women Beware Women* begins with a visually differentiated tableau. In the earlier play, the passage of the ghost across the stage is watched and commented upon by two sentries; in Middleton's play, a similar enactment of the gaze occurs between Leantio (who is as yet unnamed) and his mother on the one hand, and Bianca on the other. This staging logic marks out both plays immediately as embodying a differentiated play world; the stage spacing elaborates a visual split between those who gaze and comment, and the one who is subjected to their discussions. The difference inscribed here accords with Weimann's theorizing of the *locus* and *platea*, the upstage and downstage position on the open platform stage respectively.[16]

The concept is a deceptively simple one. The *locus* is the upstage area that corresponds most closely with the static proscenium arch stage, since it is located farthest from the audience and presents a relatively unified field of view. It is important to note that this relation is only provisional, since the architectural space of many Renaissance theatres permitted a much more diverse set of audience positions and, correspondingly, audience gazes. The *platea* is the more open downstage position, right in the middle of the audience in at least some of the apron stage playhouses. This is the position from which actors closest to the audience can comment on the action and the *locus* in ways that are extremely difficult to understand, let alone reproduce, on most modern stages. Additionally, this is the area or zone in which some of the play action most closely accords with the expectations of audiences in Renaissance performance and play-going culture.[17] The term 'zone' is especially useful here because it denotes relative rather than absolute spheres of influence. It implies that movement is possible between the *locus* and the *platea*, turning the differentiation between the two into an interweaving of performative possibilities on the Renaissance stages.

Such a dynamic relation is exactly what occurs in the first scene of *Women Beware Women*. Leantio's mother, in her downstage position of collusion with the audience, says to her son 'What's this gentlewoman?' (1.1.11). Her question comes after Leantio's 'aside' to the audience, directly describing his own view of his mother to them. The *platea* enables direct audience address by means of conventions such as the aside; it is the space from which Bianca in the *locus* zone is pointed out, as if by someone in the midst of the audience itself. I will return to the implications of this technique later, as they relate directly to the question of characterization and the status of the audience in its own right.[18] What matters for the moment is the spatial logic of the relationship between the two zones. It must be noted in this context that Bianca stands there for 110 lines before her new mother-in-law crosses the threshold from one zone to the other in order to kiss her. This visual objectification of Bianca is the choreographic equivalent of Leantio's warning to his mother about the ramifications of his marriage at 1.1.46–567, which establishes the importance of money, status and sexual relations in this dramatic world. The dynamic complexity here can only be treated by recognizing the layering effects of the spoken word and its relationship with dramatic action; neither is necessarily privileged over the other and indeed both must operate effectively for the play to be successful. Weimann's portmanteau German term for this very specific element of Renaissance performance is *figurenposition*.[19] It should be noted that the scene ends with another convention, that of the soliloquy (1.1.151–76).

The action now moves to the play's second grouping of relations between the sexes, and it does so in ways that directly recall the first scene. The character denoted as 'Guardiano' comments directly to the audience, employing the convention of the aside in the same manner as Leantio in the previous scene; in particular, Guardiano's description of Isabella at 1.2.69–73 parallels Leantio's earlier description of Bianca. Significantly, it is exactly at this moment that Fabritio orders Isabella to mask herself – it would not be too far-fetched in performance for the company to have Bianca initially veiled or masked, as in scene 1, so as to point up the parallels even further. Conventionally, of course, the masked woman is often seen as a woman silenced. Costuming here could become a visual echo of Fabritio's attempts to silence any reservations Isabella might have about the stupidity of the Ward he has chosen to be her husband.

However, the play very quickly subverts any easy assumptions about such an attempt to objectify the silent woman by revealing in this very scene the possibility of incestuous desire and Isabella's own ambivalent status as a desired object and desiring subject.

The third scene of the first act returns to Leantio, his mother and Bianca, but in ways that significantly change the exposition. Leantio enters in soliloquy, almost picking up from where he left off at the end of scene 1. Bianca and her mother-in-law enter separately after this above the stage. In an open air theatre similar to the Swan or the Globe, the two characters would presumably be located at an aperture in the upper gallery of the tiring house. The symbolic location is again the *locus*, but this time with a difference: the vertical dimension could be used further to isolate them from Leantio in the *platea* (and thus, by extension, the audience as well).[20] Leantio reinforces the importance of the gaze here as he describes to the audience the effect this sight has upon him by repeating the verb 'see' at 1.3.13 and 1.3.17. His first use of the term is a typical *platea* injunction to the audience.

Leantio leaves on business and is replaced in the *platea* by citizens preparing for the Duke's procession. It is clear by this point that the two women above the stage are effectively looking out of the main façade of the house. The placing of the citizens reinforces the communality of the audience and *platea*, while the simultaneous staging of Bianca and Leantio's mother continues as the latter describes for the former what is about to take place. The clarity of the stage division inevitably draws attention to the acts of specularity: not only is the pair upstage (and up high) about to watch a procession, but those down below will be able to see the two women, Bianca included, which is precisely what Leantio was so desperate to avoid. And, at the same time, the audience sees all of this unfolding.[21] The complex logic of this kind of staging of multiple viewpoints enables Middleton to take advantage of the rich potentialities of the Renaissance stage. Interestingly, however, the play does not force the issue by immediately denoting some form of recognition or acknowledgement on the part of the Duke. Rather, it postpones this stage business by simply using the convention of the procession in dumb show, thus varying the exposition still further. The possibilities are left open:

Bianca: Did not the Duke look up? Methought he saw us.
Mother: That's everyone's conceit that sees a duke (1.3.105–6)

However, such staging does allow for the possibility of 'wrong seeing', an element that the play will go on to develop much more fully.

Rather than expand immediately upon the various possibilities left open by the third and final scene of Act 1, the action now shifts back again to the other main plot strand. In a sense this patterning is now becoming a form of ironic counterpointing by close dramatic association: the sexual conversation that takes places between Livia and Hippolito contaminates the hitherto separate world of Bianca. In the meantime Livia spins Isabella a tale that effectively bastardizes her niece, and in a paradoxically positive manner, because it means that there is now a way out from Fabritio's dictates for Isabella (2.1.92–177). The thematic importance of sexual deceit is being brought more and more into the open in a network of associations of wealth and social status: according to Livia, Isabella's real father was the Marquis of Coria. Livia's explanation ostensibly clears the way for Hippolito to make his advances to Isabella – if Fabritio is not her father, then Hippolito is not her uncle. In this way the second main strand of the plot is used to introduce obliquely, as it were, the tragedy's obsessive interest in upper-class corruption and sexual incontinency that will inevitably infect the Bianca plot. In strictly literary critical terms, there is nothing new in making these points, but what I am trying to do is provisionally reconstruct how the staging itself is utilized to produce the same meanings, in a kind of double relationship of the kind envisaged by Weimann.

The latter part of 2.1 is acted out by means of a series of 'asides' interspersed among the conversations between characters. This includes a direct address by Livia to the audience about her craftiness at 2.1.178–79 as she is on her way out. She encounters Hippolito as he enters the stage, and there is a short epigrammatic utterance as Livia tells him 'She's thine own. Go' (2.1.179). Not only does this complete the second line of her aside, it makes use of another dramatic convention, the conversation between some characters that is not overheard by others, the 'mishearing' equivalent of 'wrong seeing'. The interaction between Isabella and Hippolito that follows is structured by means of 'asides' which constitute separate addresses to the audience. What happens here is not just a series of short comments; these are long descriptions by each character made directly to the audience while the other character is still onstage. Presumably each is to one side of the stage in the *platea*, splitting the location further and reinforcing the sense of audience collusion. The fact that so many characters have now used the technique of the aside means that it becomes a vehicle, in this play at least, for simultaneous staging of multiple character viewpoints, all within the purview of the audience's direct engagement. Middleton uses this well-established stage convention to invigorate the plot element of character motivation and manipulation, reinventing its purpose as a tool of more than just one character at a time. In other words, the *platea* aside functions emblematically as a visual enforcement of a play world in which almost everyone has a hidden purpose, and only the audience is made fully aware of what is going on. Indeed, Hippolito directly draws attention to the events that unfold by means of a soliloquy after Isabella has left him alone on the stage.

Such shifting engagements produce a skilful use of the physical resources available to the Renaissance stage. Perhaps the single most commonly cited performance element of the play now begins to unfold in 2.2, the game of chess. However, it should be noted that this emblematic game occurs in the context of a particularly complex long scene that consists of many internal shifting sub-scenes. It begins by picking up on the potential options deferred from the Duke's earlier procession. The conversation between Guardiano and Livia leaves the audience in no doubt that the Duke desires Bianca. Guardiano has been charged with enabling the Duke to gain access to the unknown lady and Livia will help out by manipulating her old neighbour, Leantio's mother. The character developments glimpsed here will be revisited later; what is important for the moment is the exploitation of sexual favours for political gain is not confined to one sex alone. Moreover, it is interesting to note that the subsequent onstage

OUT OF THE REPERTOIRE   49

antics and sexual punning of the 'useless' Ward and his foil, Sordido, act as a visual enactment not just of a related plotline, but of the excesses of acting that are part and parcel of the expectations of this performance culture.

As the two fools leave, the Mother comes on, and the game of chess is set up, symbolizing the *motif* of human manipulation in evidence throughout the play. The Mother is inveigled by Livia to send for Bianca, and then to allow Bianca to be taken off by Guardiano to see the rest of the house. At this point (292ff) the full resources of the Renaissance stage are brought into play. Not only is there simultaneous staging, possibly with Guardiano and Bianca (and then the Duke) vertically removed from the chess game, but the rape of Bianca takes place off stage. The layering of effects that results again reveals the multiple relationships of surveillance between the characters. And in direct comparison with many of Shakespeare's plays, the singular importance of the crucial act of violence is emphasized by the fact that it exists in a life beyond the stage: compare, for example, the death of Duncan in *Macbeth*, the supposed sexual incontinence of Hero in *Much Ado About Nothing*, and the drowning of *Ophelia*.[22] These unshown scenes carry so much symbolic weight that subsequent cultures have felt a requirement to fill them in, as it were, with their own interpretations. One only has to think of the Romantic and pre-Raphaelite obsession with painting Ophelia in the water, or indeed the need felt by modern film directors directly to show such events to their audiences. Nor is this a trivial point; the later necessity to represent these unpresented events may hint at a major difference between later cultures and the Renaissance. Given the often volatile nature of sixteenth- and seventeenth-century society, a Renaissance company would have had to be very careful about staging something like regicide – if staging it were a possibility in the first place. But there is a further paradox: not to show such a major plot element draws attention to it as something crucial to the play's representations. Thus, the meanings generated by the event will be represented in different ways by different people, as well as providing plot momentum. On this stage, absence has its own dynamic.

The scene ends with a split in Bianca's own speech patterns after she returns to the main part of the stage. Her conversation with her mother-in-law is interspersed with imprecations made aside to Livia before the latter is left on stage alone. Her final soliloquy sets the seal on an extremely complicated series of movements; it also links her indissolubly to a very specific set of performance requirements which are, in turn, shaped by the larger culture for which the tragedy was produced. To recap: since these circumstances are historically precise, it does not take a great shift in the cultural environment to render the play as a performance piece problematic indeed, perhaps even alien to subsequent generations – and thus unplayable.[23]

Character in Performance

Livia's soliloquy at the end of the second act also draws attention to characterization in performance, as indeed does the whole scene. At first sight, this may seem an obvious point to make, but in terms of Renaissance dramatic exposition it is not trivial. As the antics of the Ward and Sordido in this very long scene remind us, there is a logic of dramatic performance for its own sake that is embedded in the very structure of this drama.[24] The contemporary audience expects the acting it sees and hears not only to advance the story, but also to be worth watching in its own right, over and above any plot exigencies or requirements of dramatic writing. *Women Beware Women* provides a very sophisticated example of this dramatic art at its richest, with characters moving dynamically across the stage, exploiting the full range of its zonal organization. Additionally, at least some of them must move between roles, in order that the full potentialities of the *figurenposition* may be teased out. There is a productive tension between the role played and the person playing the role; the historical root of the Brechtian *gestus* in which the actor enacts a part and at the same time shows great awareness of the process of acting itself.[25] The actor does not submerge himself entirely in another (fictional) psychology; this is not a theatre for Stanislavski.

All of which brings me to the second important issue raised by the play's performance history: this kind of characterization may provide another part of the explanation for the play's peculiar history in performance. In direct comparison with the earlier consideration of performance techniques, characterization in *Women Beware Women* can be examined in the context of the prevailing dramatic conventions. For example, Livia and Guardiano can both be seen as stage types common to Jacobean tragedy. As a manipulator, the figure of Livia compares well with, say, Beatrice in *The Changeling*, another woman who operates by undermining the ideological basis for codes of sexual behaviour. Guardiano can similarly be compared with Bosola in *The Duchess of Malfi*. Both are malcontents because of their lack of social advancement, and both initially operate on behalf of powerfully corrupt patrons at the apex of the social pyramid. Such figures recognize the innocence of the people they are to victimize, and the ethical dubiety, to put it mildly, of those they serve. Bosola and Guardiano change from this knowing acquiescence to agency against their employers. It is perhaps this shifting logic of character presentation that is at the root of the historical problem of *Women Beware Women* in performance. Moreover, Guardiano is not alone in changing in this way – Leantio also tries to become a kind of revenger figure, moving radically away from his initial passivity.

It seems reasonable to suggest that such a movement depends on something other than what a later period might consider to be consistent or realistic internal character psychology. However, this is a performance point, differing in its implications from other forms of critique: 'the most striking thing about *Women Beware Women* is the very consistent and comprehensible human and psychological motivation of the characters, given the social circumstances, a consistency uncommon in Jacobean drama'.[26] Here Margot Heinemann argues that the social world of the play produces consistent character motivation in a uniform manner. While this is persuasive within a narrative of literary criticism, the fact that several of the onstage figures change, and not all at the same time or at the same speed, disturbs any easy assumptions of a primacy of coherence, at least for a modern audience. The comparison between Bosola and Guardiano is a case in point: in the long second scene of Act 2, Guardiano begins to assume the role of plot motor familiar from Webster's play, enacting the convention of the outsider.

> 'Tis for the Duke; and if I fail your purpose,
> All means to come by riches or advancement
> Miss me and skip me over. (2.2.28–30)

He speaks these lines to Livia, enacting a cue to the audience that will enable them to recognize his character type. Guardiano is now becoming a lynchpin to the double plots of sexual corruption, both Livia's and the Duke's. His unspecified position in the households of Fabritio and Livia makes him useful in such business, as well as rendering him available to the Duke as part of his plans. The *figurenposition* thus generated for Guardiano is crucial, marking him off as a socially and dramatically liminal personage. The way the actor puts this role into action makes him a dramatic threshold, precisely because he is able to comment on his own conduct and that of others while still remaining a participant in the intrigue.[27]

The way in which the Guardiano *figurenposition* is able to do this is by occupying the *platea* and acting as an 'intervenient' figure.[28] A good example occurs when Bianca curses him in an aside at 2.2.425–43. His response is particularly illuminating:

> Well, so the Duke love me,
> I fare not much amiss then. Two great feasts
> Do seldom come together in one day;
> We must not look for 'em. (2.2.443–46)

His comment is noted in the stage directions as an aside, but again it is much more a direct address to the audience, encapsulating his success in both plotlines. Of course, it is important to note in this context that Guardiano does not necessarily always act in this way: the 'intervenient' pose is one that is conventionally available to him as one of many stage personae.

In addition, dynamic characterization is not limited to him alone; in the next scene, Bianca also begins to show signs of a rapidly-changing stage presence. This is prepared for by another character in soliloquy, this time Leantio's mother, as she tells the audience about the difference she has noticed in Bianca since the visit to Livia's house. Bianca then enters, argues with her mother-in-law about the meanness of the house, and exits. The Mother then speaks a second soliloquy and withdraws to another part of the stage, the cue for Leantio's entrance. When Bianca returns to greet him, she does so rather frostily, employing a number of sexual puns. The conflict becomes more and more open as a messenger arrives from the Duke, inviting Bianca to a banquet at Livia's house; this leads to a full-scale argument because Leantio is shocked by the fact that the Duke knows about his wife. Bianca and her mother-in-law now ally against Leantio and go off to get ready for the banquet against his orders. The messenger reappears to invite Leantio as well. This short overview of the scene does not do justice to its complex staging and use of asides, but in the context of the discussion of characterization it raises the major issue of change in several figures at once.

The differences in Bianca are perhaps the most obvious, and as part of the sexually corrupt world depicted in the play, her role has attracted the most critical attention.[29] Understandable as this may be in terms of the play's sexual politics, an analysis of the effects of her rape on her character and the beginning of her change into accepting the role appointed for her in the moral economy of the Duke (as well as that of her husband), can underplay the performative element of the play's treatment of Bianca. This is a particularly difficult point to unpick, because it requires a way to see such character change via the actor's performance, in addition to the words provided by the dramatic text. In this instance, one has to assume provisionally that Bianca's sexual vocabulary combines with her own more aggressive use of asides in this scene to highlight exactly the associations noted earlier. To reiterate: in this play, the aside is never simply a neutral utterance and its prior uses by Livia and Guardiano in particular associate the aside with the play's preoccupation with sexual and politic manoeuvring. The fact that Bianca now participates fully in this usage marks her out as having become another such figure. It could, of course, be argued that this is over-reading; but the point is, precisely, that reading is not enough – this is a point which continues to be neglected on account of the modern privileging of literary culture, even on the stage. However, *Women Beware Women* was written for a radically different stage culture and we should not underestimate its performance assumptions, even if they have subsequently become alien to the conventions of our own theatre experiences.

In the next scene, change comes to Livia as well as she falls in love/lust with Leantio at the banquet. Initially, she warns the Duke about him and, interestingly, she begins to fall for him after the Duke rewards him with the Captainship of the citadel of Ruinse – perhaps his social elevation has something to do with her attraction. Leantio, in the meantime, is also changing, as denoted by his use of the aside. He sees that there is some sort of relationship between the Duke and Bianca, but is not powerful enough to say or do anything about it; interestingly, he confides in the audience as a result. Leantio begins his character shift to revenger in aside at lines 89–98 as he sees the Duke and Bianca drinking together. The distance between husband and wife might be emphasized by placing the Duke and Bianca in the *locus* zone, with Leantio in the *platea* commenting to the audience. Leantio's conversion to an active character seeking vengeance adds to a steadily growing list of changing figures, and this is important. Almost all of the major figures are now shifting, in one way or another, as they take turns to use the aside and the *platea*. It would seem sensible to suggest as a result that character change alone is not sufficient to account for the play's difficulty for subsequent readers and audiences, but that the extent of multiple change to a range of characters has posed real challenges to generations of readers and actors. There is a good historical reason for such difficulty: the growth in importance of the individual as a concept in subsequent centuries has created an appetite for less fluid and more coherent characterization than is to be found in *Women Beware Women*.[30] Later reception of the play may well be affected by the extravagance and rapidity of change in multiple characters, such that for an audience used to a more managed form of characterization, simultaneous changes in so many figures may result in affective and moral disengagement.

A great deal more than this occurs in 3.2, but the focus on the performance of character needs to be glossed further with reference to the Isabella plotline. As the banquet progresses, Guardiano is seen at a different part of the stage trying to deal with the Ward and Isabella, just as the Duke finishes off the arrangements for their marriage. This is developed further in 3.3, and here again we find another use of the aside convention. At 3.3.33–42, Isabella develops upon her previous asides in the company of Hippolito, commenting ironically on her arranged marriage with the Ward. The broad comedy in this scene is reminiscent of the Ward's earlier appearances on stage, but this time it occurs in the context of Isabella's grudging acquiescence in a match that is necessary to conceal her interest in Hippolito. The scene as a whole is framed in movement by Guardiano; he sets up the encounter between Isabella, Sordido and the Ward. He leaves the scene to take its course, and returns when it is over. The result is to emphasize Guardiano's liminal function and role as surveillant.

The beginning of Act 4 now requires a further series of changes related in this instance to the Duke. Bianca, who is now his in the fullest sense of possession, tells him about Leantio's knowledge of their affair. The Duke decides to make use of Hippolito in an aside at 4.1.132–41 that marks him out as an expert machiavel. The relentless logic of change marches on, with so many characters now undergoing radical transformations that only an audience steeped in this performance culture will be able to attend to these shifts. What is needed to make this work is ensemble performance of the highest order, with no one single character predominating, something that is again extremely difficult to pull off on the modern stage. Even Hippolito changes, as the Duke reveals to him the relationship between Leantio and Livia, putting all the blame on the former, of course. It is only when this final movement takes place that the Cardinal finally appears on stage. Even though he witnesses some form of repentance in his brother, it is only provisional. After the Lord Cardinal's exit, the Duke re-emerges as a machiavel, this time in soliloquy.

It is clear that character is not some stable unity of coherent psychology. Rather, it is a set of performative possibilities over and across which a multiplicity of meanings can be played out. Such a dynamic conception of how meanings occur in and through performance serves as a critical foil to historically subsequent assumptions that the prime generator of meaning is the text.

Audience engagement

If techniques of performance and character in *Women Beware Women* are culturally and historically specific, what about the assumptions held by the play's contemporary audiences? This is the last of our three major elements under investigation, and it is inevitably linked with the first two. This drama is structured by a prior recognition of the accepted parameters of playing. As successful practitioners of the craft, the company of players has a professional working knowledge of what will succeed on these stages for its paying contemporaries.

But recovering such audience assumptions is perhaps an even more difficult task than imagining performance or character techniques: 'For the audience itself to be acknowledged as the supreme court of appeal is an act of authorization that goes beyond that of the representation of dramatic action'.[31] Weimann goes on to explore this formulation. However, in the context of a discussion of *Women Beware Women*, a further operation needs to be managed so as better to understand the reasons for this play's peculiar performance history. Taking into account the critical perspectives of Weimann and our earlier discussions of performance and characterization, it is possible to discern here a complex dramaturgy that is aimed very precisely at a specific culture, that of the contemporary play-goers. And if the two interrelated elements of performance and character are difficult for later cultures to decipher, this situation should also give us cause in terms of a possible shift in audience tastes which has led to the sustained neglect of plays such as *Women Beware Women*.

At 4.2 Hippolito does indeed kill Leantio, but this action leads to a further dynamic of revenge. In her grief, Livia reveals to everyone present his lust for Isabella as well as her lies about Isabella's ties of kinship. There now follows a swift sequence of multiple shifts: Guardiano decides to become an agent of revenge; Isabella scorns Hippolito and vows revenge on Livia; and this results in a final extravagant commitment to deceit on the part of all the major players.[32] It is clear that the logic of character change is by Act 4 so fundamental that it becomes the driving force of the drama as it moves inexorably towards its conclusion in the traditionally excessive bloodbath. The death of Leantio and the reactions of the characters who become involved engender as a kind of psychologized chaos before the final catastrophe is enacted on stage. The logic that underpins the play's representations of sexual and political power becomes so entangled that it unravels. In the case of *Women Beware Women*, the signal to audiences that this play will indeed fulfil their expectations comes with the announcement of the Duke's marriage and the wedding masque that will accompany it. Guardiano makes the required performative comment: 'The plot's full then' (4.2.214).

The appearance in a Renaissance play of such self-artifice is well known in terms of the self-referentiality so beloved of literary critics, but here it has added meaning. It points to the play-within-the-play, completing Middleton's display of his command of the full repertoire of Renaissance techniques of enactment. However, at the same time it also acknowledges the audience's expectation of an explosive finale.[33] The play prepares the way for its own use of the sub-play by sweeping on through two short scenes. In 4.3 the wedding procession is interrupted by the Lord Cardinal, who is then disdained by Bianca and the Duke. The Lord Cardinal is left alone on the stage to utter his prophetic epigram:

> Lust is bold,
> And will have vengeance speak ere't be controlled. (4.3.71–72)

The anticipated bloodbath arrives in a quite spectacular fashion. In turn, Livia starts to die from poisonous fumes exuded by Isabella's censer; Livia retaliates by throwing fire on Isabella's lap, which kills the niece; Guardiano falls onto his own caltrop when Hippolito stamps in anger at Livia's death; Hippolito is shot by the masqued Cupids with poisoned arrows and finishes himself off by running

OUT OF THE REPERTOIRE   55

onto a halberd; the Duke dies of the poisoned cup Bianca had intended for the Cardinal; and Bianca kills herself with the same poison. The sheer performative excess generated by all of these accidental and stage-managed deaths inscribes Renaissance performance culture onto the play, as does the Lord Cardinal's final four-line comment.

There is a very good reason for rehearsing the final bloodbath at such speed: it points not only to the conventions of early seventeenth-century tragedy, but also the problem posed for subsequent performance cultures. On its own stage, the ending of *Women Beware Women* may have been a specific requirement, even an expectation. And when the play is finally revived for modern audiences who are perhaps more than ready for its multiple treatments of sex and politics (the more easily available textually generated meanings), the problem of performing it looms large, precisely because it can seem so absurd. John Jowett describes the strategy adopted by Howard Barker for the 1986 Royal Court Theatre production:

> a pared-down text of the first four acts was followed by a second part in modern idiom written entirely in Barker's own hand. Barker notes that in Middleton 'lust leads to the grave'; in his own version, which rejects the Cardinal's moralizations as a lie, 'desire alters perception', becoming a frenzy that leads towards political revolution.[34]

Such massive cutting of the finale could be seen as the solution to an insurmountable problem. It could also, of course, point to a structured historical shift, since Barker's production is aimed at a modern audience who might accept the play's dealings with sexual and social power politics, while at the same time being irretrievably alienated from at least some of the staging techniques it uses. Indeed, the Lord Cardinal's final epitaph may in fact have drawn attention to the inadequacy of the wider moral culture of this dramatic world.[35]

Jowett's 'Introduction' to the play replays its recent performance history in exactly the terms delineated above. The way in which the play disappeared from the stage for so long is a direct result of its fidelity to its own performance culture in the three areas of technique, characterization and the relationship with its own audience. This seems persuasive enough, but what is particularly interesting is that even its modern revivals have a sense of partiality to them, as though the production of meaning is somehow demeaned by some of the play's own stagecraft. I would contend, rather, *pace* Robert Weimann, that a very precise structural change in the conditions of reception has inevitably led this play to a history of non-performance. This is not to denigrate modern performances; rather, it takes cognisance of the fact that at root they recognize that a long-term change has occurred – it is not possible for modern productions simply to *replay this play*.

In this context, it is important to note that one of the most recent major revivals of the play took such issues as a major point of departure. The Red Bull Theater's New York production of the play ran from December 2008 to January 2009 and received a number of reviews.[36] Some of these are shorter than others, but a distillation gives some flavour of the production. First of all, the costuming was very sumptuous, giving a gloss of excessive luxury to the play world. Secondly, the staging was elaborately designed so as to give a sense of elaborate intertwining between levels and stage areas, a labyrinthine visual reminder of the play's intertwining plots. Thirdly, the language was somewhat pared down, presumably to relieve a contemporary New York audience of some verbal excesses that would be difficult to convey. Fourthly, some interaction was enacted between the cast and the audience. And, finally, the Cardinal was rewritten to be just as corrupt as the rest of the characters. All of these directorial/cast choices make judicious choices in restaging the play in a meaningful way for a much later audience.

Our own conditions of performance are radically distinct from those of Middleton's contemporaries, especially given the rise of the individual and the appetite for more psychologically coherent characterization. Singleness of purpose in playing and character is a completely different cultural *milieu* from the liminal locations of theatrical practice operational in Renaissance London,[37] not to mention the threshold characteristics of Renaissance characterization. The primacy of the unitary gaze associated with the proscenium arch theatre reaches its *apogee* with modern visual media: Granada Television broadcast a televised performance in 1965.[38] It is difficult to conceive of a play less suited to the gaze of an individual directed towards a single point of light in a corner, cut off from all possible audience interaction.

Notes

1   For a reminder of the literary and cultural bias of the early editorial business, see Robert Weimann, *Author's Pen and Actor's Voice: Playing and Writing in Shakespeare's Theatre* (Cambridge: Cambridge University Press, 2000), pp. 31–36.
2   Recently recounted in Margreta de Grazia, *Hamlet Without Hamlet* (Cambridge: Cambridge University Press, 2007), pp. 7–22.
3   A representative sample would include Steven Mullaney, *The Place of the Stage: License, Play, and Power in Renaissance England* (Chicago and London: University of Chicago Press, 1988); Louis Montrose, *The Purpose of Playing: Shakespeare and the Cultural Politics of the Elizabethan Theatre* (Chicago and London: University of Chicago Press, 1996); Pauline Kiernan, *Shakespeare's Theory of Drama* (Cambridge: Cambridge University Press, 1998); W. B. Worthen, *Shakespeare and the Authority of Performance* (Cambridge: Cambridge University Press, 1997); Leeds Barroll, *Politics, Plague and Shakespeare's Theater: The Stuart Years* (Ithaca: Cornell University Press, 1991); Meredith Anne Skura, *Shakespeare the Actor and the Purposes of Playing* (Chicago and London: University of Chicago Press, 1993). All of these works could be considered as sympathetic to my own present endeavour, in that they attempt to theorize the relationships between dramatist, actors/players and audiences, rather than simply use them to account for the pre-eminence of Shakespeare. The most important body of work in this respect is that of Robert Weimann, *Shakespeare and the Popular Tradition in the Theater: Studies in the Social Dimension of Dramatic Form and Fiction*, ed. by Robert Schwartz (Baltimore and London: Johns Hopkins University Press, 1978), and his updating and extension of that work, in Robert Weimann, *Author's Pen and Actor's Voice: Playing and Writing in Shakespeare's Theatre*, ed. by Helen Higbee and William West (Cambridge: Cambridge University Press, 2000). See also Andrew Gurr, *Playgoing in Shakespeare's London*, 2nd edn (Cambridge: Cambridge University Press, 1996) for the impact of the socially disparate composition of the audiences. There is of course a much longer (and uneven) history of attempts to address the void in studies of Renaissance performance. The texts cited above seem to me to attempt most directly to account for this much neglected aspect of the period's output.
4   Weimann, *Shakespeare and the Popular Tradition*, pp. 73–84.

OUT OF THE REPERTOIRE 57

5   Robert Weimann, *Authority and Representation in Early Modern Discourse*, ed. by David Hillman (Baltimore and London: Johns Hopkins University Press, 1996).
6   Weimann, *Author's Pen and Actor's Voice*, p. 7. Compare the comments on modern assumptions about textual primacy even in drama in Worthen, *Shakespeare and the Authority of Performance*, p. 27.
7   Weimann, *Author's Pen and Actor's Voice*, p. 8.
8   Weimann, *Author's Pen and Actor's Voice*, pp. 10–11.
9   Weimann, *Author's Pen and Actor's Voice*, pp. 20–21. He goes on later to adopt a similar technique in relation to Marlowe's *Tamburlaine the Great* at pp. 58–61. By way of comparison, see also Leah Marcus, *Unediting the Renaissance: Shakespeare, Marlowe, Milton* (London: Routledge, 1966), pp. 38–67, a chapter in which she analyses in subtle depth the nuances of the two texts of Marlowe's *Dr Faustus*.
10 Weimann, *Author's Pen and Actor's Voice*, p. 39.
11 Stephen J. Greenblatt, *Shakespearean Negotiations: The Circulation of Social Energy in Renaissance England* (Oxford: Clarendon Press 1988), p. 3; quoted in Weimann, *Author's Pen and Actor's Voice*, p. 38.
12 Weimann, *Author's Pen and Actor's Voice*, p. 40.
13 Weimann, *Author's Pen and Actor's Voice*, p. 55.
14 I make no apologies for my shameless use of Weimann's work in this way. It seems to me to be the most sophisticated and complex work to date that analyses both the context and practical exigencies of Renaissance dramatic production.
15 The alternative would be to adopt a purely thematic methodology, reading the whole play in three different ways. In one sense this would be a more sophisticated argument, but there is the danger that the three main issues would become relatively isolated one from another. By reading the text in sequence, but subdividing it into three categories for investigation, I am trying to get to a baseline for each that will help to explain the play's disappearance from the performance record.
16 Weimann, *Shakespeare and the Popular Tradition*, pp. 73–84, and as further developed in Weimann, *Author's Pen and Actor's Voice*, pp. 180–95.
17 For the term 'zone', see Weimann, *Author's Pen and Actor's Voice*, p. 202. Paul Innes, '"Pluck but his name out of his heart": A Caesarean Cross-section', in *Refiguring Mimesis: Representation in Early Modern Literature*, ed. by Jonathan Holmes and Adrian Streete (Hatfield: University of Hertfordshire Press), pp. 79–98 (p. 89), discusses a moment in Shakespeare's *Julius Caesar* at which a character in one part of the stage points to another in exactly the same way as occurs at the beginning of *Hamlet* and *Women Beware Women*, albeit in the context of a different argument. This is glossed later in the same essay at pp. 92–95, with specific reference to Weimann, *Shakespeare and the Popular Tradition in the Theater*.
18 'technique' seems such a weak term for what is in fact a major constituent element of a performance culture that is alien to later stages.
19 Weimann, *Shakespeare and the Popular Tradition in the Theater*, pp. 224–36.
20 Adrian Streete makes a similar point in relation to performance in his article on the religious iconography of the play: '"An old quarrel between us that will never be at an end": Middleton's *Women Beware Women* and Late Jacobean Religious Politics', *Review of English Studies*, published online at http://res.oxfordjournals.org/cgi/content/full/hgm167v1 2008), 12.
21 Kiernan, *Shakespeare's Theory of Drama*, uses the suggestive term 'layering' to describe a similar complexity in *Measure For Measure* at p. 103.
22 For some useful comments on the representation of offstage events, see Kiernan, *Shakespeare's Theory of Drama*, pp. 71–72.
23 Again, a comparison with Shakespeare's fortunes is illuminating. The ways in which the older writer's plays were removed from history and subsumed under the rubric of a literary and increasingly psychologically focused culture are radically different from the reception of *Women Beware Women* by later audiences and readers. Indeed, the occlusion of his contemporaries that goes hand in hand with Shakespeare's elevation to Bardhood depends on their plays being seen as somehow second-rate by later cultures, at least in the terms by which they familiarized his plays. Much work has

58 WOMEN BEWARE WOMEN

been done on the idolatry of Shakespeare, of course, but far less on the effects of the process on the reputations of his peers in the profession.
24　On antic acting of the old, antique style in Hamlet see Weimann, *Author's Pen and Actor's Voice*, pp. 161–68, and also de Grazia, *Hamlet Without Hamlet*, pp. 171–96.
25　Worthen, *Shakespeare and the Authority of Performance*, pp. 95–150, investigates these issues and their implications.
26　Margot Heinemann, *Puritanism and Theatre: Thomas Middleton and Oppositional Drama under the Early Stuarts* (Cambridge: Cambridge University Press, 1980), p. 181.
27　By way of comparison, see Weimann's analysis of the figure of Apemantus in *Timon of Athens* (*Author's Pen and Actor's Voice*, pp. 208–15). Interestingly enough, this play is included in *Thomas Middleton: The Collected Works* (ed. Taylor, Lavignano et al.) because of Middleton's collaboration with Shakespeare.
28　The term is Weimann's, used of Apemantus (Weimann, *Author's Pen and Actor's Voice*, p. 211).
29　See the comments made summing up critical judgements of Bianca in Martin White, *Middleton and Tourneur* (Basingstoke and London: Macmillan), p. 117.
30　For some comments on the primary importance of the unified subject that comes about as a result of the rise of individualism, see Worthen, *Shakespeare and the Authority of Performance*, p. 91.
31　Weimann, *Author's Pen and Actor's Voice*, p. 218.
32　See Weimann, *Author's Pen and Actor's Voice*, p. 225. Here, he discusses how the ending of a play may be fashioned in such a way as to meet the audience's expectations and approval.
33　Weimann explicitly links the play-within-the-play to the doubled logic of textual representation and played presentation; see Weimann, *Author's Pen and Actor's Voice*, p. 83.
34　Jowett, *Women, Beware Women*, p. 1488.
35　See Weimann, *Author's Pen and Actor's Voice*, pp. 226–40 for a thorough discussion of the endings of Renaissance plays, and Kiernan, *Shakespeare's Theory of Drama*, pp. 98–100.
36　Website citations as follows:.
www.theepochtimes.com/n2/content/view/9601/.
www.variety.com/review/VE1117939211.html?categoryid=33@cs=1.
http://berkshirereview.net/theater/womenbeware.html.
http://newyork.timeout.com/articles/theatre/69953/women-beware-women.
www.theatremania.com/off-broadway/news/12-2008/women-beware-women_16594.html.
www.theatrescene.net/ts/articles.nsf/OBP/BAA88011C6A87B158525752600567115.
www.curtainup.com/womenbewarewomen.html.
www.villagevoice.com/2008-12-24/theater/vile-italians-in-women-beware-women-and-caligula/.
www.playbill.com/news/article/124286_Red_Bull's_Women_Beware_Women_Opens_Off-Broadway_Dec_13.
www.nytheatre.com/nytheatre/showpage.php?t=wome7699.
www.highbeam.com
37　See Mullaney, *Place of the Stage*.
38　Jowett, *Women, Beware Women*, p. 1488.

CHAPTER THREE

In The Repertoire:
Women Beware Women on Stage

Annaliese Connolly

We do not know when *Women Beware Women* was first performed. It was entered in the Stationers' Register in 1653 and was finally published in 1657 by the printer Humphrey Moseley, 30 years after Middleton's death in 1627.[1] This first octavo was accompanied by a dedicatory verse by the dramatist Nathaniel Richards, who claims to have seen the play performed but does not say where or when:

> *Women beware Women*: 'tis a true Text
> Never to be forgot. Drabs of State vext,
> Have plots, poisons, mischiefs that seldom miss
> To murder virtue with a venom kiss.
> Witness this worthy tragedy, expressed
> By him that well deserved among the best
> Of poets in his time. He knew the rage,
> Madness of Women crossed; and for the stage
> Fitted their humours, hell-bred malice, strife
> Acted in state, presented to the life.
> I that have seen't, can say, having just cause,
> Never came tragedy off with more applause.[2]

There are no further records of the play's performance history until the twentieth century when Middleton's dramatic works, particularly *Women Beware Women*, *The Changeling* and *The Revenger's Tragedy* underwent a revival during the 1960s and have continued to be performed regularly up to the present day.[3] In this chapter I will focus upon the following productions: Royal Shakespeare Company (1962, 1969 and 2006), Oxford Playhouse Company (1982), Royal Court (1986), Birmingham Repertory (1989), Buttonhole Theatre Company (1994), Glasgow Citizens' Company (1995), Red Bull Theater (2008) and National Theatre (2010).

Theatrical Productions: The 1960s

The first professional production of *Women Beware Women* in the United Kingdom was performed by the newly formed Royal Shakespeare Company in London at the New Arts Theatre Club in 1962. Reviewers such as Philip Hope-Wallace identified this RSC production and its revival of Middleton's play as part of a new innovative chapter in theatre history:

> If anything more was needed to justify the Royal Shakespeare Company's virile and enlightened artistic policy as followed at this small theatre, here it is in the shape of a classic so long kept off the stage that to see it is to be gripped from start to finish as if much learned writing on the subject had only hinted at its theatrical quality.[4]

Kenneth Tynan also considered Middleton's play in the context of recent theatrical developments, including the decision to build a National Theatre in London. Indeed, he made a direct plea to the recently formed Arts Council to provide funding for existing London theatres including the Arts Theatre Club

> I am fired to make this plea partly because I should like to go on enjoying my job and partly because of the Royal Shakespeare's striking revival of Thomas Middleton's *Women Beware Women*.[5]

Tynan went on to make several related points about the play's realism, a quality which is a recurring theme in subsequent performance criticisms of the play and is frequently contrasted with the stylized final act. He began by commending the acting of the company for its 'muted intensity', in particular the parts of Livia, Bianca and Leantio: 'Pauline Jameson as the seductress, bland and insatiable; Jeanne Hepple as the wife unable to flower outside the hothouse of luxury; and best of all Nicol Williamson as the cuckold'.[6] Tynan suggested that there was truthfulness in Williamson's depiction of Leantio (the 'factor') which spoke to a contemporary audience, and suggested that Williamson was an exemplar of the method style of acting:

> Mr Williamson makes the rhetoric of his speeches ring true and newly-coined by the simple expedient of finding a psychological justification for every word he utters: his performance is a triumphant reminder that, even in blank verse, the Stanislavsky method works.[7]

Tynan then proceeded to claim that Middleton's handling of sexual relationships was more authentic than those found in the Shakespearean canon:

> Where sexual vagaries are concerned there is more authentic reportage in *The Changeling* and *Women Beware Women* than in the whole of the First Folio.[8]

Despite this complimentary flourish, Tynan described the masque in the final act of the play as a 'farcical massacre', underlining the critical tradition of comparing the final scene with the rest of the play.[9] Irving Wardle later praised the production as

> One of those rare pieces of theatrical alchemy that seizes on an old text

and releases a forgotten voice stonily telling the unchanging truths about human affairs.[10]

In 1965 Granada Independent Television dramatized the play for their 'ITV Play of the Week' series. Directed by Gordon Flemyng and adapted by Philip McKie, the production made use of period costume and boasted some of the best known actors and actresses of the period, including Diana Rigg as Bianca, William Gaunt as Leantio and Gene Anderson as Livia.[11]

The RSC revived the play in 1969, developing the studio production of 1962. Directed by Terry Hands, this production employed period costume from the mid-seventeenth century, with the contrasting styles of the Civil War era to indicate the court versus city class divide in the play. Leantio (Richard Pasco), for example, wore a sober outfit made up of brown jerkin and trousers and knee-length boots, whereas the other male characters linked to the court wore sumptuous colours of red, purple and green with velvet jackets and trousers. Livia played by Elizabeth Spriggs, wore a striking gown of deep burgundy velvet with white lace collar and feather cuffs. Bianca, played by Judi Dench, wore a simple white dress covered by a brown travelling cloak. The Mother (Anne Dyson) was dressed as though she were a member of a religious order in a black and white outfit with a large black cross and rosary beads hanging at her waist. The set design was also striking in that the action took place on a stage which was presented as a large chess board of black and white squares, thus magnifying the play's famous chess game between Livia and the Mother and indicating the ways in which Florentine society is engaged in game playing.[12] The stage was sparsely decorated except for a large female nude sculpture which, for Irving Wardle, was 'reminiscent of the Palazzo Signoria'.[13] This square in Florence in front of the Palazzo Vecchio is famous for its sculptures, particularly the copy of Michaelangelo's *David*. The sculpture ironically had a hand placed over her breasts and genitals as though she was the only model of female modesty left in Florence. While this aspect of set design nodded to the play's Italian location, the costuming underlined the way in which Middleton's Florence was really London. Critics also remarked on the way in which the play spoke to a twentieth-century audience, with Philip Hope-Wallace describing it as 'astonishingly modern in feeling' and suggesting that a Jacobean revenge play with its conventions of murderous revenge and corruption also encouraged comparison with the work of recent dramatists such as *Antigone* by Jean Anouilh (1943) and the novelist Iris Murdoch:

> The Jacobean idea of a Florentine court in all its corruption may superficially seem to take us into the familiar world of Victor Hugo or Verdi, yet for all the facile recourse to poison and poniard, it is to the world of Anouilh and Iris Murdoch that our minds keep reverting as these creatures, scheming to advance their lustful ambitions, get hoist with their own petards.[14]

One of the issues raised by this production was the development of individual characters, particularly Bianca. Irving Wardle noted, for example, that Dench's Bianca 'radiant as ever in the opening scenes, continues to project a sense of angelic incorruptibility in defiance of the lines'[15] and Ronald Bryden for *The Observer* remarked that

Judi Dench's Bianca, though poised and kittenishly vicious never grows into the kind of lovely monster who litters the stage of the finale with poisoned bodies'.[16]

Theatrical Productions: The 1980s

In 1982 the Oxford Playhouse Company's production updated the play to the twentieth century, specifically Italy of the 1930s and 40s. The set design was described as 'high fascist chic' with a 'shining imitation black marble floor with trap door, and a wedge-shaped back piece equipped with sliding panels to reveal high steps and recess doors, allows spectacular movements and transformations'.[17] *The Guardian*'s reviewer, Nicholas de Jongh, felt that the director Gordon McDougall 'daringly transposes the action to Mussolini's Italy, and the Duke who snatches Bianca away from her husband and brings her into Dolce Vita society looks suspiciously like Il Duce himself'.[18] This historical period offered a blend of glamour, alongside a violent political regime, which spoke to the play's themes of sex and corruption. While the set design was praised, the production was criticized for putting style before substance, as de Jongh complained: 'We seem to be in a highly decorous no man's land where the actors look Italian and sound and behave as if they have been schooled in RADA or some such'.[19] So, for many, while this period 'look' was successful in underlining the modernity of the play's themes, the emphasis upon design seemed to eclipse the passion of the characters.

McDougall's production used modern dress to suggest the relevance of Middleton's play-world for Britain at the start of the 1980s, but, by the middle of the decade, a more radical and politically informed approach was adopted by Howard Barker in his adaptation of the play. This landmark production had its roots in several theatrical traditions of the twentieth century: the first of these being Bertolt Brecht's Epic theatre and the idea of dialectics, whereby drama should establish a debate between the play and the audience with the aim of prompting social and political change outside the theatre. Barker objected to what he regarded as the moral tone of Middleton's play and the didactic nature of the retributive masque. Barker's adaptation can be situated among plays such as Tom Stoppard's *Rosencrantz and Guildenstern Are Dead* (1966) and *The Real Thing* (1982) as well as Edward Bond's *Saved* (1965) as examples of the appropriation of Renaissance plays (respectively, *Hamlet*, Ford's *'Tis Pity She's A Whore* and *King Lear*) by modern dramatists. Barker was keen to underline the parallels between Middleton's Florentine society and the yuppie culture of 80s Britain, remarking that 'England in this era is a money and squalor society also'.[20] Barker's emphasis upon how this Renaissance play allowed his audience to reflect upon their own historical moment was an approach which had been gathering pace during the early part of the 1980s, and was developed as a literary theory by the British academics Jonathan Dollimore and Alan Sinfield under the label 'cultural materialism'. Whereas one approach to a Renaissance play might be to consider what the play can tell us about the society in which it was produced and the power relations at work at that time, cultural materialists will look at the role of that play in modern society, and how the study of literature could effect social and political change in the here-and-now. This point was made clear in the preface to *Political Shakespeare: New Essays in Cultural Materialism* published in 1985 by Dollimore and Sinfield:

> the relevant history is not just that of four hundred years ago, for culture is made continuously and Shakespeare's text is reconstructed, reappraised, reassigned all the time through diverse institutions in specific contexts. What the plays signify, how they signify, depends on the cultural field in which they are situated. This is why this book discusses also the institutions through which Shakespeare is reproduced and through which interventions may be made in the present.[21]

Barker's adaptation of the play was informed by such ideas, explored by Dollimore and Sinfield, concerning how a play like *Women Beware Women* could intervene or challenge contemporary attitudes towards sex and power. In the programme notes for the production written by Dollimore, he outlines the terms of the debate

> This is a play which dramatises *both* conceptions of desire: desire at the mercy of power, desire as subversive of power. Or rather, by creatively vandalising the earlier play, Barker sets up a violent dialectic between the two. And it's a dialectic which we're living now, in a society which both incites and represses sexuality.[22]

Barker termed the play a 'collaboration' since he retained the first three acts of Middleton's play, albeit lightly edited and turned the verse into prose. The play was divided into two parts with the second half written entirely by Barker, using modern diction. In Barker's conclusion to the play, Middleton's masque was removed and the relationships between Bianca and the Duke and Leantio and Livia were given particular emphasis. Barker's premise for his section of the play was to challenge what he perceived to be Middleton's moral emphasis – that the consequences of lust are death and destruction. For Barker, lust or sexual freedom have the potential to be revolutionary, providing an opportunity to challenge and overthrow the status quo, and he insists upon 'the redemptive power of desire, opposing your [Middleton's] view on the inherent corruptibility of power'.[23] Livia was therefore transformed by her sexual relationship with Leantio: she was now capable of seeing society as though for the first time and positioned herself outside of the political and social hierarchy. The former pander now plotted the downfall of the Duke and his corrupt regime by making an example of Bianca, who had come to stand as an exemplar both of state corruption and power. Livia used Sordido (who was now given a more prominent role) to rape Bianca as a redemptive act. Physical rape was here being employed to point up the figurative rape of Bianca by Florentine society, a place where greed and power violated individuals. During the rape Sordido is interrupted by the Duke who stabbed him. The Duke then rejects Bianca, the wedding is abandoned and she resolves to go in quest of her true identity. The play ends with the question of who will govern in the Duke's place since his abdication. The Ward (an intelligent figure in Barker's play, who feigns stupidity) rejects the position in favour of Livia and Leantio who are proclaimed Duchess and Duke.

Writing in *The Times* newspaper on 6 February 1986, Barker engaged in an imagined discussion with Middleton about his project. In the interview Middleton claimed that in his play 'the characters got what they deserved' and that Barker was wrong to alter the character of Cardinal whom he describes as the 'moral spokesman from my play'.[24] Barker's response to Middleton's didacticism was to consider the place of such a view in Thatcherite Britain in 1986:

> Contemporary reactionary ethics would make such a viewpoint welcome. They are reviving a medieval social theology in which human nature is deemed incurably corrupt in order to reconcile the poor with poverty, the sick with sickness, and the whole race to extermination [...] We require a different form of tragedy in which the audience is encouraged, not by facile optimism or useless reconciliation, but by the spectacle of extreme struggle and the affirmation of human creativity. Failure is unimportant, the attempt is all.[25]

Here, the influence of Brechtian dialectics is clear and Barker was clearly unwilling to endorse, what he perceived as, the deterministic worldview promoted by the status quo. Barker argued that whereas Middleton's title was a straightforward warning about the behaviour of women towards one another, without a trace of irony, his Livia had not become the tool of patriarchy, but was motivated by a new-found political zeal:

> In [your play] a woman engineers the fall of a woman, for a man. That is the role of women in your time. In mine a woman engineers the fall of a woman, but for her own enlightenment. But the pain is terrible. So the title finds an irony it never had in your play.[26]

The production, directed by William Gaskill, galvanized critical opinion when it opened in February 1986. The set designed by Kandis Cook underlined the moral bankruptcy and stagnation of this society with its 'rust pocked black columns', black-streaked walls and bare stage, it was 'austere to the point of stasis'.[27] The end of each scene in the second part of the play was marked by a complete black out. The pertinence of the play's concern with different forms of power for Britain in the mid-80s and the sense in which Barker's adaptation was a product of its own historical moment was quickly noted by critics:

> Its thematic preoccupation with sex and violence – though no less pervasive than among Jacobeans – is nevertheless markedly a product of the *second* Elizabethan age.[28]

Thus, the preparations for the wedding between Bianca and the Duke revealed the political cynicism which informed this public pageantry as the Duke regards his wife, wedding and potential offspring as ways of exerting control over his subjects:

> My popularity was never higher, and she dangles from me, flashing like some encrusted gem, blinding discontent and dazzling the cynic [...] The dossers will applaud my wedding and go home warmer than they would be after a meal, there is great nourishment in pageantry. Later, the royal

birth will have them gasping who cannot conceive themselves, and those
that can will name their brats after ours immaculate.[29]

The contemporary resonance of these remarks by the Duke could hardly have
been lost upon the audience, seeing that in February 1986 the preparations for
the wedding of Prince Andrew to Sarah Ferguson were well underway with a
date set for July of that year. The decade had begun with the media frenzy
surrounding the wedding of Prince Charles to Lady Diana Spencer in 1981,
followed by the births of their sons William (1982) and Harry (1984) and
continued unabated until the death of Diana in 1997. William Hutchings remarks

> Like Brecht's literary use of history for didactic purposes of his own – and
> indeed like Shakespeare's too – Barker's expropriation of Middleton's play
> is the pretext for commentary on decidedly contemporary social and moral
> issues [...] contemporary Britain [...] like Middleton's Florence, has been
> preoccupied with a profligately celebrated royal wedding in a time of
> widespread hardships caused by the state's dire economic problems.[30]

The fact that Barker had rewritten the conclusion to a Middleton play (which
had a history of being perceived as unperformable) was largely welcomed in
principle by critics. Irving Wardle described Middleton's play as an 'imperfect
masterpiece' because of the tone of the final act. For Wardle, the first four acts of
the play offered realism, but the final act descended into the creaky conventions
of Jacobean revenge tragedy:

> But at the moment you have come to trust the author as a modern voice
> speaking clearly across the centuries the play abruptly subsides into period
> convention and surrenders all its complex truths and detailed humanity
> for the rusty machinery of a Jacobean revenge plot.[31]

Barker's conclusion, however, produced difficulties of its own for critics, with
Wardle forced to admit that he hankered for the return of Middleton's masque:
'I was left mainly wishing that Joanne Whalley's delicately cruel Bianca had been
given the chance to play the original text, poisoned arrows and all'.[32] The second
rape of Bianca produces a similar response in critic Michael Ratcliffe:

> The virginal sewer rat Sordido, whose avenging rape of Bianca, corrupt
> symbol of the state (Joanne Whalley), precipitates a denouement no more
> credible, and even more extraordinary, than Middleton's masque of
> death.[33]

Barker's assertion that Middleton's play offered a clear moral message was
also challenged by Michael Billington who queried Barker's political message:
'there is a lack of logic in Mr Barker's argument that desire cleanses perception.
If Livia is redeemed by desire, then why not the Duke, who has had everything in
sight?'[34] He argued that the idea that Bianca's rape would lead to her
enlightenment is 'morbid', while Donald J. Hutera was similarly troubled by
Barker's own brand of morality:

> I was troubled by the suggestion that the rape shows Bianca what a pawn
> both the Duke and her own greedy wants had made of her. It is surely a

specious, confused morality that would justify rape as a means to free a woman from her partially self-created oppression.[35]

Feminist critics, such as Kathleen McLuskie, also questioned the depiction of female sexuality in Barker's play and the *apparently* liberating effect of sex upon the female characters. Livia celebrated the knowledge sex with Leantio had given her, declaring 'Touch me and I know I live! [...] this was light and transformation',[36] but, as McLuskie pointed out,

> the knowledge is not arrived at by her own perception but by the overwhelming power of Leantio's phallic energy. Her language describes sexual experience in terms of male fantasies of the all-dominating phallus [...] the knowledge which this coitus brings fuels her determination for political change. However, the change is to be brought about by humiliating Bianca and destroying her as a false image of purity.[37]

The Birmingham Repertory Company's production in 1989 was in many ways a response to both the 'creative vandalism' of Barker's play, and to the critical tradition surrounding the rape of Bianca in Middleton's play. The set design of Paul Brown dominated John Adams's production, creating an atmosphere of surveillance and treachery. For Peter Smith, this recalled 'Piranesi's *Image of Confinement* with balconies and stairs that offered an unobserved haven for spies'.[38] The play also made use of Catholic iconography, including a huge statue of the Madonna, from behind which the Duke emerged to rape Bianca, and before which Isabella and Hippolito both prayed and kissed, indicating that 'this is a society full of pretend piety and religious protestation'.[39] Whereas Barker suggested that his characters could take control of their own lives and channel their passions into political revolution, Adams's production offered a much bleaker view of Middleton's play through the inclusion of an additional character, a Master of Ceremonies figure, played by David Moylan. This character oversaw events, but remained invisible to the cast. Dressed in a monk's cowl and habit with a shaven head and assuming a maniacal laugh, he appeared, for Smith, as a 'cross between the disaffected henchman Bosola and the mischievous wit of Mosca'.[40] As this master of ceremonies responded to the action of the play there was a sense that the fate of the characters was preordained: 'The evil, the production insisted, was less a consequence of the characters' machinations and more a pre-fatalistic inevitability'.[41]

As is apparent from the chapters in this volume treating the critical history of *Women Beware Women*, critics have repeatedly referred to the rape of Bianca during the famous game of chess in Act 2, scene 2, as 'seduction'. This response is partly due to the speed with which the encounter takes place. If the rape takes place offstage, after the Duke's line 'We'll talk together / And show a thankful joy for both our fortunes' (2.2.386–87), Bianca then re-emerges just over thirty lines later. Despite her responses to Livia and Guardiano, Bianca may seem quickly resigned to her position as the Duke's mistress. This has led to the contention that Bianca welcomes the Duke's attentions because he can provide her with material goods and repair her social status. The depiction of the Duke and Bianca in the rape scene in the Birmingham Rep's production was carefully nuanced and allowed for a number of reactions and interpretations to be considered. Smith

IN THE REPERTOIRE   67

notes that in this production when the Duke saw Bianca at the window as he followed the statue of the Madonna in a religious procession, 'the procession freezes and the light changes to an eerie blue. He stares at her dumbstruck – the lights change back and he moves on and Bianca's "Did not the duke look up? Methought he saw us" is thereby tinged with nervous excitement'.[42] This girlish excitement was clearly important because of the ambiguity it communicated: 'this production did the play full justice in articulating the dangerous assumption that the duke's assault is in some way subliminally welcomed by Bianca'.[43] Here, the assault was 'brutal and revolting', and yet there appeared during the physicality of this moment actions which indicated Bianca's acquiescence: 'as he places a hand on her breast and the other between her legs, her hand moves to meet and hold his', and they exit 'still holding hands'. Smith stressed that 'Judy Dumas's Bianca and Ian Barritt's duke succeeded in delineating the profoundly disturbing sexual politics of the scene without demystifying it – half rape, half seduction, but neither one thing nor the other'.[44]

Theatrical Productions: The 1990s

During the 1990s Bianca continued to provoke varying responses from directors of productions of the play. The Buttonhole Theatre Company in 1994 chose to employ cross-racial casting in order to underline Bianca's position as an outsider in Florentine society. Here, Bianca was played as an African princess by Noma Dumezweni. Elizabeth Schafer argued that the costuming was 'strongly evocative of central African cultures. [Her] class was also emphasised by stage business such as Bianca's refusing to help the widow with the washing up.' This casting decision seems to have been made largely as a means of clarifying Bianca's motivation in the play as the production indicated that Bianca welcomed the Duke's attention from the outset: 'when she was seduced by the Duke (this Bianca was not raped), there was a strong sense of Bianca's return home in terms of class'.[45] To support this interpretation Leantio was cast as a working-class Londoner with an 'East End accent [who] was always out of his depth with the Machiavellian upper classes'.[46] While class is an important factor in the play, it remains unclear whether the issue of race as presented by the production added to an audience's sense of Bianca as anything more than a two-dimensional character. The suggestion that Bianca willingly consents to the Duke's demands in order to rehabilitate her social standing tends to flatten out both her character and the gender politics of the play. Indeed, this decision served to coarsen the play's complex presentation of her reaction and position, leaving little scope for the possibility that at the beginning of the play Bianca was an innocent young woman.

In the following year the Glasgow Citizens' Company performed *Women Beware Women* at the Glasgow Citizens' theatre. The company had built a reputation during the 70s and 80s for its productions of Renaissance revenge tragedies. The artistic director Philip Prowse had been responsible for a number of productions of Renaissance tragedies in the preceding years, including those of Webster's *The White Devil* in 1971, 1984 and in 1991 for the National Theatre, *The Duchess of Malfi* in 1985 for the National Theatre, and *'Tis Pity She's A*

Whore in 1988. This production of *Women Beware Women* signalled both the power and corruption of the state through its striking set design. *The Observer's* critic, Michael Coveney, found that the staging presented Florence as both 'corrupt state and religious abattoir: helicopters and sirens accompany the Duke's procession; rows of rotting corpses hang from meat-hooks above the action'.[47] Prowse developed Leantio's feminized images of 'fair-eyed Florence' (1.1.161) and linked them with the character's image of a whore, who is fair on the outside but rotten within

> When I behold a glorious dangerous strumpet
> Sparkling in beauty, and destruction too,
> Both at a twinkling, I do liken straight
> Her beautified body to a goodly temple
> That's built on vaults where carcasses lie rotting; (3.1.95–99)

In contrast to the 'serried ranks of clothed skeletons suspended over the action like a permanent memento mori',[48] the costumes were modern, with class difference indicated at the level of clothing: 'the aristos drift about in dinner-jackets and cocktail dresses and the proles go barefoot'.[49] The production was also notable for the way in which Prowse edited Middleton's play. The subplot was trimmed with the Ward reduced to a non-speaking role. Despite this decision, however, Coveney argued, 'he [Prowse] compounds the horrors even when cutting. The idiot Ward [...] is a speechless, filthy-minded epileptic in a wheelchair'.[50] Prowse also adapted the masque – a decision which once again prompted a mixed reaction among the critics. Coveney acknowledged that while Prowse had cut the text, he was congratulated for keeping 'the spirit by simply enveloping his cast of lechers and schemers in a poisoned fog (they are incensed by incense) while the victims meekly descend into burning pits'.[51] Michael Billington felt that Prowse's editing of the masque 'brilliantly solves the problems of the fifth act'. While changes to the masque were considered a success, Billington argued that staging the rape upstage rather than on a balcony was a mistake: 'Only in the last act, where an incensed-filled marriage ceremony continues regardless of corpses sliding into subterranean graves does the staging marry perfectly with the text'.[52] Thus, from some quarters, the production was criticized for not fulfilling the directions laid out in Middleton's playtext, and yet commended at other points for doing exactly that. Other reviewers felt that Prowse's masque was a missed opportunity, and that the characters 'deserved to die more stylishly'.[53] Victoria Scarborough, as Bianca, was praised for charting her 'persuasive development from sweet-voiced bride, radiant in her beauty, shocked into a ducal near-rape when her diction becomes piteously slurred and emerging as a fierce unbridled killer'.[54] Anne Lambton's Livia, despite the sophisticated modern dress of the production, was described as 'a gypsy-like pander in jangling bangles'.[55]

Theatrical Productions: The Twenty-first Century

The RSC's third production of *Women Beware Women* was staged at the Swan in 2006. This small intimate venue with its thrust stage contributed to the production's dark, claustrophobic design. The stage was sparsely decorated with a bronze backdrop and black glittering tiles which recalled the earlier chess design of the flooring in the RSC's 1969 production. The period costuming was early seventeenth-century with a modern twist – notably, a mix of Elizabethan slashes on doublets alongside punkish zips and safety pins. The colours were monochrome with characters wearing either all black, charcoal or white which served to point up the chessboard analogy as well as problematizing the colour system as an index to characters' morality. The Duke, played with a wonderfully repellent unctuousness by Tim Piggott-Smith, wore a black doublet and padded hose which became a white doublet and hose covered in slashes of black silk for the wedding scene. Bianca began the play in a gown of grey taffeta covered in silken twists of material, gradually changing into a cream dressing gown during the scene in which Leantio pronounces her a whore and finally appearing in a white wedding dress for the play's concluding scenes. Isabella, on the other hand, wore a black gown and changed into a white dress, reminiscent of a shepherdess and complete with straw hat for her role in the antemasque. Livia's sumptuous black gown was covered in open zips which revealed petal shaped pieces of grey fabric beneath, mimicking the slashes on the doublets of the male aristocratic characters. While the zips gave the gown a modern edge, the overall effect of the shapes on Livia's gown was to suggest the iconic image of power and surveillance in the Hatfield portrait of Elizabeth I, where the Queen's gown is covered in tiny eyes and ears to indicate her omniscience and absolute power. Leantio, played by Elliott Cowan, wore black studded trousers and a black hoodie, rather than doublet and hose; subsequently, the material benefits of his liaison with Livia were indicated by the replacement of the hoodie with a cream silk shirt which was covered by a piece of black corsetry. Sordido wore a black punk doublet which was held in place with safety pins and he also sported an aggressive-looking dildo from his codpiece. The Ward wore large padded hose which were held up by braces, together with grey and white striped knee-length socks, a doublet and a sweatband. Later, the colour scheme of his outfit changed from black to red and his hose were covered in what appeared to be pink plastic tongues. Richard Hudson's design prompted mixed responses, with Michael Billington remarking:

> Even if the play has a modern cynicism about sex, it seems decidedly eccentric to costume Bianca's cuckolded husband in studded trousers and a mugger's hood.[56]

Kate Bassett was unimpressed by the mix of modern synthetic fabrics, zips and pins, but suggested that perhaps the effect was to underline 'that the nobility and the social climbers around them are morally shoddy'.[57] Paul Taylor for *The Independent* indicated that the costuming worked as visual shorthand to 'suggest an overlap of values between Middleton's world and our own'.[58] The casting of Penelope Wilton as Livia, the play's central character, was the subject of much discussion, partly because Middleton's character was perceived to be a departure from Wilton's usual roles, who is perhaps best remembered by UK audiences for warmer television characters, such as Anne alongside Richard Briers in *Ever Decreasing Circles* during the 1980s, and her film roles in *Calendar Girls* (2003) and *Pride and Prejudice* (2005). Wilton managed to capture the complexity of Livia's character, so that she demanded sympathy as well as condemnation, with reviewers noting that

> her behaviour can't be excused, but it can be partly explained as the proxy continuation of her own sex life and as the prostitution of a high intelligence that can't find another outlet. She wastes her relative freedom on doing men's dirty work.[59]

Wilton's abilities as a comic actress were praised, with her Livia described as 'a magnificently witty and amused predator': indeed, she offered the widow 'a beamingly draconian hospitality that would intimidate Ghengis Khan'.[60] Michael Billington observed that 'Wilton brings out the comedy as well as the chicanery, and even overcomes the awkward transition that allows Livia herself to become a slave of passion'.[61] Wilton's skilful handling of the role of Livia meant that the chess game was not simply an opportunity for a comic masterclass which can serve to distract and therefore shield the audience from the implications of the encounter between Bianca and the Duke. The rape was given greater prominence as it took place downstage from the chess game and was indicated symbolically by Piggott-Smith inserting his bejewelled finger into Bianca's mouth.

The production adhered to the text in its handling of the masque, indicating director Laurence Boswell's confidence in Middleton's own directions and his theatrical competence as a dramatist. This decision on Boswell's part may have been a consequence of the way in which Middleton's reputation as a dramatist had been on the rise for a number of years, and the fact that the publication of the Oxford Middleton project (2007) would soon see his complete works in print. In any event, the masque was a triumph. One review made an interesting parallel between the masque and the play-within-the play in *A Midsummer Night's Dream*, comparing Middleton's Duke with Shakespeare's:

> Like a darkly ironic version of Duke Theseus in *A Midsummer Night's Dream*, Piggott-Smith consults his programme in bemusement, remarking that the entertainment seems to be diverging from the plot synopsis.[62]

This observation clearly indicates that members of a modern theatre audience unfamiliar with all the conventions of a Jacobean masque are still able to think of comparable dramatic scenarios which will contribute to their understanding and enjoyment of the play, without the director having to resort to cutting elements of the final scene.

For the masque a small raised stage appeared in the centre of the main stage and here Isabella placed her bowl of burning incense. The nymphs who accompanied her were dressed in costumes of bright lurid pinks, greens and yellows, while Wilton's Juno outshone them all. Appearing as the mother of the gods Livia descended from the flyspace on a wire in a magnificent gown of violet blue covered in yellow and orange eyes suggestive of peacock feathers, the peacock being a bird sacred to Juno. The production seemed to combine the right amount of menace and humour in the final scene with reviewers remarking that 'dark gleefulness is the spirit of this beautifully staged production',[63] while

Billington noted that 'even the climatic masque is done with the right black gaiety as hurtling arrows, deadly flame and poisoned chalices do their work'.[64]

In 2009 Jesse Berger, founder and director of the Red Bull Theater in New York, produced the company's second staging of a play by Middleton. Founded in 2003, the company is dedicated to performing plays by Shakespeare's contemporaries as well as those more neglected plays by Shakespeare. Recent productions by the company include *Pericles* (2003), *The Revenger's Tragedy* (2006), Marlowe's *Edward II* (2008) and *The Duchess of Malfi* (2010). The production of *Women Beware Women* bridged the gap between Middleton's Florence and the present day through costuming, which was a mixture of period costumes from the seventeenth century and the mid twentieth century. The Duke and Leantio, for example, wore heavy velvet brocade jackets and cloaks, while the female characters such as Livia and Bianca wore brightly coloured 1950s-inspired dresses and hairstyles. Kathryn Meisle was praised for her depiction of Livia who was not played simply as a villainess 'but rather as a character who passionately and enthusiastically argues for the rightness of her actions, even when they are so obviously wrong'.[65] Berger adapted Middleton's play, but rather than focusing upon the masque, he turned his attention instead to the Cardinal, who in this production is successfully poisoned. The elimination of the Cardinal (so often identified as the play's moral spokesperson) meant that the play's conclusion remained extremely bleak.

In 2010 the National Theatre's production of *Women Beware Women* was directed by Marianne Elliott, who had had recent successes with *Much Ado About Nothing* for the RSC at the Swan in 2006 and with *All's Well that Ends Well* at the National in 2009. The production made use of the drum revolve under the stage of the Olivier theatre to dramatize the bifurcated world of Middleton's Florence. On one side of the revolve stage was the opulence of the Duke and his court indicated by two dove-grey pillars flanked by a large sweeping staircase on each side. Between the columns was a burnished bronze backdrop with a glass-fronted balcony. Above the balcony was the lettering COSMVS MEDICE, indicating the historical context of the play, with the programme notes for the play providing a helpful biography of those members of the Medici family whose lives and loves provide some of the sources for Middleton's play. In the case of Cosimo de' Medici, he was the father of Middeton's Duke Francesco de' Medici, although Cosimo is also the name of Francesco's son.[66]

Despite the nod to history the set design with its black and grey marble floor tiles and live jazz band was more night club than Renaissance palace. When the stage rotated the shabby mercantile world of Leantio, the travelling salesman, was revealed with its rusty scaffolding and fire escape. The costuming for the production was 1950s glamour with Bianca arriving in Florence in a white Jackie-O two-piece suit and pillbox hat. For a moment Bianca could have been mistaken for Blanche Du Bois who also arrives in a strange city in a white suit and is clearly out of place there. The set design with its fire escape was also evocative of Williams's Elysian Fields. Leantio, played with a boyish enthusiasm by Samuel Barnett, was dressed in a modern plain blue suit which was slightly too big for him and reinforced the sense that certainly in the first part of the play he is really a boy in a man's world. The introduction of Harriet Walter's Livia and later Isabella, played by Vanessa Kirby, took place on the steps of a church, and here the men wore dark modern suits and the women wore Dior-inspired dresses. Isabella wore a pale blue dress with white veil and gloves, while Livia wore a black veil and lace gloves as befits her status as a widow. As in earlier productions the costumes of the Ward and Sordido were inspired by punk couture, with spiky hair, jeans and waistcoats. The Ward sported a Morrissey-esque quiff and during the scene in which he dances with Isabella wore an outlandish combination of white trousers, white frilly shirt, golfing socks and a dickie bow. Hippolito wore a long military coat over black trousers and a bronze-coloured shirt and waistcoat. Later in the play, when Leantio becomes Livia's lover, he too wore a bronze coloured shirt which hinted at the play's incest theme as Leantio becomes Livia's substitute for her own brother. Livia's costuming employed the cliché of the scarlet woman as she changed from the demure mourning weeds of the opening scenes to a startling red and black velvet dress, complete with gloves, in order to seduce Leantio. The mix of styles employed in the production prompted polarized responses from reviewers. On the one hand the updating of the play suggested a particular period with its own set of scandals, as Kate Bassett noted:

> [the play] is translated to somewhere near Kensington in the 1950s. So Middleton's darkly comic-going-on-punitive vision of affluence and corruption chimes with more modern High Society sleaze, as exposed by the Profumo affair and subsequent scandals.[67]

Michael Coveney for *The Independent* agreed that updating the costumes reinforced the relevance of the play for a modern audience:

> You don't have to dress this rarely seen lust-fest in modern garb to make its feminist points but Marianne Elliott's magnificent and disturbing National Theatre revival does benefit from updating the Italian Renaissance to a period mish-mash of New Look couture, dead cool jazz and punk primitivism.[68]

On the other side of this debate was the view that the play was necessarily a product of its own historical moment, and that some attention should be paid to the differences between the seventeenth century and the present day. Benedict Nightingale made the following point:

> Nothing wrong with the updating in Marianne Elliott's production except that the play is Jacobean to its core, reflecting a pessimism, a paranoia about foreigners and lurid tastes even more extreme than our own era.[69]

Michael Billington put the case more strongly when he asked,

> How do we keep the classics alive? Partly by reimagining them. But also occasionally by rooting them in their historical period. And, although Marianne Elliott's modern-dress production of Middleton's 1621 play is wittily inventive, I found myself wishing it owed more to Medici Florence than to Fellini's Rome: La Dolce Vita has become a lazy reference point for these Italianate Jacobean plays.[70]

The periodization of this production criticized by Billington is certainly a form of shorthand employed by directors and designers, but, in many ways, it was successful in conjuring up a world of aspirational glamour, of greed and of wealth. As for Billington's desire for more Medici rather than Fellini, the play managed to combine the two persuasively in the chess scene when a white muslin curtain hangs down in front of the balcony. An image of a white nude sculpture was then projected onto the muslin as the Duke appeared from the fire escape at the side of the balcony and approached Bianca. The sculpture was of a female nude caught in the arms of a male figure and was reminiscent of Giambologna's sculpture of the *Rape of the Sabine Women* in Florence's Piazza della Signoria.

One of the strengths of the production was the ways in which it encouraged the audience to consider the parallels between the male characters in both the main and the subplots. For example, the Duke's rape of Bianca was presented as a rape in this production and Lauren O'Neil's sensitive depiction of Bianca was of a woman who did not really have a choice. At the banquet, for example, she indicated her continued affection for her husband through her looks and gestures. The Duke, despite his position, was shown to be no different from the Ward; both men were motivated by lust and can act with immunity because of their social and financial positions. Sordido referred to one of the Ward's conquests: 'You never shot at any but the kitchen wench, / And that was a she-woodcock, a mere innocent' (3.3.21–22). It seemed that the only thing to differentiate between the Duke and the Ward is geography: the Ward operates in the kitchen while the Duke selects Livia's art gallery to commit his rape. The production also foregrounded the disturbing nature of the dance which took place before the Duke and his court between Isabella and the Ward. Here, the dance was not merely a ridiculous parody of the passionate tango performed by Isabella and Hippolito moments before, but was itself a kind of rape as Isabella was forced to perform mock fellatio upon the Ward while the court laughed and cheered. Harriet Walter as Livia is no stranger to interpretations of flawed leading ladies, having played Lady Macbeth opposite Antony Sher (1999) and the Duchess of Malfi (1989), both for the RSC. Walter, like Wilton, was praised for the insights she gave to Livia's character

> She's like a snake coiled in a basket of slowly putrefying fruit. Even her shape is serpentine: her leanness is clothed in clinging gowns and her hair puffed out at both sides to give her head that triangular look that fashionable adders favour. Still, she is never simply a hissing villainess. Subtle, elaborate and quick-thinking, she's a woman whose ability has no fruitful outlet.[71]

Walter's bouffant hairstyle caused Michael Coveney to suggest that Livia is 'played in the very likeness of the Duchess of Windsor'.[72] The comparison is telling not just in terms of hairstyles, but also for the parallels between the twice-widowed Livia and the twice-divorced Wallis Simpson (who acquired the title Duchess of Windsor upon her marriage to Edward VIII in 1937). While Livia engaged in an affair with a commoner, Wallis Simpson, an American commoner, married the recently abdicated king of England. (In the spring of 2010 Wallis Simpson was back in the media spotlight as plans were made public that a new film involving Madonna was to be made of Simpson's life.) Elliott chose not to deliver the final masque in its entirety, choosing instead to rework the detail and to make use of the rotating stage for the enactment of the final murders. Here the production was indebted to Philip Prowse's production of 1995: Elliott used the concept of deadly smoke (this time from cigarettes smoked by an array of masked assassins) to envelope the characters. Again, opinion was divided on the success of this aspect of the play. For Coveney, the final scene was

> A seamless, if slightly blurred, atmospheric extension of the whole show, with Walter priming a body double, Barnett returning as a ghost, the incestuous Isabella (Vanessa Kirby) expiring in a balletic gang bang (instead of the stipulated shower of gold) and her love-struck uncle (Raymond Coulthard) impaling himself on a convenient dagger.[73]

Billington, however, was scathing about the handling of the final scene in which 'the climactic masque, with its multiple murders, is cut to be replaced by a phantasmagoric jazzy ballet which suggests an unusually wild night out at Ronnie Scott's'.[74] The critical pendulum here seems to have swung back in favour of the masque as detailed in playtext.

The diverse performance history of *Women Beware Women* illustrates the ways in which Middleton's play has captured audiences' imaginations throughout the course of the twentieth century and beyond. It is testimony to the play's engaging characters and the questions it raises about power, corruption and the individual that *Women Beware Women* will no doubt continue to be a staple of modern theatre repertories in the twenty-first century.

Reviews of Productions

Bassett, Kate. *The Independent on Sunday*, 2 May 2010 (Elliott).
Bassett, Kate. *The Independent on Sunday*, 26 February 2006 (Boswell).
Billington, Michael. *The Guardian*, 24 February 2006 (Boswell).
Billington, Michael. *The Guardian*, 28 & 29 April 2010 (Elliott).
Billington, Michael. *The Guardian*, 6 February 1995 (Prowse).
Billington, Michael. *The Guardian*, 7 February 1986 (Gaskill).
Bryden, Ronald. *The Observer*, 6 July 1969 (Hands).
Clapp, Susannah. *The Observer*, 2 May 2010 (Elliott).
Coveney, Michael. *The Independent*, 29 April 2010 (Elliott).
Coveney, Michael. *The Observer*, 12 February 1995 (Prowse).
De Jongh, Nicholas. *The Guardian*, 22 October 1982 (McDougall).
Fisher, Philip. *The British Theatre Guide*, 2009 (Berger).
Hanks, Robert. *The Independent*, 2 March. 1994 (Geelan).
Holder, Heidi. *The Berkshire Review* 18 February 2009 (Berger).
Hope-Wallace, Philip. *The Guardian*, 4 July 1969 (Hands).
Hope-Wallace, Philip. *The Guardian*, 5 July 1962 (Page).
Howard, Tony. *RORD*, 2 (1986–87), 70–71 (Gaskill).
Hutera, Donald J. *Theatre Journal* 38.3 (October 1986), 366–67 (Gaskill).
Isherwood, Charles. *The New York Times*, 16 December 2008 (Berger).
Kingston, Jeremy. *The Times*, 6 February, 1995 (Prowse).
Loup-Nolan, Richard. *The Independent*, 14 February 1995 (Prowse).
Nightingale, Benedict. *The Times*, 29 April 2010 (Elliott).
Paul Taylor. *The Independent*, 27 February 2006 (Boswell).
Ratcliffe, Michael. *The Observer*, 9 February 1986 (Gaskill).
Schafer, Elizabeth. *RORD*, 34 (1995), 139 (Geelan).

Smith, Peter. *Cahiers Elisabéthains*, 36 (1989), 90–91 (Adams).
Smith, Peter. *Shakespeare Bulletin*, 24.4 (2006), 100–2 (Boswell).
Taylor, Gary. *The Guardian*, 21 February 2006 (Boswell).
Trotter, David. *Times Literary Supplement*, 21 February 1986 (Gaskill).
Tynan, Kenneth. *The Observer*, 8 July 1962 (Page).
Tyrrell, Rebecca. *The Daily Telegraph*, 2 March 2006 (Boswell).
Wardle, Irving. *The Times*, 4 July 1969 (Hands).
Wardle, Irving. *The Times*, 5 July 1962 (Page).
Wardle, Irving. *The Times*, 7 February 1986 (Gaskill).

Notes

1. Gerald Eades Bentley, *The Jacobean and Caroline Stage*, 5 vols (Oxford: Oxford University Press, 1956), IV, pp. 906–7.
2. Nathaniel Richards in Thomas Middleton, *Women Beware Women*, 2nd edn, ed. by William C. Carroll (London: A & C Black, 1994), p. 3.
3. For useful performance history resources for Middleton's play and other Renaissance plays see Lisa Cronin, 'A Checklist of Professional Productions in the British Isles since 1880 of plays by Tudor and Stuart Dramatists (excluding Shakespeare)', *Renaissance Drama Newsletter*, Supplement Seven (University of Warwick: Graduate School of Renaissance Studies, 1987) and more recently the open access online resources provided by the University of Warwick for Renaissance dramatists 'Elizabethan and Jacobean Dramatists'. Resources for Middleton include criticism and a performance history of *Women Beware Women* and *The Changeling*. It contains a guide to reviews and includes performance stills. http://www2.warwick.ac.uk/fac/arts/ren/elizabethan_jacobean_drama/middleton/
4. Philip Hope-Wallace theatre review, *The Guardian*, 5 July 1962.
5. Kenneth Tynan theatre review, *The Observer*, 8 July 1962.
6. Tynan review (1962).
7. Ibid.
8. Ibid.
9. Ibid.
10. Irving Wardle theatre review, *The Times*, 5 July 1962.
11. See '*Women Beware Women* – Film Productions' for stills of the production:. http://www2.warwick.ac.uk/fac/arts/ren/elizabethan_jacobean_drama/middleton/women_beware_women/stage_history/film/
12. See J. L. Styan, *The English Stage: A History of Drama and Performance* (Cambridge: Cambridge University Press, 1996), pp. 228–29.
13. Irving Wardle theatre review, *The Times*, 4 July 1969.
14. Philip Hope-Wallace, *The Guardian*, 4 July 1969.
15. Wardle review (1969).
16. Ronald Bryden theatre review, *The Observer*, 6 July 1969.
17. Nicholas de Jongh theatre review, *The Guardian*, 22 October 1982.
18. Ibid.
19. Ibid.
20. Howard Barker, 'The redemptive power of desire', *The Times*, 6 February 1986.
21. Jonathan Dollimore and Alan Sinfield, *Political Shakespeare: New Essays in Cultural Materialism* (Manchester: Manchester University Press, 1985), p. viii.
22. Cited in David Trotter, 'An end to pageantry', *Times Literary Supplement*, 21 February 1986, p. 194.
23. Barker, 'The redemptive power of desire'.
24. Ibid.
25. Ibid.
26. Ibid.
27. Irving Wardle theatre review, *The Times*, 7 February 1986.
28. William Hutchings, '"Creative Vandalism" Or, A Tragedy Transformed: Howard Barker's "Collaboration" with Thomas Middleton on the 1986 Version of *Women*

Beware Women', in *Text and Presentation: The University of Florida, Department of Classics, Comparative Drama Conference Papers*, VIII, ed. by Karelisa Hartigan (Lanham, MD: University Press of America, 1988), pp. 93–101.
29   Thomas Middleton and Howard Barker, *Women Beware Women* (London: John Calder, 1986), pp. 25–26.
30   Hutchings, '"Creative Vandalism" Or, A Tragedy Transformed', p. 99.
31   Irving Wardle, *The Times*, 7 February 1986.
32   Ibid.
33   Michael Ratcliffe theatre review, *The Observer*, 9 February 1986.
34   Michael Billington theatre review, *The Guardian*, 7 February 1986.
35   Donald J. Hutera, 'Women Beware Women and Les Liaisons Dangereuses', *Theatre Journal*, 38.3 (October 1986), 366–67.
36   Middleton and Barker, *Women Beware Women*, p. 20.
37   Kathleen McLuskie, *Renaissance Dramatists* (Hemel Hempstead: Harvester Wheatsheaf, 1989), pp. 21–22. Michelle O'Callaghan echoes McLuskie's concerns in *Thomas Middleton: Renaissance Dramatist* (Edinburgh: Edinburgh University Press, 2009), pp. 120–22.
38   Peter Smith, '*Women Beware Women*', *Cahiers Elisabéthains*, 36 (1989), 90–91 (p. 90).
39   Ibid.
40   Ibid.
41   Ibid.
42   Ibid.
43   Ibid.
44   Ibid.
45   Elizabeth Schafer, *Research Opportunities in Renaissance Drama*, 34 (1995), p. 139.
46   Ibid.
47   Michael Coveney theatre review, *The Observer*, 12 February 1995.
48   Michael Billington theatre review, *The Guardian*, 6 February 1995.
49   Richard Loup-Nolan theatre review, *The Independent*, 14 February 1995.
50   Michael Coveney theatre review, *The Observer*, 12 February 1995.
51   Ibid.
52   Michael Billington, *The Guardian*, 6 February 1995.
53   Jeremy Kingston theatre review, *The Times*, 6 February 1995.
54   Ibid.
55   Billington review (1995).
56   Michael Billington theatre review, *The Guardian*, 24 February 2006.
57   Kate Bassett theatre review, *The Independent on Sunday*, 26 February 2006.
58   Paul Taylor theatre review, *The Independent*, 27 February 2006.
59   Ibid.
60   Ibid.
61   Michael Billington, *The Guardian*, 24 February 2006.
62   Kate Bassett, *The Independent on Sunday*, 26 February 2006.
63   Rebecca Tyrrel theatre review, *The Daily Telegraph*, 2 March 2006.
64   Billington review (2006).
65   Heidi Holder theatre review, *The Berkshire Review*, 18 January 2009.
66   National Theatre programme note.
67   Kate Bassett theatre review, *The Independent on Sunday*, 2 May 2010.
68   Michael Coveney theatre review, *The Independent*, 29 April 2010.
69   Benedict Nightingale theatre review, *The Times*, 29 April 2010.
70   Michael Billington theatre review, *The Guardian*, 28 & 29 April 2010.
71   Susannah Clapp theatre review, *The Observer*, 2 May 2010.
72   Michael Coveney theatre review, *The Independent*, 29 April 2010.
73   Ibid.
74   Billington review (2010).

CHAPTER FOUR

The State of the Art

Joost Daalder

In accepting, with gratitude, an invitation to write this chapter, I greatly underestimated the complexity of the task that would be involved. It soon became clear that such are the masses of critical material that have been published on Middleton in recent years that inevitably there would be items that I overlooked. Nevertheless, I am confident that there is probably little of genuine significance that I have not seen. Some items that seemed to me not in need of individual attention have deliberately not been mentioned below. Readers will be able to form their own opinion of 'the state of the art' by reading those writings which I do analyse and evaluate to the best of my ability. I have not refrained from giving personal views, which any discussion on 'the state of the art' is bound to do. Hence, I do not merely summarize what others say, but critically engage with it. I now turn to the issues that seem to me to stand out in work done between 1995 and 2009.

Editions

Editions of *Women Beware Women* have generally been of a very high standard in modern times (and, one could say, well before). The first thorough edition based on modern bibliographical and critical procedures was that of J. R. Mulryne, for the Revels Plays (now published by Manchester University Press), in 1975. Ultimately, this was based on Mulryne's unpublished PhD thesis (Cambridge University, 1962), which even by itself has been much used by other editors. Roma Gill consulted it for her New Mermaids edition (then published in London by Ernest Benn) in 1968, and it helped her in producing a sound text with a critical account which was very much her own, and remains important.

Mulryne's 1975 edition has not really been surpassed or equalled, though other editors have added to it in valuable ways, and there have been numerous comments on specifics in it. To provide some insight into its worth, I move straight to consideration of the most recent substantial edition, that which was executed by John Jowett for the Oxford Middleton in two volumes: (1) Thomas Middleton: *The Collected Works*, and (2) *Thomas Middleton and Early Modern*

Textual Culture: A Companion to the Collected Works, both edited by Gary Taylor and John Lavagnino.[1] The Oxford Middleton produces the texts of plays, with brief critical introductions and rather thin explanatory notes in the *Collected Works* (2016 pages), and related material on authorship, date and textual matters in what I shall for convenience call the *Companion* (1183 pages). This means that anyone with a serious interest in the qualities of an edition like that of *Women Beware Women* constantly, and most awkwardly, has to move between these very heavy and thick volumes. Nonetheless, it is worth underlining that Jowett's respect for the 1975 Mulryne edition is such that in his section on textual matters (pp. 1140–48) he writes: 'The list of press corrections in this edition is based on Mulryne's collation' (p. 1140).

It is a policy of the Oxford Middleton that editors must face the primary sources for a text afresh, and produce edited texts that dare break with editorial convention. Jowett amply fulfils these expectations and the result is that (as elsewhere in the Oxford Middleton) we suddenly see a title we are not used to, namely *Women, Beware Women*. The comma is chosen to convey Jowett's sense that the verb is an imperative. Of course, this is a tempting enough interpretation and it may even have been intended by Middleton. Nevertheless, many have found the very ambiguity of the more conventional *Women Beware Women* attractive, not least because its puzzling nature may be seen as compatible with that of the play itself. In addition, Jowett proposes a number of new emendations for the text which are all worth considering. At least one of them seems to me definitely right and in need of acceptance. In 2.2.95–97, he presents Sordido's speech about Isabella as follows:

> I have a plaguy guess. Let me alone to see what she is;
> if I but look upon her cony-way, I know all the faults
> to a hair that you may refuse her for.

Here *cony-way* is Jowett's emendation of the 1657 primary source, which instead contains a long dash followed by 'way'. As his suggestion is revolutionary and requires some explanatory comment, he makes the basic points about it in both the annotation to his text in the *Collected Works* (p. 1507) and in the *Companion* (pp. 1142–43). To use the note in the *Collected Works*: Jowett explains that his *cony-way* would mean 'rabbit burrow' and that *cony* puns on 'cunt'. I must add that it actually would pun on *cony* in the sense of 'cunt' (see *OED* cony sb. 5b), not on 'cunt' *per se*, but the key point is that his reading makes sense in the context, as he demonstrates, especially as 'to a hair' would allude to both pubic hair and *hare*. He also claims, plausibly, that the 1657 edition probably deliberately omitted the obscenity presented by *cony*, printing in its place a decent but incomprehensible long dash.

The dash was a problem to Mulryne and other editors, who read *way* as *'way* and unconvincingly took that to mean 'away; leave it to me'. This kind of emendation shows the Oxford Middleton at its best, though it must also be added that Jowett's conjecture is aided by the fact that during the last two decades we have learned a good deal about 'indecent' punning in Middleton. In this respect Mulryne was not as coy as many others in 1975, frequently picking up the presence of bawdy senses, but unfortunately too rarely explaining just what they were. Jowett has no inhibitions on this score in his commentary, perhaps at times seeing bawdy where none occurs. However, it remains surprising that Jowett totally ignores William C. Carroll's New Mermaids edition.[2] Carroll is more explicit about sexual puns than is Mulryne and in all respects there is a great deal of value, both in his commentary and in his Introduction. But Jowett does justly acknowledge 'Women Beware Women' and Other Plays, edited by Richard Dutton.[3] Dutton's Introduction is superb, and very much worth reading for many comprehensive and penetrating comments on the play. His good (but all-too-short) explanatory comments are unfortunately printed at the end of the edition and thus will not be consulted as often by many readers as they should be.

From these unsatisfactorily brief remarks, it will perhaps be obvious that I do not consider that there is anything like a really suitable 'standard edition' of the play at present. Mulryne's 1975 volume, based on extensive textual work, with a very sensible and comprehensive Introduction and (for 1975) very full and helpful notes, remains to my mind the closest thing that we have.

'Religio-political' Issues

Much writing on Middleton in recent decades has been concerned with what is argued to be the 'religio-political' content of his work, suggesting that it presents religious and political matters as connected. Thus, to take an obvious example, the Cardinal in Women Beware Women, whose views are expressed in religious terms, in effect comments on political behaviour and this is at least as important as his theology per se. Also, as Richard A. Levin has persuasively and extensively suggested in a significant contribution, the Cardinal speaks as a first-class political schemer.[4]

The first, and also the lengthiest and most extreme exercise as a study of Middleton's supposed religio-political writing has been, and remains, Margot Heinemann's Puritanism and Theatre.[5] Its influence has been enormous. Heinemann's study was ground-breaking, which is no doubt one important reason for its impact. If a number of scholars have increasingly come to take issue with its theses, Puritanism and Theatre still has a central place in Middleton studies, to such an extent that several of Middleton's writings are now discussed predominantly with religio-political concerns in mind, including Women Beware Women. As Richard Dutton has highlighted, Heinemann 'attempts to impose an intelligible shape' on Middleton's career in her study. Nonetheless, he points out, quite correctly, that when we try to bring Middleton into focus by identifying him as a 'Puritan', as Heinemann does, we are treading in a minefield. Among literary scholars, Dutton is unusual in expressing commendable reservations in his widely available edition, published in 1999, which draws on excellent work by previous scholars.[6]

Not only did Heinemann argue that Middleton was a 'Puritan' throughout his life, but she sees his Puritanism as in essence controlling his writing, and as the dominant emphasis in his works. However, she never clearly defines what she means by 'Puritanism', though the word could and did mean quite different things, both to different people, and at different times, while Middleton was alive. Most importantly, for Heinemann, Middleton's 'Puritanism' is especially significant in the political sphere: her interest in religious aspects of 'Puritanism' is small, but her preoccupation with its supposed political role large. As Dutton points out, her title suggests that 'she identified Middleton's Puritanism with a strain of political resistance to the absolutism of James I and to a range of associated court policies and practices.' She saw Middleton as writing 'opposition drama' (drama opposed to James and his court), particularly (but by no means solely) in *A Game at Chess*. Heinemann views that satirical play as not only criticizing Roman Catholic and Spanish ambitions, but also James himself for supposedly supporting them. But, as Dutton justly emphasizes:

> This thesis has, nevertheless, been attacked on a number of counts. The whole concept of 'opposition drama' has been called into question for applying twentieth-century concepts of ideologically polarized party politics to an early modern world of faction and patronage which simply did not operate in that way. Revisionist historians, in particular, have argued that her view of the early Stuart era was uncritically based on dated Whiggish prejudices, reinforced by a tendency to read the conflicts of the Civil War back into earlier generations. In respect of *A Game at Chess*, her suggestion that Middleton's Puritanism was ideologically consonant with the grouping around the earl of Pembroke, who had for many years resisted Buckingham's influence and advocated anti-Spanish policies, and who as Lord Chamberlain would have been well placed to facilitate the staging of so 'dangerous' a play, has been challenged on several counts. It has particularly been pointed out that by the time the play was staged all the key political players – the King, Prince Charles, Buckingham, and Pembroke (the latter pair having come to a reconciliation) – were agreed on an anti-Spanish policy, so that the play was neither so controversial nor so 'oppositional' as she suggested.[7]

In the same year as Dutton, N. W. Bawcutt produced what is so far the most sustained and detailed critical analysis of Heinemann's understanding of Middleton and his drama.[8] During the course of an important discussion, Bawcutt points out, for example, that Heinemann's claim that Middleton was 'sympathetic to Puritanism' is challenged by the fact that the numerous references to Puritans in his writings are contemptuous in tone. Damagingly to Heinemann's argument, Bawcutt underlines that she simply overlooks (or suppresses) evidence to that effect.[9] A further major faultline in Heinemann's book is that she speaks regularly of Middleton as writing about 'the Parliamentary Puritan Opposition', as though, in Bawcutt's words, 'all Puritans and all members of parliament were joined together in a mass movement strongly hostile to James I'.[10] No such thing as this 'Opposition' party existed in the 1620s or before, and if such a term is to be used at all it is best applied to a grouping in the 1630s and 1640s, that is, a period after Middleton's death in 1627. Indeed, Heinemann herself later admitted that an expression like 'the Parliamentary Puritan Opposition' was quite wrong, although many academics had meanwhile come to believe in its validity. Not only does Heinemann, in *Puritanism and Theatre*, construct an opposition party where there was none, but she also, as Bawcutt demonstrates, calls people Puritans quite arbitrarily and without convincing evidence, such as in the case of Richard Fishborne.[11]

While Heinemann sees Middleton as an 'Opposition' writer, his work for the City of London habitually praises James I, without any innuendo or hint to the contrary.[12] William Heminges's oft-quoted lines about Puritans saying 'Middleton thay seemd much to Adore / fors learned Excercise gaynst Gundomore' (i.e. Gondomar in *A Game at Chess*) derives from a poem which in Bawcutt's view 'is clearly a surrealist fantasy, with a strong anti-Puritan bias, not a sober study of Middleton's reputation'. Thus, the attitude of the Puritans in the poem cannot be held to indicate that Middleton was, as Heinemann claims, 'the Puritans' favourite dramatist'.[13] Indeed, there is evidence to indicate that some notable Puritans objected to Middleton's plays as much as they did to those by others.[14] With particular reference to a play such as *Women Beware Women*, one curious omission in Heinemann's argument which Bawcutt overlooks but to which Dutton does draw attention is that she does not explain how we are to understand, if Middleton is a Puritan, his frequent and abundantly obvious preoccupation with sex. The latter is most certainly not viewed in anything like a Puritanical way, either in Middleton's dramatic presentation of it or in the language which he so frequently applies to it. For example, in *Women Beware Women* we have a very apparent preoccupation with incest in more than one place, and lust plays a major part in the play, as it does often in Middleton's work. Moreover, Dutton stresses with reference to *A Game at Chess* that 'there is even a scene (3.2) which revolves almost entirely around sodomy and homosexual subjection', and – even by extremely broad Jacobean standards – 'Middleton sometimes achieves levels of sexual suggestiveness and innuendo that few of his contemporaries could match'.[15] It is not as though only those who are sceptical about the idea of a 'Parliamentary Puritan Opposition' have difficulty seeing Middleton as a Puritan. Julia Gasper, for example, who insists on calling Marlowe, Chapman, Dekker, Heywood, Webster, Fletcher and Massinger 'militant Protestants',[16] does not include Middleton in this lengthy list, though one would have thought that if he were a Puritan he would qualify.

We are forced to conclude then that much of Heinemann's case for regarding Middleton as a Puritan does not withstand serious examination. However, more generally (and importantly in this discussion of scholarly responses to Middleton's tragic drama), there has been ongoing confusion surrounding the word 'Puritan' in literary criticism, not least because of a failure to distinguish between 'Puritan', 'Calvinist', and 'Protestant'. In his 1973 essay 'Puritanism, Arminianism and Counter-Revolution', Nicholas Tyacke laid down the groundwork of much that he developed more imposingly in his later *Anti-Calvinists*.[17] At the beginning of his essay he explains that for Marxists like Christopher Hill Puritanism 'was the ideology of the newly emergent middle classes, or *bourgeoisie*, as they are sometimes called'. It is not difficult to see that, for all its vagueness, Heinemann's notion of 'Puritanism' is, at least in practice, strongly influenced by this view of society, as she is intensely preoccupied with what she sees as a Puritan Parliament battling the aristocratic Court, and notably the King. Another traditional view has it that the Puritans were 'a religious fifth column within the Church of England' whose numbers greatly increased during the early seventeenth century and who thus eventually (by the early 1640s) were 'able to take over at least in the religious sphere'.[18]

Tyacke sees a very different scenario from these two positions. His principal contention is that indeed Puritans gained in influence during the early years of the seventeenth century, but that their views came to be strongly opposed by the growing power of the Arminians, who rejected much of Calvinism (all in all the most important influence on Puritanism). Subsequently, and as a reaction to the Arminians, Puritanism re-emerged, so to speak, as a much stronger force in what became the Civil War. This view is obviously drastically different from the two earlier ones which Tyacke mentioned and which used to have great currency – and it is completely at odds with the theses put forward in Heinemann's *Puritanism and Theatre*. Furthermore, what Tyacke stresses and what is even now not generally realized is that doctrinally, at least, from the latter sixteenth century onwards 'a majority of the clergy from the Archbishop of Canterbury downwards were Calvinists, and the same was probably true of the more educated laity'.[19] Although the Thirty Nine Articles agreed upon as part of the Elizabethan Settlement in 1562 are capable of more than one interpretation, it is difficult, I agree with many others, not to see them as substantially Calvinist.[20] But, if officially the doctrinal position of the Church of England from 1562 was Calvinist, in what sense was it not 'Puritanical', or how did 'Calvinism' and 'Puritanism' differ from each other? Tyacke further underlines that 'Puritanism around the year 1600, and for more than two decades subsequently, was thought of in terms either of a refusal to conform with the religious rites and ceremonies of the English Church, or as a Presbyterian rejection of church government by bishops. At that date conformists and nonconformists, episcopalians and Presbyterians all had in common Calvinist predestinarian ideas'.[21] From this it should be apparent that it might be reasonably easy to argue that, in Middleton, we find Protestant, i.e. Calvinist, ideas, but that it is much harder to conclude that he was a 'Puritan'. That there are Calvinist traits to be found in the 'specifically Protestant' texts by Middleton has been demonstrated convincingly by G. B. Shand.[22] However, while such traits encourage us to see Protestant traits in these documents, they do not in any sense indicate that Middleton was a Puritan, 'moderate' or otherwise.

The supposedly 'strongly Calvinist' vocabulary and psychology in Middleton's major tragedies is arguable, and has been treated in depth by John Stachniewski.[23] Written in 1989 and published in 1990, Stachniewksi's 'Calvinist Psychology in Middleton's Tragedies' seeks to establish an inevitable connection between the author's Calvinism and his psychological analysis, and the case is most persuasively made with reference to *The Changeling*. However, interestingly in the context of this discussion, Stachniewksi does not seem to see *Women Beware Women* as particularly concerned with the unconscious. Most recently, Adrian Streete's article '"An old quarrel between us that will never be at an end": Middleton's *Women Beware Women* and Late Jacobean Religious Politics'[24] draws attention to the fact that several allusions can be found in the tragedy which may well have been inspired by Calvinism, in particular many phrases that are apocalyptic. The dramatist definitely shows a very close and detailed biblical knowledge, but it seems to me, in reading this otherwise excellent piece of scholarship, that *Women Beware Women* might not be wholly imprisoned by the doctrine which Streete appears to see as totally pervading the play, as when he says: 'For a Calvinist, Hippolito, Isabella, and Livia would all be viewed as unregenerate sinners.'[25]

'For a Calvinist' that might well be – probably is – true: but is it necessary to assume that Middleton saw them only from that perspective? Or, even more importantly, would he have expected the members of his audience to have been so steeped in biblical knowledge that they would inevitably have seen the play in a particular theological manner? I rather doubt that he would, or could, have assumed such a response, or at least as a universal one, among his quite varied spectators. In other words, while the theological component may be undeniably present, it does not seem to me to provide an adequate explanation for the total effect and impact of the play. Later in this discussion, Streete contends 'When, just before his death, Leantio refers to "that glist'ring whore [who] shines like a serpent, / Now that the court's sun's upon her" (IV.ii.20–21), the identification that the play has been hinting at since Act 1 is made clear: Bianca is the whore of Babylon.'[26] Of course, the identification is possible, and I would not wish to rule it out as *one* meaning that may be conveyed, yet surely, even in biblical terms, the most immediate notion that an audience would seize on is that a serpent represents the devil. Moreover, Streete's interpretation ignores that the 'serpent' is 'glist'ring' because the sun *of the court* is upon her, a matter which takes us away from Rome and the Catholic church. In addition, if Bianca is nothing other than the whore of Babylon, this would utterly dehumanize her – and the tragedy refrains from doing this: it presents her at various times as subject to changing, very human emotions, and even evokes some audience sympathy for her towards the end, as many have noted, when she refers to her own 'leprous soul' and adds, having poisoned herself by kissing the dying Duke: 'What make I here? These are all strangers to me, / Not known but by their malice, now thou'rt gone; / Nor do I seek their pities' (5.1.247–49).

The current solemn emphasis on religio-political issues does not seem to me to do any justice to the fact that Middleton himself appears to be very capable of standing apart from them. In this context, Dutton persuasively argues that what happens at the end of *Women Beware Women* remains consistent with a Calvinist reading. He suggests that the characters 'remain blind sinners, unable to read the plots of their own damnation any better than that of the masque', but significantly adds that the development of the masque is at the same time 'disconcertingly funny, a strangely postmodern distraction from the high seriousness in which they are unwitting players, exposing the fictionality of the medium even as the medium itself purports to be dealing with absolutes. In such self-consciousness Middleton seems to question, even to undermine, the theological certainties he depicts'.[27] Indeed, one might go further in contending that if we look at what happens at the end – that is, who dies and who stays alive – we can only conclude that Middleton offers to us a picture of a universe which makes no moral sense. This is not the view of a person who can simply be described as a Calvinist, but of one who realizes that the world is a far more complex place than such an ideology as Calvinism can satisfactorily account for. Middleton seems to bring this out also in his portrayal of the Cardinal, if we consider that at its most simple level. Whatever the merits of the Cardinal's moralizing may superficially seem to be, they are annulled by the ease with which he joins an evil world. Although in theory he disapproves of the Duke and Bianca, the Duke expresses his wish for a reconcilement between Bianca and the Cardinal, who amazingly answers: 'I profess peace, and am content' (5.1.51).

Paul Yachnin is also timely in his varied vision on early modern dramatic worlds. While seeing Middleton as an 'authentic Protestant', Yachnin adds pertinently that most probably he, 'like most people, had a multifaceted sense of identity, so that whatever his beliefs in the sphere of religion, his view of his plays – and the plays themselves – would tend to be conditioned by his professional identity. Certainly, there are zealots whose sense of self galvanizes around a single idea, but it seems unlikely that Middleton was such a person or that anyone who was a religious zealot would have also been a professional playwright.'[28]

Matters of Gender

Matters of gender have been a central concern in criticism of Renaissance drama in recent decades, and discussions of *Women Beware Women*, too, have to a very large extent chosen to focus on them. Interestingly, the most frequently debated question has been whether, in Act 2, scene 2, we should see Bianca as 'raped' or 'seduced'. The possibility that she is both 'raped' *and* 'seduced' is rarely considered, let alone thoroughly explored. The 'older' argument was usually to the effect that Bianca was 'seduced', even if it was admitted that the Duke also used threats as part of his argument. Thus Mulryne, in his 1975 Revels edition, wrote that 'the Duke [...] deals with her with splendid poise, in a superbly calculated mixture of reassurance, sexual play, flattery and threats'.[29] While 'threats' are mentioned, Mulryne nevertheless speaks of 'the seduction-scene'.[30] When he revised his edition for student use, however, and updated it in 2007, Mulryne declared instead that Bianca's 'seduction by the Duke, with its abuse of authority and, on her part (at most) questionable consent, would properly in a modern court of law be called rape'.[31] Apart from the radical change in emphasis we can immediately observe that a difficulty has been introduced in the claim that the 'seduction' would in a *modern* court of law be called rape. Our first duty is, obviously, to try and understand what the play would have meant *in 1621*: we may then go on to consider what we think of it now, but that is a different exercise. From the way in which most discussions of gender issues in the play at some point or other confront this matter, it is clear that there is agreement that the episode in question is in many ways central within the play, and essential to concentrate on if we are to gain reasonable insight into Middleton's attitude to relations between the sexes.

In her 1998 discussion 'Middleton: silence and sound', Celia R. Daileader invokes the community of 'modern editors', adding parenthetically 'all of whom, by the way, happen to be male'.[32] In the course of this study, Mulryne and his 1975 edition are mentioned, but Roma Gill's 1968 Revels edition not at all.[33] The supposition that an homogeneous group of male modern editors, to whom she refers, could hardly be expected to show sympathy for a young woman in

THE STATE OF THE ART 85

Bianca's position is linked apparently to the reluctance to provide adequate stage directions for this key scene, for example. However, from this point of view, Gill cannot be seen as doing any better than her male counterparts. The editions of the tragedy which Daileader does consider (the most recent item is David L. Frost's 1978 anthology)[34] were produced at a time when stage directions were only rarely added anyway, and this fact has nothing to do with the question of whether the editor was a man or a woman. In 1994, four years before Daileader's study was published, William C. Carroll's very noteworthy New Mermaids edition appeared, but this is not mentioned.[35] This omission matters, not so much in terms of Carroll's handling of the text, but because of what he actually has to *say*, in his Introduction, about the seduction/rape section, which in any discussion of an editor's attitude surely cannot be simply disregarded. Daileader would in fact have had to consider the following passage as highly congenial to her point of view:

> The site of the Duke's assault on Bianca is the famous chess scene (II.ii), its lower-stage chess game and upper-stage and off-stage rape of Bianca one of the most brilliantly managed pieces of stagecraft in all of Jacobean drama. Many critics of the play once argued the supposed question of Bianca's consent to the Duke – [Samuel] Schoenbaum, in a notorious phrase, said she 'is able to lose her virtue only because she never really possessed it' [*Middleton's Tragedies: A Critical Study*; New York: Columbia University Press, 1955] – but their encounter is usually read with a different sensibility now. The Duke's cunning is paralleled with Livia's below, in any event, and his language is filled with the rhetoric of masculine power ('Strive not to seek / Thy liberty', 'you shall not out till I'm released', 'I should be sorry the least force should lay / An unkind touch upon thee', 'I can command: /Think upon that') which asserts a familiar pattern of masculine domination/female subjection as well as the more gender-neutral master/subject hierarchical relation. In such a context, Bianca's 'choice' is really non-existent.[36]

The case that Bianca is raped is argued vigorously and extensively in Anthony B. Dawson, '*Women Beware Women* and the Economy of Rape' (1987), which has perhaps become the *locus classicus* for this critical approach, and indispensable reading for all those who reject the 'seduction' scenario. He contends that the play 'examines the pressures of sexual power in a quite startling way. At its center stands a rape, presented [...] as an emblem of hierarchy and an image of the domination that characterizes most of the play's relationships'.[37]

I would read matters differently, as follows. In analysing the details of this scene, it is clear that Bianca speaks intriguingly about the Duke as seemingly unappetizing: 'Infectious mists and mildews hang at's eyes. / The weather of a doomsday dwells upon him' (2.2.421–22). This description implies that the Duke is corrupted, probably suffers from a physical illness, and that he is contagious. Many have suggested that the infectious mists and mildews are caused by his having venereal disease, which c. 1620 was, indeed, common among people in his position. (Interestingly, however, in *The Changeling* De Flores sounds similarly distasteful when Beatrice describes him while yet she is – at first unconsciously – magnetized by him as a huge sexual force.) But Bianca's initially negative comments after the sexual incident cannot and should not be regarded in isolation: while she describes her honour as leprous (2.2.423), she feels that this condition was in part triggered by her own sexual beauty, so wonders 'why should I / Preserve that fair that caused the leprosy?' (2.2.423–24). Is she surrendering here to an evil which she associates with her own being? Similarly, we have to consider that although she rebukes Guardiano, she also affirms: 'I'm made bold now, / I thank thy treachery. Sin and I'm acquainted, / No couple greater; and I'm like that great one / Who, making politic use of a base villain, / He likes the treason well, but hates the traitor' (2.2.438–42).

Although Leantio in 1.1 speaks of his marriage to Bianca as 'theft, but noble' (37), he stresses that it is 'sealed from heaven by marriage' (45), and there is no sign at all that Bianca was anything other than a willing participant in the elopement. Strikingly, one may conclude, what has motivated her has, in effect, been *lust*, which the play reveals as perhaps the most ruinous emotion for one to be guided by. Bianca abandoned her parents for the sake of her erotic ambitions, and thus also relinquished the prospect of a marriage to a much richer person who could have offered her comforts that Leantio cannot possibly afford, as his mother points out reprovingly (1.1.65–66). Bianca's own statement, 'I have forsook friends, fortunes, and my country, / And hourly I rejoice in't' (1.1.131–32) soon is shown to be evidence of her lack of self-knowledge. Leantio, because of his life as a humble 'factor', has actually very little time for her. This, because of what I take to be her sensual nature, cannot fail to disappoint her: 'But this one night, I prithee' (1.3.49). She cries when he sets forth (1.3.62–63), but matters are made far worse again by the fact that Leantio in effect imprisons Bianca, considering his mother good enough 'to look to keys' (1.1.176).

All in all, Leantio has created an explosive and most unsatisfactory situation for a young bride to be in, and not least one that has been strong-willed enough to elope without regard for her parents, for the sake of a desire now largely left unfulfilled, and deprived of wealth such as she had known and could have looked forward to. We also learn later that when she was an unmarried girl at her father's house she was 'kept short of that / Which a wife knows she must have – nay, and will, / Will, Mother, if she be not a fool born' (3.1.54–56). In 4.1.31, she complains that she was kept strictly in her young days. These, and there are many others, are all details from Middleton's dramatic world which we must remember when we consider what happens when she first meets the Duke. That does not happen in Livia's home, but long before, in 1.3, when Leantio has left Bianca in tears in his poor mother's house, who is to keep her under lock and key with no other company present. Hardly has Leantio left when the Duke comes past Leantio's mother's house. A citizen makes plain that this event excites women, saying to an Apprentice (and probably punning bawdily), 'You sirrah, get a standing for your mistress, / The best in all the city' (1.3.75–76). Bianca has bid her farewells to Leantio from a window 'above' and is still there when the Duke passes. While she remains there, the men below change, with the Duke symbolically replacing Leantio in her vision. The interest in the Duke is plain. The Mother says 'now you shall see / Our Duke, a goodly gentleman of

THE STATE OF THE ART   87

his years' (1.3.89–90). One meaning of 'goodly' is 'handsome, attractive', and as the Mother draws attention to the Duke's 'years', I think that this is the meaning which (for whatever reason) she intends. We may be sure, in any case, that Bianca has taken it in. Told that the Duke is 'some fifty-five', she remarks: 'That's no great age in man he's then at best / For wisdom and for judgement' (1.3.92–93). Clearly, her interest in the Duke is piqued and, indeed, later she asks: 'Did not the Duke look up? Methought he saw us' (1.3.105).

He certainly did, and the whole purpose of Livia's staging a meeting between the Duke and Bianca in 2.2 is to satisfy his desire for her. However, in saying this, the tragedy clearly insists that we proceed with care. If the Duke wished, he could, given his authority, have approached Bianca much more brusquely than he does. This remains a real difficulty for those who believe that the Duke is merely planning to 'violate' Bianca off-stage. Undeniably, he does imply, and in more than one place, that he has power over her, which he says he could use but would prefer not to use. And this must be one factor influencing her in listening to him. But the Duke does not, in fact, drag her along with him, but sets about wooing her. The reason is, no doubt, that he is so taken with her that he does not aim for a one-off sexual assault, but something far more lasting: and we can see that he may be right to think that Bianca will suit him in the longer term, for he and she turn out to be very well matched, even if we perhaps dislike both of them. So the Duke courts Bianca by not merely threatening her, but rather by saying: 'I could compel you to surrender, but I think there are very good reasons for you to do so without my forcing you to'. And he proceeds to mention those reasons. With his worldly insight, he has an excellent understanding of what she might respond to, positively and lastingly. Indeed, he has clearly done his homework:

> Do not I know you've cast away your life
> Upon necessities, means merely doubtful
> To keep you in indifferent health and fashion –
> A thing I heard too lately, and soon pitied –
> And can you be so much your beauty's enemy
> To kiss away a month or two in wedlock
> And weep whole years in wants for ever after?' (2.2.374–80)

Given Bianca's circumstances – particularly the way they have developed since her arrival in Florence – what the Duke says here is likely to make a very potent impact upon her and may explain why she exits with him, soon declares that she likes '*the treason well*', and very easily adjusts to her new situation. I believe that the interpretation which I provide here makes consistent sense, ignores no important evidence, and does justice to Middleton's dramatic and psychological art as both logical and complex, though by no means incomprehensible. I would suggest that it does so far more than those readings which present the Duke simply as a rapist. The Duke does conjure up the idea of possible coercion, but in particular persuades Bianca in quite different ways: his success is real and lasting, because the element of coercion is far less important than the various attractions (including sexual magnetism) which he is able to offer, and which ultimately make it very easy for Bianca to reject Leantio. It is not sexist to insist that both the Duke and Bianca have faults and that both may consent to adulterous behaviour on the basis of their own needs, as they see them, without regard for others. I do not think that my reading has actually been presented by any critic so far, which is why I do so here. It enables me to explain why I think that this matter has been inadequately dealt with in contemporary criticism, although parts of my argument turn up here and there in work done by others. On the whole, I feel that those who see the Duke as seducing Bianca are more justified in that conclusion than those who consider him a rapist.

Murray Biggs's 'Does the Duke Rape Bianca in Middleton's *Women Beware Women?*'[38] reads the dialogue in the scene well and very thoroughly, but I do not find his approach comprehensive enough: much of our understanding, particularly of Bianca's state of mind before and after this episode, can only be derived from equally thorough analysis of earlier and later parts of the play.[39] Another important reading of this dramatic action is performed by Emily Detmer-Goebel.[40] Her essay concentrates very much on the matter of consent. Detmer-Goebel says that 'Middleton dramatizes Bianca's choice to end resistance and "consent after" as morally corrupt but altogether reasonable'.[41] This makes some sort of sense, but the failure of the essay is that Bianca's complex psychology, as presented by Middleton throughout the play, is not sufficiently examined and hence neither her personality nor her very particular circumstances are sufficiently taken into account. Instead, we are confronted with the disappointing ideological claim that Middleton fears women's 'agency' because, if granted it, they 'might just think they have the right to decide when and with whom they can consent to sex. Men's interests are not served, the play suggests, by investing women with unlimited agency'.[42] One may object that the Duke's interest is actually very much served by Bianca's consent. There is no hint, moreover, that *all* women would invariably misuse their 'unlimited agency'. Finally, to the extent that the women in the play do so, this does not place them in any special position: the men misuse their unlimited agency just as much. The reservations communicated in *Women Beware Women* about male a- or immorality are just as stringent as those concerned with the female characters. The charge of anti-feminism could only arise if Middleton saw women as worse than men: in fact, his negativistic view is remarkably even-handed.

Amongst those essays which treat the rape/seduction question, one by Anne M. Haselkorn remains illuminating.[43] Exceptionally, Haselkorn notes that 'the fifty-three-year-old [he is actually 55] duke, urbane and enamored of Bianca, realizes that gentleness and paternalism rather than "command" will win a sixteen-year-old'.[44] And she offers an ingenious explanation as to why the Duke's threatening language might actually be helpful to Bianca: 'It is too disquieting for her to accept responsibility for her self-assertion [i.e. in rejecting Leantio], and she can reproach herself less if, embedded in her decision, is an element of coercion'.[45] Nonetheless, concerning this rape/seduction debate, very few of the discussions offered in recent times depart from the portrayal of the Duke as a brute patriarch who through his 'violent' language as a 'social superior' rapes Bianca, at the least mentally, and certainly physically. Some do adopt a more cautious stance; but they are in the minority.[46] Interestingly, several critics have more of interest to say on Isabella than on Bianca, not least because Isabella thinks that, in having sex with her uncle, she avoids incest (as a result of Livia's lie about her parentage), but, oddly, is prepared to marry the crude Ward at the same time. Her reasons for doing this are found puzzling. Perhaps, with the problem of incest solved, Isabella finds it easier to accommodate her father's desire that she marry the Ward, to whose money she appears to be attracted? Her punishment at the end would indicate that her wish for gold (which is poured into her lap) is the source of her undoing, not incest. Thus, from this perspective, Middleton appears to view her alliance with the Ward as a kind of prostitution.

Richard A. Levin writes a very full piece on Leantio's mother, whom most critics rather tend to ignore. He sees the Mother as a sophisticated schemer rather than the somewhat naïve victim that she may appear to be at first sight.[47] Livia is, of course, another interesting character in the play, who is often examined more cursorily than Bianca or Isabella (though with more attention than Leantio's mother). Lisa Hopkins is probably the most interesting critic on Livia, and, in general, has been one of the most original and searching writers on Renaissance tragedy in recent times. In her *Female Hero* she collects some very important material on *Women Beware Women*, providing a substantial overview of matters that interest her.[48] It is worth mentioning that she comments on Bianca and the Duke in terms of art and nature rather than discussing the all-too-frequent rape/seduction question, but it is in her treatment of Livia that her discussion really demands attention. While, as she is aware, the play is at times very much seen as preoccupied with quasi-family relations in which older characters seem to play more or less parental roles, nevertheless her view of Livia as a mother, even if a surrogate mother, is perceptively and interestingly developed. In this discussion, Livia may be seen rather too much, at times, as 'typical' for a mother figure such as the Renaissance often thought of when discussing mothers, but the thesis is powerfully argued. Peculiarly interesting is the fact that Livia may be showing maternal inclinations in her attitude to others, but actually *is not* a mother. Hopkins does touch on this substantial oddity: 'What women most need to beware of, it seems, is this fundamental aspect of their own womanhood, seen as so deeply rooted in the feminine psyche that it manifests itself as a mothering instinct even in the literally childless'.[49] As I see it, the most important matter is ultimately that Livia herself is not aware that much of what she does is prompted by this maternal drive, which is in many cases fatally misdirected. In other words, she is one of those characters in Middleton who understands herself badly because her actions are at least in part prompted by what is in the unconscious, and thus she is potentially destructive. Hopkins seems to me entirely persuasive when she observes that 'Livia in fact represents impulses not so much of uncontrolled evil as of uncontrolled gratification'.[50]

We can see in some places just how this comes about. Livia says, for example: 'I have buried my two husbands in good fashion, / And never mean more to marry' (1.2.50–51). Hopkins comments: 'Livia here proposes to exercise a restraint very rare amongst the middle-aged women of Renaissance drama [...] she seems ready to renounce her sexuality and take her place as one of the older generation rather than among the still marriageable'.[51] Given Livia's attitude to sexuality generally, I am not sure that she is not rather saying that she wants to be free-ranging rather than to be restricted by a husband. Hopkins's reading, however, is also perfectly possible: Livia may be willing to encourage sexuality in, for example, Bianca or Isabella while planning to be chaste herself. Either way, what I think needs to be stressed is that Livia is not conscious of the fact that what she is choosing for herself will prove an impossible task. She underrates her ability to channel her sexuality (whether as a promiscuous woman or a chaste one), embarks on an impulsive affair with Leantio as her toyboy, and pays for her lack of self-knowledge with her life. Her lack of awareness of her own nature is characteristically what interests Middleton particularly, as in so many other instances, e.g. that of Beatrice in *The Changeling*. Hopkins has initiated an important way of thinking about characters in *Women Beware Women*, but I feel that a yet more penetrating investigation of them, along these lines, remains a desideratum.

Matters of Place

Some very interesting and valuable essays concern themselves with questions to do with locality in the play. Ann C. Christensen's 'Settling House in Middleton's *Women Beware Women*' is to my mind one of the very best essays to emerge among the many that have been written since the early nineties,[52] and I felt I learned much from it not only because of its insights but also its scholarship, which is never ponderous, but illuminating and to the point. The way the rules of households are broken indicates much, Christensen shows, of what is amiss with the characters and the social world portrayed in the play. Thus she demonstrates in fine and totally persuasive detail that 'The tragedy of the main plot in *Women Beware Women* stems from Leantio's failure to observe the rites not only of marriage but specifically those of the inauguration of the household.' For various reasons (all specified) his 'domestic establishment is shaky from the start, lacking both the public, communal sanction fundamental to an occasion as important as a wedding and the solid economic foundation necessary to the family's continuation'. Moreover, in her view, 'The play's other domestic arrangements, not properly based in marriages, are likewise secretive and prove morally unsound'.[53] Even many seemingly inconspicuous details are given meaningful point by Christensen's approach. For example, Livia claims that Isabella's mother engaged in adulterous sex while her husband was away from home on business (a situation increasingly seen as a threat to marriage at this time). As Christensen points out: 'The story, albeit fictive, matches all the marriages staged or discursively represented in the play in which husbands leave on business and wives make do with lovers at home'.[54] As a result of Livia's story, 'Isabella's view of house-keeping lends an especially cynical cast to the whole enterprise of settling house'.[55] This fine essay deserves thorough reading and, indeed, re-readings.

Another essay which offers some sound insights into its chosen domestic territory is Leonardo Buonomo's 'Domestic Themes in Thomas Middleton's *Women Beware Women*'.[56] Again, houses and what happens within them are seen as important markers of morality and psychology. Thus Leantio's house 'reflects the simplicity and ordinariness of its occupants', and the play's movement into degradation is indicated by the shift to Livia's house which, 'with the sophisticated disposition of its rooms, becomes the objective correlative of Livia's (as well as the court's) craftiness'.[57] In fact, trouble is already apparent in the first house, where 'the immature, almost childish aspects of the personalities of Leantio and Bianca' are on display, as well as a 'helpless' mother unassisted by 'paternal authority and guidance'.[58] Much of the essay concentrates on marriage, arguing persuasively that 'The meaning of the institution, grossly distorted by Bianca and Leantio, is utterly trivialized and parodied by the proposed marriage between Isabella and the Ward (who is himself a poor imitation of a man)'.[59]

There are larger and more complicated critical issues involved in considering essays dedicated to the function of another place: Florence as the city within which the play is set. In an essay for the collection *Shakespeare's Italy*, Zara Bruzzi and A. A. Bromham are ultimately less interested in the Italian setting *per se* than in the way it enables them, as they see matters, to locate allusions to English politics, particularly the Jacobean court.[60] The general approach is perhaps reasonably well indicated by this statement: 'Recent work on censorship and political comment in Jacobean drama has shown that it was a widely adopted formula to find a plot which had suggestive analogies with the forbidden material to be treated, frequently one based on a different historical period. The technique was one of intermittent implication of comparability rather than the continuous narrative parallel of allegory'.[61] The intermittent nature of the allusions is perhaps a problem for those individuals who are sceptical about political allusions *per se*, and even for those who are not, as at times the connections are not necessarily firm; and, as the authors realize, the persuasiveness of their case also depends upon what one could reasonably suppose the audience to have perceived. For those of us open to the allusions as at least a possibility, and at times very likely to be 'real', the material opens up many interesting parallels. The approach can also be seen at work in a later essay by Bruzzi on much the same topic.[62] Again, the emphasis is very strongly on allusions to politics in England. To an extent, the argument is at times at risk of moving rather far outside the text, as when Bruzzi says, 'if one looks at Bianca's career, there are similarities with Buckingham's'.[63] The context makes plain that here we are to think not only of James's favourite, Buckingham, who is not part of *Women Beware Women*, but also of the historical Bianca rather than the Bianca of the play, all of which would require some real intellectual gymnastics on the part of an audience witnessing the play on stage. Yet, even if one were to concentrate on the Bianca of the play, Bruzzi's suggestion seems quite persuasive: she makes a case for believing that there is a strong parallel between this Bianca and the two favourites of James's reign. The similarities are often quite striking. The idea may also help us to interpret, in the way that Bruzzi does, the Cardinal's comment at the very end of the play.

With a rather more specific emphasis upon the *Italian* world of the play, J. R. Mulryne, also in *The Italian World*,[64] concentrates on 'a broader cultural rather than political literacy'.[65] His argument is that 'Middleton turned to Florence for the socially and politically inclusive image he needed to represent the London of his own cultural moment'.[66] Thus, Middleton employs Florence for its setting 'because his audiences might be expected to see in a fictionalized Florence a working model of a possible future for London and England'.⁶⁷ Mulryne stresses the sophistication of Florence, for example in the area of the visual arts and collections of art objects. He draws attention to the fact that around 1620 major Italianate art collections were being built up in England and that connoisseurship had become a mark of prestige, as had ostentatious buildings. The masque at the end is for one thing used because 'in the Jacobean public mind the authority of the Florentine court was directly associated with festival display'.⁶⁸ Thus Mulryne argues for interpreting the Florentine setting of the play 'more seriously as a cultural referent than is usual in Middleton commentary'; *Women Beware Women* 'made its contribution to the circulation of cultural energy in London through overt recollection and (re)construction of a recognizable but fictional image of Florence'.⁶⁹

Final Words

I have enjoyed reading a good many discussions on the play that appeared during the last fifteen years or so, but also have some serious reservations about others. That in some respects Middleton must have been at the least 'a good Protestant' with some Calvinist leanings is something I accept, but that is quite different from believing, as several critics do, that his writings should be approached, and can somehow be fairly readily understood, by assuming that he predominantly wrote from a particular religious perspective. I think that the evidence – even the perplexing ending of *Women Beware Women* – shows that Middleton had an altogether more complex view of life and the universe and was very capable of looking beyond any ideological perspective. Thus I think that this approach to him is damagingly reductive and have come to agree with the contention of Derek B. Alwes that 'Whatever Middleton's own religious beliefs may have been, the world he depicts in his city comedies is one in which religious practices failed to guarantee ethical human behaviour.'⁷⁰ Much of the oddity and complexity of Middleton's view of the world in fact still remains to be fully explored and to be accepted as extraordinary.

I see a similar reductive tendency at work in many gender studies that would impute simplistic ('sexist' or 'non-sexist') views or portrayals to Middleton. By contrast, I think that his interest in psychological complexity, on the part of members of both sexes, is still under-explored. Middleton's characters often behave with striking peculiarity compared with those in the works of most other dramatists and this is where I think that, for example, Lisa Hopkins's approach to the character of Livia as a surrogate mother is promising and should be further developed as a line of inquiry into the individuality of the characters generally. The Ward, for example, is a curious mixture of shrewdness and a-social behaviour and his psychological make-up has been far too little examined.

Most of all, I was struck by the fact that, during the period with which I was concerned (c. 1995–2009), there were strikingly few discussions of the play *as a whole*. Many writers concentrated on various more or less interesting aspects. Often the discussions revealed late-twentieth-century preoccupations that told me much about the critics, sometimes at the expense of Middleton. In any case, many commentators did not seem to be sufficiently aware that the play is structured very carefully and subtly, so that one's view of matters is constantly affected by the dramatic changes (many of them unsettling and unorthodox). In any appreciation of any important matter in the play the fact that *it is a play* should, I believe, be constantly kept in focus. We need, to stress just some important things, a more 'organic' approach to the wholeness of the play in its theatrical development, more thorough investigation of many artistic matters such as its prosody (e.g. just how Middleton achieves an effect very different from Shakespeare's), and a much stronger emphasis on matters of genre. In this respect Lisa Hopkins wrote an all-too-short but still useful essay, 'City Tragedy: Middleton, Shakespeare and Ford', which in principle helps one to understand what expectations of such a genre an audience might bring to bear on its reception of *Women Beware Women*.[71]

In many recent discussions the matter of the *final* reception, in particular, as related to the play as a whole, is not really addressed, even if the masque is analysed. An overall grasp of the structure and effect of a play is often lacking these days, such as was still demonstrated by critics writing not so very long ago. For example, Alexander Leggatt in *English Drama: Shakespeare to the Restoration 1590–1660* seems to me to reveal just such an illuminating, comprehensive view of the play as is now only very rarely produced.[72] He does, in fact, almost immediately justify the term 'city tragedy' for *Women Beware Women*: 'Middleton's city comedies, then, present a low view of humanity. When he turns to tragedy in *Women Beware Women* (c. 1621) the effect is not very different, and the result is a tragedy that has many affinities with satiric comedy: the wide focus, quite unlike Shakespeare's concentration on a single hero; the heavy irony; the lack of any compensating dignity'.[73] All the points here seem to me meaningful, perceptive, and helpful, and part of a critical mode of writing that we need to return to more.

Finally, although I greatly admire *Women Beware Women*, we need some research into not just this play but into our own reactions to Middleton. Why is it, precisely, that his status has risen so hugely during the last two decades or so? Many comment on his interest in power, money, and sex as a reason. If so, that may mean that we overrate this author. I would hope we can find better reasons: perhaps Middleton speaks to us with peculiar force, not least in the case of this play, because the society he portrays has lost all its valuable roots and moral/ spiritual beliefs. His diagnosis may be that of a profound social upheaval. We need to come to a more exact assessment of both his and our own views. For example, do we run the risk that we think of Middleton more highly than we should simply because our own period in history happens to resemble his in some significant ways? I would suggest the need for a more critical examination both of him and of ourselves in relation to him.

Notes

1 Thomas Middleton, *The Collected Works*, gen. ed. by Gary Taylor and John Lavagnino (Oxford: Clarendon Press, 2007); Gary Taylor and John Lavagnino, eds, *Thomas Middleton and Early Modern Textual Culture: A Companion to the Collected Works* (Oxford: Clarendon Press, 2007).
2 Thomas Middleton, *Women Beware Women*, ed. by William C. Carroll, New

Mermaids, 2nd edn (London: A & C Black; New York: W. W. Norton, 1994).
3   Richard Dutton, ed., *'Women Beware Women' and Other Plays* (Oxford: Oxford University Press, 1999; repr. 2009).
4   Richard A. Levin, 'The Dark Color of a Cardinal's Discontentment: The Political Plot of *Women Beware Women*', *Medieval and Renaissance Drama in England*, 10 (1998), 201–17.
5   Margot Heinemann, *Puritanism and Theatre: Thomas Middleton and Opposition Drama under the Early Stuarts* (Cambridge: Cambridge University Press, 1980).
6   Richard Dutton, ed., *'Women Beware Women' and Other Plays* (Oxford: Oxford University Press, 1999; repr. 2009), pp. xiv–xv. The predecessors Dutton refers to are J. Limon, *Dangerous Matter: English Drama and Politics in 1623/4* (Cambridge: Cambridge University Press, 1986) and T. H. Howard-Hill, 'Political Interpretations of Middleton's *A Game at Chess*', *Yearbook of English Studies*, 21 (1991), 274–85. But see also, for further discussion, Thomas Cogswell, 'Middleton and the Court 1624: *A Game at Chess in Context*', *Huntington Library Quarterly*, 47 (1984), 237–88.
7   Dutton, *'Women Beware Women' and Other Plays*, pp. xiv–xv.
8   N. W. Bawcutt, 'Was Thomas Middleton a Puritan Dramatist?', *Modern Language Review*, 94.4 (1999), 925–39.
9   Bawcutt, 'Was Thomas Middleton a Puritan Dramatist?', p. 926.
10 Bawcutt, 'Was Thomas Middleton a Puritan Dramatist?', p. 928.
11 Bawcutt, 'Was Thomas Middleton a Puritan Dramatist?', pp. 929–30.
12 Bawcutt, 'Was Thomas Middleton a Puritan Dramatist?', pp. 930–33.
13 Bawcutt, 'Was Thomas Middleton a Puritan Dramatist?', p. 933.
14 Bawcutt, 'Was Thomas Middleton a Puritan Dramatist?', p. 934. Another curious point in Heinemann's book which Bawcutt draws attention to is her confidently presented contention that no doubt a powerful patron shielded Middleton from punishment for writing his provocative play, and that this person was an influential Puritan. Her candidate is William Herbert, third Earl of Pembroke and Lord Chamberlain, but her argument remains utterly speculative.
15 Dutton, *'Women Beware Women' and Other Plays*, p. xiii.
16 Julia Gasper, *The Dragon and the Dove: The Plays of Thomas Dekker* (Oxford: Oxford University Press, 1990), pp. 2–9.
17 Nicholas Tyacke, 'Puritanism, Arminianism and Counter-Revolution', pp. 119–43. in Conrad Russell's *The Origins of the English Civil War* (London: Macmillan, 1973); and Tyacke *Anti-Calvinists: The Rise of English Arminianism c. 1590–1640* (Oxford: Clarendon Press, 1987; rev. pb. edn, 1990). See also Russell *The Origins of the English Civil War* (London: Macmillan, 1973), specifically pp. 1–31. The literature on Puritanism is, of course, extensive. Among other recent works the following seem to me useful for our purpose: Christopher Durston and Jacqueline Eales, eds, *The Culture of English Puritanism, 1560–1700* (New York: St Martin's Press, 1996) and Laura Lunger Knoppers, *Puritanism and Its Discontents* (Newark: University of Delaware Press; London: Associated University Presses, 2003).
18 Tyacke, 'Puritanism, Arminianism and Counter-Revolution', p. 119.
19 Tyacke, 'Puritanism, Arminianism and Counter-Revolution', p. 120.
20 To understand what is meant by Calvinism one of course needs to read Calvin himself. Those who want to inform themselves of his views at least broadly, yet accurately, might start by reading Willem van 't Spijker's excellent *Calvin: A Brief Guide to His Life and Thought*, trans. by Lyle D. Bierma (Louisville, KY: Westminster John Knox Press, 2009), and take matters further by consulting the clear-headed book on Calvin – and, importantly in our context, Calvin's followers – by Paul Helm, *Calvin and the Calvinists* (Edinburgh: The Banner of Truth Trust, 1982), which, in answering R. T. Kendall's *Calvin and English Calvinism to 1649* (Oxford: Oxford University Press, 1979) provides a lucid and comprehensive exposition of Calvin's thought. The most thorough and extensive treatment, widely praised, of the early history of Protestant theology is Richard A. Muller's *Post-Reformation Reformed Dogmatics: The Rise and Development of Reformed Orthodoxy, ca. 1520 to ca. 1725* (Grand Rapids, MI: Baker Academics, 2003).

21 Tyacke, 'Puritanism, Arminianism and Counter-Revolution', pp. 120–21.
22 G. B. Shand, 'The Elizabethan Aim of *The Wisdom of Solomon Paraphrased*', in *'Accompaninge the Players': Essays Celebrating Thomas Middleton, 1580–1980*, ed. by Kenneth Friedenreich (New York: AMS Press, 1983), pp. 67–78.
23 John Stachniewski, 'Calvinist Psychology in Middleton's Tragedies', in *Three Jacobean Revenge Tragedies: A Selection of Critical Essays*, ed. by R. V. Holdsworth (Basingstoke: Macmillan, 1990), pp. 226–47. I think that Stachniewski has a case, but it is not unassailable, and in any case what he points at is a Calvinist element in the tragedies, not a Puritan one.
24 Adrian Streete, '"An old quarrel between us that will never be at an end": Middleton's *Women Beware Women* and Late Jacobean Religious Politics', *Review of English Studies*, 60.244 (2009), 230–54.
25 Streete, '"An old quarrel between us that will never be at an end": Middleton's *Women Beware Women* and Late Jacobean Religious Politics', p. 247.
26 Streete, '"An old quarrel between us that will never be at an end": Middleton's *Women Beware Women* and Late Jacobean Religious Politics', p. 252.
27 Dutton, *'Women Beware Women' and Other Plays*, p. xi.
28 Paul Yachnin, 'Reversal of Fortune: Shakespeare, Middleton, and the Puritans', *English Literary History*, 70.3 (2003), 757–86. I greatly admire the good sense of this article.
29 *Women Beware Women*, ed. by J. R. Mulryne, The Revels Plays (London: Methuen, 1975; reprinted Manchester: Manchester University Press, 1975), p. lxix.
30 *Women Beware Women*, ed. Mulryne, p. lxx.
31 *Women Beware Women*, ed. by J. R. Mulryne, Revels Student Editions (Manchester: Manchester University Press, 2007) p. 26.
32 Celia R. Daileader, 'Middleton: silence and sound', in *Eroticism on the Renaissance Stage: Transcendence, Desire, and the Limits of the Visible* (Cambridge: Cambridge University Press, 1998), pp. 25–34.
33 *Women Beware Women*, ed. by Roma Gill (London: Ernest Benn, 1968).
34 *The Selected Plays of Thomas Middleton*, ed. by David L. Frost (Cambridge: Cambridge University Press, 1978).
35 See note 2 for details.
36 *Women Beware Women*, ed. Carroll, p. xxiv.
37 Anthony B. Dawson, '*Women Beware Women* and the Economy of Rape', *Studies in English Literature. 1500–1900*, 27.2, Elizabethan and Jacobean Drama (1987), 303–20.
38 Murray Biggs, 'Does the Duke Rape Bianca in Middleton's *Women Beware Women?*', *Notes and Queries*, n.s. 44.1 (March 1997), 97–100.
39 However, in a later discussion seeking to refute Biggs's readings, Mark Hutchings argues that 'if Bianca submits, she does so, surely, because the only alternative is a brutal rape'. See Mark Hutchings, 'Middleton's *Women Beware Women*: Rape, Seduction – or Power, Simply?', *Notes and Queries*, n.s. 45.3 (September 1998), 366–67 (p. 367).
40 Emily Detmer-Goebel, 'What more could woman do?: Dramatizing Consent in Heywood's *Rape of Lucrece* and Middleton's *Women Beware Women*', *Women's Studies*, 36 (2007), 141–59.
41 Detmer-Goebel, 'What more could woman do?', p. 156.
42 Ibid.
43 Anne M. Haselkorn, 'Sin and the Politics of Penitence: Three Jacobean Adultresses', in *The Renaissance Englishwoman in Print: Counterbalancing the Canon*, ed. by Anne Haselkorn and Betty Travitsky (Amherst, MA: University of Massachusetts Press, 1990), pp. 119–36.
44 Haselkorn, 'Sin and the Politics of Penitence', p. 127.
45 Haselkorn, 'Sin and the Politics of Penitence', p. 128.
46 It would become repetitive to summarize the arguments concerning this matter from all recent criticism, so I at this point simply list a number of them here: Ingrid Hotz-Davies, '*A Chaste Maid in Cheapside* and *Women Beware Women*: Feminism, Anti-Feminism and the Limitations of Satire', *Cahiers Élisabéthains*, 39 (1991), 29–39;

Jennifer L. Heller, 'Space, Violence, and Bodies in Middleton and Cary', *Studies in English Literature*, 45.2 (2005), 425–41; Cristiana Ziraldo, 'Thomas Middleton's *Women Beware Women*: A Portrayal of Feminism or Misogyny?', *Rivista di Letterature Moderne e Comparate*, 17.1 (2004), 1–28; Catherine MacGregor, 'Undoing the Body Politic: Representing Rape in *Women Beware Women*', *Theatre Research International*, 23.1 (1998), 14–23; A. A. Bromham, ' " A Plague Will Come": Art, Rape, and Venereal Disease in Middleton's *Women Beware Women*', *EnterText*, 3.1 (2003).

47   Richard A. Levin, 'If Women Should Beware Women, Bianca Should Beware Mother', *Studies in English Literature*, 37.2 (1997), 371–89.

48   Lisa Hopkins, *The Female Hero in English Renaissance Tragedy* (Basingstoke: Palgrave Macmillan, 2002), see especially Chapter 1. Hopkins herself mentions in her Acknowledgements (p. vii) that, and where, some of this material on Livia had been published before.

49   Hopkins, *The Female Hero in English Renaissance Tragedy*, p. 37.

50   Hopkins, *The Female Hero in English Renaissance Tragedy*, p. 36

51   Hopkins, *The Female Hero in English Renaissance Tragedy*, pp. 32–33.

52   Ann C. Christensen's 'Settling House in Middleton's *Women Beware Women*', *Comparative Drama*, 29.4 (1995), 493–518.

53   Christensen, 'Settling House', p. 495.

54   Christensen, 'Settling House', p. 501.

55   Christensen, 'Settling House', p. 502.

56   Leonardo Buonomo, 'Domestic Themes in Thomas Middleton's *Women Beware Women*', *Prospero* 7 (2000), 21–33.

57   Buonomo, 'Domestic Themes', p. 28.

58   Buonomo, 'Domestic Themes', pp. 22–23.

59   Buonomo, 'Domestic Themes', p. 25.

60   Zara Bruzzi and A. A. Bromham, 'The soil alters; Y'are in another country': multiple perspectives and political resonances in Middleton's *Women Beware Women*', in *Shakespeare's Italy: Functions of Italian locations in Renaissance drama*, ed. by Michele Marrapodi et al. (Manchester: Manchester University Press, 1993; rev. edn 1997), pp. 251–71.

61   Bruzzi and Bromham, 'The soil alters', p. 263.

62   Zara Bruzzi, 'A Device to Fit the Times: Intertextual Allusion in Thomas Middleton's *Women Beware Women*', in *The Italian World of English Renaissance Drama: Cultural Exchange and Intertextuality*, ed. by Michele Marapodi and A. J. Hoenselaars (Newark: University of Delaware Press; London: Associated University Presses, 1998), pp. 302–17.

63   Bruzzi, 'A Device to Fit the Times', p. 312.

64   J. R. Mulryne, 'Thomas Middleton, *Women Beware Women*, and the Myth of Florence', in *The Italian World*, ed. by Marapodi and Hoenselaars, pp. 141–64.

65   Mulryne, 'Thomas Middleton, *Women Beware Women*, and the Myth of Florence', p. 141.

66   Mulryne, 'Thomas Middleton, *Women Beware Women*, and the Myth of Florence', p. 148.

67   Mulryne, 'Thomas Middleton, *Women Beware Women*, and the Myth of Florence', p. 151.

68   Mulryne, 'Thomas Middleton, *Women Beware Women*, and the Myth of Florence', p. 156.

69   Mulryne, 'Thomas Middleton, *Women Beware Women*, and the Myth of Florence', pp. 161–62.

70   Derek B. Alwes, 'The Secular Morality of Middleton's City Comedies', *Comparative Drama* 42.2 (2008), 101–119 (p. 115).

71   Lisa Hopkins, 'City Tragedy: Middleton, Shakespeare and Ford', *Compar(a)ison*, 1 (1994), 71–76.

72   Alexander Leggatt, *English Drama: Shakespeare to the Restoration 1590–1660* (London: Longman, 1988), 147–52.

73   Leggatt, *English Drama: Shakespeare to the Restoration*, p. 147.

CHAPTER FIVE

New Directions: *Women Beware Women* and Jacobean Cultural Narratives

Anne McLaren

The common people are unruly by nature, and magistrates are easily corrupted through avarice or ambition. There is just one blessed stay in this tide of evils – the unsullied character of the prince. If he, too, is overcome by foolish ideas and base desires, what last ray of hope is there for the state?

– Erasmus, *Education of a Christian Prince*[1]

The closing words of *Women Beware Women* belong to the Cardinal. Surveying the dead bodies left onstage after the wedding masque, he concludes:

Sin, what thou art these ruins show too piteously.
Two kings on one throne cannot sit together,
But one must needs down, for his title's wrong;
So where lust reigns, that prince cannot reign long. (5.1.263–66)

By the time Middleton wrote his play in the early 1620s, the saying that 'two kings in one kingdom cannot reign at once' had become proverbial. So too had its linkage with lust. For contemporaries, the saying expressed a truth that was simultaneously personal and political. The Cardinal's words would have gained their power because early modern people regarded all men and women, up to and including the king, as engaged in a life-long battle that pitted the soul against the body, reason against lust. When reason was king, the individual attained to the best state possible in the postlapsarian world, one that compensated to some extent for the ineradicable effects of the Fall. 'Thou mayst compare [...] a man [...] to a commonwealth or realm, where is king, lords and the common people', wrote Erasmus, in his seminal *Enchiridion*, and early modern men and women took this comparison very seriously indeed.[2] Collective success in establishing the kingship of reason, up and down the ranks of society, amplified this individual attainment. It established social and political harmony and made the earthly commonwealth an image of God's will for the world. Conversely, failure, at any and each level, raised the spectre of a world turned upside down. It portended moral and social collapse and, by taking man away from God, threatened divine retribution.

Many historians agree that early modern England witnessed a crisis of order that began in the second half of the sixteenth century and peaked around 1650.[3] The perceived correspondence between good order within the individual and throughout society produced intense anxiety about anticipated disorder, and focused attention on the person of the king with new immediacy. It also gave every individual a stake in public as well as personal morality. For contemporaries, *Women Beware Women* would have dramatically illustrated the consequences of lust's usurpation in two interrelated spheres: the body and the state. As we shall see, these interconnections between the personal and the political gave the play much of its force, making it both universal and highly topical. In this chapter I want to explore that axis to locate Middleton's vision of a profoundly disordered society. The first half of the essay considers the play itself in the light of its early modern cultural context. I will then refer outward by looking at the world of present politics that Middleton and his audience would have confronted when they left the playhouse.

A Phallocentric Social Order

For early modern men and women all God's children were enlisted in the struggle to actualize their better selves by subordinating lust to reason. Because they were made in God's image, their task in the world was to reconstitute that identity as best they could in a fallen world. Yet this was a strongly hierarchical and patriarchal world. To contemporaries it was axiomatic that, because of their position in the hierarchy, men acted as officers, as it were, in the army of humanity. God gave greater powers of reason to men than to women, and thus greater power of self control (see Illustration 3). In his immensely popular book on marriage *A bride-bush, or A wedding sermon: compendiously describing the duties of married persons* (1617), the Church of England clergyman William Whately used military metaphors to explain the significance of this fact for marital relations. 'Without question it is a sin for a man to come lower than God hath set him', he wrote. 'It is not humility, but baseness, to be ruled by her, whom he should rule. No general would thank a captain, for surrendering his place to some common soldier, nor will God an husband, for suffering his wife to bear the sway'.[4] Nurtured by appropriate education (including, very importantly, paternal example), this natural endowment for command could develop to its full extent in male children as they matured. This process enabled some men – but not all – to be, and to be recognized as, fully realized human beings. This is man as Hamlet extolled him: 'What a piece of work is a man, how noble in reason, how infinite in faculties, [...] in action how like an angel, in apprehension how like a god! The beauty of the world, the paragon of animals' (2.2.302–12).

Although not all men attained this status, which tended to be regarded as the prerogative of the elite, as a sex they were naturally equipped with the tools to do so. If women were to be successful in the endeavour (albeit in their lesser degree), they needed the infusion of reason that only their near male relations could provide. A slew of proverbs, generally credited to Aristotle, reinforced the

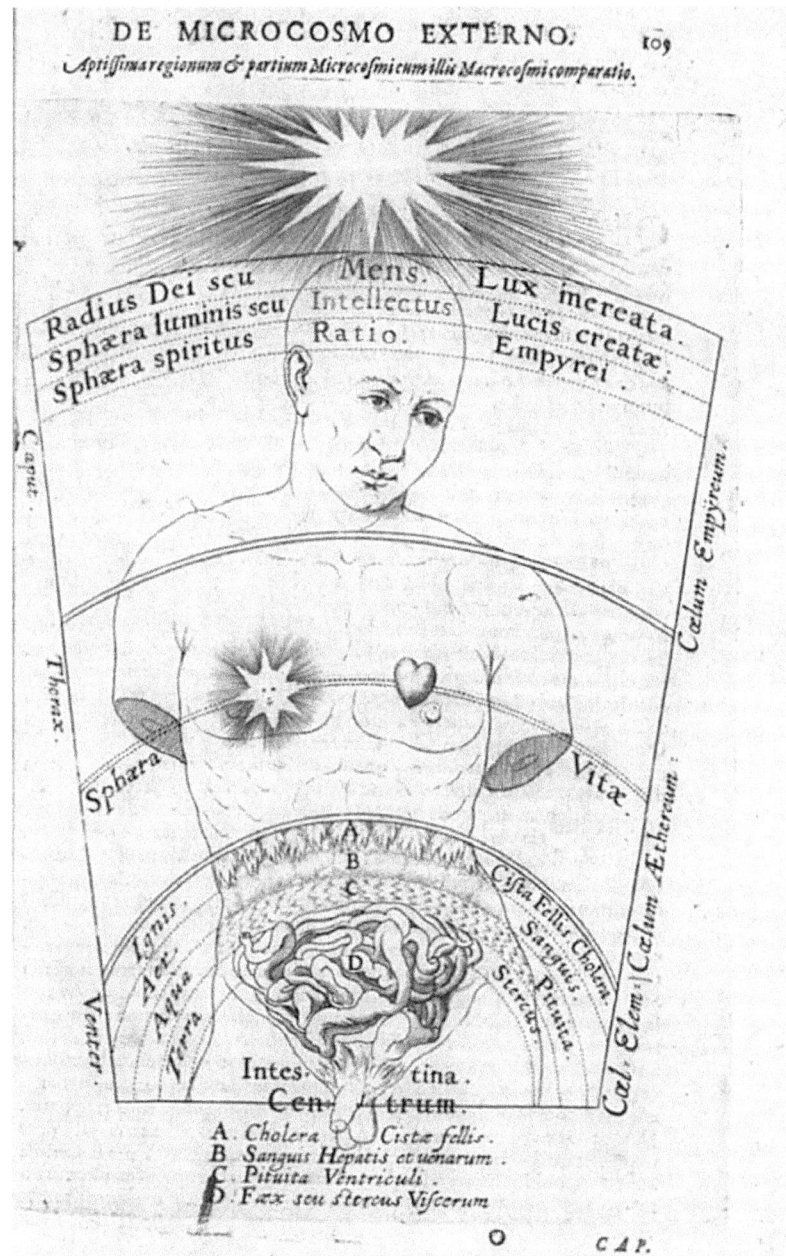

3 Robert Fludd's depiction of the relationship between man's body and the created world (Tract. I. Sect. I. Lib. V, *Utriusque Cosmi, Maioris scilicet et Minoris, metaphysica, physica, atque technica Historia* (1617–1619), p. 105.
This image is reproduced by kind permission of The Bancroft Library

truism that 'women by men receive perfection'.[5] Women required completion in this way not only because they possessed reason in smaller measure than men but also because, as Clare McEachern notes, in the early modern world 'the female body [...] was always more of a body than a male one'.[6] Locked into her body by nature, women were less subject than men to the control of reason; this had been the case since Eve was seduced by the serpent in the Garden of Eden. Unlike male children, who might and should outgrow the need for tutelage, a woman would need male supervision throughout her life to compensate for her natural defects. So strong was this association of men with reason and women with the body that it raised the question once again as to whether women and men possessed the same spiritual entitlement. Did women, for example, have souls? The Duke's announcement in Act 3 that Bianca's perfections will have him believe that 'they have every one a soul' refers to this debate (3.3.26). At the same time it is disturbingly ironic. He takes this pledge in honour of the physical perfections of a woman who has imperiled her soul by breaking her marital vows. Under the Duke's influence she has committed to her passions, becoming a 'harlot'; undoubtedly the audience would have been attuned to the word's use to denominate a wayward soul as well as a lust-driven woman.[7]

These conventional views about human nature, male and female, acquired new force over the sixteenth and seventeenth centuries as reformers – humanist, Anglican and Puritan – sought to make every household an outpost of the True Church. This project attributed a sacerdotal role to the male head of household because of his special, and potentially immediate, relationship with God.[8] John Knox addressed his male congregants as 'brethren' – a newly resonant term – telling them that they were 'ordained of God' to rule in their houses: 'Within your houses, I say [...] you are bishops and kings: your wife, children, servants are your bishopric and charge.'[9] The relocation of spiritual authority from priests to laymen inaugurated a discourse that turned on the correlative identities of father and husband as 'brethren', and it opened the door to a new kind of political authority in the public sphere. For if godly men were 'kings' in their own households, if they there exercised true government after the model of God himself, then a difference of degree only, not of kind, separated them from the monarch. Moreover, their common subjection to God the Father renegotiated (although it did not erase) the absolute division between 'king' and 'subject' that divine right theorists were intent on establishing. Describing the exemplary husband, Whately marvels that his 'just, wise, and mild government is government indeed' and makes him 'as it were, God in the family'.[10] We see evidence here of the shift towards a sense of political inclusion centred on notions of fatherhood, biological and social, that Lyndal Roper has identified as dating from this period.[11]

Protestant commitment to the holy household ensured that the meaning of this changing status was often rehearsed and discussed in tracts on marriage. For, as George Hakewill reminded the future Charles I in a 1621 sermon, '[e]very householder is *parvus Rex* a little king in his own family [...] [T]he greatest monarch, upon the matter, is but *magnus Pater-familias* a great householder, or a common father of the public family of the state.'[12] Marriage tracts proved to be a lastingly popular *genre* whose influence extended beyond the domestic sphere into the world of public politics. Through them men (and women) learned what was required of the *parvus Rex* within the household. This discourse of rights and responsibilities in turn informed expectations of the *magnus Pater-familias*, the king. In England the effects of this crossover appear in the increasingly combative relationship between James and the House of Commons that developed especially over the 1620s, and to which I will return in the conclusion.

To take one notable example of the *genre* of conduct books, Whately's *The Bride-bush* went through three editions in the 1620s, and many more during the following 150 years. The last edition was published in 1794: only the typesetting and the title page distinguished it from the first edition of 1617. Whately provided a representative summary of the male householder's rights and responsibilities, figured as those of the husband in relation to his wife:

> [A]s our Lord Jesus is to his church, so must [the husband] be to his wife, an head and saviour [...] [For] every man is bound to maintain himself in that place in which his maker hath set him, and to hold fast that reverence and precedency which both God and nature have assigned him. Nature hath framed the lineaments of his body to superiority, and set the print of government in his very face [...] he must not suffer this order of nature to be inverted.

To enact true magistracy the husband must provide a godly example, first and foremost in relation to his wife. No matter how 'peevish' by nature, she will then 'willingly give him the better place', for 'no inferior can choose but in his soul stoop to that superior in whom grace and God's image doth appear according to his place'.[13] Because of her special relationship to the husband, the wife presents the test case of the husband's authority. When he has successfully conquered her by love, order extends through the ranks of the household to include other 'inferiors', children and servants. Whately is at pains to give due weight both to the wife's elevated status relative to other members of the household, and yet not to exempt her from the same duty of obedience. 'All inferiors owe reverence', he affirms. 'The wife owes as much of that to her husband, as the children or servants do to her, yea as they do to [the father].' Their special relationship entitles her to 'more familiarity' with her husband, and his conduct towards her will in turn be 'sweetened with more love'. This does not, however, promote her beyond the ranks of the other inferior members of the household: she is 'more dear' to her husband, 'not less subject than they'.[14]

At its best, marriage was an educative process that elevated women beyond their sex, for it was believed that women's bodies were most effectively controlled through carnal (or 'mutual') conjunction with their husbands.[15] A long tradition, reinvigorated by Protestantism, presented sexual relations as necessary to maintain and enhance the marital bond, and also to preserve both partners in a state of married chastity. These ideas underpinned the concept of the 'conjugal debt', which required that each spouse give to the other sexual access whenever it was sought – providing such requests were not contrary to God's decrees. In this context marriage was regarded as a mechanism that continued and, indeed, fulfilled, a process of edification begun in the household under the father's auspices. Fathers gave their daughters to husbands that they had chosen. The couple's carnal conjunction wedded them, making them, in accordance with God's expressed will, one indissoluble person under the governorship of the husband. John Calvin affirmed Protestant orthodoxy when he glossed St Paul's statements on marriage in these terms: '[T]he man consisteth not without the woman, because otherwise he should be a head cut off from the body: neither doth the woman stand without the man, because then she would be a dead body.'[16] At first glance, the concept of the marital debt would appear to promote equality between men and women because it applied equally to both husbands and wives. But the well established view of women as more at the mercy of their passions than men, thus at least potentially sexually voracious, put that duty of care squarely in the male camp. Indeed, the husband's duty was proactively to anticipate her sexual needs, to ensure that she did not look outside marriage for satisfaction of longings over which she had little control. One early modern moralist wrote that 'a man is required to render the debt to his wife not only when she expressly seeks it, but also when she appears to desire it by signs'.[17]

Women, children and servants were thus regarded as being 'subsumed' in various ways into the personalities of their betters – husbands, fathers, masters – and through them, above them all, the king, the *pater patriae* to whom everyone naturally owed obedience.[18] At one level this powerfully affirmed the king's supreme status as both man among men and vicar of God. On the other hand, because 'reason is king in a man', one corollary of these ideas about men and women was that all men participated in the Christian commonwealth in some form. This might be understood as the *respublica Christiana* – but it might be conceptualized more immediately as the nation, the 'body of the whole realm' as it was commonly envisaged. Richard Hooker followed what had become an established tradition over the sixteenth century when, in *Of the Laws of Ecclesiastical Polity*, he stated that 'with us [that is, in England] one society is both Church and commonwealth'.[19] That society was given visible expression in meetings of Parliament: the representative assembly that conjoined the three estates of kings, lords and commons.

Only male heads of households were admitted to any share of public political power, but even low-born men enjoyed this relative entitlement, at least theoretically, as a function of their manhood. In *Women Beware Women* Middleton exaggerates the disparity between such 'normal' men and the Ward and Sordido to emphasize how irrevocably they stand outside the bounds of Christian manhood. The Ward is simple-minded and sunk in wilful ignorance; 'I am past schooling', he proudly, and correctly, announces (1.2.127), while Sordido's coarse and base character is all that his name implies. Within the normal spectrum, however, this masculine endowment meant that every man was charged with a twofold obligation. He had to obey reason's dictates and guide all his actions by its laws. By the same token he had also to equip his dependents – the subordinates and inferiors for whose physical and moral welfare he was responsible – to do likewise. His example, and the education he provided, was the only sure means of compensating for their lesser powers of reason and self-control. This twofold duty fell on men differentially. It depended in large measure on their personal circumstances, and especially on the number and quality of their dependants. It weighed far more heavily on men who were husbands, fathers and masters of servants than it did on young, unmarried men who did not own property, and more heavily still on men whose status as magistrates made them also responsible for public order. It weighed most heavily on the king, vicar of God, chief magistrate and *pater patriae*, whose household comprised the realm and all of its inhabitants.

Women Beware Women and Early Modern Patriarchy

This vision of a phallocentric social order may well have led to the anxieties about masculinity that scholars have identified as unusually pervasive during the period.[20] As Cynthia Herrup has recently written, masculine dominance was regarded as critical to order at every level of society, yet, especially when set against this exceptionally high standard for its full accomplishment, it appeared to be a desperately fragile commodity.[21] Similarly, Su Fang Ng has explored how the figure of the father functioned as a 'crucial node' in political debate of the period, as early men and women contested the extent and limits of both paternal and royal power within and across various literary genres.[22] Inevitably, these anxieties focused particular attention on the 'common father of the public family of the state', the prince. I now want to consider how Middleton anatomizes this crisis of paternal authority in *Women Beware Women*, first at the level of the household, and then at the level of the dukedom, before turning to the Jacobean polity.

At a time when the religious standards of morality were tightening, these domestic responsibilities were taken with the utmost seriousness, certainly among the men and women for whom Middleton wrote his plays.[23] They required men to enact a god-like paternal role, and this in turn depended on them internalizing the behavioural norms envisioned by Protestant reformers. In the world that Middleton portrays, however, women must 'beware women' because the male figures, who should protect them from their baser instincts, are incapable of doing so. Leantio and Fabritio either misunderstand or resoundingly pervert their natural authority as husbands and fathers; at another, more dangerous level, so too does the Duke. Their failure of paternal care leaves the women in their care vulnerable to corruption. This gradually permeates the world of the play, as the disparity between 'is' and 'ought' sets the stage for tragedy.

The play begins by introducing us to a single parent family: the factor Leantio, newly returned to Florence, and its acting head, his overly affectionate Mother. His father is nowhere in evidence; later it is suggested that he fled the country much earlier in order to avoid being imprisoned for manslaughter. Leantio's return as a married man offers him the opportunity to take charge of the household. Yet, after introducing Bianca to her new mother, he abandons her in order to tend to his business affairs. He asserts that he is acting the part of a true man by rationing their sexual congress – which he describes as 'ruling wanton love' – but the audience appreciates that this is self-deception. In fact his avarice gets the better of him, leading him to ignore what is required of him in his new role as husband. It is his responsibility to impart himself to her, sexually, once he perceives that that is her desire. When, instead, he praises himself for pursuing 'love that is respective for increase', we hear a perverted echo of the Biblical injunction to 'be fruitful and multiply':

> Leantio [to Bianca]
> I could well wish myself where you would have me;
> But love that's wanton must be ruled awhile
> By that that's careful, or all goes to ruin.
> As fitting is a government in love
> As in a kingdom. Where 'tis all mere lust,
> 'Tis like an insurrection in the people
> That, raised in self-will, wars against all reason;
> But love that is respective for increase
> Is like a good king that keeps all in peace. (1.3.40–48)

Because he regards Bianca as his possession, as 'treasure', he believes that his duty of care requires him simply to lock her away from the world, rather than to edify her to withstand its lures. Significantly, the place he lights on is the 'dark parlour' that had been his father's hideout (3.1.243–47).

Similarly, Fabritio's abuse of his paternal authority is flagged early in the play. In Act I he roughly informs his daughter Isabella that, in the matter of her marriage, his will is law. That she will marry the grotesque but wealthy Ward is a *fait accompli*:

> Fabritio   How do you like him, girl? This is your husband.
> Like him or like him not, wench, you shall have him,
> And you shall love him. (1.2.130–32)

In *Locksley Hall*, written over two hundred years later, Tennyson wrote 'As the husband is, the wife is: thou art mated with a clown, / And the grossness of his nature will have weight to drag thee down'. These lines encapsulated what remained conventional wisdom about the marital bond throughout the nineteenth century; they also neatly summarize the fate into which Fabritio has bullied his daughter. In Act 3, Fabritio discusses Isabella with the Duke. As she enters holy matrimony – and we know that she does so in order to pursue her incestuous relationship with her uncle – the conversation reveals Fabritio to be little better than a panderer. Rather than edifying her in righteousness, he has objectified her. His educational programme has consisted of enhancing her sexual attractiveness and highlighting her sexual availability. His goal was not to prepare her to become a good wife to a carefully chosen husband, and thereby to secure her spiritual betterment, but rather to solicit the attention of a wealthy prospective suitor. In the speech which follows 'stir' carries an erotic overtone:

> Fabritio   She's a dear child to me.
> Duke   That must needs be; you say she is your daughter.
> Fabritio   Nay, my good lord, dear to my purse, I mean,
> Beside my person, I ne'er reckoned that.
> She has the full qualities of a gentlewoman.
> I have brought her up to music, dancing, what not
> That may commend her sex and stir her husband. (3.2.106–12)

Utterly blind to the true end of marriage, which was, as contemporary homilists endlessly explained, instituted by God Himself for the spiritual betterment of both men and women, Fabritio complacently concludes that the expense he has incurred in Isabella's upbringing has paid off. Using Isabella as bait, he has been able to arrange a marriage that brings the Ward's 'broad acres' into his purview. The Ward's uncle and guardian, the ironically named Guardiano, has nothing but contempt for Fabritio, whom he regards as a fool. However, they are as one in viewing marriage as ordained for their own self-aggrandizement, and in using their dependants as exploitable resources in its pursuit. In his pompous speech to Fabritio, Guardiano's repeated use of the word 'tender' undercuts his sanctimonious protestations about his reasons for arranging the Ward's marriage to Isabella, and renders their kinship unmistakeable:

> *Guardiano* He has been now my ward some fifteen year,
> And 'tis my purpose, as times calls upon me,
> By custom seconded, and such moral virtues,
> To tender him a wife. [...]
> [...] If now this daughter
> So tendered – let me come to your own phrase, sir –
> Should offer to refuse him, I were handselled. (1.2.3–6, 8–10)

Fabritio's paternal incapacity adds another layer of meaning to Livia's dramatic revelation to Isabella in Act 2 that Fabritio is not in fact her father. When Livia tells Isabella that she is the product of her mother's adulterous liaison, she is lying. She wants to encourage Isabella to embark on a sexual relationship with her uncle Hippolito by persuading her that there is no impediment of near kinship. It is a sign of Isabella's ill education, even at this early point in the play that she receives the news with joy, despite what it suggests about her mother's character and thus her own maternal inheritance.

Livia argues that Isabella's bastard birth frees her twice over. Released from paternal constraint, she can now follow in what Livia claims are her mother's footsteps. Isabella too will be able to indulge her adulterous inclinations under the cloak of marriage. More generally, Livia declares – in terms that must have caused a *frisson* of apprehension, at least, among the audience – that Isabella's fatherlessness liberates her to follow nothing but the dictates of her own will:

> *Livia* How weak his commands now whom you call father
> How vain all his enforcements, your obedience!
> And what a largeness in your will and liberty,
> To take, or to reject, or to do both!
> For fools will serve to father wise men's children. (2.1.158–62)

Livia's speech may refer to the common law principle that because the bastard child could not inherit from parents as of right, he (or she) was legally *filius nullius*, the child of nobody.[24] But metaphorically, certainly, Isabella is *filius nullius*. Her birth mother is nowhere in evidence; her progenitor Fabritio is incapable of exercising fatherly authority, defined by Whately as the use of 'mild, gentle, and wise proceeding'. 'Sharp, tart carriage, consisting of reviling, striking, and other furious words and gestures' – the 'fathering' that Fabritio has displayed – is 'tyrannical'. It 'works hatred and [...] must needs be a great underminer of authority'.²³ Fabritio's failure as a father thus gives plausible status to Livia's lies, and encourages Isabella to rebel. In the early modern world, that perverted female empowerment came viscerally to life in the linked figures of the cuckold and the bastard which Livia's speech invokes.

As elsewhere throughout the play, at this point a female character makes a profoundly true remark that simultaneously reveals her lack of moral awareness; this emerges as a shared trait among the play's female characters. The intimation of an alternative maternal line of descent, forged in licence, not true liberty, recurs in Act 2 scene 2, when the Duke seduces Bianca. He tells her that she will honour her maternal inheritance should she agree to become his mistress – while the parallel action taking place below reveals the Mother, Bianca's new 'mother' and her sole parent, to be foolish, greedy and duplicitous:

> *Duke* [to Bianca]
> But I give better in exchange: wealth, honour.
> She that is fortunate in a duke's favour
> Lights on a tree that bears all women's wishes.
> If your own mother saw you pluck fruit there,
> She would commend your wit, and praise the time
> Of your nativity. Take hold of glory. (2.2.368–73)

What then of the duke, the *magnus Pater-familias*? This model of social organization gave the example set by 'great men', and pre-eminently the prince, a uniquely powerful ordering force, one that was both moral and political. The prince's example extended beyond the household, reaching and reforming especially the ranks of the inferior males who constituted the common people. They, like women, children and servants, were always more at the mercy of their 'vile appetites' than elite males and, like them, needed to be ordered by their husbands, fathers and masters. But good order resided first and foremost in the person of the prince. 'Go through your ancient history', Erasmus urged his readers, 'You will find the life of the prince mirrored in the morals of his people. No comet, no dreadful power affects the progress of human affairs as the life of the prince grips and transforms the morals and character of his subjects.'²⁶ In Act 4 of the play, the Cardinal invokes this network to try to recall the Duke of Florence to his princely duty. The sins of the 'love-private man [...] seldom stretch beyond his own soul's bounds', he tells him, but the great man's moral declension 'sets a light up to show men to hell'. ''[T]is example proves the great man's bane', he continues:

> The sins of mean men lie like scattered parcels
> Of an unperfect bill; but when such [great men] fall,
> Then comes example, and that sums up all. (4.1.203, 205, 228, 217–20)

The syntax is hard to follow here, but Middleton's meaning is very clear. When good order reigns, ordinary men's sins – unavoidable since the Fall – constitute deviations from the norm. Of course they imperil the soul of the sinner, but the Cardinal's references to 'love-private' and 'mean' men emphasizes their limited impact, because such men are unlikely to have dependents or to carry public responsibilities. The prince's fall from grace stands at the other end of this elongated hierarchy because it affects the whole realm. His impurity corroborates and validates not only their moral lapses, but also those of all the intervening ranks: men like Leantio, Fabritio, and Guardiano, who have dependants in their care. By changing the social norm from virtue to vice his declension poses the greatest imaginable danger. It threatens the moral integrity of all members of society, and it makes the prince a tyrant.

Effeminate Kings and Tyrants

These well-established correspondences between the personal and the political took on a particular significance in Jacobean England. By the time that Middleton's play was produced, James's character as *magnus Pater-familias* had become a burning issue. The ubiquity of the habits of mind that we have been considering meant that debate on the subject was often referred to good and bad models of manhood, fatherhood and effeminacy respectively. I now want to turn to this topical dimension, looking first at how Middleton presents these linked discourses in the play and, from there, how they informed political debate in the 1620s.

The hinge of the closing couplets of the play is the Cardinal's use of the word 'lust'. Over the seventeenth century the word acquired what has remained its main meaning: 'libidinous desire or degrading animal passion', its use signalling 'intense moral reprobation' on the part of the speaker. But the early modern era was the period of transition. Before, 'lust' could mean simply pleasure, delight, or a particular relish or longing for something. To take one example, in the Sternhold and Hopkins psalter – widely used during the early modern period, on both sides of the Atlantic – King David tells God that 'From my youth I had a lust still to depend on thee.'[27] Moreover, the competing, negative definition – sensuous appetite or desire, considered as sinful or leading to sin – was not yet fully equated with carnality. This is one reason why the adjective 'fleshly' is so often attached to 'lust' during our period. It functioned as a means of specifying that the desire at issue was a bodily, and specifically sexual, one.

Women Beware Women occupies the cusp of these linguistic developments, which reflect the impact of religious reformation. The elite characters who die in the last act pay the price for acting out their immoral sexual desires. These 'fleshly lusts' most dramatically (and theatrically) signify a more general refusal to live a moral life, but they are not the only ones. In the play they correlate to greed, that sin of the belly that afflicts the Mother and the Ward and his man, Sordido, and to the avarice that deforms the characters of Leantio, Fabritio and Guardiano. By allowing lust to reign in reason's seat, they too have turned away from God. Presiding over this disordered realm stands the Duke of Florence: the great man whose example has blasted the commonwealth. The Duke sinned by lusting after Bianca, despite her being another man's wife, and prostituting his regal office in order to possess her. But his carnality also signified his willingness to subordinate the public good to his own personal desires, of whatever description. In the personal monarchies of early modern Europe, that was a more damning character flaw, and one that impugned his political legitimacy. For, as Erasmus put it in *The Education of a Christian Prince*:

Only those who dedicate themselves to the state, and not the state to themselves, deserve the title 'prince'. For if someone rules to suit himself and assesses everything by how it affects his own convenience, then it does not matter what titles he bears: in practice he is certainly a tyrant, not a prince.

'No matter what the prince is deliberating about,' he concludes, 'he always bears in mind whether it is to the advantage of all his subjects.'[28]

Middleton establishes this Erasmian paradigm in the opening stages of the play, during the Duke's entry procession and in the exchange between Bianca and the Mother:

Boys	Now they come, now they come!
2 Boy	The Duke!
3 Boy	The state! [...]
Mother	How like you, daughter?
Bianca	'Tis a noble state.
	Methinks my soul could dwell upon the reverence
	Of such a solemn and most worthy custom.
	Did not the Duke look up? Methought he saw us.
Mother	That's everyone's conceit that sees a duke:
	If he look steadfastly, he looks straight at them,
	When he perhaps, good careful gentleman,
	Never minds any, but the look he casts
	Is at his own intentions, and his object
	Only the public good (1.3.73, 102–11)

Three points are notable here. The first is Middleton's insistence that the Duke personally embodies – he *is* – the 'state'. The widespread acceptance of this equivalence during this period made the character of the ruler – his desires, virtues, vices – a matter of the greatest importance. Only gradually over the seventeenth century did the word 'constitution' begin to take on an abstract political significance in addition to a humoral one; the first cited reference in the *Oxford English Dictionary* dates from 1610.

The second is the Mother's misreading of the Duke's behaviour. Using the entirely conventional terms that described good rulers, she credits him with casting a virtuous radiance equally on all his subjects as a by-product of his primary desire, the realization of the public good. The same orthodoxy underpinned the belief that subjects absorbed something of that virtue through participating in such public spectacles, and primarily through seeing virtue embodied and in action in the person of the prince.[29] This is the godly ruler as alpha male, and we see again the force of example. It is what Bianca, especially vulnerable given her status as newly married, a stranger in Florence – and, at this point in the play, forsaken by her husband – anticipates here. By regarding Bianca with lustful intent rather than, disinterestedly, as one of his subject-children, the Duke jettisons his exemplary status. That lapse constitutes the first step in her seduction, and it leads inexorably to the social collapse that we see in the last act.

Finally, Bianca's reference to her soul is a telling one. Humanist attempts to harmonize the Bible with Platonic philosophy led to a view of man as composed of three parts: mind or spirit, body, and soul. Through our spiritual capacity we are drawn to God and can be made one with him. The body or the flesh is the lowest part. After the Fall, its promptings and demands seduce us away from God and towards the devil. It is perpetually at war with the spirit, the highest part of man, which is modelled on God's own nature. For Erasmus, 'the spirit makes us gods, the flesh makes us brute animals'; St Paul envisaged two men stuck together and contending for control, yet bound to go together either to heaven or to hell. Trapped between these two forces and drawn to both is the third part, the soul.

In *Enchiridion*, Erasmus described the ensuing struggle between the body and the soul in gendered terms:

> The body verily as he himself is visible, so delighteth he in things visible. As he is mortal, so followeth he things temporal. As he is heavy, so sinketh he downward. On the other part, the soul mindful of her celestial nature enforceth upward with great violence and with a terrible haste striveth and wrestleth with the heavy burden of the earthly body. She [...] loveth things immortal and celestial, and rejoiceth with things of like nature, except she be utterly drowned in the filth of the body and by contagiousness of him hath gone out of kind from her native gentleness.[30]

In the play Middleton dramatizes this psychodrama in the character of Bianca, who commits to passion after her seduction by the Duke. The terms of that psychodrama help to explain her seemingly abrupt and, in the eyes of some critics, unpersuasive transformation from the innocent young woman who engages our sympathies in the play's early stages, to the brazen 'harlot' who flaunts her immorality once she becomes the Duke's mistress. At the beginning of the play, Bianca believes that, in her husband's absence, her soul, and thus her whole being, can be confirmed in virtue by absorbing the Duke's influence. For contemporaries part of the play's fascination would lie in the dawning realization that, because the Duke has given in to his passions, the truth is exactly the opposite. She ends 'drowned in the filth of the body' through her seduction by the Duke.

At the same time Middleton personifies the conflict in the characters of Bianca and the Duke, who represent the soul and the body respectively. In the early modern cultural lexicon, however, those gender identities would have been complicated, in ways that would have challenged the Duke's masculine status. Erasmus was not alone in characterizing the soul as female, regardless of whether it was encased in a male or a female body.[31] At one level the figuration conveyed the soul's innocence and vulnerability, hence the need for it to be protected by masculine *virtus*. It also strikingly exemplified the great disparity in power between the body and the other two elements, the spirit and the soul. Since the fall in most men the body – 'the flesh, the most vile part of us [...] wherewithal we be provoked to filthiness' – always holds the upper hand; Erasmus suggested by a ratio of twenty four to one.[32]

Yet, as we have seen, the gendered binary of passion and reason associated women with untrammelled appetite and men *qua* men with sufficient self-control to keep their passions (and their women) under control. Referring to Biblical examples of the warfare between the body and the mind, Erasmus reminds his readers that in all cases 'The woman figureth affection, the man reason'; 'affection' meaning a powerful or controlling emotion.[33] When the Duke chooses pleasure over duty, he betrays his manhood twice over. First, he reneges on his status as *dominus* or lord, given by God to Adam in the Garden of Eden, and by extension to all men. He does so again, in a related degree, because he perverts the power of supreme magistracy that God invested in Samuel, the Old Testament king, and, again by extension, to all subsequent kings. But this transaction also has immediate implications for the Duke's own character. In succumbing to the pleasure principle, he gives the upper hand to the lower female elements in his nature, and it is this inversion that makes him a tyrant.

The meaning of this transaction becomes clear if we look again at Illustration 3 and compare it with Erasmus's description of where in the body God has located reason, the soul, and the passions. As befits a king, reason, or the spirit, occupies the 'highest part of the body, [...] next to heaven', because it is 'most far from the nature of a beast'. Because of its mixed nature the soul resides in the middle ranges, between the neck and the midriff. Last on the list, and lowest down, is passion, which drives us towards bodily pleasures. This God 'banished utterly away from the king's palace'; that is, the head. Desire fittingly dwells in the genital region 'that as it were a certain wild beast untamed he should there stable and dwell [...] for because that power is accustomed to raise up motions most violent, and to be disobedient to the commandments' of reason.[34] A modern reader is likely to associate the 'wild beast' with the male penis. For contemporaries it could as easily, and indeed would more likely, refer to the womb, whose tendency to wander uncontrollably throughout the body made women (and effeminate men) peculiarly prone to hysteria.[35]

But there is more to the connection between tyranny and effeminacy. In *The Obedience of a Christian Man* (1528) William Tyndale built on the distinction between the 'tyrant' and the 'effeminate tyrant' to convict the latter of inaugurating the worst sort of tyranny. Because he is incapable of self-mastery, he is unable to command:

> For a tyrant though he do wrong unto the good / yet he punisheth the evil and maketh all men obey [...] A king that is soft as silk and effeminate / that is to say turned unto the nature of a woman / what with his own lusts / which are as the longing of a woman with child / so then he cannot resist them / and what with the wily tyranny of them that ever rule him / shall be much more grievous unto the realm than a right tyrant.[36]

Rebecca Bushnell has shown how in Renaissance political discourse these layers of meaning of the term effeminacy could lead to it being attached to even securely heterosexual princes, specifically to convict them of tyranny. The association worked at several levels. Like a woman, the tyrant loves pleasure; like a woman, he indulges his desires. Both allow lust to usurp the sovereignty of reason.[37] Finally, because he has succumbed to the female in himself, the effeminate king will be at the mercy of favourites who will take advantage of his bodily lusts to rule over him. Unsurprisingly, in this phallocentric society, where 'sodomy', was regarded as a horrific sin as well as a crime against the state, this perverted relationship was often figured as an explicitly homosexual one.

The Jacobean Polity

Thus, in this world the antithesis of the effeminate tyrant was the god-like king, husband to the realm and father to his subjects – the man who the Duke claims to be, but is not. The cultural centrality of this model of human identity ensured that the political tensions that developed during James's reign would be debated in terms of effeminacy and tyranny. I now want to locate Middleton's play as a contribution to that debate by exploring that wider context.

'I am the husband and the whole isle is my lawful wife', James announced to his new subjects when he came to the English throne after Elizabeth I's death in 1603. In addition to restoring patriarchal norms at the level of the crown (and thus affirming it throughout society), James's explicit invocation of these paternal identifiers worked to his political advantage because of his bodily fertility. He was the first king of England since Henry VIII to have proved his manhood by producing children; when he arrived in England he brought with him, among other children, two male heirs and a marriageable princess. His advice to his son, communicated in the pages of *Basilikon Doron*, was a popular best-seller, appearing in several editions after its publication in 1599. Some argued that this testimony to his character as a godly father, in tandem with his demonstrable fecundity, played a significant role in easing his passage to the English crown.[38] 'A king is truly *parens patriae*, the politic father of his people', he reflected on another occasion. He becomes 'a natural father to all his lieges at his coronation'.[39] James's personal status as a fully empowered adult male – husband, father and king – convincingly presented him as embodying cosmic order, and thus as a gift from God to the English nation. Realizing the godly empire of Great Britain required only that his English subjects acknowledge his superior status, embracing their identity as his subject-children, wives to his husband.

In 1615 he dilated on his vision of kingship in the pages of a book called *God and the King*, possibly by Richard Mocket, and 'imprinted by his Majesty's special privilege and command'. The burden of the message, which was couched in these familiar familial terms, was that all subjects owed the king absolute obedience. The duty of obedience is the bulwark of all social order, Mocket affirmed. It is 'grounded upon the law of nature', and it begins at birth. The particular 'law' to which he referred was the absolute identification of fathers and sons: 'For as we be born sons, so we are born subjects; his sons from whose loins; his subjects in whose dominions we are born.' Note the fifth commandment, he directed, 'where, as we are required to honour the fathers of private families, so much more the father of our country and the whole kingdom'.[40] Nor could this natural bond be dispensed with, any more than it would be possible to divorce the husband and the wife once they had been made one in the body of Christ:

> In the marital conjunction of the husband and wife, there is a lively resemblance of the obligation of subjects in civil allegiance unto their

prince: for as the coupling of the wife unto the husband in dutiful obedience, so of subjects unto their prince in loyalty and fidelity [...] and as the husband is the head of the wife, so is the prince of his subjects.[41]

God and the King pleased James so much that a proclamation was issued commanding 'the universal dispersing, and teaching of all youth in the said book'. Presumably the instruction would be conducted by male householders, those vicarious 'kings', and thereby ensure that all James's 'children', of whatever degree, would be edified and instructed by its contents. A year later the Aberdeen general assembly similarly decreed that all Scottish children should learn this 'catechism' by heart.[42]

Historians now generally agree that James did not make such claims in order to forward Stuart 'absolutism', as earlier generations were taught. Instead they served to mobilize support for the two key planks of his political vision. First, he wanted to forge a lasting union between his two inherited realms, England and Scotland. That in turn would facilitate his second goal, the reunification of Christendom. Under the auspices of 'Great Britain's Solomon' – James himself – this early modern version of the League of Nations would preserve Protestantism and end the religious warfare that, since the Reformation, threatened to become endemic in Europe.[43] Over time, however, his status as *pater patriae* was increasingly contested. The Thirty Years War (1618–48) made continental Europe the epicentre of a battle that pitted Protestants against Catholics. Many Englishmen understood the conflict in apocalyptic terms. For them its outcome would determine whether Protestantism would survive or be crushed by resurgent Catholicism, powerfully figured by the Spanish crown. After 1618 English public opinion grew more militant, and more militantly Protestant. It favoured military intervention, both to shore up the Protestant cause and to preserve national honour. This was regarded as immediately involved in the contest since the marriage in 1613 of the king's eldest daughter, Elizabeth, to the head of the Protestant union, Frederick V, Elector Palatine and, for a brief time, King of Bohemia.

But James refused to take up the gauntlet. Remaining true to his vision of a united Christendom, he continued to negotiate with Spain in order to broker a diplomatic solution. Central to the negotiations was the proposal for a marriage to be arranged between James's son, the future Charles I, and the Spanish Infanta. Among other outcomes the Spanish Match was intended as the diplomatic counterpart to the 'Protestant' marriage between Elizabeth and Frederick V. In effect it would confirm England's disinterested stance between the warring Protestant and Catholic factions in Europe, and thereby strengthen James's credentials as peacemaker. In England, however, these manoeuvres fuelled fears within the political nation about the king's policies, unleashed potent anti-Spanish xenophobia, and finally, inevitably, raised doubts about the king himself. As God's will for the world increasingly seemed to demand the martial commitment that James eschewed and that his Protestant subjects were more than willing to provide, his assertions of his godlike authority in the role of *Rex pacificus* sounded ever more shrill – even unmanly.

We see evidence of this shift in perception in attacks on James's kingship that were written or published during the 1620s. In 1620 one anonymous author attacked the king for refusing to lead a pan-European crusade in support of his 'children', ambiguously Elizabeth and Frederick (his children in blood), and his subject-children, James's fellow Protestants. He acknowledged that in the earlier years of James's reign, his commitment to reigning as (like Christ) a 'king of peace' had been allowable, even, perhaps, commendable. Now, however, 'there is question of God's glory, as well as your own', and 'the cause of both your children [which] lies equally a bleeding'. Now James's failure to act makes men suspect that 'your peaceable disposition all this while hath not proceeded so much out of Christian piety, and love of justice, as out of mere impotency, and desire of ease'; 'impotency' here meaning the antithesis of male-gendered qualities that we would call moral fibre or self-discipline.[44]

He was not alone. In the polarizing political climate of the 1620s, James's commitment to peace seemingly at any price began to be read as evidence of a problem more fundamental than his disposition: his nature or character. Did his shortfall in *virtus* – the manly and martial qualities of prudence, self-control, and courage – convict him of effeminacy? Rumours of his fearful nature began to spread throughout the country. In 1622 the censorious puritan Sir Simonds D'Ewes confided to his diary as a commonly held view that it was 'the king's base fear' that prevented him from fighting for religion abroad and effecting a thorough reformation at home. This was as much as to convict the Supreme Head of the Church of England of lukewarmness in religion: truly, for Protestants, a cardinal sin. D'Ewes soberly recorded that James's 'base and cowardly nature', all too apparent in negotiations with the Spanish ambassadors, was 'laughed at by the vulgar, but considered and lamented by the wise sort'.[45] No doubt this reported concern stemmed in part from the conviction that James's example, if it did not, in the Cardinal's words, 'set[ ] a light up to show men to hell', threatened national wellbeing. It seemed to many to set the tone for a court that was perceived as being sexually, politically and religiously corrupt. As such it diverged from – and might, in the view of some, come to contaminate – the strongly Protestant, virtuous and uncorrupted 'Country' with which Middleton identified.[46]

And if 'impotency' ruled at the centre, for how long could the nation retain its manhood? Thomas Scott's *Vox Populi Or Newes From Spayne*, published c. 1620, purported to be a report written for his paymasters in Madrid by the widely hated Spanish ambassador Don Diego Sarmiento de Acuña, Count of Gondomar. Scott's 'Gondomar' assures his compatriots that Englishmen will not be able to resist their forward march towards world domination because their minds have been 'effeminate[d]'. 'I have certain knowledge', he continues:

> [...] that the commons generally are so effeminate and cowardly as that they at their musters [...] of a thousand soldiers, scarce one hundred dare discharge a musket, and of that hundred, scarce one can use it like a soldier [...] Thus stands the state of that poor miserable country, which had never more people and fewer men.[47]

Vox Populi was commonly taken for a piece of genuine reportage and aroused considerable consternation. Increasingly men looked back longingly to the reign of Queen Elizabeth – when, under a female ruler, men had been men, and England had ruled the waves. The anonymous author of *Tom Tell-Troath* reported as widespread talk that since James's accession the nation had become 'less in reputation, less in strength [...] less in all manner of virtue' than it had been during the reign of his predecessor. Who would have thought, he pondered, posing a damning paradox to his sovereign, that England, having changed 'the weaker sex, for your more noble, to be our commander', would have lost by the transaction?[48]

These attacks give some indication how widespread these concerns became during the crisis years of 1618–23, and how immediate was the perceived connection between effeminacy and political crisis. Reading the play in this context reveals the accuracy of Margot Heinemann's assertion that Jacobean plays were 'shot through with politics at every level' – even those that, like *Women Beware Women*, do not at first glance appear to be overtly 'political'.[49] And from this perspective we can see a closer affinity than scholars usually posit between *Women Beware Women* and Middleton's follow-up play, the phenomenally successful, and nakedly anti-Spanish, *A Game at Chess* (1624).[50]

Fears of national declension also found expression in parliament and led to increasingly combative relations between the king and especially the House of Commons. In the early 1620s, all could recognize and abhor the resulting breakdown in loving kindness between the head and the body politic of the realm, and be alarmed about its political consequences. But how to explain it? Who was to blame for the king's reluctance to summon parliament, and the short and bitter sessions that resulted when they met? In this climate efforts by the king's councillors to 'manage' the House of Commons, in the hope of securing more harmonious relations and hence more fruitful sessions, began to look to a growing number of MPs like a conspiratorial determination to curtail parliamentary liberties, with a view to imposing court policies on the 'country'. By this point the term referred both to the nation and, if not yet what we would recognize as a political party, at least to a nascent opposition alliance. Did responsibility for these tactics – and for the policies themselves – lie with the king himself, or with his councillors and favourites? To phrase these questions in the early modern lexicon, had James become tyrannical, acting now in his kingship as a 'cruel master' rather than *pater patriae*?[51] Or did his effeminacy give the upper hand to minions who seduced the king and corrupted the body politic?

At this juncture William Tyndale's nightmare vision of 'effeminate tyranny' seemed to many to have been realized in England. This version featured James's favourite, George Villiers, Duke of Buckingham, in the role of chief minion. After having caught the king's eye in 1616, Buckingham rose from relatively humble origins to become the most powerful courtier of the age. He exercised unequalled formal and informal political influence during James's reign and achieved the unparalleled feat of maintaining his hold on power after the king's death, when he succeeded in becoming the favourite of James's son and successor, Charles I. Buckingham's ascendancy came at a cost. A steady stream of hostile reports, often in the form of verse libels, represented him as uniquely corrupt and vicious, and dilated on the deleterious effects for national well-being of his alleged control of the king. His celebrity made him almost universally feared and hated; in the words of his most recent biographer, 'he aroused a hatred among the public at large that was without precedent'.⁵² This found expression in 1628, three years after James's death, when he was assassinated by a disgruntled infantry lieutenant named John Felton. Outside the confines of the court, Felton's act triggered widespread rejoicing. To many it seemed to offer the chance of a new beginning that would reunite king and the nation in support of those militant Protestant policies that James had so determinedly rejected. In the words of one anonymous poet, Felton had endeavoured

> [...] by one stroke to make
> The King and commons (by him put asunder)
> Join all in one, and resolution take
> To mend all things unto the world great wonder.⁵³

As we might expect (and as Alaistair Bellany has reported), the deluge of reports that followed the assassination frequently depicted Felton as the hero of the 'country', and as the manly antithesis of the effeminate Buckingham – and by extension, of his master the king.⁵⁴ Turning the clock back, it is significant that speculation that the relationship between king and favourite was a homosexual one first became widespread in the crisis years around 1620. Equally telling is the fact that this was the point at which some men, at least, began to envisage the violent removal of Buckingham that Felton would finally effect in 1628.⁵⁵

So base and cowardly in the eyes of some, but was James, as some historians allege, homosexual?⁵⁶ The question of James's sexuality remains unanswered and is likely unanswerable. Certainly allegations of his effeminacy proliferated, especially from the 1620s onwards, and these segued into assertions that he was 'more addicted to love males than females', as Edward Peyton claimed in 1652. Specific allegations date overwhelmingly from the civil war period, however, and are often blatantly ideologically charged.⁵⁷ Peyton, for example, hoped that revealing the 'chamber abominations of the last two kings' – James I and Charles I – would satisfy public opinion that the regicide and the establishment of the Commonwealth government were actions that had been ordained by God specifically to punish the Stuart line.⁵⁸

Undoubtedly many contemporaries condemned the corruption and immorality of James's court. A growing number feared that God would punish the nation for these and other moral failings, notably the refusal to battle against Antichrist by going to war with Spain. But during James's reign, as we have seen, the charge of effeminacy more often pointed to a perceived imbalance between male and female traits in a man's character than even to homosexual inclination, much less what we would recognize as a fixed homosexual identity. Even the charge of 'sodomy' did not carry the specifically sexual meaning that we now attach to it. Instead it denoted a general state of sinfulness so deplorable that it threatened to provoke God's wrath. It could be signified by widespread 'unnatural' sexual and related practices: bestiality, promiscuity (especially in women), and especially male homosexuality, as well as cross-dressing and female insubordination. But it also referred to other forms of pollution, including religious heterodoxy, political corruption, and witchcraft. Increasingly, over our period, it was related to 'papistry', especially covert commitment to Roman Catholic beliefs and practices.⁵⁹ This is the understanding of sodomy that informs Sir Simonds D'Ewes's 1622 *Diary* entry. He reports that he conversed with a friend

> Of things [...] that were secret as of the sin of sodomy, how frequent it was in this wicked city, and if God did not provide some wonderful blessing against it, we could not but expect some horrible punishment for it; especially it being as we had probable cause to fear, a sin in the prince as well as the people, which God is for the most part the chastiser of himself, because no man else indeed dare reprove or tell them of their faults.[60]

His specific meaning is lost to us, but D'Ewes's utterance is nonetheless significant. Whatever it may have been, his statement convicts James of having lost the 'unsullied character of the prince' that, according to the Erasmian model with which we began, alone sustained good government.

Conclusion

To draw together the threads of the discussion, I want to conclude with a brief vignette from 1623. This shows James attempting to reclaim that unsullied character by drawing on the template of phallocentric social order that I have explored in this essay. As we have seen, the Thirty Years War fuelled increasing dissonance between James's view of Christian kingship and that of the 'Country', now powerfully communicated by MPs in the House of Commons. In this context the decade-long negotiations for a marriage between the heir to the throne and the Spanish Catholic princess, central to James's vision of a united Christendom, exacerbated tensions nearly to the breaking point. There was palpable relief when the project finally collapsed in 1623. This was a moment of the greatest danger for James's kingship. The Spaniards' arbitrary withdrawal from the negotiations seemed to confirm the view of him as a toy of the masterful Spaniards. It also required him to summon a parliament – an exigency that he had avoided for the previous seven years. From James's point of view, the collapse of negotiations must not be allowed to be interpreted as a triumph for MPs and confirmation of their apocalyptic reading of foreign affairs. That would directly challenge his political legitimacy and push him inexorably down the road to war. Faced with this challenge, in a speech to MPs in the House of Commons, he shored up his credentials as a godly prince by invoking his superior male status and explaining his and their political relationship in gendered terms. In this speech the parallels with Whately's depiction of marital relations with which we began are particularly telling.

'This I can truly say, and will avouch it before God and his angels, that never king governed with a more pure sincerity, and uncorrupt heart, than I have done', he began. Secure in his incorruptibility, he continued 'I [...] say unto you as Christ said to the Church, I am your husband, and you are my spouse.' The fact that he has convened Parliament, inviting MPs to give their 'free and faithful counsel', confirms his status as the exemplary 'good husband'. It reflects his will, not theirs, and it does not elevate them beyond their subordinate role in the partnership. Interestingly, he describes their harmonious relationship in the sexualized terms favoured by the authors of marriage manuals such as Whately's. '[A]s it is the part of a good husband to procure, and maintain the love of his wife; which he usually doth by often visiting her, and upon extraordinary occasions communicating the secrets of his affairs unto her, and by all gentle and affable ways to gain her love', so he has acted in summoning Parliament. Through his speech he has entrusted them with the secrets of his and the nation's affairs. At this point he changes gears, to depict MPs as husbands and fathers, not wives. As reasoning creatures, as men, they must now extend a reciprocal trust and recognize his and their fundamental kinship as true Protestant men: 'I am the husband, and you the wife', he affirms. '[I]t is subject to the wife to be jealous of her husband, [but] let this be far from you!'[61] He thus invites them to participate vicariously in his exercise of divine-right rule by invoking the risk of social disorder, figured as female insubordination.

At the time the speech evidently made exactly the impact upon its hearers that James must have hoped it would do, and went some way to repairing the rift between king and country. But his success proved to be ephemeral. In his *History of [...] the life and reign of King James the First* (1653) the historian Arthur Wilson articulated the viewpoint of the 'Country' in identifying the failures of James I's reign. He argued that they were caused by the king's *constitutional* incapacity.[62] The king 'would be called *Rex Pacificus* to the last; his heart was not advanced to glorious achievements'. Enfeebled in this way, he did not find favour in God's eyes. 'God will not (many times)', he concluded, 'make use of some men to do great things by them' – even when such men occupy the role of king. Moreover, for Wilson, James's effeminacy set England on the road that would end in civil war:

> If the king's spirit had been raised up to a war, when the voice of God (the voice of the people) called him to it, happily it might have hindered the great effusion of blood amongst ourselves, that happened after in his son's time.

This was so in part because of the legacy that he imparted to his son. Like father, like son. Rather than learning lessons in true kingship, Charles imbibed from his father 'the pattern of breaking parliaments, and contesting with his subjects, til ruin succeeded to him and his posterity'.[63] His sour comment on James's 1623 speech reveals the continuing relevance of the narratives of effeminacy and fatherhood that informed Middleton's play to political enactments in James's reign and beyond. It showed, he said, 'the temper of the times; where, men made themselves less than men, by making kings little less than gods'.[64]

Notes

1   Desiderius Erasmus, *The Education of a Christian Prince*, ed. by Lisa Jardine, Neil M. Cheshire, Michael John Heath (Cambridge: Cambridge University Press, 1997), p. 23. For the extent of the influence of Christian Humanism, and particularly Erasmus, on the early modern political, see Margo Todd, *Christian Humanism and the Puritan Social Order* (Cambridge: Cambridge University Press, 2003).
2   Desiderius Erasmus, *A Book Called in Latin Enchiridion Militis Christiani and in*

English *The Manual of the Christian Knight, replenished with the most wholesome precepts made by the famous clerk Erasmus of Rotterdam, to which is added a new and marvellous profitable Preface* (London: Methuen, 1905). Chapter: *Of the outward and inward man: Chap. iv.* Accessed from http://oll.libertyfund.org/title/191/5516 on 20 February 2009.
3   Susan Dwyer Amussen, *An Ordered Society: Gender and Class in Early Modern England* (Columbia: Columbia University Press, 1988), pp. 122–23.
4   William Whately, *A bride-bush, or A wedding sermon: compendiously describing the duties of married persons* (London, 1617), p. 51.
5   Arthur Tilley, ed., *A Dictionary of Proverbs in England in the Sixteenth and Seventeenth Centuries* (Ann Arbor: University of Michigan Press, 1950), p. 748.
6   Claire McEachern, *The Poetics of English Nationhood, 1590-1612* (Cambridge: Cambridge University Press, 1996), p. 129. See also Ian Macewan, *The Renaissance Notion of Woman: A Study in the Fortunes of Scholasticism and Medical Science in European Intellectual Life* (Cambridge: Cambridge University Press, 1983).
7   Adrian Streete, '"An Old Quarrel Between Us That Will Never Be at an End": Middleton's *Women Beware Women* and Late Jacobean Religious Politics', *The Review of English Studies*, Advance Access published on 18 January 2008; doi: doi:10.1093/res/hgm167
8   Christopher Hill, *Society and Puritanism in Pre-revolutionary England* (London: Secker & Warburg, 1964), pp. 466, 457. For an alternative view that emphasizes women's relative empowerment in the holy household see Margo Todd, 'Humanists, Puritans and the Spiritualized Household', *Church History*, 49 (1980), 18–34.
9   Quoted in Norman Jones, *The English Reformation: Religion and Cultural* (Oxford: Blackwell, 2002), p. 37.
10 Whately, *A bride-bush*, pp. 49–51.
11 Lyndal Roper, '"The Common Man", "the Common Good", "Common Women": Gender and Meaning in the German Reformation Commune', *Social History*, 12 (1987), 1–21 (p. 20).
12 George Hakewill, *King Davids Vow for Reformation of Himselfe. His Family. His Kingdome. Delivered in twelve sermons before the Prince his Highness upon Psalm 101* (London, 1621), pp. 94–95.
13 Whately, *A bride-bush*, pp. 49–51.
14 Whately, *A bride-bush*, p. 83.
15 See for example, Tilley, *Dictionary of Proverbs*: 'women by mutual conjunctions receive their perfections from men', p. 758.
16 Jean Calvin, *A commentarie vpon S. Paules epistles to the Corinthians. Written by M. Iohn Caluin: and translated out of Latine into Englishe by Thomas Timme* (London, 1577), fol. 130r.
17 Quoted in Joyce Salisbury, 'Gendered Sexuality', in *Handbook of Medieval Sexuality*, ed. by Vern L. Bullough and James A. Brundage (New York: Taylor & Francis, 2000), pp. 88–131 (p. 95). See also James A. Brundage, *Law, Sex, and Christian Society in Medieval Europe* (Chicago: University of Chicago Press, 1987).
18 J. P. Sommerville, *Politics and Ideology in England 1603–1640* (London: Longman, 1986), pp. 9–56.
19 Quoted in Jeffrey Goldsworthy, *The Sovereignty of Parliament: History and Philosophy* (Oxford: Oxford University Press, 1999), p. 73.
20 Mark Breitenberg, *Anxious Masculinity in Early Modern England* (Cambridge: Cambridge University Press, 1996).
21 Cynthia Herrup, 'The King's Two Genders', *Journal of British Studies*, 45 (2006), 493–510.
22 Su Fang Ng, *Literature and the Politics of Family in Seventeenth-Century England* (Cambridge: Cambridge University Press, 2007), p. 25.
23 Margot Heinemann, *Puritanism and Theatre: Thomas Middleton and Opposition Drama under the Early Stuarts* (Cambridge: Cambridge University Press, 1980).
24 Chris Given-Wilson and Alice Curteis, *The Royal Bastards of Medieval England* (London: Routledge & Kegan Paul, 1984), p. 43.
25 Whately, *A bride-bush*, pp. 51–52.

26 Erasmus, *Education*, p. 21.
27 Thomas Sternhold, *The whole booke of Psalmes, collected into English meter* (London, 1565), p. 164.
28 Erasmus, *Education*, pp. 24–26.
29 Gordon Kipling, *Enter the King: Theatre, Liturgy, and Ritual in the Medieval Civic Triumph* (Oxford: Clarendon Press, 1997).
30 Erasmus, *Enchiridion*, Chapter: *Of the outward and inward man: Chap. iv.*
31 See, for example, William Irwin Thompson, *The Time Falling Bodies Take to Light: Mythology, Sexuality, and the Origins of Culture*, 2nd edn (Basingstoke: Palgrave Macmillan, 1996).
32 David Marsh, 'Erasmus on the Antithesis of Body and Soul', *Journal of the History of Ideas*, 37 (1976), 673–88 (p. 675).
33 Erasmus, *Enchiridion*, Chapter: *Of the outward and inward man.: Chap. iv.*
34 Erasmus, *Enchiridion*, Chapter: *Of the outward and inward man.: Chap. iv.*
35 Some medics regarded men as also possessing wombs, although theirs did not play a role in reproduction. See for example Thomas Vicary's 1548 work (reissued in 1577), *The Anatomie of the Bodie of Man*, ed. by F. J. Furnivall and Percy Furnivall, Early English Text Society (London: N. Trubner, 1888), pp. 64–65.
36 William Tyndale, *The Obedience of a Christian Man* (1528), fol. 34iv–r.
37 Rebecca W. Bushnell, *Tragedies of Tyrants: Political Thought and Theater in the English Renaissance* (Ithaca, NY: Cornell University Press, 1990), p. 69.
38 James Doelman, '"A King of Thine Own Heart": The English Reception of King James VI and I's *Basilikon Doron*', *Seventeenth Century*, 9 (1994), 1–9.
39 James VI and I, 'A Speech to the Lords and Commons of the Parliament at White-Hall, on Wednesday the XXI of March. Anno 1609', in *King James VI and I: Political Writings*, ed. by Johann P. Sommerville (Cambridge: Cambridge University Press, 1994), pp. 179–203 (p. 181); James VI and I, *The True Law of Free Monarchies; And, Basilikon Doron*, ed. by Daniel Fischlin and Mark Fortier (Toronto: Centre for Reformation and Renaissance Studies, 1996), p. 57.
40 Richard Mocket, *God and the King* (London, 1615), p. 83. John Bossy, *Christianity in the West* (New York: Oxford University Press, 1985), comments that 'Nobody seems to have taken much notice that commandment put mothers on a level with fathers', noting that the 'failure to read past first three words of commandment was general' (p. 116). He adds that 'The immediate beneficiary of the Protestant insistence on fatherhood was the metaphorical prince rather than the literal father' (ibid.).
41 Mockett, *God and the King*, pp. 83, 19.
42 Bertha Porter, 'Mocket, Richard (1577–1618)', rev. Glenn Burgess, *Oxford Dictionary of National Biography*, ed. by H. C. G. Matthew and Brian Harrison (Oxford: Oxford University Press, 2004) < http://www.oxforddnb.com/view/article/18866 > (accessed 21 February 2009).
43 For James's European agenda, see William Brown Patterson, *King James VI and I and the Reunion of Christendom* (Cambridge: Cambridge University Press, 1997).
44 [Thomas Scott?], *Tom Tell-Troath: or, a free Discourse touching the Manners of the Time. Directed to his Maj by waye of humble advertisement*, in J. Somers, *A Collection of Scarce and Valuable Tracts, Chiefly Such as Relate to the History and Constitution of These Kingdoms*, ed. by Walter Scott, 2nd edn, 10 vols (London: James Ballantyre, 1809–1815), II, pp. 470–92 (p. 476).
45 Elisabeth Bourcier, ed., *The Diary of Sir Simonds d'Ewes 1622–1624* (Paris: Didier, 1974), pp. 85, 113.
46 For the role of the Spanish Match in forging a 'Country' opposition, see Thomas Cogswell, 'England and the Spanish Match', in *Conflict in Early Stuart England: Studies in Religion and Politics, 1603–1642*, ed. by Richard Cust and Ann Hughes (London: Longmans, 1989), pp. 107–33. Cust identifies its elements as antipopery, anti-Spanish chauvinism, suspicion of corruption in high places, and fear for the continuance of parliaments. Richard Cust, 'Politics and the Electorate in the 1620s', in ibid., pp. 134–67 (pp. 155–59). I use capitals and inverted commas to signal its status as a proto-political party. For Middleton's political convictions, see Margot Heinemann, *Puritanism and Theatre*.

47 Thomas Scott, *Vox Populi Or Newes From Spayne* (London, 1620), fols B3v, C2v.
48 *Tom Tell-Troath*, pp. 471, 475.
49 Margot Heinemann, 'Political Drama', in *Cambridge Companion to English Renaissance Drama*, ed. by A. R. Braunmuller and Michael Hattaway (Cambridge: Cambridge University Press, 2003), pp. 164–96 (p. 168).
50 See Richard Dutton, 'Thomas Middleton's A Game at Chess: A Case Study', in *The Cambridge History of British Theater, Volume 1: Origins to 1660*, ed. by Jane Milling and Peter Thomson (Cambridge: Cambridge University Press, 2004), pp. 424–38.
51 Erasmus, *Education*, p. 26.
52 Roger Lockyer, *Buckingham: The Life and Political Career of George Villiers, First Duke of Buckingham: 1592–1628* (London: Longmans, 1981), p. 463.
53 For the poem see 'Early Stuart Libels: an edition of poetry from manuscript sources', ed. by Alastair Bellany and Andrew McRae, *Early Modern Literary Studies*, Text Series I (2005) < http://www.earlystuartlibels.net/htdocs/buckingham_assassination_section/Pii18.html > (accessed 31 March 2010). For commentary see the website and, in particular, Alastair Bellany, '"Raylinge Rymes and Vaunting Verse"': Libellous Politics in Early Stuart England', in *Culture and Politics in Early Stuart England*, ed. by Peter Lake and Kevin Sharpe (Stanford: Stanford University Press, 1993), pp. 285–310.
54 Bellany, ' "Raylinge Rymes and Vaunting Verse"', p. 305.
55 Bellany, ' "Raylinge Rymes and Vaunting Verse"', p. 299.
56 See, for example, Michael Young, *King James and the History of Homosexuality* (New York: New York University Press, 2000).
57 Robert Shephard, 'Sexual Rumours in English Politics: The Cases of Elizabeth I and James I', in *Desire and Discipline: Sex and Sexuality in the Premodern West*, ed. by Jacqueline Murray and Konrad Eisenbichler (Toronto: University of Toronto Press, 1996), pp. 101–22 (p. 115).
58 Edward Peyton, *The divine catastrophe of the kingly family of the house of Stuarts or, a short history of the rise, reign, and ruine thereof. Wherein the most secret and chamber-abominations of the two last kings are discovered, divine justice in King Charles his overthrow vindicated, and the Parliaments proceedings against him clearly justified* (London, 1652), pp. 28–29.
59 Alan Bray, *Homosexuality in Renaissance England: With a New Afterword* (New York: Columbia University Press, 1995), pp. 19–30.
60 Elisabeth Bourcier, ed., *The Diary of Sir Simonds D'Ewes*, pp. 92–93.
61 Arthur Wilson, *The history of Great Britain being the life and reign of King James the First, relating to what passed from his first access to the crown, till his death* (London, 1652), pp. 260–61.
62 See above, p. 00. For Wilson, see Graham Parry, 'Wilson, Arthur (*bap.* 1595, *d.* 1652)', in *Oxford Dictionary of National Biography*, ed. by H. C. G. Matthew and Brian Harrison (Oxford: Oxford University Press, 2004), < http://www.oxforddnb.com/view/article/29640 > (accessed 31 March 2010).
63 Wilson, *History of Great Britain*, pp. 172–73.
64 Wilson, *History of Great Britain*, p. 263.

CHAPTER SIX

New Directions: *Women Beware Women* and the Arts of Looking and Listening

Helen Wilcox

'Wormwood' or 'nectar'? Tragedy at Work on the Senses

Thomas Middleton's 1621 tragedy, *Women Beware Women*, is a deeply sensual play. Its subject-matter is human desires – material, sexual, forbidden, incestuous – and these impulses are fully represented and experienced through (and on) the *senses* of characters and audience alike. Livia, the pivotal character who unites the play's two plots and propels it to its climax, asserts that she can

> bring forth
> As pleasant fruits as sensuality wishes
> In all her teeming longings. (2.1.30–32)[1]

The tragedy concerns the impact of such 'teeming longings' on the four Florentine families whose fates are interlocked in Middleton's drama. In enacting and embodying the power of desire, the play draws upon virtually every imaginable 'fruit' of 'sensuality', and presents us with the effects of all five senses: taste, smell, touch, sight and hearing.

The sense of taste is perhaps the most subjective of the five – an observation upheld by the closing words of the second act of *Women Beware Women*. Livia complains that Bianca's scruples after her enforced seduction by the Duke are 'but a qualm of honour', a temporary bitterness: 'Sin tastes at the first draught like wormwood-water, / But, drunk again, 'tis nectar ever after' (2.2.473, 475–76). How can the senses be trusted, when foul wrongdoing can come to taste like 'nectar'? The play's centrepiece (3.3) is a great banquet, an ostentatious celebration of the delights of food and material consumption, yet it becomes a distorted reflection of 'Cupid's feast' (2.2.401). With its undercurrents of manipulation and envy, this mouth-watering but disturbing moment in the play symbolizes the unworthy desires of those many characters who long to taste 'sweetmeats' and, as the play proceeds, 'grow so greedy' (3.1.268, 3.2.77). The anticipation and memory of eating and drinking are also among Middleton's most persistent metaphors. As the play's marriageable young woman, Isabella, is being scrutinized by her potential husband and his servant, she takes quiet relish in the fact that she already has a lover of her own choice, unbeknown to the foolish Ward who is appraising her, and she secretly notes that

> the comfort is
> He's but a cater's place on 't, and provides
> All for another's table. Yet how curious
> The ass is like some nice professor on 't,
> That buys up all the daintiest food i' th' markets,
> And seldom licks his lips after a taste on 't. (3.3.37–42)

The Ward is shown here as one who thinks he is getting a tasty meal for himself but is in fact furnishing another man's table, and merely looks on without savouring it himself. The physicality of the simile in these last lines, referring to the strange scruples of those who would choose dainty food and yet do not lick their lips with enjoyment, transforms the mercantile imagery into a tantalizing account of taste and suppressed desire.

The senses of taste and smell are closely connected. Which of the two is predominant, for instance, in Leantio's unpleasant reference to 'a sallet growing upon a dunghill' (3.2.52)? The two senses are virtually indistinguishable in the Ward's reaction to his first kiss of Isabella: 'O, most delicious scent! Methinks it tasted as if a man had stepped into a comfit-maker's shop to let a cart go by all the while I kissed her' (3.3.61–63). The spectacular masque in the final scene of the play goes over the top (almost literally) in mingling sensual effects. In devising ingenious ways to kill off almost all his protagonists, Middleton makes use not only of relatively conventional poisoned drinks, but also of a notorious deadly vapour. Traditionally associated with the sensuality of Catholic worship, the 'precious incense' which wafts to the theatre's top balcony like prayer towards the heavens is transformed by Isabella into a weapon against her enemy. In contrast to the 'scent [...] of blessings' hoped for earlier in the play (3.1.86–87), poisoned odours now 'ascend' to Livia, who is playing the exalted part of the goddess Juno in the wedding masque; the fumes cause her to become 'sick to th' death' (5.1.137, 168). At the very moment when she is being overcome by the 'savour' of the poisonous smoke (5.1.151), Livia herself makes use of another sense – touch – to wipe out the purveyor of the incense. As the stage direction vividly puts it, Livia 'throws flaming gold upon Isabella's lap'. This deceptive 'sign of wealth and golden days' (5.1.152), visually dazzling but primarily at work on the character's tactile sense as it showers Isabella and burns her to death, finds its treacherous equivalent in the poisonous darts fired by the masque's Cupids at Isabella's lover, Hippolito. Again, the sensual devastation caused by fire (ironically associated with love's passion) is highlighted in the intense pain felt by Hippolito as Cupid's shafts pierce his skin; he cries out that 'death runs through my blood, in a wild flame too' (5.1.177).

Tempting though it is to pursue these three senses further within the profoundly physical world of *Women Beware Women*, these brief preliminary examples of Middleton's use of taste, smell and touch must give way to a more prolonged focus on the remaining two of the five senses, sight and hearing. The reason for this is twofold. First, looking and listening are given greater emphasis and prominence in the action and mood of the tragedy than the activities of the other three senses, and more significantly underpin the play's basic assumptions concerning society, gender and morality. Second, visual and musical elements (the practical consequences of an emphasis on sight and hearing) occupy a more central role in the interpretation and performance of a play and particularly influence its impact on the audience. Taking these premises as my starting-point, and drawing on my own experience of teaching the text and participating in a production of *Women Beware Women*,[2] this essay will explore the insights to be gained from approaching the play through its appeal to the eyes and the ears.

'Here's my masterpiece': The Art of Looking

From the very first line of the play, Middleton's dramatic focus is on the visual dimension of human interaction. As Leantio returns home to Florence, his widowed Mother exclaims: 'Thy sight was never yet more precious to me' (1.1.1). The literal meaning of 'thy sight' – the sight of thee – focuses on the Mother's experience of seeing her son once again, but as the play unfolds it becomes clear that Leantio's own 'sight' is fundamental to his attitude to the world about him, and particularly to his attitude towards women. Later in the same scene, he talks proudly of his new wife, Bianca, beginning with a very telling phrase:

> As often as I look upon that treasure
> And know it to be mine – there lies the blessing –
> It joys me that I ever was ordained
> To have a being ... (1.1.14–17)

The peculiar and disconcerting quality of the play's sensuality emerges here: Leantio's pleasure in his marriage is not only based on feasting his sight on his 'treasure', but this delighted looking is bound up with the pride of possession, and the true 'blessing' he receives is to 'know it to be *mine*'. Leantio's choice of pronoun, 'it', is a further tell-tale sign of the society brought to life by the play. A woman is an object to be looked at and bought: Bianca is to Leantio 'the most unvalued'st [invaluable] purchase / That youth of man had ever knowledge of' (1.1.12–13). He urges his Mother, in unmistakeably boasting tones, 'View but her face', and 'Look on her well, she's mine' (1.1.54, 42).

With such a beginning, it comes as no surprise that the play is dominated by the language of looking, and explores a culture of personal interaction based on visual judgements. Sordido, the Ward's 'man', is eager to assess the nature of the Ward's intended bride, and claims that he will be able simply 'to *see* what she *is*' (2.2.96). This seems to be the superficial basis of all social encounters in the play, wherever they occur; we learn that 'gallants' go to church 'only to see faces' (1.1.33), suggesting the shallowness of Florentine society and the early seventeenth century London that it mirrors. The interlinking of 'faces' and faith is an idea recalled towards the end of the play when Isabella realizes the incestuous nature of her love for Hippolito:

> 'Tis time we parted, sir, and left the sight
> Of one another; nothing can be worse
> To hurt repentance, for our very eyes

Are far more poisonous to religion
Than basilisks to them. (4.2.137–41)

Relationships and moral states are both defined in visual terms, and Isabella's only hope of redemption is expressed to Hippolito as a request that 'I ne'er may see you more' (4.2.143).

The driving force of the play's main plot, the Duke's desire for Bianca, is equally couched in the language of looking, and is itself based on one transitory visual encounter, as Bianca and her widowed mother-in-law stand on the balcony and watch the Duke's annual procession, a 'sight' that is not to be 'lost' (1.3.89). When Bianca notes that the Duke seemed to 'look up' and see them (1.3.105), she is treated to a speech from the Mother on the nature of looking:

> That's everyone's conceit that sees a duke:
> If he looks steadfastly, he looks straight at them,
> When he perhaps, good careful gentleman,
> Never minds any, but the look he casts
> Is at his own intentions, and his object
> Only the public good. (1.3.106–11)

This ideal is soon shown to be far from the truth: the Duke does indeed concentrate on 'his own intentions', but these are sensual rather than governmental. As Guardiano comments, 'How strangely that one look has catched [the Duke's] heart' (2.2.21); later, the Mother astutely points out that 'one spark' can set fire to a whole house (3.1.238). Bianca may have glanced down at the Duke out of curiosity, but his interpretation of her look (and her looks) fires his desire. The result is a radical shift and an ensuing chaos, for the Duke's gaze has power and his wishes must be satisfied. One brief glimpse rapidly results in the seduction and rape of Bianca.

Both Isabella and Bianca are presented as visual commodities to be put on display for the benefit of men. Isabella is expected to be 'handsomely tricked up' by her father in order to be shown in the best light to her suitor (2.2.59), but when it comes to the crunch the foolish Ward is more interested in checking the quality of her teeth, as though he were attending a horse-market: 'But, Sordido, how shall we do to make her laugh, that I may see what teeth she has?' (3.4.82–83). However, this obsession with using their eyes to assess the world around them is not limited to male characters' encounters with women. There is a general emphasis on value being visible, whether this is Bianca's demand for 'some fair cut-work' to be 'pinned up in my bedchamber' (3.1.20) or Leantio's interjection, 'Stay, stay, let's see your cloth-of-silver slippers' (4.1.55). The detail with which material items such as these – furnishings, clothing, watches, jewels – are put on display in the language of the play not only offers hints for performance[3] but also suggests connections with the visual culture of the early seventeenth century. The play's fascination with textures, colours, craftsmanship and ostentation recalls the lavish still life paintings of contemporary artists in the Dutch republic, for example, where the Protestant paradoxes of materialism and propriety, success and piety, were encapsulated in attentive representations of fruit, cheese, textiles and silverware.[4] However, drama adds movement and

NEW DIRECTIONS: THE ARTS OF LOOKING AND LISTENING 125

4   'Gedekte tafel' [Laid table] by an unknown artist of the Flemish or Dutch school,
    c. 1615. This image is reproduced by kind permission of the Museum Boijmans van
    Beuningen, Rotterdam.

variety to such images: the visual and moral world of *Women Beware Women* is one of rapid change and instability. As Bianca confesses to her bemused husband,

> I would not stand thus
> And gaze upon you always; troth, I could not, sir.
> As good be blind and have no use of sight
> As look on one thing still. What's the eye's treasure
> But change of objects? (3.1.141–45)

In a play obsessed with the 'use of sight', this argument is a clear sign of the moral chaos in which the drama culminates.

The art of looking, so central to *Women Beware Women*, is focused during much of the play on female bodies and domestic accoutrements, but it is not exclusively concerned with these aspects of the visible environment. Considerable reference is also made to the fine arts, which play a crucial function in the seduction of Bianca by the Duke. Bianca is tempted 'above', where the Duke awaits her, by an invitation to see Livia's 'rooms and pictures', particularly a 'monument' that is 'worth sight indeed' (2.2.272, 276, 278). Bianca is overwhelmed by the collection shown to her by Guardiano – 'Mine eye ne'er met with fairer ornaments' – and it is later revealed that her guide specifically prepares Bianca for her sexual encounter with the Duke by manipulating her gaze: 'I showed her naked pictures by the way: / A bit to stay the appetite' (2.2.310, 402–3). However, just before the Duke emerges from the shadows and reveals himself, Bianca is assured that 'There's a better piece / Yet than all these' (2.2.313–14), suggesting that the Duke himself is the mysterious 'monument' that she is destined to admire. There is an uncanny link here with Leantio's account of his earlier wooing of Bianca in Venice, when he

> [...] received thee from thy father's window
> Into these arms at midnight, when we embraced
> As if we had been statues only made for 't,
> To show art's life, so silent were our comforts,
> And kissed as if our lips had grown together? (3.2.259–63)

The idea of the lovers as statues, works of art given breath, renders yet more complex the relationship of looking and being looked at, or seeing and being, in this highly visual play.

If human beings are sculpted into life, then there is, by implication, an artist at work on their creation. In the case of the 'monument', the stage-manager (if not the artist) is Livia, who sets up the circumstances in which the Duke can come forward as a living statue and thereby seduce Bianca. There is in this a darker echo of the benevolent Paulina in Shakespeare's *The Winter's Tale*, another character with inside knowledge who, in her case, encourages Leontes and Perdita to admire the 'statue' of Hermione which turns out to be 'warm' with life.[5] In *The Winter's Tale*, the encounter with the 'statue' leads to reunion and the restoration of love; in the tragic context of *Women Beware Women*, the outcome is the fulfilment of lust and the beginning of destruction. Earlier in Middleton's play, Bianca herself has been presented as the artistic creation of her own husband, Leantio, who announces to his mother: 'here's my masterpiece; do you now behold her' (1.1.41). The Duke echoes this as he in turn woos Bianca, describing her as

> A creature so composed of gentleness
> And delicate meekness, such as bless the faces
> Of figures that are drawn for goddesses
> And makes art proud to look upon her work, (2.2.340–43)

Bianca's beauty is likened to that depicted by artists as they search for a visual representation of the divine, and the group gazing upon this apparently otherworldly woman is widened in this speech to include personified and proud 'art' itself.

Once again we find that the women in Middleton's play are objects of visual attention, the focal points of the art of looking. For this purpose they are also sometimes their own artists, through the familiar trope of women as 'made up' to be artificially attractive. When Livia plans to express her desire for Leantio, she resolves to 'paint tomorrow, / So follow my true labour day by day' (3.2.142–43), suggesting that to use cosmetics (a female artistry with 'paint') is not only effective but actually a woman's 'true' activity. When Isabella is on parade in front of the critical eyes of the Ward and Sordido, one of the more outrageous questions put to her is, 'And is that hair your own?' (3.4.68). We may well be reminded of the conversation between Cesario (that is, Viola in male disguise) and Olivia in *Twelfth Night*, when Olivia unveils her face as though it were a 'picture' and asks, 'Is't not well done?' Cesario's response, 'Excellently done, if God did all', also plays with the idea of female beauty as (perhaps) more the result of artistry than of nature's gifts (1.5.233, 235–36). Whatever the source of the beauty, in all these instances the emphasis is on women as conscious compositions and the object of intense visual scrutiny, just as a work of art might be.

This metaphor of the female character as an artistic creation lies at the heart of the play's assumption that life is a kind of show. The drama moves from one troubled set piece scene to another: the game of chess below while Bianca is raped above (2.2); the banquet with its parody of social etiquette and stately dances (3.2); the crude observations of the Ward and Sordido as they (and the audience) eye up Isabella (3.3); and the final, deadly masque with its tableaux and special visual effects (5.1). Before he dies, the Duke surveys the scene around him and, tellingly, commands a guard to 'remove these ruined bodies from our eyes' (5.1.212). The very last speech of the play, delivered by the Cardinal who alone has survived, begins: 'Sin, what thou art these ruins show too piteously' (5.1.263). Right to the end, this play is in the business of *showing*, and in many ways its use of the visual is stylized, like a game of chess itself. Several productions have used the idea of the black and white squares of a game board as the basis of their stage design,[6] inspired by Middleton's evident fascination with the symbolic and strategic relationships in chess. This fundamentally visual and manipulative understanding of human interaction is strongly indicated by the metaphors of being 'cunning at the game' of social and sexual success in *Women Beware Women* (2.2.294) and by the overall structure of Middleton's *A Game at Chess*.[7] In both cases, the sense of characters as figures to be watched – statues who may think that they can control their own destinies but are in fact pawns in a larger and more sinister game – underlines the tragedy of the drama.

The art of looking, in all these different ways, is fundamental to the effect of *Women Beware Women* – but there is also considerable reference to the absence or impossibility of vision, through darkness or blindness. Knowing the significance of the sight (active and passive) of his wife, Leantio jealously guards her in a hidden closet 'at the end of the dark parlour' (3.1.243), upholding his principle of keeping 'choice treasures in obscurest places' (1.1.166). Having discovered the hidden treasure that Bianca represents, the Duke declares to his court that 'we sat all in darkness / But for that splendour' (3.2.101–2). The desires that drive Florentine society, however, are shown to flourish in darkness. Hippolito refers to the night as the 'blind time' made for vicious and guilty acts, suited to 'closeness, subtlety, and darkness' (4.2.5, 7). Light and darkness, sight and blindness, delineate a moral system: sin is a 'monster with all forehead and no eyes' (4.1.94) and, as the final masque is prepared, the Ward refers to an earlier court pageant in which 'a devil with one eye' rose up through a trap-door (5.1.8). This remembered visual effect, alerting us to the spectacle of hatred with which the play ends, again connects what is seen with that which lies hidden inside – a lack of conscience or ethical insight. All within is ignorance, 'darker' than the 'womb' (4.1.104).

The power of the play to evoke and explore the shadowy realms of human longings, brilliantly linking the pervasive emphasis on sight and looking with the potential for error and blindness, brings to mind another useful parallel with the visual arts. In the early seventeenth century, painters were exploring the capacity of visual representation to suggest the absence of light, or the contrast of darkness and, say, a lone candle. Gary Taylor has drawn attention to the similarities between Middleton's staged world and the paintings of Caravaggio or Frans Hals,[8] but in their effects of light and darkness the experimental compositions of Georges de la Tour, particularly focusing on the female image, may also be compared with *Women Beware Women*. The art of looking – by characters and by audience – is a difficult process of discernment, frequently carried out in the half light as in de la Tour's meditative paintings; in the play's dark parlours, half-lit balconies and shadowy masques, issues of morality and mortality must be discerned. When Fabritio urges his daughter Isabella to cover her face as she watches her future husband, the moral complexity of these relationships is all too clear:

> On with your mask, for 'tis your part to see now,
> And not be seen. Go to make use of your time.
> See what you mean to like; nay, and I charge you,
> Like what you see. (1.2.74–77)

While Isabella's sight is manipulated by older relatives in order to arrange her marriage, Bianca's viewing of works of visual art, especially the 'monument', is used as a means to trap her into adultery. With superb irony, Middleton assigns to Bianca's cuckolded husband, Leantio, the realization that it is

> [...] As much madness
> To set light before thee as to lead blind folks
> To see the monuments, which they may smell as soon
> As they behold; marry, oftimes their heads,
> For want of light, may feel the hardness of 'em. (4.1.96–100)

The sensual confusion in Leantio's simile here – showing visual art to those unable to see it, and substituting smell and touch for sight – is a reminder of the 'madness' of the play's moral and social system. What you see is, and yet simultaneously is not, what you get.

'Here's a tune indeed!': The Art of Listening

When we consider the hierarchy of the senses in Middleton's writing, it becomes evident that he was not only fascinated by the multiple implications of sight but also profoundly aware of the dramatic and sensual impact of sound.[9] It is not so much that he took advantage of the music of language itself; in the nineteenth century, Swinburne noted the theatrical ability inherent in the 'noble eloquence' and 'rhetorical affluence' of *Women Beware Women*,[10] but the effect of Middleton's language is generally more material and psychological than lyrical or harmonious. Rather, as the many musical stage directions in *Women Beware Women* indicate, Middleton saw the importance of *actual* music to his drama.[11] From biographical and textual evidence it seems likely that the playwright was, at the very least, knowledgeable about music and well accustomed to working with its practitioners, if not musically accomplished himself. His wife was the grand-daughter of the leading Tudor church composer, John Marbecke, and in a

Latin pun on his own name Middleton referred to himself as 'Thomas Medius et Gravis Tonus', making the most of the musical associations of 'tonus' (note or pitch) along with 'medius' and 'gravis' (mid and low) to suggest his familiarity with music.[12]

A production of *Women Beware Women* demands extensive music in a variety of kinds – processionals, songs, dance tunes, masque – though, sadly, it appears that none of the work composed for the early performances has survived, in spite of the fact that there is a substantial corpus of extant music linked with Middleton's plays as a whole.[13] Instrumental music, often for dances, would also have been performed between the acts of the play, according to the custom of the theatres for which Middleton wrote; however, none of this musical material has been discovered either.[14] It is necessary, therefore, to use and adapt the music of Middleton's contemporaries – such as Robert Johnson, John Dowland, Orlando Gibbons, Thomas Tomkins and John Ward – if historical accuracy is the aim of a production. Some traditional material may also be incorporated – dances, ballad tunes and so on – since the practice of setting new words or steps to existing tunes was common in early modern music. On the other hand, commissioning new compositions can result in strikingly appropriate dramatic effects, and was, no doubt, what Middleton and his companies did. Crucially, whatever kinds of music are employed, the play is an intensely aural experience and contains scenes in which a more than casual *listening* is demanded of both characters and audience.

The two main musical interludes of *Women Beware Women* – the song and lovers' dances at the courtly banquet, and the masque in the final act – are set in the context of a society permeated by music. We learn that Isabella, for instance, has been well groomed in readiness for marriage: her 'courtly' upbringing means that she 'can sing and dance' (4.2.105–6), and her performance of a song during the banquet is said to provide evidence that 'Florentine damsels are not brought up idley' (3.2.133). Indeed, women are closely associated with the performance of music in the play, and it is no coincidence that the foolish and bawdy Ward judges female bodies in terms of music and dance: he 'cannot abide a splay-footed woman' whose 'heels keep together so as if she were beginning an Irish dance still, and the wriggling of her bum playing the tune to't' (3.3.112–15). Rhythm, melody and movement, here rendered with vulgar physicality, are the metaphorical principles on which relationships in the play are based. The Duke asserts that 'music bids the soul of man to a feast' (3.2.130), and Livia talks of being awakened by 'love's music' (3.2.306), recalling the early seventeenth-century emblem headed 'Amor Docet Musicam' [Love teaches music] depicting Cupid with a lute.[15] Later, an apparently well-meaning conversation between Isabella and Livia is described by the listening Guardiano as being sociably 'tuneful' (4.2.187). Musical forms, with their implicit symbolism of a more divine harmony, even remind the audience (briefly) of the spiritual values which seem remote from most of the play's characters. When the Cardinal believes that he has moved his brother the Duke to abandon his adulterous liaison with Bianca, the churchman exclaims that this religious 'conversion' will be 'Sung for a hymn in heaven' (4.1.260–61). The Duke's subsequent amorality, in plotting the murder of Leantio so that Bianca can become his Duchess and therefore no longer his 'strumpet' (4.1.270), converts the heavenly melody into a far more hellish tune.

The arts of listening, actual as well as metaphorical, are widely and fully exploited in *Women Beware Women*, beginning with the music which heralds entrances and signifies the nature of the occasion or the status of the persons involved in the ensuing scene. When the Duke is first observed by Bianca (and the audience), he and his entourage are announced by 'variety of music and song' (1.3.101) and the innocent Bianca's 'soul' is stirred by 'the reverence / Of such a solemn and most worthy custom' (1.3.103–4). Music here implies stately grandeur and solemnity; the Duke's capacity to command both instrumentalists and singers in his procession is a sign of his wealth and importance. When the Duke subsequently makes his entrance to the grand banquet – 'Fall back, here comes the Duke' (3.3.22) – the accompanying stage direction indicates that 'Cornetts' should sound, neatly combining the association of military authority with this instrument's festive overtones appropriate to a banquet. Similarly, as the banquet ends and the Duke and Bianca depart to the sound of a 'flourish' of cornets, the music confirms the general splendour lavished by the Duke on Bianca, who leaves in a fine 'caroche' (a particularly luxurious mode of transport) and is assured that the Duke has taken 'special care' of her (3.2.241, 237, 239). On the occasion of their marriage, however, the couple do not make their entrance to the music of cornets but of 'Oboes' (4.3.1), which produce a reedier and less martial sound, appropriate to the sensual delights associated with a wedding.

The effects of music within the play are vividly attested in the dialogue of its characters as well as by its stage directions. When Isabella is prevailed upon to sing at the banquet, her choice of song is fully commented upon by the Ward, beginning with his sarcastic exclamation, 'Here's a tune indeed!' (3.2.153). In his uneducated view, the song is one of the 'simpering tunes' associated with the court, 'played upon catsguts, and sung by little kitlings' (3.2.156–57). This suggests a decorated vocal line accompanied by one or more instruments with gut strings: a lute, perhaps, or a small consort of viols. The 'kitling' (a young cat, presumably referring back to the 'catsguts' as well as to Isabella's youth and high voice) no doubt sings a melody which embellishes the words with an affective and melismatic style in which one syllable might well be set to several bars of music. This is contrasted with the simple, syllabic settings of less courtly songs such as ballads: as the Ward protests, 'Pish, I had rather hear one ballad sung i'th' nose now of the lamentable drowning of fat sheep and oxen' (3.3.153–55).[16] The impact of Isabella's performance is shown by Middleton to be dependent on the state of mind of those who listen. While the Ward is disappointed by the 'simpering' music of his potential bride, Isabella's father Fabritio takes great pride in his product (as it were) and invites the Duke to comment approvingly on her voice. The instrumental music which introduces and accompanies the song reminds the listening Leantio that he has lost his beloved Bianca to the Duke, and thus he despairingly whispers, 'O, that music mocks me!' (3.3.137). The same harmonies can convey disgust to one listener, joy to a second and intense sorrow to a third – but in all cases the impact of music is to 'play upon' the emotions of those who hear it. As Hamlet cries out in exasperation to Rosencrantz and

Guildenstern, 'You would play upon me, you would seem to know my stops [...] 'Sblood, do you think I am easier to be play'd on than a pipe?' (3.2.364–65, 369–70).

Drawing on the dramatic impact of music, simultaneously entertaining the audience and revealing the characters, Middleton employs a variety of aural effects in the banquet scene to convey the seductive yet deceptive powers of human desire. Isabella's voice makes a sensual impression – positive or negative – on the listeners around her on the stage, but the words she is singing are a lament for the way in which women are led into marriage with a 'thing for no use good' (3.2.149). Her song's musical effect induces passion, even while its words are critical of the passionless social trap in which she finds herself: 'She that would be / Mother of fools, let her compound with me' (3.2.151–52). Music and words are here deliberately at odds with one another. When Isabella is made to show off 'another quality' (3.2.165) – her ability to dance – she again works with *and* against the music in demonstrating the paradox of her situation. First she dances with her secret and forbidden lover, her uncle Hippolito, a man described by the Ward as a 'fine-timbered reveller' (3.2.183). The stage direction suggests that theirs is an elegant and harmonious dance, in which Isabella and Hippolito make 'honours to the Duke, and curtsey to themselves both before and after' (3.2.201). But this perfectly balanced dance is followed by an enforced repeat performance for Isabella, now partnered by the Ward who 'ridiculously imitates Hippolito', as the stage direction tells us (3.2.229). The two performances highlight the power of 'love's music' (3.2.306): Isabella dances perfectly with her real lover, while the performance with her undesired husband-to-be is hideous mimicry. However, the contrast also encapsulates the moral complexity of the entire plot, in which incest is equated with aesthetic beauty while marriage is rendered ridiculous.

The choice of music for this scene plays an important part in confirming or challenging the moral perspectives offered by it. The first demonstration should be an elegant, harmonious dance – an 'almain', 'pavan' or other stately form[17] – though this could suggest that the love between Isabella and Hippolito is an honourable ideal,[18] an expression of genuine desire which defies social restrictions. Perhaps an affected or cloying musical style would be more appropriate, if the production aims to imply the dangerous immorality of the relationship. The choice of instruments can also carry symbolic significance: sweet recorders with interweaving lines, for instance, conventionally convey a mood of overwhelming sensuality and obsessive love, as in the lovers' duets in Blow's masque, *Venus and Adonis*.[19] When it comes to Isabella's second dance, more directorial choices must be made: should the music itself be a parodic echo of the preceding dance, or would it be more effective simply to repeat the same music, thereby leaving the element of parody to the dancing, heightening the contrasts between the accomplished Hippolito and the clumsy Ward? If the music of the second dance is itself to provide a contrast, there are several ways of doing this: the second tune can be a carefully composed variation on the first, for example, or a deliberately discordant and ugly tune. A different sort of dance may also be introduced, contrasting in its very nature with the stately and sensual skill of Isabella and Hippolito's demonstration. Before the Ward dances his 'ridiculous' caper, he lists the kinds of dances he knows about: 'Plain men dance the measures, the cinquapace, the gay / Cuckolds dance the hornpipe, and farmers dance the hay' (3.2.216–17). It might, therefore, seem most apt to play a rough 'hornpipe' for this husband who is a cuckold even before he is married – or, as he adds that a 'whore and bawd' dance 'the jig', perhaps a fast and furious jig would be doubly appropriate to Isabella and the Ward in this context.

What is clear is that there is a language of music at work in this scene, functioning as psychological and moral commentary; the art of listening to these aural dimensions of rhythm, tempo, melody, style and harmony (or discord) sharpens the audience's awareness of the contradictions in the play's moral world. As the plot and subplot interconnect and gain momentum towards the great masque of the final act – when, as Ceri Sullivan has put it, 'multiple murders and a suicide come in the guise of a court entertainment'[20] – the musical references grow more intense and less ambiguous. At the moment of Leantio's death – the event which drives Livia to arrange the masque – the dying man laments the simultaneous breaking of his 'heart-string' and his 'marriage knot' to Bianca. This reference is mercilessly picked up by his murderer, Hippolito, and turned into a piece of musical wordplay: 'There I heard the sound on't, / And never liked string better' (4.2.43, 45–46). The association of parts of the human body (as well as 'catsguts') with the making of music is traditional – compare George Herbert's metaphor of Christ's 'stretched sinews' on the cross being the sacrificial inspiration for all sacred music-making[21] – but Middleton gives the idea a particularly sadistic twist here in Hippolito's delight at the death of Leantio. Hippolito's murderous action is the catalyst which brings the drama to a crisis; like Iago, though without his calculating malice, Hippolito has 'set down the pegs that make this music' (*Othello* 2.1.200) and untuned what remained of harmony around him.

The discord of Leantio's murder drives Livia to reveal the incestuous nature of the relationship between Hippolito and Isabella, a new turning-point in the play which also gives rise to musical black humour. The Ward, on being informed that his bride is already pregnant by her uncle, nonchalantly reflects upon her singing with his customary vulgarity:

> I marvelled she sung so small, indeed, being no maid. Now I perceive there's a young chorister in her belly. This breeds a singing in my head, I'm sure. (4.2.120–22)

The lewd associations between a woman's singing voice and the state of her virginity, the image of the baby in her womb as a small 'chorister', and the Ward's state of mind as a 'singing' in his head, all suggest the rich seam of musical metaphor being mined here. The response of Sordido is equally witty: ''Tis but the tune of your wife's cinquapace, danced in a feather bed' (4.2.123–24). The ironic reference to the 'cinquapace', listed by the Ward during the banquet scene as the dance associated with revelry, mocks this foolish cuckolded husband whose wife has been dancing in Hippolito's bed. However, in the context of the murder carried out by Hippolito and the 'confusion of life, soul, and honour' experienced by Isabella (4.2.131), the metaphorical music is 'jarring' and the joke is bitter indeed.[22]

The final scene of the play, the masque of 'mighty Juno' in her guise as 'the marriage-goddess' (5.1.73, 74), contains and epitomizes the moral chaos of the Florentine society depicted by Middleton. The synopsis includes a nymph 'in love with two at once', the threat of 'strife', the dangers of 'discontent', 'Slander' and 'disgrace', and the notion of judgement that 'pays him i'th' end' (5.1.71, 77–81), all of which not only occur in the play as a whole but are enacted in the masque under cover of instrumental music, song, dancing and special effects. The 'ditty' is particularly important in musical and thematic terms, since the stage direction specifies that it is sung by two nymphs and Isabella 'in parts' (5.1.109). This is an unusually precise instruction, telling the singers that the words should not be set to a melody performed in unison but must be harmonized as a part-song. This recalls the boast of Isabella's father that she 'took her pricksong earlier' than 'any of her kindred ever did' (3.2.124–25); bawdy overtones are forever present in musical references linked with women. Isabella and her nymphs sing of 'coupled bodies' and the 'amazed affection' of one who is torn in love (5.1.111, 114), and the musical setting used in performance will have a strong influence on the impression made by the masque. Is this part-song a melancholy exploration of the 'passionate conflict' within Isabella (5.1.124), or a dispassionate hymn to Juno? Should the singers' parts work in close parallel, suggesting the anticipation of a harmonious resolution of the 'strife' requested in the ditty (5.1.119), or would the antagonism of interweaving contrapuntal lines better express the tensions among those acting in the masque, which are about to burst out in a climax of ingenious killings?[23] It is also possible to set the words to a round, in which one part follows the next while singing the same melody, a musical form which would in this context ironically imply the predictable and apparently endless chasing of one lover by another in the maze of love.[24]

The enormous scope for musical interpretation in this final scene is in keeping with the play's overall emphasis on music as a source of dramatic structure, wit, entertainment, ridicule, dignity, sensuality and the exploration of emotion. Listening is no neutral or merely indulgent activity in *Women Beware Women* – whether for the characters or the audience – since it carries the weight of interpretation and insight, conveying the complex aesthetic and ethical composition of the play's world.

'Longing for performance': Looking, Listening and Reacting

As this wealth of visual and aural material from *Women Beware Women* should have made clear, Middleton made the most of these two key sensual dimensions in his drama, from monument to banquet and song to masque. This is a play in which seeing and being seen are crucial to making judgements: as the Duke revealingly comments as he enters the banqueting hall with Bianca, she has been 'Of purpose sent into the world to show / Perfection once in woman' (3.2.24–25). The most important word here is 'show': it is not that Bianca *is* perfect, but that she is seen to *show* perfection. Similarly, when Isabella sings to the guests later in the same scene, we are again made aware that listening is a social and psychological skill of vital importance. As the Duke astutely points out on hearing Bianca's song and seeing her intended husband, the Ward,

> Methinks now, such a voice to such a husband
> Is like a jewel of unvalued worth,
> Hung at a fool's ear. (3.2.162–64)

The Duke's observation not only highlights the glittering mercantile world of 'worth' in which the characters function, but also points up the role of music in the definition of individuals and relationships within it.

Hearing and sight are the most vital of the senses for the working of theatrical effect, and many of the instances of visual and aural sensuality in Middleton's tragedy, so far discussed separately, in fact produce their dynamic impact through activating the arts of looking and listening simultaneously. Two further examples will demonstrate the ways in which sight and hearing work together in this play. First, the dances between Isabella and her two partners, Hippolito and the Ward, depend equally on the music played (including its instrumentation, tempo, rhythm, style and harmony) and the visual effect of the dance steps (including the success or otherwise of the manoeuvres, and their impact on the dancers and those watching). As Gary Taylor and Andrew J. Sabol have noted, the dances have a powerful 'aesthetic and emotional effect' which is both visual and musical at once.[25] Second, it is the nature of masque as a genre to be dependent both on visual stimuli and on the impressions made by music. The onlookers' eyes can feast on dance, colourful costume[26] and elaborate stage machinery, as well as other related sensual effects such as smell and touch, while their ears are assailed with dance tunes, incidental music and song-setting. In describing a 1967 Toronto production of *Women Beware Women*, J. R. Mulryne refers to the combined impact of the masque's visual and aural effects: 'every move and word was choreographed strictly to the music', while all the characters 'wore white domino masks and long white kid gloves, to strengthen the sense of a nuptial dance turning to a dance of death'.[27] The arts of looking and listening, in spectacle, music and dance, are inseparably invoked here.

The masque with which the play ends, ironically named a 'marriage-triumph' (4.2.164) but in effect a triumph of ingenious destruction, is the culmination of a series of shows and tableaux structuring the play, beginning with the parade of the Duke and proceeding to the game of chess, the banquet with its song and symbolic dances, the wedding procession and finally the masque of Juno. When Guardiano shares with Livia his idea of carrying out revenge under the cover of this last 'invention' (4.2.205), her response is to express 'longing for performance on't' (4.2.168). Her phrase compresses the sensuality of 'teeming longings' (2.1.32) with 'performance', a key word which encapsulates the play's combination of showing and playing. A 'performance' is something laid on to be watched, listened to and experienced; it suggests the drama and music, but also the dissembling and sexual prowess at the heart of the play.[28] A theatrical or musical performance requires players and stage managers – of whom there are several in *Women Beware Women*, chiefly Livia, Guardiano and the Duke – but performers also expect active interpreters. Bianca observes the Cardinal as he castigates the Duke on their marriage, and her subsequent comments highlight the way in which characters watch one another in Middleton's play, even outside the special moments of pageant or show:

NEW DIRECTIONS: THE ARTS OF LOOKING AND LISTENING   135

> Sir, I have read you over all this while
> In silence, and I find great knowledge in you,
> And severe learning; yet 'mongst all your virtues
> I see not charity written, which some call
> The first-born of religion, and I wonder
> I cannot see't in yours. (4.3.47–50)

The judgement of a character depends here, as throughout the play, on the capacity of others to 'read' an individual's nature in his or her performance. The problem with this interpretative task is that mistakes can be made: after all, as Isabella points out, a fool is 'but the image of a man', yet it is all too easy to fall into 'idolatry' (1.2.167, 166) and treat the image as though it were the real thing.

This prevailing sense of the danger, and yet the necessity, of performance reminds us that the arts of looking and listening are moral skills in the end, and particularly closely bound up with the enacting and the implications of gender roles that, as we have seen, are the subject of the play from its very title onwards.[29] In a drama that is so concerned with watching, it is notable that women are visually 'scrutinised'[30] to an almost obsessive degree, typified in the Ward and Sordido's cataloguing of Isabella: 'Now to her, now you've scanned all her parts over' (3.3.43). In a play that demands so much listening, it is significant that the songs are both performed by a woman. It was conventional in the early modern period to consider music itself to be feminine and to associate women in sensual and often bawdy ways with the making of music,[31] and in the banquet scene Middleton unmistakeably draws on this tradition. When Isabella has finished singing for the guests, her father turns to the Duke and enquires, 'How like you her breast now, my lord?' (3.2.158). The phrase 'a sweet breast' is used earlier in the scene to mean an attractive voice (3.2.122), but the sexual overtones of Fabritio's question are picked up by Bianca, who comments in an aside to the Duke:

> Her breast?
> He talks as if his daughter had given suck
> Before she were married – as her betters have.
> The next he praises, sure, will be her nipples. (3.2.158–61)

This is a play in which daughters, wives and mistresses are considered and presented as possessions, 'masterpieces' on a par with statues or compositions. Thus an understanding of the role assigned by Middleton to looking and listening in *Women Beware Women* is not only fundamental to an appreciation of the sensual, theatrical and moral world of the play, but takes us in the end to its central question: of what or whom should women *really* beware?

136 WOMEN BEWARE WOMEN

5   Pieter de Grebber, 'Musicerend gezelschap' ['Music-making group'], c. 1623. This image is reproduced by kind permission of the Museo de Bellas Artes de Bilbao.

Notes

1   Thomas Middleton, *Women Beware Women*, ed. by John Jowett, in *Thomas Middleton: The Collected Works*, gen. ed. Gary Taylor and John Lavagnino (Oxford: Clarendon Press, 2007), pp. 1488–1541.
2   The performances took place in the Eleanor Rathbone Theatre of Liverpool University in spring 1980; the production was designed and directed by Brean Hammond, and I was musical director. I am grateful to Brean Hammond for the loan of his notes and production photographs.
3   See Inga-Stina Ewbank, 'Realism and Morality in *Women Beware Women*', *Essays and Studies*, 22 (1969), 57–70 (p. 62).
4   For a lively study of this era of Dutch social, religious and cultural history, see Simon Schama, *The Embarrassment of Riches: An Interpretation of Dutch Culture in the Golden Age* (London: Collins, 1987). See Illustration 4.

NEW DIRECTIONS: THE ARTS OF LOOKING AND LISTENING 137

5   Shakespeare, *The Winter's Tale*, 5.3.109, from *The Riverside Shakespeare*, ed. by G. Blakemore Evans et al. (Boston: Houghton Mifflin, 1974). All further Shakespearian references are to this one-volume edition. The concept of a relationship between artist and work of art recalls the myth of Pygmalion, and the sinister overtones introduced by Middleton anticipate Browning's 'My Last Duchess'.
6   This was true of the Liverpool 1980 production, as well as the RSC's pioneering production of 1969 directed by Terry Hands and starring (among others) Judi Dench as Bianca and Brewster Mason as the Duke.
7   The title-page of *A Game at Chess* (1625 edition) includes an engraving of a group of courtly figures seated around a table playing chess – while they are also themselves chess pieces.
8   See *Collected Works*, pp. 25–26.
9   The work of Bruce Smith among others has drawn attention to the importance of listening to the early modern soundscape: see his *The Acoustic World of Early Modern England: Attending to the O-Factor* (Chicago: University of Chicago Press, 1999).
10 Swinburne, introduction to *Thomas Middleton* in *The Best Plays of the Old English Dramatists*, ed. by Havelock Ellis, Mermaid Series (London, 1894), I, xxviii, cited by J. R. Mulryne (ed.), in Thomas Middleton, *Women Beware Women* (London: Methuen, 1975), p. lii.
11 See 1.3.101, 3.2.20, 3.2.135, 3.2.145, 3.2.201, 3.2.228, 3.2.241, 4.3.1., 4.3.71, 5.1.36, 5.1.85, 5.1.108, 5.1.109. For a discussion of the significance of musical stage directions, see Alan C. Dessen and Leslie Thomson, *A Dictionary of Stage Directions in English Drama, 1580–1642* (Cambridge: Cambridge University Press, 1999).
12 The pun occurs in the dedication of Middleton's poem, *The Ghost of Lucrece*, in *Collected Works*, p. 1989, lines 20–21, and its implications are fully discussed in *Thomas Middleton and Early Modern Textual Culture: A Companion to the Collected Works*, ed. by Gary Taylor and John Lavagnino (Oxford: Clarendon Press, 2007), p. 120.
13 See *Companion*, pp. 119–81.
14 See *Companion*, p. 123.
15 Crispijn de Passe de Oude, from Gabriel Rollenhagen, *Nucleus Emblematum* (Cologne, 1611), cited in *Judith Leyster: Schilderes in een mannenwereld*, ed. by James A. Welu and Pieter Biesboer (Zwolle: Waanders Uitgevers, 1993), p. 126.
16 'Melisma' is the musical term for a melody which sets one syllable of the text to many notes, and can therefore employ expansive phrases for emotive purposes; syllabic word-settings use one note for each syllable, as in most hymn tunes, for example. A ballad is likely to be sung 'i' th' nose' as it would probably be unaccompanied and sung in a more raucous fashion than a lute song or madrigal.
17 These dance types, popular with early modern composers, are both characterized by a dignified four beats to a measure, as opposed to the faster movements of other courtly dances such as courantes and galliards with which they were often paired for the sake of contrast.
18 The association of dancing and honour is also suggested by the 'honours' or respectful bows made to the Duke at the beginning and end of Isabella and Hippolito's dance. For the implications of the cultural language of choreography, see Barbara Ravelhofer, *The Early Stuart Masque: Dance, Costume, and Music* (Oxford: Oxford University Press, 2006).
19 John Blow, *Venus and Adonis: A Masque for the Entertainment of the King* (1683), ed. by Bruce Wood, Purcell Society Edition Companion Series, II (London: Stainer and Bell, 2008). In Blow's work (the setting of a libretto by Anne Finch), the lovers' vocal lines are anticipated, and then accompanied, by decorated contrapuntal lines played on soft 'flutes' (that is, recorders). For the dances in the banquet scene of *Women Beware Women* in the 1980 Liverpool production, we took contrasting dance tunes from Playford's *The English Dancing Master* (1651), the most important seventeenth-century collection of pre-existing dance music, and embellished the melodies in appropriately contrasting styles using recorders.
20 Ceri Sullivan, 'Thomas Middleton', in *Teaching Shakespeare and Early Modern*

Dramatists, ed. by Andrew Hiscock and Lisa Hopkins (London: Palgrave, 2007), p. 155.
21 George Herbert, 'Easter' line 11, in *The English Poems of George Herbert*, ed. by Helen Wilcox (Cambridge: Cambridge University Press, 2007), p. 139.
22 The 'hellish jarring sounds' referred to in John Dowland's song, 'In Darkness Let Me Dwell' (1610), set to jagged and chromatic music, would be (paradoxically) in tune with the emphasis on discord and darkness at the end of the play. Dowland was one of the leading musicians of his day and his work has been linked with Middleton's plays; see *Companion*, pp. 137–38.
23 For the Liverpool production, we commissioned new musical settings for this 'ditty' and for the song performed at the banquet. The composer, Keith Orrell, set the words in a dignified mock-Renaissance manner, in a minor key in both cases, and in a harmonic rather than contrapuntal style.
24 Compare the musical setting of the words 'up and down they wandered' in John Farmer's madrigal of secular love, 'Fair Phyllis' (*Madrigals a 4*, 1599), where the four voices appear to 'wander' around in hopeless pursuit of one another.
25 *Companion*, p. 132.
26 See the stage direction preceding 5.1.87: 'Enter Hymen in yellow, Ganymede in a blue robe powdered with stars, and Hebe in a white robe with golden stars'.
27 See Mulryne, p. lxxviii.
28 See *OED* 'performance' 2 and 3.
29 See Judith Butler on gender itself as performance: *Gender Trouble: Identity and the Subversion of Identity* (New York: Routledge, 1999).
30 The stage direction at 3.3.32, referring to the Ward and Sordido observing Isabella, reads: 'They pry at Isabella'. The equivalent in Mulryne (3.4.22) reads: 'They scrutinize her intently'.
31 See, for example, the discussions of courtship through close encounters over a musical instrument in Thomas Whythorne's *Autobiography* (c. 1576), ed. by James M. Osborn (Oxford: Clarendon Press, 1961), pp. 20, 30–31, 77. Whythorne, a poet, composer and music teacher, also describes how his chamber is decorated with 'the figure and image of a young woman playing on the lute' (p. 20). Compare seventeenth-century Dutch paintings of women receiving musical tuition, such as Vermeer's 'The Music Lesson', and studies of women singing or playing musical instruments, such as Jan Miense Molenaer's 'Girl with Recorder' or Pieter de Grebber's mixed 'Music-making Group' (1623) – see Illustration 5.

CHAPER SEVEN

New Directions: *Women Beware Women* and Genre Theory

Edward Gieskes

either for tragedy, comedy, history, pastoral, pastoral-comical, historical-pastoral, tragical-historical, tragical-comical-historical-pastoral, scene individable, or poem unlimited: Seneca cannot be too heavy, nor Plautus too light.

Shakespeare, *Hamlet*

Genre theory has a long and distinguished history, from Aristotle to Bakhtin and beyond, and has taken a wide variety of forms from the descriptive to the analytical and the prescriptive. This discussion will attempt to negotiate between the extremes of description and prescription which have characterized much generic criticism, especially in the Renaissance, as it presents a survey of genre theory. Generic categories have been used in the production, explanation, categorization and evaluation of cultural production, from ancient Greece to the modern bookstore and theatre. In what follows I will be interested in all four of these aspects as they relate to a discussion of Middleton's *Women Beware Women*. Early modern drama is notoriously free with generic mixing and innovation and Middleton, as with so many of his contemporaries, is an inveterate inventor and mixer of forms. Middleton produced plays which have been categorized as tragedy (of various subtypes), history, comedy (also of various subtypes), and tragicomedy – all the major modes of drama in the period.[1] The play at the centre of discussion here, *Women Beware Women*, is a tragedy, of course, but, as with most early modern plays, it is a tragedy whose effect depends on the deployment of generic resources beyond the strictly tragic and as such intervenes in the generic system into which it places itself. If the critical commonplace that Jacobean tragedy is somehow different from Elizabethan has any truth to it, an historical genre theory is the most logical tool to use in order to characterize that change.

Early Modern Genre Theory

But besides these gross absurdities, how all their plays be neither right tragedies, nor right comedies, mingling kings and clowns, not because the matter so carrieth it, but thrust in the clown by head and shoulders to play a part in majestical matters with neither decency nor discretion, so as neither admiration or commiseration, nor the right sportfulness, is by their mongrel tragicomedy obtained [...] So falleth it out that, having indeed no right comedy, in that comical part of our tragedy, we have nothing but scurrility, unworthy of any chaste ears, or some extreme show of doltishness, indeed fit to lift up a loud laughter, and nothing else: where the whole tract of a comedy should be full of delight, as the tragedy should be still maintained in a well-raised admiration.
Sir Philip Sidney, *A Defence of Poesy* (1579)

Gentlemen, so nice is the World, that for apparell there is no fashion, for Musique no Instrument, for Diet no Delicate, for Playes no Inuention but breedeth satietie before noone, and contempt before night. Come to the Taylor, hee is gone to the Painters, to learne how more cunning may lurke in the fashion, then can be expressed in the making. [...] Time hath confounded our mindes, our minds the matter, but all commeth to this passe, that what heretofore hath beene serued in seuerall dishes for a Feast, is now minced in a Charger for a Gallimaufrey. If we present a mingle-mangle, our fault is to be excused, because the whole World is become an Hodge-podge. We are iealous of your iudgements, because you are wise; of our owne performance, because wee are vnperfect; of our Authors deuice, because he is idle. Onely this doth encourage vs, that presenting our studies before Gentlemen, though they receiue an inward mislike, wee shall not be hist with an open disgrace. *Stirps rudis vrtica est: stirps generosa, rosa*.[2]
John Lyly, *Midas* (1592)

WIFE: I have a plot in my head, son – i'faith, husband, to cross you.
SAM: Is it a tragedy plot or a comedy plot, good mother?
WIFE: 'Tis a plot that will vex him.
Thomas Middleton, *A Trick to Catch the Old One* (1605)

I begin with these three discussions of genre and generic mixing as a way of exploring the period's thought about generic categories – a persistent topic for early modern writers. Sam Lucre's question about his mother's plot is a question that is often asked of early modern plays and critics have spent a great deal of intellectual energy in developing solutions to the problem of classification.[3] Her answer to this common question is instructive and will serve as a guiding principle of the discussion that follows. As far as Jenny Lucre is concerned, it does not matter whether the plot is comic or tragic, so long as it produces the desired effect of vexation on its intended audience. Thus, her 'plot' will be composed of whatever generic elements necessary to achieve her desired effect and that effect is the plot's principle of structure rather than the other way around. If the question of whether a play is comedy or tragedy (or tragicomedy or history etc.) is a vexing one, it may be because it is not exactly the right question. We might more usefully begin with the effects of the plot and proceed to a discussion of how various generic elements contribute to those effects. This may not be a surprising approach, but it is one that critics like Rosalie Colie have used to produce major insights about Renaissance literature. In her book, *The Resources of Kind*, Colie argues that 'kind' (a term that she prefers to genre) needs to be thought of as a set of representational tools that can achieve certain responses from readers or auditors.

Sidney's complaint that the improper mingling of kings and clowns in the drama of the 1570s leads to neither right tragedy nor right comedy has less to do with a global condemnation of mixing genres than it does with the improper, indecorous, or gratuitous mixing of forms. The 'mongrel tragicomedy' criticized by Sidney cannot achieve properly tragic 'admiration or commiseration' or comic 'sportfulness' because the play is not judicious in its deployment of distinct generic types. His complaint here is specifically that these mixtures, which are not dictated by the matter of the play, prevent the work from achieving the full effect of either tragedy or comedy. Indeed, it is almost the effects that define the genres – tragedy is to produce 'right' admiration and comedy 'sportfulness' not scurrility or doltishness – rather than some list of specific formal characteristics. This condemnation is sometimes taken to be absolute – particularly as it appears in the context of a broader critique of English drama's failure to observe the unities – but it is important to stress that Sidney's focus here is on the effect such drama has on its audience and his criticism is not of mixing *per se*, but mixing with problematic results. Earlier in the *Defence* he argues that mixing is not a problem if the parts 'be good':

> Now in his parts, kinds, or species (as you list to term them), it is to be noted that some poesies have coupled together two or three kinds, as the tragical and the comical, whereupon is risen the tragicomical. Some, in the manner, have mingled prose and verse, as Sannazaro and Boethius. Some have mingled matters heroical and pastoral. But that cometh all to one in this question, for if severed they be good, the conjunction cannot be hurtful.[4]

The tragicomical here is good because, unlike the works he criticizes later, it mingles good (or right) tragedy and comedy. It is only when the contrary is true that the hybridizing of genres is to be condemned.

The prologue to John Lyly's play takes a somewhat different position with regard to the mixing of genres. Lyly admits that at one time the sundry dishes of comedy, tragedy, and pastoral were served as separate courses at the Ordinary of Literature, but that now all of them are 'minced' together 'for a Gallimaufrey'. Formerly firm distinctions between genres erode and this erosion causes the players to present a 'mingle-mangle' of forms: 'If we present a mingle-mangle, our fault is to be excused, because the whole World is become an Hodge-podge.' Where Sidney complains about the bad effects of careless mixing, Lyly shrugs and attributes it to the mingle-mangle condition of the world, requesting the audience pardon the play as being simply a reflection of the mixed nature of the whole world. Lyly's mingle-mangle is a deliberate one, designed to appeal to his audience at Paul's – the *rosa generosa* of the epigraph.

Both Sidney and Lyly posit the existence of more or less distinct genres that organize the production and reception of dramatic art – even though they both also allow that genres often mix and purity of kind is rarely seen. As these examples demonstrate, generic categorization is a preoccupation of early modern authors. Lyly in particular points out that generic mixing responds to the condition of the world and that the representation on stage mixes kinds in much the same way that the times confound them under the pressure of a demand for the new. It is a critical commonplace that early modern English dramatists invented genres, mixed existing ones, and generally treated more traditional notions of generic decorum with a certain amount of skepticism. Nevertheless, those received categories of classification and expression remained important for them and for later audiences, readers, and critics. In what follows, I will begin with a discussion of some important theorists of genre and I will then turn to Middleton's play to discuss how *Women Beware Women* deploys, parodies and transforms the genres it combines.

Genre Expectation

Aristotle's *Poetics* exerts a powerful influence over genre theory and has often been taken as a prescription for the production of what Sidney might call 'right tragedy'. I do not propose to offer an extended reading of the *Poetics* here, but do wish to point to a few of the most salient features of that text as they structure much later thinking on genre. In particular, the definition of tragedy in Chapter 6 has drawn a great deal of commentary. Aristotle writes:

> Tragedy, then, is a representation of an action that is worth serious attention, complete in itself, and of some amplitude; in language enriched by a variety of artistic devices appropriate to the several parts of the play; presented in the form of action, not narration, by means of pity and fear bringing about the purgation of such emotions.[5]

This passage combines a description of the form of tragedy – representation of a serious action of some significant size in appropriate language – with a definition of the effect this representation is meant to achieve. Other, more learned, commentators have written extensively on what Aristotle means by catharsis; my interest is in indicating that the attention here is to the effect tragedy ought to produce and to point out that successful tragedy is as much marked by this as by any particular element of structure it may possess.[6] Elsewhere in the *Poetics*, Aristotle discusses the history of the form, presenting a developmental narrative about how tragedy developed into the form it had at the time he wrote. He does not, however, propose 'to consider whether or not tragedy is now developed as far as it can be in its various forms, and to decide this absolutely and in relation to the stage'.[7] Aristotle's reservation here demonstrates that his approach to thinking about genre is historical, that he does not suppose that tragedy (or, by extension, any particular genre) has or will reach some final form beyond which there is no further development. The only category of judgement that might remain fixed is the evaluation of what the effect of tragedy is – in his terms, whether it produces and purges the emotions of pity and fear. This historically dynamic and less restrictive notion of genre is picked up by Rosalie Colie in another important work of genre theory.

In her posthumously published collection of lectures, *The Resources of Kind*, Rosalie Colie presents an extended consideration of the usefulness of genre to writers in the Renaissance and makes an argument for the similar usefulness of genre-theory for critics working in the period.[8] The title itself is a clear statement of that argument: for writers of the Renaissance, kind (as she prefers to call genre) was a rich resource of forms that enabled rather than restricted expression. In contrast to what Barbara Lewalski in the introduction calls 'the modern prejudice that genre is some kind of straightjacket', Colie's book points out how essential genre is to communication, whether artistic or otherwise.[9] The prejudice Lewalski alludes to seems to me to have faded somewhat since the publication of Colie's book, partly due to the strength of her argument, but I would argue it still exerts an effect in the way that genre criticism tends more to the descriptive and classificatory than to the analytical. Colie's book begins with a discussion of how rhetorical education encouraged Renaissance writers to think in terms not only of styles but of structures:

> Rhetorical education, always a model-following enterprise, increasingly stressed *structures* as well as styles to be imitated in the humane letters – epistles, orations, discourses, dialogues, histories, poems – always discoverable to the enthusiastic new man of letters by kind.[10]

This stress on structure, she argues, tended towards the development of poetics which became an important Renaissance genre itself. Colie's analysis of these poetics along with the literature of her long Renaissance lead her to a version of genre theory that serves as a means to account for 'connections between topic and treatment within the literary system' as well as a way 'to see the connection of the literary kinds with *kinds* of knowledge and experience'.[11] This is an approach that combines the descriptive and the analytical in productive ways. She wishes to investigate, in her words, 'what the *literary* gain may be, both in having genres and refusing to allow generic categories to dictate or predestine the size, scope, content and manner of any particular literary work'.[12] This disposition – being aware of the usefulness of different genres for expression but sceptical about their determining power – allows for an approach to the question of genre that can account for both tradition and innovation. It is neither purely descriptive nor prescriptive and this makes it an important tool for thinking about plays like *Women Beware Women* which combines a series of older forms into something distinctively new.

Shortly after the publication of Colie's book, Fredric Jameson's seminal essay 'Magical Narratives: Romance as Genre' appeared in *New Literary History*. The essay complements Colie's approach by considering generic innovation as, at least in part, a response to historical change – romance emerges as an imaginative solution to historical contradictions. Jameson points out that:

> Traditional genre theory has been understood as performing the distinct but related functions of furnishing specifications for the production of this or that type of composition, and of providing a typology according to which the various existing compositions may be sorted out by genus and species.[13]

This combination of functions is important to literary history, as Jameson concedes, but leads genre criticism to alternate between the functions of prescribing and sorting, and eventuates in what he describes as an intractable division between a semantic and a syntactic approach to genre. In the semantic approach, Jameson writes that 'the object of inquiry is not the individual work but rather something like the comic vision, which may be seen as a more general or universal attitude towards life or form of being-in-the-world'.[14] This kind of inquiry is interested in the meaning of a genre. The syntactic approach, in contrast, proceeds from:

> a view of comedy as a determinate laughter-producing mechanism with precise laws and requirements of its own, whose realization in the various media of theater or narrative, in film or in daily life, may be the object of analysis and synthetic reconstruction, resulting, not in the expression of a meaning, but rather the building of a model.[15]

Jameson's solution to the intractability of the distinction between these approaches is to attempt to turn the 'dilemma into a solution' through an historical approach to genre. Jameson locates romance in the historical moment of its emergence and in a passage worth quoting at length, describes it as an imaginative response to a specific historical contradiction:

> When, in the twelfth century, this kind of social isolation is overcome and the feudal nobility becomes aware of itself as a universal class, with a newly elaborated and codified ideology, there arises what can only be called a contradiction between the older positional notion of evil and this emergent class solidarity. Romance may then be understood as an imaginary 'solution' to this contradiction, a symbolic answer to the question of how my enemy can be thought of as being evil, that is, as other than myself and marked by some absolute difference, when what is responsible for his being so characterized is simply the identity of his own conduct with mine, which —challenges, points of honor, tests of strength — he reflects as in a mirror image.[16]

Emergent genres can be seen as imaginative responses to historical developments and this view makes an historical approach to genre essential. Early modern dramatic genres respond not only to developments within the theatre, but also to external pressures and the work of thinkers like Jameson is profoundly important in understanding those responses. In the next section of this discussion, I will turn to the work of M. M. Bakhtin and Pierre Bourdieu as they offer ways to account for generic innovations like those of Middleton and his contemporaries.

Bakhtin, Bourdieu and Genre

> The novel as a whole is an utterance just as rejoinders in everyday dialogue or private letters are (they do have a common origin), but unlike these, the novel is a secondary (complex) utterance.
>
> The work, like the rejoinder in dialogue, is oriented towards the

response of the other (others) [...] The work is a link in the chain of speech communion. Like the rejoinder in dialogue, it is related to other work-utterances: both those to which it responds and those that respond to it.
Utterances are not indifferent to one another, and are not self-sufficient; they are aware of and mutually reflect one another [...] each utterance is filled with various kinds of responsive reactions to other utterances of the given sphere of speech communication.
M. M. Bakhtin, 'The Problem of Speech Genres'[17]

Changes as decisive as an upheaval in the internal hierarchy of different genres, or a transformation within genres themselves, affecting the structure of the field as a whole, are made possible by the *correspondence between internal changes* (themselves directly determined by the transformation in the chances of access to the literary field) *and external changes* which offer to new categories of producers (successively, the Romantics, Naturalists, Symbolists, etc.) and to their products consumers who occupy positions in social space which are homologous to heir own position in the field, and hence consumers endowed with dispositions and tastes in harmony with the products these producers offer them.
Pierre Bourdieu, *The Rules of Art*[18]

Despite Bakhtin's alleged hostility to drama, his work offers productive ways to engage with the question of generic change in the dramatic field of the first decades of the seventeenth century.[19] In 'The Problem of Speech Genres', Bakhtin argues that while utterance remains the fundamental category of analysis in the study of language and that each utterance is irreducibly individual, language tend to develop 'relatively stable types' of utterances: 'these we may call *speech genres*'.[20] He goes on to argue that literary works can be understood as utterances engaged, like speech, in dialogue but with other works as interlocutors. In this conception, the work is necessarily oriented towards both its predecessors and its successors in the meta-dialogue of a literary history imagined as dialogue. What this suggests is that individual plays can be usefully conceptualized as interventions in an ongoing debate or conversation about the nature, purpose, capacities and form of drama. In addition, the play-utterance is actively linked to both the play-utterances that come before and those that come after.[21] As an example, Jonson's *Poetaster* explicitly attempts to define the boundaries of good dramatic language by caricaturing and expelling bad dramatic verse while at the same time presenting a play that is a statement about dramatic form. Verbal interaction, here at the level of the work, is thus oriented towards both past and future and each intervention necessarily alters the genre in which it takes form.
Bakhtin also suggests ways to link changes in literary language to concrete social and historical developments. He writes:

Historical changes in language styles are inseparably linked to changes in speech genres. Literary language is a complex, dynamic system of linguistic styles. The proportions and interrelations of these styles are constantly changing [...] In order to puzzle out the complex historical dynamics of these systems and to move from a simple (and, in the majority of cases, superficial) description of styles, which are always in evidence and alternating with one another, to a historical explanation of these changes, one must develop a special history of speech genres [...] that reflects more directly, clearly, and flexibly all the changes taking place in social life. Utterances and their types, that is, speech genres, are the drive belts from the history of society to the history of language.[22]

Bakhtin's metaphor of a drivebelt can be more productively (and less reductively) replaced with the idea of refraction. Genre, in this account, is the primary link between language and society and generic innovation can then be argued to occur as a refraction of social change. If generic change at least partly results from social change, then generic innovation may serve as a marker of social change – but not in any direct or transparent way. Bakhtin also here identifies a central problem of genre theory – the way that discussion of genre has tended to function in a descriptive rather than an analytical or historical register – calling for a 'special history of speech genres' that would move beyond what he criticizes as the 'simple description of styles'.

The final epigraph at the outset of this section comes from Bourdieu's most extended treatment of artistic production – *The Rules of Art* – a book that contributes to the development of a more clear and flexible history of genre. His comments about generic upheaval bear a clear resemblance to Bakhtin's discussion of genre and, like Bakhtin's, offer a productive way to characterize generic change that moves beyond description or catalogue towards a more adequate historicization of generic change. Bourdieu argues that upheavals within genres or in the hierarchy of disparate genres depend on the coincidence of historical developments with aesthetic innovations. I will here be interested in transformations within genres – transformations amounting to the development of new subgenres like the 'tragedy of blood'. For such transformations to be successful, changes internal to the field like the advent of new playwrights with different dispositions and backgrounds must coincide with changes in audience that are dependent on external – social or historical – changes that alter that audience's tastes. Lynda Boose has discussed what she terms the 'sexualization' of the Jacobean stage as a result of the 1599 ban on satire promulgated by the Archbishop of Canterbury and the Bishop of London.[23] The ban legislatively closed the print market for verse satire which, Boose argues, led a group of writers including Middleton and Marston to turn to the stage as a venue for their work. It is tempting to think that as the authors turned to an alternative publication medium so too did their audience. What is striking, nevertheless, is the degree to which satirical railing of the kind that Middleton and Marston write before the ban makes its way into the drama after 1600. Its presence suggests the existence of an audience well-suited to appreciate such productions.

Genre, History, Theory

What we need, in effect, is a form of structural history that is rarely practiced, which finds in each successive state of the structure under examination both the product of previous struggles to maintain or to transform this structure, and the principle, via the contradictions, the tensions, and the relations of force which constitute it, of subsequent transformations.

Pierre Bourdieu, *Invitation to Reflexive Sociology*[24]

Bourdieu often argues for a historicism that attempts to locate elements of diachrony in the synchronic moment of study. Each successive state of a social structure thus must be thought of as containing both traces of the past and indications of possible future trajectories of change. This call for a 'structural history' seems especially appropriate in literary history and I believe will be useful in this essay's examination of genre theory and the drama of Middleton. In the first decades of the seventeenth century, Middleton, like many of his peers, was writing plays that challenged and transformed more or less established boundaries of genre, literally confusing history, tragedy and comedy in plays like *The Revenger's Tragedy* and *Hengist, King of Kent*. Any effort to investigate genre and generic change must also look to the materials this process of combination transforms. Thus, this effort at establishing a structural history of genre will necessarily be a kind of source study, but one that focuses on technique and narrative form rather than specific textual or plot echoes.

Source study has a long history in English studies and has recently begun to be reconsidered by such scholars as Douglas Bruster, among others. Bullough's invaluable *Narrative and Dramatic Sources of Shakespeare* might serve as an exemplar of the field. It focuses on sources of event, of character, of language, and of plot, more than on technique or of form. It allows scholars to perceive how Shakespeare worked with the given materials of his cultural milieu and to determine the kinds of transformation effected as, say, prose romance moved to the stage. However, it seems that this model tends to emphasize the content of the source over the form of the source and perhaps overlooks sources of techniques by virtue of this emphasis. In his *Shakespeare and the Question of Culture*, Douglas Bruster suggests that source study 'is a formalism [...] not only through its interest in the parts that make up a textual whole, but also through its sensitivity to the histories of those parts'.[25] He goes on to describe 'the new formalism' which in turn has what he calls a 'sub-genre' concerned with sources. Robert Miola describes source study as moving between the traditional notion of a source being 'an imitated text that manifests its presence in verbal or stylistic echo or adaptation' that is, despite its power and usefulness, limited 'by a tendency to rely almost exclusively on verbal iteration as proof of influence' and a notion of source as 'an intermediated text (i.e. tradition) that manifests its presence in verbal or stylistic echo or adaptation', a notion that is itself limited by a tendency to 'succumb to a vague impressionism that timorously avoids committing itself to any single text as source'.[26] Miola advocates a synthetic, eclectic approach that uses both notions strategically. This chapter will attempt to do the same, but with narrative structure as the source rather than a myth (as in Miola's article) or other element of a text's literary background.

These changes need to be located in their historical contexts, as well as their literary-historical context, and I hope that it will suffice here to say that the kinds of appropriations and transformations under discussion in this chapter will necessarily be linked to changes both within and without the literary field. As

Bakhtin reminds us, 'utterance and their types, that is, speech genres, are the drive belts from the history of society to the history of language', and while I might qualify the directness of the link Bakhtin imagines here, literary change necessarily relates to broader social changes and a fuller understanding (insofar as such things are possible) of generic changes – and literary influence must include a consideration of historical developments that get refracted into literary work.[27]

Bakhtin's late essay on 'The Problem of Speech Genres' offers another tool for this study – the idea that genre and generic change arise out of a literary metadialogue wherein influence operates at the level of the word, at the level of structure, and between whole works. Bakhtin's conception of literary works as part of an enormous dialogue of utterance and rejoinder suggests alternative ways to conceptualize relations between works and between writers. Works are inevitably oriented towards other works (not to mention audiences) and that orientation, like that of the rejoinder in spoken dialogue, comprehends in various ways the utterance to which it is responding. As Bakhtin writes:

> Utterances are not indifferent to one another, and are not self-sufficient; they are aware of and mutually reflect one another [...] each utterance is filled with various kinds of responsive reactions to other utterances of the given sphere of speech communication.[28]

This mutual awareness and reflection operates at both the level of the individual word (the domain of the 'iteration' version of source study) and of the whole work (in terms of both style and content). This reflection operates across generic boundaries as much as within them. I would substitute or emend 'reflection' to 'refraction' in order to better characterize the transformation of style or form across generic boundaries. A play like *Women Beware Women* draws on a wide variety of forms, especially comic forms, transforming them in the process in ways that affect both Middleton's tragedy and comedy more generally.

Many early modern comic and tragic plays are set in distinct social and physical locations – comedy tending to either country or urban settings while tragedy tends to be set at court. This, of course, has much to do with the social classes normally associated with the two genres.[29] The association between setting and genre is close in genre theory. M. M. Bakhtin uses the term chronotope in the essay 'Forms of Time and the Chronotope in the Novel: Notes Towards a Historical Poetics', to describe the specific form that time and space take in particular works of literature.[30] He writes that the chronotope refers to the 'intrinsic connectedness of temporal and spatial relationships that are artistically expressed in literature'.[31] There are, in this view, ways of representing space and time that are particular to particular forms – the example of 'adventure time' in Greek romance is widely commented on. 'Adventure time' is a chronotope in which space and time function only as a background for the characters' adventures, exerting no particular influence over those adventures or the characters. Chronotopes necessarily stand in close relation to genres. If a speech genre (or literary genre) is the characteristic mode of speech of some specific sphere of communication, then chronotopes could be said to be the modes of representing time and space characteristic of those spheres.[32] In much the same way that genres bring with them more stable expectations, so too do chronotopes. These expectations are part of the resources of kind that Rosalie Colie discusses in her work, and in the next section I will discuss how Middleton draws on the resources of tragedy, history and comedy to produce the complex effects *Women Beware Women* achieves.

Middleton and *Women Beware Women*

> *Women beware Women*: 'tis a true text
> Never to be forgot. Drabs of state vexed
> Have plots, poisons, mischiefs that seldom miss
> To murder virtue with a venom kiss.
> Witness this worthy tragedy, expressed
> By him that well deserved among the best
> Of poets in his time. He knew the rage,
> Madness of women crossed; and for the stage
> Fitted their humours, hell-bred malice, strife
> Acted in state, presented to the life.
> I that have seen't can say, having just cause,
> Never came tragedy off with more applause.
>   Nathanael Richards, dedicatory poem to the
>   1657 Quarto[33]

Nathaniel Richards's poem, titled 'Upon the Tragedy of My Familiar Acquaintance, Thomas Middleton', locates Middleton's play in a series of contexts of evaluation. First, it indicates the veracity of the 'text' of the title read as an aphorism. Then Richards calls the play a 'worthy tragedy, expressed / By him that well deserved among the best of poets in his time' (5–6), offering both a judgement of the play and an endorsement of the author as highly ranked among his fellow poets. Finally, Richards informs the reader that 'never came tragedy off with more applause' (12), claiming the sanction of audience approval for the play. All three of these evaluative contexts depend on a sense of the play's effect on an audience – the truth of the text lies in the accuracy of the warning, the worthiness of the tragedy in the rank of the poet and the accuracy of the representation, and the success of the play, marked by applause, necessarily depends on the audience. The poem also attests to Middleton's awareness of the 'rage, / Madness of women crossed' and his ability to properly represent them on stage. By this description, Middleton's play might appear to fit nicely into the Aristotelian description of the tragic – representing action of some amplitude, with proper language and spectacle, and inducing knowledge in the audience, witnessed by their applause. However, the play does contain elements of other genres, like city comedy, and because of this it has been seen by later readers as being problematic in terms of form and effect.[34]

In his 1955 book *Middleton's Tragedies: A Critical Study*, Samuel Schoenbaum discusses *Women Beware Women* and *The Changeling* together, describing them both as 'impressive' and 'in their own ways, even masterpieces. Yet for masterpieces they are curiously imperfect and uneven.'[35] This unevenness he attributes to several causes: that he loses interest in the plays, that he becomes exhausted, or that he 'was finding it increasingly difficult – possibly even distasteful – to try to reconcile the sensational melodrama of his age with the psychological drama toward which he aspired'.[36] Schoenbaum attributes some of the so-called unevenness of the play to a conflict between the playwright's desire to write one kind of play and the audience's desire for another – this is a conflict of the type that Bourdieu discusses as productive of generic upheavals and, without speculating on Middleton's possible 'distaste' for melodrama (a distaste I am not convinced he had), this idea provides a useful way to begin a closer examination of the play.

Women Beware Women dates to 1621, a year in which Middleton had collaborated with Shakespeare on *Measure for Measure*, a year in which Massinger's revision and retelling of his play *Trick to Catch the Old One* had appeared under the title *New Way to Pay Old Debts*, and he was at work on his city comedy *Anything for a Quiet Life*. Middleton also was the playwright for the Lord Mayor's Show that year. The range of his work in just this one year demonstrates that he was experimenting with city comedy, tragicomedy, and other forms. It is clear that this experimentation extends to the formal structure of *Women Beware Women*, which draws on historical materials for its plotline, but transforms that material by presenting it through a series of shifting genres that move from comic to tragic.

As Schoenbaum and many other commentators note, Middleton draws on an Italian source for the main plot of the play: the history of Bianca Capello (1548–87), whose life served as a structural model for the Bianca of the play. Unlike Middleton's Bianca, the historical Bianca does not die on her wedding day, but lives for almost ten years as the wife of the Grandduke Francesco de'Medici before succumbing to either malaria or poison on the same day as her husband.[37] Many of the details of the play's plot echo this historical narrative – from the secret wedding between Bianca and Leantio to the efforts to placate Leantio with offices. My interest here is in how the play transforms history into fiction by deploying the resources of multiple genres. The revisions of the historical plot depend in some degree on form and on dramatic economy – the historical story spans many years and ends inconclusively, where Middleton's plot comes to a rapid and spectacular end. The play begins in the conventional territory of city comedy with the first characters we see being part of the merchant class, but is inflected by motifs characteristic of other genres. I intend to argue that the play takes what are fundamentally comic materials and, by moving them into what might be considered the social and literary territory of tragedy, produces a play that mixes these forms to produce what Sidney might have considered a 'right' play. I do not purpose to offer a comprehensive reading of the play; my goal is to demonstrate the usefulness of genre theory for developing an understanding of how the play works.

Leantio enters with his mother and Bianca in 1.1 and introduces her as his wife. For him, the marriage is a heroic act, his 'masterpiece', while at the same time in need of concealment because her rich parents are against the marriage. He tells her:

> You must keep counsel, mother, I am undone else;
> If it be known, I have lost her. Do but think now

What that loss is; life's but a trifle to't.
From Venice her consent and I have brought her,
From parents great in wealth, more now in rage;
But let storms spend their furies now we have got
A shelter o'er our quiet innocent loves.
We are contented. Little money sh'as brought me.
View but her face, you may see all her dowry,
Save that which lies locked up in hidden virtues
Like jewels kept in cabinets (1.1.47–56).

Leantio presents the marriage as a love-match. It is her consent that brings her from Venice, and the parents' rage at the marriage will, in his view, expend itself while they enjoy their quiet loves. He attributes more value to her face and virtue than any dowry and that will content both of them. The language of possession and wealth pervades his speech throughout this first scene and Middleton appears to be linking this vocabulary with his social position. This linkage is made more explicit in his scene-ending soliloquy in which he decides to keep Bianca obscure:

[...] 'tis great policy
To keep choice treasures in obscurest places:
Should we show thieves our wealth, 'twould make 'em bolder.
Temptation is a devil will not stick
To fasten upon a saint; take heed of that.
The jewel is cased up from all men's eyes (1.2.165–70).

This plan to keep her hidden from sight has comic antecedents, not least being Corvino in Jonson's *Volpone,* whose efforts to hide Celia only result in the predations of Volpone and his own punishment as a fool. Leantio and his Mother seem clearly to belong to the world of city comedy and, at least at the beginning of the play, so does Bianca.

The Duke and his family, however, are more closely associated with a court of the type seen in *The Revenger's Tragedy* if, perhaps, a less universally pathological one. From the incestuous desire of Hippolito to the lust of the Duke, Middleton links the Florentine court to the tragic. Hippolito's words at the end of 1.2 after avowing his incestuous love for her to his niece Isabella, point to this in no uncertain terms: 'The worst can be but death, and let it come. / He that lives joyless, ev'ry day's his doom' (1.2.231–32). The satisfaction of his desire can only be tragic, despite the role of the clownish Ward and the weird intervention of Livia, his sister. The play brings these populations together at court in the second and later acts and this movement is one of the elements that constitute it as tragedy.

Probably the best-known and most discussed example of this movement is the chess-playing seduction/rape scene in Act 2. The Duke, after seeing Bianca at her window, is consumed with desire for her. This moment has a comic antecedent in Volpone's sighting of Celia from the street and produces the same effect of lust in him. But, whereas in *Volpone* adultery is avoided but lust is punished, *Women Beware Women* does not avoid the adultery. Moreover, lust *is* punished in the end, and it is punished in a tragic mode. The sighting in the street here brings Bianca into the ambit of tragedy. After the Duke seduces (or rapes) her, she says:

> Now bless me from a blasting! I saw that now
> Fearful for any woman's eye to look on.
> Infectious mists and mildews hang at's eyes.
> The weather of a doomsday dwells upon him.
> Yet since mine honour's leprous, why should I
> Preserve that fair that caused the leprosy?
> Come, poison all at once! (2.2.419–24)

Bianca shifts from the language of domestic happiness she uses in the first act with Leantio and into the tragic register of disease and doomsday here. The Duke, far from being the goodly gentleman the Mother labels him in 1.3, is here surrounded by a cloud of corruption. In the aftermath of this, Bianca's character shifts, she becomes discontented with the 'shelter o'er [her] quiet innocent loves' (1.1.153) and is cold to the husband she was reluctant to be parted from for even an hour in the first act.

Leantio's character and fate is likewise shaped by his movement from the comic world of the merchants to the tragic world of the court. When Livia falls in love with him, he accedes to her advances as a means of revenge on Bianca and as a means of social advancement. He banters with Bianca about their 'advancement' in 4.1 and he leaves her with a warning that his revenge will come to her 'at such an hour when thou least seest of all. / So to an ignorance darker than thy womb / I leave thy perjured soul. A plague will come' (4.1.103–5). His adoption of the language of revenge signals his absorption into the tragic plotline of the play and his brief career as a courtier ends when Hippolito kills him in 4.2. Hippolito challenges him in the name of his sister Livia's honour and Leantio recognizes that had he remained a poor factor he would have been safe from such attacks:

> How close sticks envy to man's happiness!
> When I was poor, and cared little for life,
> I had no such means offered me to die;
> No man's wrath minded me (4.2.32–35)

Had he remained where he was, in other words, he would not have been exposed to a world in which such dangers are normal (and that he is ill-equipped for). He is the first direct casualty of the tragic aspect of the play and his fate has much to do with his movement away from the social and generic world of comedy. Moreover, his death precipitates the series of killings in the final scene of the play – the multiple revenge plots all derive directly or indirectly from Livia's response to Leantio's death.

My suggestion here is that the change in Bianca's character and Leantio's fate, while both are plausible for reasons deriving from the plot, are also supported by the movement from the territory of comedy, from trade and domesticity, to the world of the court, often the territory of tragedy. Middleton deploys the resources of different genres as the play moves to its tragic dénouement, using the effects made possible by the contrast between the comic elements of the first act and the developing tragedy of the rest of the play to create and intensify the sense of imminent catastrophe, part of which depends on the audience's sense that characters like Leantio are doomed in the tragic world into which they enter when they move to the court.

Genre theory and an awareness of the historical resources of kind available to Middleton allow for readings of the play that can account for some of the apparent 'problems of the play'. Samuel Schoenbaum, to return to the critic with whom I began this section of the discussion, suggests that the play at its most brilliant is 'not too far removed from the spirit of comedy'.[38] He goes on to point out that the settings of the play are closer to those of city comedy and that the play develops a 'blurring of the distinction between tragedy and comedy'.[39] On the basis of this blurring, Schoenbaum argues that 'In *Women Beware Women* Middleton appears to have been on the verge of creating a novel kind of drama – a drama that occupies a middle ground between comedy and tragedy.'[40] Recognizing this new kind of drama requires the tools of genre theory and so too does analysing the social, literary and historical forces that support and drive such generic innovation. It is beyond the purview of this discussion to develop a full account of those changes, but one could speculate that what Schoenbaum represents as the 'lowering' of tragedy from the palaces of the nobility to the houses of the gentry may be what Jameson calls an imaginative solution to a social contradiction whose outlines might be suggested by the resources of an historical genre theory.

Notes

1   For tragedy, see *The Revenger's Tragedy* and *Women Beware Women*, for history see *Hengist, King of Kent*, for comedy see *The Roaring Girl*, and for tragicomedy see *The Old Law*. Only Shakespeare was comparably successful in these major genres. Middleton also wrote civic pageants as well as prose work in various modes. See Gary Taylor, 'Thomas Middleton: Lives and Afterlives', in *Thomas Middleton: The Collected Works* (Oxford: Oxford University Press, 2008), pp. 25–58, for an extended discussion of Middleton's life and the diversity of his work.
2   'The nettle is of rude stock; the rose, of noble stock.' This probably refers to the audience in Paul's in 1590 who are being flattered here as being more gentle than the audiences of the amphitheatres.
3   City comedy alone has been the subject of many books since at least L. C. Knights's work on Jonson in *Drama and Society in the Age of Jonson* (London: Chatto and Windus, 1937).
4   Sir Philip Sidney, *A Defence of Poetry*, ed. by J. A. Van Dorsten (Oxford: Oxford University Press, 1996), p. 43.
5   Aristotle, *The Poetics*, in *Classical Literary Criticism*, trans. by T. S. Dorsch (London: Penguin Books, 1965), pp. 38–39
6   For more developed commentary on the *Poetics*, see Gerard Else's work including *Aristotle's 'Poetics': The Argument* (Cambridge, MA: Harvard University Press, 1957).
7   Aristotle, *Poetics*, p. 36
8   She uses Renaissance to designate a period that starts with Petrarch and ends with Swift. This is a deliberately broad designation of period that encompasses multiple language traditions. Her contention is that any approach to questions about genre must be comparative.
9   Rosalie Colie, *The Resources of Kind: Genre Theory in the Renaissance*, ed. Barbara Lewalski (Berkeley: University of California Press, 1973), p. vii. In this, her position is

akin to Bakhtin's in the speech genres essay (see below note 17) which holds that all expression depends on some notion of kind without which meaning would be difficult to produce.
10 Colie, *Resources of Kind*, p. 4.
11 Colie, *Resources of Kind*, p. 29.
12 Colie, *Resources of Kind*, p. 103.
13 Fredric Jameson, 'Magical narratives: Romance as genre', *New Literary History*, 7.2 (1975), 135–63 (p. 136).
14 Jameson, 'Magical narratives', p. 136.
15 Jameson, 'Magical narratives', p. 137.
16 Jameson, 'Magical narratives', p. 161.
17 In M. M. Bakhtin, *Speech Genres and Other Late Essays* (Austin: University of Texas Press, 1986).
18 Pierre Bourdieu, *The Rules of Art* (Palo Alto: Stanford University Press, 1996)
19 This hostility has always been more putative than actual and pretty clearly does not apply to the plays of early modern playwrights like Middleton or Shakespeare. In *The Dialogic Imagination*, when Bakhtin suggests that drama is inherently monological, he seems to be referring specifically to plays of the nineteenth century. Shakespeare figures in Bakhtin as fundamentally dialogic and heteroglot. See James R. Siemon's *Word Against Word: Shakespearean utterance* (Amherst: University of Massachusetts Press, c.2002) for a discussion of Bakhtin and early modern drama.
20 Bakhtin, *Speech Genres*, p. 60.
21 *Troilus and Cressida*'s armed prologue responds to the armed prologue of Jonson's play, for example.
22 Bakhtin, *Speech Genres*, p. 65.
23 Lynda Boose, 'The 1599 Bishop's Ban, Elizabethan Pornography, and the Sexualization of the Jacobean Stage', in *Enclosure Acts*, ed. by Richard Burt and John Michael Archer (Ithaca: Cornell University Press, 1994), pp. 185–200.
24 Pierre Bourdieu, *Invitation to Reflexive Sociology*, trans. L. J. D. Wacquandt (Cambridge: Polity, 1992), p. 91.
25 Douglas Bruster, *Shakespeare and the Question of Culture* (New York: Palgrave, 2003), p. 168.
26 Robert S. Miola, 'Othello *Furens*', *Shakespeare Quarterly*, 41 (1990), 49–64 (p. 49).
27 Bakhtin, *Speech Genres*, p. 65.
28 Bakhtin, *Speech Genres*, p. 76.
29 Aristotle writes that comedy concerns people of the middling or lower sorts while tragedy concerns the better sort. These social distinctions are picked up by Renaissance thinkers like Sidney.
30 M. M. Bakhtin, 'Forms of time and the chronotope in the novel: Notes towards a historical poetics' in *The Dialogical Imagination: Four Essays* (Austin: University of Texas Press, 1981).
31 Bakhtin, 'Chronotope', p. 84.
32 Bakhtin refers to spheres of communication in relation to speech genres in 'The Problem of Speech Genres'. I am using his language here as the most appropriate to this discussion.
33 I cite the dedicatory poem from the 1657 edition (I have modernized the spelling).
34 For discussions of city comedy as a form see L. C. Knights, *Drama and Society in the Age of Jonson* (London: Chatto and Windus, 1937), Brian Gibbons, *Jacobean City Comedy* (London: Methuen, 1980) and Theodore Leinwand, *The city staged : Jacobean comedy, 1603-1613* (Madison: University of Wisconsin Press, 1986). City comedy is closely associated with the first decades of the seventeenth century and with playwrights like Ben Jonson, Thomas Dekker, and Middleton. Jonson's *Volpone* and *The Alchemist* along with Middleton and Dekker's *Roaring Girl* might serve as exemplars.
35 Samuel Schoenbaum, *Middleton's Tragedies: A Critical Study* (New York: Columbia University Press, 1955), p. 102.
36 Schoenbaum, *Middleton's Tragedies*, p. 103. Schoenbaum also asserts that the 'most brilliant episodes in *Women Beware Women* reflect a mood not too far removed from

the spirit of comedy' (p. 103). This seems like a persuasive characterization of part of the generic resources from which the play draws. One of the primary non-tragic genres that Middleton deploys here is city comedy, a form to whose development he was an important contributor.
37 Schoenbaum's discussion of the Bianca Capello story asserts that the tale was well-known, but that Middleton likely drew on Celio Malespini's version of 1609. See Schoenbaum, *Middleton's Tragedies*, pp. 104–9.
38 Schoenbaum, *Middleton's Tragedies*, p. 103.
39 Schoenbaum, *Middleton's Tragedies*, pp. 128–29.
40 Schoenbaum, *Middleton's Tragedies*, p. 130.

CHAPTER EIGHT

New Directions: 'Two kings on one throne':
Lust, Love, and Marriage in *Women Beware
Women*

Coppélia Kahn

In the last moments of *Women Beware Women*, Bianca drinks the same poison that her lover the Duke has fatally drunk by mistake. Her dying word is 'love'. The Cardinal then brings the tragedy to a close in four ringing lines:

> Sin, what thou art, these ruins show too piteously.
> Two kings on one throne cannot sit together,
> But one must needs down, for his title's wrong;
> So where lust reigns, that prince cannot reign long. (5.1.263–66)[1]

The Cardinal's moralizing summary responds to Bianca's last word: the audience hears 'love', then 'sin'. The 'two kings' to which he refers are 'lust' and the Duke now lying dead onstage: a ruler who is ruled by lust, says the Cardinal, 'cannot reign long'. What Bianca calls love is to the Cardinal, lust – sinful love. Bianca and the Cardinal have been enemies ever since he denounced the Duke's liaison with her as 'a strumpet's love' (4.1.195, 245) that would bring him eternal damnation. At that earlier moment, their union, which the Duke celebrated and blatantly displayed in the face of Bianca's husband Leantio, is clearly illicit and Bianca a plainly adulterous wife. The Duke, however, makes an honest woman of her two scenes later when (after having her husband murdered), he marries her. It is easy to dismiss the marriage as merely a cynical nod to convention, and to condemn it – founded on murder as it is – as a gross perversion of religion and morality that puts a greater value on marriage than on human life. But it is also an interesting marriage, in that it assays to convert 'lust' to 'love' and 'sin' to virtue' according to the definition of wedlock promulgated by the Church of England – albeit by doing away with Bianca's inconvenient husband.

In dramatizing three compromised marriages – those of Bianca and Leantio, Isabella and the Ward, and Bianca and the Duke – Middleton tackles yet again a cluster of contradictions attending marriage, love, lust, and female sexuality that he treats in several other plays.[2] Constructions of male and female, whore and wife, husband and cuckold are built into the idea of companionate marriage advocated in the stream of sermons and domestic conduct manuals flowing from English presses during Middleton's career. Critics have tended to focus on Middleton's treatment of Bianca's transformation from wife to courtesan, but I find his treatment of Leantio's transformation from husband to wittol equally compelling, because Leantio's anxieties about his bride echo the anxieties of the sermons and manuals. Their spoiled marriage counterpoints that of the Ward and Isabella. Both marriages begin with the full consent of the parties involved, and end as mere shams, travesties of the consensual union on which companionate marriage is supposed to be based. Both couplings dramatize the problematics of an institution understood to join man and woman as 'one flesh', but which instead serves as the troubled and contested dividing line between lust and love, two princes that cannot reign together in the state of marriage.

'One Flesh' and the Institution of Marriage

In the sixteenth and seventeenth centuries, both Puritan and Anglican preachers read Genesis to mean that the creation of woman was synonymous with the invention of marriage.[3] For example, in his popular treatise *Of Domesticall Duties* (1627), William Gouge identifies Adam and Eve as the first husband and wife because God makes Eve to supply that 'help meet for him' that Adam wants. Both woman and marriage are already enfolded within the idea that woman is subordinate to man, which is reaffirmed and given an additional rationale in the punishments God decrees for Adam and Eve after the Fall. To Eve, he declares that she will suffer pain in childbirth, that her desire will 'yet' be for her husband, and that he will rule over her (Gen. 3.16), which implies that her subordination to Adam in marriage is associated with her sexuality. As Gouge says, 'she who first drew man into sin should now be subject to him, lest by the like weakness she fall again'.[4] Repeatedly, Gouge and others insist that 'the husband is the head of the woman, as Christ is the head of the Church'.[5]

They also elaborate, however, a new conception of marriage that stresses, in addition to the traditional reasons for it – avoiding mere lust or fornication and procreation – a third reason: mutual affection. Though the medieval church had attempted to confine sexuality within monogamy, in the wake of the Reformation, the more fully articulated idea of companionate marriage, married love that comprises sexual pleasure, emotional intimacy and mutual affection, put marriage under strain. For one thing, insofar as companionate marriage depends on the mutual consent of the partners, it implies that women, like men, are agents of choice, and thus contends uneasily with the basic doctrine of wifely subordination.[6] Furthermore, as it now becomes important for men to love their wives and to enjoy sexual pleasure with them, 'whoredom' – the pleasure associated with sex outside marriage – becomes an internal threat as much as an external one. Paul's dictum that man and wife should be 'one flesh' – as God tells Adam in Genesis 2.24 – begins to seem truly a matter of the flesh, specifically enmeshed with profound mistrust of, if not outright disgust at, woman's sexuality.

For example, in his *Christen State of Matrimony* (1575), Heinrich Bullinger assures readers that 'the work of matrimony is no sin', but goes on to caution them:

> Therefore must not we as shameless persons cast away good manners and become like unreasonable beastes. God hath given and ordained marriage to be a remedy and medicine unto our feeble and weake flesh. [...] But if we rage therewith, and be shameless in our words and deeds, then our mistemperance and excess make it evil that is good, and defile it that is clean.[7]

This passage exemplifies what Stephen Greenblatt calls 'the colonial power of Christian doctrine over sexuality'; in this instance, its power to endorse sexual pleasure within marriage by constructing that pleasure in terms of a binary opposition between sex that is 'good' and 'clean' and sex that is, in the term most often used, 'whoredom', or as Bullinger says, 'unreasonable', bestial, evil 'mistemperance'.[8]

In *A Godlie Forme of Household Government* (1598), the first comprehensive manual of domestic conduct written in English, John Dod and Robert Cleaver provide two lists of the four gender-specific 'duties' that husbands owe to wives and *vice* versa.[9] For the husband, 'to love his wife as his owne fleshe' comes first, taking priority over 'to govern her' and 'to dwell with her' (145). For the wife, the first three duties all concern obedience to her husband: she must 'submit and subject herself' to him, 'be an helpe unto him', and 'obey his commandments in all things' (146). For both husband and wife, the fourth duty is rendering 'due' or 'mutual benevolence' to their spouses, a Pauline euphemism for sex in marriage (see 1 Cor. 7.3). The operative word, Dod and Cleaver repeatedly imply, is 'due'. As Paul says in 1 Cor. 7.4, husband and wife *owe* each other the pleasures of the body: when they voluntarily and mutually consent to be married to each other, they promise that 'the Wife hath not the power of her owne body, but the Husband: and likewise also' (145): 'they are in each other's power, as touching the body', the authors solemnly repeat (189). This mutual sexual indebtedness, this subordination to each other's desires, divinely decreed, resonates strongly with the idea that they are 'one flesh', a phrase repeated four times within five pages (145, 147, 149, 150).

Echoing Bullinger, the authors declare that the contract of marriage 'serveth as a strong bridle, to pull backe the force and headinesse of Carnall, Naturall, and brutish lust' (164). Yet a hazard remains:

> True it is, that the honour of marriage, grounded upon God's ordinance, doth cover the shame of incontinencie; yet not so, as that married folks should defile and pollute that holy estate [...] but that they should so use it, as there might be no excesse in dissolutenesse [...] to abuse it in lascivious excess is Fornication. (209)

Going farther than Dod and Cleaver, in his *Bride-bush: or, a direction for married persons* (1617), William Whately names the 'two principall duties' of marriage as chastity and due benevolence, giving sexual pleasure priority over the 'less principall duties' of mutual love and the husband's command of the wife's obedience. In other words, he separates sex from love and puts sex first.

'Was not marriage intended to prevent whoredome?' he asks. It is clear that the pleasures of the marriage bed are the means of such prevention, but yet

> the married must not provoke desires for pleasure's sake, but allay desires [...] Excessiveness inflameth lust [...] The married must no oftener come together, than for the extinguishing of this passion in grated in the body [...] To incite themselves by mutual dalliance for pleasure's sake, and to awake the sleeping passions [...] this is a fault, even betwixt yoke-fellows.[10]

For Whately and for Dod and Cleaver, sex belongs within marriage, marriage transforms lust into legitimate pleasure, and sex outside marriage is mere whoredom. Yet sex also threatens to become a sort of whoredom within marriage. Nonetheless, it is through the sexual pleasures of marriage that the mystery of man and wife as 'one flesh', decreed by God when he created woman for man, is enacted, and sexual pleasure is integral to companionate marriage.

Leantio: 'Then what's marriage good for?'

Middleton altered his source for the story of Bianca and Leantio, two novellas by Celio Malespini in his *Ducento Novelle* of 1609, relegating their romance and elopement to the past, so that the play opens with the couple unsteadily beginning married life, Bianca a stranger in Florence, Leantio an anxiously vigilant husband, their new household pinched and meagre. In the scenes leading up to and away from Bianca's fateful encounter with the Duke, the playwright renders Leantio's state of mind with extraordinary attention and insight, giving him no fewer than five soliloquies, and a sequence of asides in 3.2 that amounts to a soliloquy. Bianca, in contrast, does not find her own voice until after the Duke rapes her, in a soliloquy at the very end of the scene (2.2), and thereafter, is limited to one soliloquy (4.1.23–40), though we hear much from her in dialogue. It is Leantio who registers the hazards of marriage as the Church conceived it and as ordinary middle-class men such as he tried to practise it. As J. R. Mulryne notes, Leantio lives 'in the world of merchant-class and lower-nobility manners' and 'suffers from a kind of inhibiting religiosity'.[11] He isn't free, even as a married man, simply to take his pleasure; he must justify it as morally good, the opposite of lust.

Beginning with the opening scene, Middleton puts a spotlight on this husband's anxiety about keeping the wife whom he first calls a 'purchase' (1.1.12) and then admits to be a 'theft' (1.1.37), alluding to their elopement. However he obtained her, though, the important point for him is that *he* possesses her:

> As often as I look upon that treasure
> And know it to be mine – there lies the blessing –
> It joys me that I ever was ordained
> To have a being, and to live 'mongst men [...] (1.1.14–17)
>
> And here's my masterpiece: do you now behold her!
> Look on her well, she's mine, look on her better – [...] (1.1.41–42)

The barely suppressed anxiety behind these declarations of possession is that other men will covet such a beautiful woman – indeed, she is a 'masterpiece' – and perhaps steal her. This fear emerges full-blown in the soliloquy that concludes the first scene:

> But 'tis great policy
> To keep choice treasures in obscurest places.
> Should we show thieves our wealth, 'twould make 'em bolder [...]
> The jewel is cased up from all men's eyes.
> Who could imagine now a gem were kept
> Of that great value under this plain roof? (1.1.165–67, 170–72)

And so Leantio inaugurates the containment policy that will backfire when the Duke sees Bianca – and she, him – in the annual procession that establishes his power and authority in Florence. The contrast of concealment and display establishes the vast difference in rank between a factor and a duke, and the difference in styles of masculinity between commons and nobility.[12] A poor man keeps his wife at home; a man of rank displays her.

Leantio worries not only about keeping Bianca hidden away from the sight of other men, but equally about the internal threat of his passion for her. The alliteration of his lines 'But beauty able to content a conqueror / Whom earth could scarce content keeps me in compass' (1.1.26–27) and the repetition of 'content' stresses his need to contain within himself the desire that is already contained by marriage. This containment is also linked to the exigencies of his poverty and low social status, elegantly conveyed in the contrast between 'business' as sexual pleasure and as the rigid demands of time and attention that his work as factor enforces:[13]

> Though my own care and my rich master's trust
> Lay their commands both on my factorship,
> This day and night I'll know no other business
> But her and her dear welcome [...]
> That pleasure should be so restrained and curbed,
> After the course of a rich workmaster
> That never pays till Saturday night. (1.1.151–54, 157–59)

In the scene of leave-taking between Leantio and Bianca, her entreaties that he stay at home with her exacerbate the conflict between business and pleasure. ''Tis e'en a second hell,' he moans, 'to part from pleasure / When man has got a smack on't' (1.3.5–6). 'Farewell, all business,' he cries, 'I desire no more / Than I see yonder' (1.3.16–17). What he sees 'yonder' is what the Duke will also see: the lovely Bianca framed by the window out of which she gazes. To Leantio, the sight of Bianca is a temptation he must resist in order to maintain her in the plain style with which she seems to be satisfied. To the Duke, the sight of Bianca is an invitation to exercise something like *droit de seigneur*, and seize his pleasure. Thus Middleton dramatizes the imbrication of class with gender, gender with class, in the constraints that mould this marriage.

After the Duke rapes Bianca, the unknowing husband returns home to claim his Saturday-night pleasures, in 3.1.[14] Now Middleton restates and knits tightly

NEW DIRECTIONS: LUST, LOVE AND MARRIAGE 161

together the concerns that Leantio voiced in the first scene, all of them associated with the house as it represents his marriage and what he as a householder must control and contain within it.[15] The scene opens before his arrival with Bianca's complaints to Mother about the defects of 'your old house here', and her demands for 'A silver and gilt casting-bottle', 'a green silk quilt', etc. (3.1.41, 21, 27). Now that Bianca has escaped concealment, she no longer echoes her husband's ideal of marital 'content'; she has a mind of her own. Thus Leantio's smug satisfaction in 'the concealed comforts of a man / Locked up in woman's love' as he approaches home are poignantly ironic (3.1.85–86). Now his imagery is more elaborate, and more revealing, than in the first scene. He pictures his marriage as a house that serves to purify a desire that would otherwise be whorish:

> I scent the air
> Of blessings when I come but near the house.
> What a delicious breath marriage sends forth!
> The violet bed's not sweeter. Honest wedlock
> Is like a banqueting-house built in a garden
> On which the spring's chaste flowers take delight
> To cast their modest odours; when base lust
> With all her powders, paintings, and best pride
> Is but a fair house built by a ditch side. (3.1.86–94)

Banqueting houses were the prerogative of rich nobility, lavish structures removed from common sight and devoted to feasting on culinary fancies quickly consumed.[16] At the probable time of the play's composition c. 1621, they would have been associated with the financial and sexual excesses of the Jacobean court, so it is striking that the lowly Leantio associates his humble, constrained pleasures with aristocratic excess. At the same time, he makes those pleasures seem almost virginal, likening them to the 'modest odours' of 'the spring's chaste flowers'. In this cluster of images, Middleton captures two interlocking impulses in the young husband. Leantio wants to secure his possession of Bianca from the constant threat of poverty; if only he could afford to lock her away in a stylish banqueting house, instead of the place 'at the end of the dark parlour', 3.1.243, where he later plans to imprison her. But Leantio, sensing sex as something filthy associated with the ditches that served as open sewers, also wants to lock up his own desires in 'honest wedlock'. As Swapan Chakravorty comments, for Leantio, marriage is like 'a prophylactic against illicit sex'.[17]

Once Leantio imagines 'base lust' as a 'glorious dangerous strumpet' and 'a fair house' built on filth, however, he's carried away with the idea, and launches into another comparison of a strumpet's 'beautified body to a goodly temple / That's built on vaults where carcasses lie rotting' (98–99). In his mind, base lust and honest wedlock are opposites, but also complements to each other. Lust excites him, but marriage manages that excitement. In a visceral image, he alludes to such a sequence: 'And so by little and little I shrink back again, / And quench desire with a cool meditation. / And I'm as well, methinks' (3.1.100–2). During the ensuing conversation with Bianca, Leantio's house of honest wedlock collapses. Not only does Bianca scorn his ideal of secluded contentment by calling it 'a pigeon-house of friendship' (159), she also implicitly belittles his manhood by mocking his uxorious affection: 'Too fond is as unseemly as too churlish' (135), and immodestly voices her own desire for 'some pleasant lodging i' th' high street, sir; / Or if 'twere near the court [...] / To stand in a bay window and see gallants' (128–29, 131).[18] Clearly, she has abandoned Leantio's bourgeois sexual economy of penury and concealment, to adopt instead the Duke's economy of luxury and display.

Middleton also changed his source story to make Leantio ignorant of Bianca's sexual encounter with the Duke. Thus he created the irony that corrodes the husband's homecoming: we realize that he has already lost his 'jewel', but he doesn't. When he learns that the Duke has spotted that jewel, he can only think of locking up his 'life's best treasure' physically, in the house of which he still thinks he is master. Lena Cowen Orlin remarks that the saying 'A man's house is his castle' became proverbial during the sixteenth century, when 'The state designated the individual household, in the absence of the old authoritarian church and of a national police, as the primary unit of social control.'[19] However, when the Duke's eyes meet Bianca's during the annual procession celebrating the authority of the nobility over the individual householder (1.3), Leantio's locks and keys are rendered useless by the ideological sway of the court, its power over the hearts and minds of his mother and his wife. For the minute that Leantio tells Bianca that the Duke has sent for her, the bourgeois husband is powerless to resist the authority outside the walls of his house. She calls him 'unmannerly, / Rude, and uncivil, mad,' even treasonous to refuse such a summons, and he remains silent as she and his mother walk out the door (3.1.261–63). In the soliloquy that follows, Leantio's imagery of wedlock as a house is replaced by the imagery of 'overladen trees' bearing the fruits of the husband's 'cares' and 'jealousies,' the 'fears, shames, jealousies, costs and troubles' that are the 'issue [...] of a marriage bed' (3.1.271–95), rather than children and heirs. Middleton has reversed the construct of marriage as a house that offers the husband shelter and protection from the storms of his own desires, turning it instead into a perpetual harvest of psychological torment from which no structure can protect him. At the end of the scene, the Duke's messenger returns to summon Leantio, who meekly replies 'I'll along with you, sir' (3.1.301).

In the copious asides that Middleton writes for Leantio in 3.2 at the banquet that effectually celebrates the Duke's acquisition of Bianca while marking her husband's new identity as cuckold, the playwright eschews the clichéd imagery of horns. He portrays instead Leantio's emotional progression from a sense of disentitlement and dispossession to an entirely new grief at his emotional loss, to the psychic reintegration preparatory to becoming Livia's pampered lover. This psychological close-up contrasts with Middleton's compressed and fragmentary treatment of Bianca's equally extreme transformation, to which I will turn in the next section. The playwright is interested in how Leantio comes to terms with desire outside the conceptual framework of marriage. He does not make him a tragic figure but rather a typical one, *l'homme moyen sensuel* who changes when circumstances change, as Bianca does.

In response to the minor position that the Duke bestows on him to keep him

NEW DIRECTIONS: LUST, LOVE AND MARRIAGE   163

quiet, Leantio becomes ironic, a style previously alien to him: 'A fine bit / To stay a cuckold's stomach', he calls the captaincy of the citadel (3.2.47–48). Meditating on the incongruity of a cuckold who benefits from his humiliation, he compares himself to 'a sallet growing up on a dunghill', a fellow infected with plague that yet 'eats his meat with a good appetite', and 'the barren, hardened ass / That feeds on thistles till he bleeds again' (3.2.52–58). The imagery of food characterizes him as a man who simply wants to survive: he must eat to live, whatever the compromises involved. Even worse, the stench of the dunghill and the contamination of plague replace the 'delicious breath' of marriage and the fragrance of its violet-bed, virtually equating Leantio as cuckold with the 'glorious strumpet' who lives by a 'ditch-side'.

When the Duke orders his caroche to take Bianca to the lodging near the court that he has provided for her, however, Leantio expresses a wholly new feeling of pain, indeed devastation at the loss of Bianca not as jewel or treasure but simply as the woman he loves:

> O, hast thou left me then, Bianca, utterly?
> Bianca! Now I miss thee. [...] I ne'er felt
> The loss of thee till now. 'Tis an affliction
> Of greater weight than youth was made to bear, [...]
>   So new it is
> To flesh and blood, so strange, so insupportable
> A torment, e'en mistook as if a body
> Whose death were drowning must needs therefore suffer it
> In scalding oil. (3.2.242–52)

Now for the first time Leantio thinks of himself not as husband and householder but as lover, recalling the long nights of waiting 'in all weathers' for his secret trysts with Bianca before she eloped with him, then the thrill of receiving her

> Into these arms at midnight, when we embraced
> As if we had been statues only made for't,
> To show art's life, so silent were our comforts,
> And kissed as if our lips had grown together? (3.2.261–63)

In the grief of losing Bianca, Leantio lets down his defences against passion and re-lives it without balancing lust against love, strumpet against wife. His wracking meditations are interrupted, however, by Livia's importunate entreaties and asides, which form a comic counterpoint to Leantio's picture of his past with Bianca.

In Leantio's last soliloquy, he begins by puzzling over the condition of a husband still, in the eyes of the church, married to a wife who, by giving her body to another man, has severed the supposedly permanent bond of 'one flesh' conferred by the church:

> Is she my wife till death, yet no more mine?
> That's a hard measure. Then what's marriage good for? [...]
> What is there good in woman to be loved
> When only that which makes her so has left her? (3.2.321–22, 333–34)

Before, he valued her for her beauty, and as his possession; now he appraises her real value as her fidelity, which 'has left her'. He struggles to reconcile his continuing affection for her with the fact that as an unchaste wife she has lost her worth, on which no price can be put. As the soliloquy proceeds, he re-casts the spiritual loss into a mercantile calculus, weighing her breach of chastity against his captainship: 'a place of credit, / I must confess, but poor. My factorship / Shall not exchange means with 't' (3.2.344–46). Here he finds a certain comfort level, and Livia, the point on which she can press her suit. The scene ends with their exchange of vows, a parody of the marriage ceremony, in which the absolute commitment of bodies and souls for eternity is replaced by a worldly relativism. 'Do but you love enough, I'll give enough', Livia pledges, to which Leantio responds, 'Troth then, I'll love enough, and take enough' (3.2.375–76).

Bianca and Isabella: 'How strangely woman's fortune comes about'

Both Bianca and Isabella enter into marriage as Dod and Cleaver, Gouge and Whately et al. expect them to: with full consent implicitly intended to guarantee the mutual pleasure that underpins 'due benevolence', and renders husband and wife 'one flesh'. Both marriages, however, travesty the models set forth by the manuals. Middleton puts the two unions into intricate counterpoint, highlighting contradictions and tensions underlying an institution that, despite the manuals' emphasis on mutuality, is controlled by men to serve male interests.

Bianca married Leantio for passion: escaping the 'jealous eyes' that kept her 'so strict' (4.1.26, 31), she defied her parents' control to become a poor man's wife and a stranger in Florence.[20] In her first speech, she embraces her new condition in terms that conspicuously echo Leantio's:

> Kind mother, there is nothing can be wanting
> To her that does enjoy all her desires.
> Heaven send a quiet peace with this man's love,
> And I am as rich as virtue can be poor,
> Which were enough, after the rate of mind,
> To erect temples for content placed here. (1.1.125–30)

To Bianca as to her husband, the marriage she has freely entered into appears to be a temple of content that shelters both desire and love. In contrast, Middleton dramatizes Isabella's marriage to the Ward as a mockery of choice on both sides, in which her deception and his brutishness substitute for mutual desire. The satirical tone of this plot is at odds with the tragic tone of the Bianca–Leantio–Duke plot, but the two plots are similar in that each turns a woman initially victimized by marriage into a woman who uses it to satisfy her own desires. In the end, however, Middleton shows that marriage cannot admit or sustain the free agency of a woman. Each woman, manipulating marriage to serve her own desires, comes to a bad end. Were it not for the contriving widow Livia, however, who tricks and deceives both Isabella and Bianca, neither heroine might have foundered and died. Yet it is not women who control the world in which their attempts to circumvent marriage unfold: it is men.[21]

NEW DIRECTIONS: LUST, LOVE AND MARRIAGE 165

Isabella is, from the start, controlled by her father who gives only lip-service to Livia's conviction that 'Maids should both see and like [...] / If they love truly after that, 'tis well' (1.2.32–33). Imperiously undermining this counsel, Fabritio urges his daughter, 'See what you mean to like; nay, and I charge you, / Like what you see. Do you hear me?' (1.2.76–77). The bitterest irony of Isabella's situation is that, while the husband her father forces on her is a simpleton for whom sex is as crude as hitting a target with a stick, even that father unwittingly perceives her uncle as the true companion that marriage manuals envision a mate to be:

> Those two are ne'er asunder. They've been heard
> In argument at midnight; moonshine nights
> Are noon-days with them; they walk out their sleeps, [...]
> They're like a chain:
> Draw but one link, all follows. (1.2.63–65, 68–69)

Indeed, Hippolito confesses his love for Isabella by saying, 'As a man loves his wife, so love I thee' (1.2.219). Of course, he means to imply that he desires her sexually, but in the context of Fabritio's prior account of their relationship, that desire is part and parcel of their congeniality and companionship. In the chaste language of the marriage manuals, Isabella describes her feelings for Hippolito as 'comforts of my life' and 'good joys' (2.1.192, 195). By contrasting the grotesque union of a refined young woman such as Isabella and an unlettered bully such as the Ward, to the marriage of true minds between Isabella and her uncle, Middleton dares to suggest that forced marriage might be more of an offence than incest; that marriage to the same 'kind', if based on mutual desire and affection, might be truer to the precepts of Gouge and Whately than forced marriage to someone like the Ward who is in every sense a stranger to Isabella.

The exchange between Fabritio and Livia following Bianca's single, brief opportunity to see, and thus implicitly choose, the Ward as husband dramatizes an issue not extensively treated in the marriage manuals: a father's power over his daughter in the choice of a husband. After both Isabella and the audience take the measure of the boorish, arrogant Ward, Fabritio declares, 'Like him or like him not, wench, you shall have him', prompting Livia's objection:

> You may compel out of the harsh power of father,
> Things merely harsh to a maid's flesh and blood;
> But when you come to love, there the soil alters;
> You're in another country, where your laws
> Are no more set by than the cacklings
> Of geese in Rome's great Capitol. (1.2.135–40)

A widow subject to no man, Livia is free to speak her mind, echoing Gouge et al. in regarding free consent as the very basis of marriage, but her words have no power to sway a father's will. Referring to marriage as a financial exchange controlled by fathers, Isabella sums up its victimization of women with pungent brevity:

> When women have their choices, commonly
> They do but buy their thraldoms, and bring great portions
> To men to keep 'em in subjection; (1.2.171–73)

Though Bianca chose her husband freely and didn't buy her thralldom, having forfeited her dowry by eloping, nonetheless her marriage turns into thralldom when Leantio decides to lock up his 'matchless jewel'.

A keynote of both plots is the objectification of the women as 'erotic object[s] to be looked at'.[22] From the moment that the Duke spies Bianca innocently viewing the annual procession from the window of a private house, she unknowingly becomes an object of aristocratic display. Having been raped amidst Livia's display of paintings, and shown off by the Duke to the guests at Livia's banquet, Bianca then takes her place as chief treasure in his collection:

> Come, Bianca:
> Of purpose sent into the world to show
> Perfection once in woman; [...]
> Glory of Florence, light into mine arms! (3.2.23–25, 29)

Masked, silent, and from the sidelines, Isabella gets a look at her future husband in all his crude foolishness (1.2), but her consent is assumed if not compelled from the start. Then Middleton devotes an entire scene (3.3) to the Ward's head to toe inspection of her, which Isabella describes as being 'bought and sold, and turned and pried into' (3.3.36). Middleton grounds the scene in the making of a marriage contract, when at the start Guardiano instructs the Ward in the importance of inspecting the proposed bride before closing the deal:

> This is the maid my love and care has chose
> Out for your wife, and so I tender her to you.
> [...]
> Tomorrow you join hands, and one ring ties you,
> And one bed holds you, if you like the choice.
> Her father and her friends are i'th' next room,
> And stay to see the contract ere they part; (3.3.3–4, 9–12)

While Middleton makes it clear that the Ward too is being 'bought and sold', it is he as bridegroom who has liberty to scan and comment explicitly on each part of his intended wife's body, even to look up her dress, treating her as chattel and making it clear that he must 'like the choice' before the contract can be signed.

With shocking suddenness, both women seize agency by means of, yet also in defiance of, marriage. By not dramatizing them as deliberating or hesitating, Middleton suggests the extremity of their circumstances and the terrible pressures they are under. Once Livia convinces Isabella that Hippolito in fact is not her uncle, the girl seizes upon the revelation as 'the means to know myself' (2.1.182) and declares 'This marriage shall go forward [...] Nothing can pull me down now' (2.1.206, 211). Now she construes marriage to a fool not as humiliating subjection but rather as the only way for her to enjoy covertly with Hippolito what arguably might be called a true marriage. She identifies Hippolito with qualities befitting a husband when she says, 'So discretion love me, / Desert and judgement, I have content sufficient' (2.1.215–16). In Isabella's eyes, this incestuous union offers simply 'content,' the kind of satisfaction within limits that the marriage manuals propose.

Bianca is no less astute, and quick to size up her options. When the Duke suddenly appears before her, she instantly grasps his purpose: 'Oh treachery to honour!', she cries (2.2.319). When he makes his desire clearer, she pleads 'I have a husband' (2.2.346): she thinks of herself as Leantio's wife, whose body is in his power. The Duke dismisses her fears as 'of thine own making', but she resists, interpreting them as a sign of the vigilance that the virtuous woman must exercise when subjected to 'thunder' and 'tempests:' 'Then wake I most, the weather fearfullest, / And call for strength to virtue', she says (2.2.356–57). In this confrontation, she may be outranked and disadvantaged in every way, but she knows exactly what is at stake: 'Why should you seek, sir, / To take away that you can never give?' (2.2.366–67), she asks. As Whately explains in *The Bridebush*, any breach of chastity 'dissolveth the bond [of marriage] [...] the obligation is void, and the contract nullified'.[23] Once Bianca loses her chastity, nothing can restore it or eradicate the stigma, and her marriage is effectively over.

The Duke's behaviour is, as Ronald Huebert says, 'a carefully orchestrated sexual performance by a man who is accustomed to getting his own way'.[24] Nonetheless, the Duke concludes the scene not with threats of force or promises of reward, but rather in language strongly resonant of marriage as portrayed in domestic manuals:

> Come, play the wife, wench, and provide for ever.
> Let storms come when they list, they find thee sheltered.
> Should any doubt arise, let nothing trouble thee.
> Put trust in our love for the managing
> Of all to thy heart's peace. We'll walk together,
> And show a thankful joy for both our fortunes. (2.2.381–86)

In a witty reversal, he urges that being his mistress is actually a wifely role, because he can 'provide' for her and shelter her better than her husband can (compare Leantio's fanciful metaphor of his marriage as a banqueting house, far beyond his means). He does not press his passion, but rather his ability to insure her 'heart's peace'. Abandoning his previous threat of force, instead he offers companionship ('We'll talk together', 'both our fortunes'). Disingenuous as these promises are, their language owes more to the conception of marriage offered by the preachers than to courtly magnificence or ducal power. Disarmed, perhaps confused, by his conflation of forced sex with quasi-marital content, certainly aware that resistance is futile, Bianca does not reply, and they exit.

When she returns, she is transformed from a docile wife to a woman fully aware that in the eyes of the world she is now a contaminated outcast: 'mine honour's leprous', she declares (2.2.423). Yet unlike Lucrece – paradigm of the raped wife – she does not take upon herself the indelible stain of rape. Rather, in a fiery excoriation of Guardiano, she distinguishes between 'strumpets' who have 'been abased and made for use' and those who, like Guardiano, 'first made 'em so' (2.2.434–37). In contrast to Beatrice-Joanna in Middleton's and Dekker's *The Changeling*, she does see that she is now 'the deed's creature' – she recognizes what Dawson calls 'the inevitability of redefined power relations'.[25] 'I'm made bold now', she says: once the Duke has laid claim to her, she cannot return to being Leantio's modest wife; her body is now in the Duke's power rather than in her husband's.

When Bianca and Leantio confront each other in 4.1 – he now Livia's kept lover, she well-established as the Duke's mistress – they meet on an equal plane in the sense that she is no longer subject to him as her husband. When he tries to claim moral superiority by calling her 'whore' and 'strumpet', she sarcastically reminds him of his captaincy. Insult returned for insult, their barbed repartée dramatizes their moral and social parity. They have both abandoned their marriage vows. No longer 'one flesh', they have exchanged the 'content' and 'due benevolence' of marriage for 'whoredom', stylish courtly dress, and a life of luxury (4.1.41–112).

The sudden incursion of the Cardinal into the play puts marriage under new scrutiny. Indeed, that seems the only reason for his presence. His denunciation of his brother's liaison with Bianca prompts the Duke's carefully worded decision 'Never to know her as strumpet more' (4.1.270) – simply by virtue of marrying her, and 'knowing' her then as his lawful wife. When the Duke says, 'Now I'm chidden / For what I shall enjoy then unforbidden' (4.1.275–76), Middleton stresses the arbitrary determination conferred by the ceremony, which can transform the same act, the same relationship, from one thing to its opposite. The Duke simply thumbs his nose at the idea that in marriage, the sexual act manifests the sacred mystery of 'one flesh'; whether chidden or not, he enjoys the same pleasure. When the Cardinal then breaks into the wedding procession (4.3), Middleton restages the question of whether or not marriage has the transforming power to change lust to virtuous pleasure. The Duke claims that his marriage 'leads to lawful love' and stands on his oath: 'I vowed no more to keep a sensual woman. / 'Tis done: I mean to make a lawful wife of her' (4.3.29, 31–32). To the Cardinal, on the contrary, once a whore, always a whore. The Duke and his bride, the Cardinal claims, 'take sanctuary in marriage' like criminals, exploiting the Church to protect their essentially sinful union, in which 'lust usurps the bed that should be pure' (4.3.37, 46). Bianca then plays the trump card of charity, 'the first-born of religion,' by claiming to be 'a converted sinner', and challenges the Cardinal:

> Pray, whether is religion better served:
> When lives that are licentious are made honest,
> Than when they still run through a sinful blood? (4.3.51, 56, 65–67)

The answer to her rhetorical question arrives in the form of the wedding masque engineered by Livia. She who, as the Duke's bawd, entrapped Bianca into an adulterous affair, tricked Isabella into an incestuous union, made Bianca's husband her gigolo, and thereby defiled two marriages, plays Juno Pronuba, the goddess of marriage. Intensifying this ironic critique of the veneration accorded marriage as a divinely decreed institution is the complex aesthetic of the masque. On the one hand, masques were intended to represent the ideas they dramatized as absolute and true. On the other, as employed in revenge tragedies, and in this one especially, the masque 'exposes the fictionality of the medium even as the medium itself purports to be dealing with absolutes', and undermines the 'theological certainties' it depicts.[26]

Vainly trying to get back at the Cardinal, Bianca adds her own lethal 'antemasque' to the evening's performance of cross-cutting revenges. Like the others, it backfires, poisoning the Duke instead of his brother. Ewbank comments, 'Thus each plotter has achieved exactly the opposite of what he or she aimed at', making the masque 'an exhibition of ironic retribution'.[27] Bianca, however, stands out from the others in that she alone dies voluntarily, a suicide, and moreover, as a loving wife. When Bianca kisses her dead husband's poisoned lips to join him in eternity, she says, 'Give me thy last breath, thou infected bosom, / And wrap two spirits in one poisoned vapour' (5.1.234–35). Middleton, having eviscerated the concept of marriage as a divinely sanctioned union that welds two persons into 'one flesh', here gives it a final ambiguous twist. Is this fatal kiss a mere parody of the mystical union of 'one flesh', or however unlikely, an example of it?

Notes

1 I have also consulted the New Mermaids edition, *Women Beware Women*, ed. by William C. Carroll, 2nd edn (London: A. & C. Black; New York: Norton, 1994; rpt. 2007).
2 In Middleton's *The Patient Man and the Honest Whore*, just before marriage confers honesty on the prostitute Bellafront, she muses, 'Had I but met one kind gentleman / That would have purchased sin alone to himself / For his own private use' (6.320–22) as though marital sex is simply private 'sin'. In Mistress Allwit, who remains married to Allwit while continuing a long-term liaison with Sir Walter Whorehound, *A Chaste Maid in Cheapside* comically confounds whore with wife. In the same play, when Tim Yellowhammer, conned into marrying Sir Walter's other mistress, tries to wriggle out by citing the maxim *uxor non est meretrix* (a wife is not a whore), his intended bride declares, 'There's a thing called marriage, and that makes me honest' (5.4.111) – which it does in the dénouement. In *Hengist, King of Kent; or, The Mayor of Queenborough*, in an elegant chiasmus, the promiscuous Roxena is affirmed a virgin, and the chaste wife Castiza a whore.
3 In this section I have revised and adapted passages from my article, 'Whores and Wives in Jacobean Drama', *In Another Country: Feminist Perspectives on Renaissance Drama*, ed. Dorothea Kehler and Susan Baker (Metuchen, NJ and London: Scarecrow Press, 1991), pp. 246–60.
4 William Gouge, *Eight Treatises of Domesticall Duties*, in *Workes*, 2 vols (London, 1627), I, p. 12.
5 William Gouge, 'On Marriage', in *Certaine Sermons or Homilies*, ed. by Mary Ellen Rickey and Thomas B. Stroup (Gainesville, FL: Scholars' Facsimiles and Reprints, 1968), p. 238.
6 Lawrence Stone, *The Family, Sex and Marriage in England, 1500–1800* (New York: Harper and Row, 1977), *passim*. Stone pushes his argument for this change in *mentalité* hard and, some scholars have objected, on insufficient evidence. Nonetheless, both pulpit and stage register many times over the friction between an implicitly egalitarian idea of mutual 'due benevolence' and the insistence on the wife's subordination to the husband.
7 Heinrich Bullinger, *The Christen State of Matrimony , wherein husbands and wyves may learne to keepe house together, with love* (London, 1575), chap. 10. Bullinger's German text, translated into English by Miles Coverdale, went through three editions in five years, and two more by 1600.
8 Stephen Greenblatt, *Renaissance Self-Fashioning from More to Shakespeare* (Chicago: University of Chicago Press, 1980), p. 242.
9 John Dod and Robert Cleaver, *A Godlie Forme of Household Government* (London, 1598), rpt. in William St Clair and Irmgaard Maasen, *Conduct Literature for Women, 1500 to 1640*, 6 vols (London: Pickering and Chatto, 2000), III, pp. 25–412.
10 William Whately, *A Bride-bush: or, a direction for married persons. Plainely*

describing the duties common to both, and peculiar to each of them (London, 1617; rpt. Amsterdam: Theatrum Orbis Terrarum; Norwood, NJ: W. T. Johnson, 1975), pp. 3, 20.

11 J. R. Mulryne, ed., 'Introduction', in Thomas Middleton, *Women Beware Women* (Manchester and New York: Manchester University Press, 2007), pp. lxii, lxiv.

12 Anthony B. Dawson, in '*Women Beware Women* and the Economy of Rape', *Studies in English Literature*, 27.2 (Spring 1987), 303–20), states, 'Once Bianca is open, at the window, on display, she becomes subject to the milieu which values showing' (p. 309). Similarly, Jowett notes that while Leantio hid Bianca, 'The Duke puts her in a theater where she is object of the gaze of others' (Middleton, *Collected Works*, p. 1490).

13 Christopher Ricks, in 'Word-play in *Women Beware Women*', *Review of English Studies*, 12 (1961), 238–50, was the first to note how Middleton plays off sexual against commercial meanings of the word 'business' to convey the interpenetration of money and love in the several plots of the play.

14 Ronald Huebert, in *The Performance of Pleasure in English Renaissance Drama* (Basingstoke: Palgrave Macmillan, 2003), pp. 137–38, charts the shift in critics' interpretation of what the Duke does to Bianca, from 'seduction' (Muriel Bradbrook, 1935) to 'rape' (Suzanne Gossett, 1984). Dawson comments: '[Bianca's] submission to, and ultimate embracing of the Duke [. . .] is not the same as consent. She is caught in a fierce economy of sexual exchange – she is indeed the currency of that exchange, exactly as she had been for her husband' (Dawson, 'Economy of Rape', p. 304). Jowett characterizes Bianca as 'entrapped, threatened with violence, denied meaningful choice, restrained as she struggles' but in addition, undergoing 'a subtler form of coercion, whereby the violence is euphemized, as though the Duke did not understand the act of consent' (Middleton, *Collected Works*, p. 1489).

15 For a well-argued interpretation centring on Leantio as an embattled head of household whose fall reflects 'the emergence of an ideological if not a spatial separation of the domestic sphere from a male professional sphere within an urban mercantile milieu', see Ann Christensen, 'Settling House in Middleton's *Women Beware Women*', *Comparative Drama*, 29 (Winter 1995–6), 493–518.

16 On banqueting houses, see Patricia Fumerton, *Cultural Aesthetics: Renaissance Literature and the Practice of Social Ornament* (Chicago: University of Chicago Press, 1991), pp. 117–30.

17 Swapan Chakravorty, *Society and Politics in the Plays of Thomas Middleton* (Oxford: Clarendon Press, 1996), p. 30.

18 Ann Christensen notes 'the importance placed on patriarchal dwellings and their inability to keep women secure', comparing Bianca in the window to Celia similarly placed in Jonson's *Volpone* ('Settling House', p. 499).

19 Lena Cowen Orlin, *Private Matters and Public Culture in Post-Reformation England* (Ithaca and London: Cornell University Press, 1994), p. 3.

20 Chakravorty finds an 'anxiety of estrangement' central to the play, linking Bianca as a stranger in Florence to a split in Leantio between 'alien pleasure and native duty' (*Society and Politics*, pp. 128, 129).

21 Jowett astutely comments, 'The initial scene of each plot establishes that all later female subterfuges have a base in male oppression' (Middleton, *Collected Works*, p. 1489).

22 Dawson, 'Economy of Rape', p. 306.

23 Whately places on the title-page of *A Bride-bush* an epigraph from Heb. 13.4: 'Marriage is honorable among all men, and the bed undefiled: but whoremongers and adulterers God will judge'.

24 Huebert, *Performance of Pleasure*, p. 138.

25 Dawson, 'Economy of Rape', p. 312.

26 Richard Dutton, 'Introduction', *Thomas Middleton: Women Beware Women and Other Plays* (Oxford: Oxford University Press, 1999), p. x.

27 Inga-Stina Ewbank, ' "These pretty devices": a study of masques in plays', in *A Book of Masques: in Honour of Allardyce Nicoll*, ed. by T. J. B. Spencer and Stanley Wells (Cambridge: Cambridge University Press, 1967), p. 445.

CHAPTER NINE

Learning and Teaching Resources: Mapping Texts,[1] Spaces and Bodies

Liz Oakley-Brown*

Introduction

I teach *Women Beware Women* as part of a year-long, level 2 undergraduate course, 'Renaissance to Restoration: English Literature 1580–1688': an optional programme of study concerned with a generically diverse range of writing. Delivered by one weekly 50-minute lecture and one 50-minute seminar consisting of approximately 12 students, the syllabus is broadly underpinned by critical concepts concerned with sexualities and socio-cultural spaces such as the city, the country and the court. By the time that they encounter Middleton's play in the middle of the first term, Lancastrian students have usually explored either Ben Jonson's *The Masque of Blackness* (1605) or *The Alchemist* (1610), and should possess an overarching sense of the generic and gendered terrains of seventeenth-century drama. In what follows, I offer an approach to examining the distinctive Middletonian enterprise in seminar discussion. In doing so, I shall also provide some means of teaching the Jacobean play alongside Shakespeare, other forms of early modern textual production, and select secondary criticism.[2]

Richard A. Levin comments that 'recognized as a great play, [*Women Beware Women*] would be recognized as a greater one, were its construction not a puzzle',[3] and, in principle, the primary material proffers an unwieldy pedagogical exercise. Middleton's tale of adultery, incest and murder – beginning in the home of a Florentine mother and ending with a spectacularly macabre court masque – may challenge even those students who are fairly proficient in the conventions of Shakespearean drama. Narratological and structural complexities notwithstanding, attempts to locate the play within a fixed period of production are frustrated. Beyond its entry in the Stationers' Register on 9 September 1653 and the octavo edition included in *Two New Playes [...] Written by Tho. Middleton, Gent* (1657),[4] *Women Beware Women*'s provenance is unidentified. While scholars have reasoned that a date circa 1621 is most likely,[5] as Richard Dutton puts it, 'the fact is that we do not know when [it] was written and performed, and should beware of over-easy assumptions that we do'.[6] Many twentieth- and twenty-first century critics are divided about *Women Beware Women*'s generic definition:

> [Samuel] Schoenbaum credits the play with verging on the creation of a 'novel kind of drama – a drama that occupies a middle ground between comedy and tragedy'. And in this vein, the play has recently been classified as a 'realistic bourgeois tragedy', a 'city tragedy', a 'tragedy of judgment', 'an *anticourt* tragedy written from a citizen's perspective' and a 'domestic tragedy'. It is said to have 'many affinities with satiric comedy' and to begin 'where a romantic comedy might have ended'. Nicholas Brooke concludes, more radically, that in *Women Beware Women* Middleton 'demonstrates the absurdity of worshipping tragedy as a moral force'.[7]

In addition, J. R. Mulryne suggests that its 'cold light [...] derives in part from the factual status of the story [about the Grand Duke Francesco de Medici and Bianca Capello] it has to tell'. He goes on to say that 'It would be a step too far to call the play "faction", but it carried for its original audience, we can suppose, something closer to this type of fictional narrative than very nearly any other tragedy of its period.'[8] *Women Beware Women*'s title also defies a singular interpretation. Anthony B. Dawson, enquires 'is it ironic? Does the play really ask us to take away only a simple anti-feminist message?'[9] However, the absence of a precise point of origin, generic label or transparent heading – factors commonly used to arrest the play of signification – can help to inculcate informed and independent student responses.

The Playtext

In advance of the session, the seminar's structure (the playtext; stagecraft; mapping spaces/mapping bodies; reading Middleton) is posted on the course's virtual learning environment. I provide the above critical extracts which consider the play's generic instability and the interrogative nature of its title, and a request that each student finds 2–3 primary quotations which are suggestive of *Women Beware Women*'s 'ambivalence'.[10] I also ask the group to choose a short scene to perform in class which sums up their initial thoughts about the play and which emphasizes the dramatic qualities of Middleton's work. At the beginning of the session, we briefly discuss issues related to reading/auditing/watching drama. Markedly, some of these concerns are inscribed in the publisher's address which prefaces the 1657 edition of *Women Beware Women*:

> To The Reader
> When these amongst others of Mr. *Thomas Middleton's* Excellent Poems, came to my hands, I was not a little confident but that his name would prove as great an Inducement for thee to Read, as me to Print them: [...][11]

As a play published in the Interregnum, students readily appreciate the socio-historical conditions of the 1650s that necessarily privileged reading above performance. They find it rather more difficult, however, to envisage *Women Beware Women*'s theatricality in a twenty-first century classroom. While the study of Shakespeare's playtexts can be easily combined with a live or filmed performance, there is little opportunity to take this approach with Middleton's work. Thus, other strategies need to be developed which help students to engage with the verbal and the non-verbal semiotics of the stage.

Alison Findlay teaches the play as part of her course on 'Feminist Perspectives on Renaissance Drama'. This performance-based module uses practical workshops alongside weekly critical readings to explore the primary material, and students must choose a short extract to learn and perform for assessment. It is accompanied by a log book (an annotated photocopy of the script with notes of directorial decisions on voice, tone, blocking, and a short introduction of 1,500 words).[12] In a more conventional seminar format, an efficient way into Middleton's dramaturgy is by way of *Romeo and Juliet*, a familiar narrative which inhabits the public and the theatrical domains. Gary Taylor's review of the RSC's 2006 production of Middleton's play sets up a facilitating, intertextual relationship with its Elizabethan counterpart:

> What if Romeo and Juliet had lived? What if Romeo had been waiting there when Juliet awoke in the tomb, and the two of them had giddily eloped to Mantua, to live happily ever after? They wouldn't have any money. Romeo would need to get a job. Juliet would stay at home all day, afraid that her family would find her if she dared to venture out. Alone at home, she'd be bored out of her skull [...] She'd start peeking out of the window, wanting to escape the little domestic box in which she'd been entombed alive. One day, a rich older man would see her at her window. She would look at him, looking at her [...] Thomas Middleton's *Women Beware Women* is *Romeo and Juliet* for grown-ups. It begins pretty much where Shakespeare's vision of breathless adolescent romance ends: with a newly married couple, eloped from Venice, arriving in Florence.[13]

Providing an undemanding comparative analysis and a basic plot-summary, Taylor's article enables students to immediately examine and discuss the play's opening scene with a degree of critical purchase and confidence.

Students notice that while Shakespeare's tragedy concludes with a homosocial scene of paternal allegiance and 'glooming peace' (5.3.304),[14] Middleton's dramatic point of departure is the disrupted bourgeois household ostensibly governed by a matriarchal figure:

> Mother: Thy sight was never yet more precious to me!
> Welcome with all the affection of a mother
> That comfort can express from natural love.
> Since thy birth-joy, a mother's chiefest gladness,
> After sh'has undergone her curse of sorrows,
> Thou wast not more dear to me than this hour
> Presents thee to my heart. Welcome again.
> [...]
> What's this gentlewoman? (1.1–11)[15]

According to John Jowett, 'Space emblematizes human relationships. Middleton resists centred groupings so as to explore the stage as a site for separation, either as isolation or as a disharmonious composition of separate elements.'[16] Indeed, *Women Beware Women*'s opening dialogue foregrounds the playwright's interest in dramatizing cultural and spatial relationships. As the Mother asks 'What's this gentlewoman?', students speculate on the ways in which Bianca's onstage position conveys her eccentric social position. The question clearly anticipates the ensuing narrative's sustained objectification of young women, yet it is also noteworthy that the older female character is referred to by a 'generic social label'.[17] This observation helps to substantiate the point that merely reading the play can misrepresent its idiosyncratic fashioning of parts:

> Bianca's name appears only in Act 3 [...] Leantio is anonymous until Act 4 [...] Guardiano is not named at all [...] In this respect the play on stage has a different texture from either the play as printed, replete with speech-prefixes and stage directions, or critical discussions such as the present one. The characters themselves normatively think of each other in terms of social roles and family relationships.[18]

Rigorous textual analyses, such as Christopher Ricks's 'Word-Play in *Women Beware Women*', examine the play's linguistic invocations of social, sexual and economic discourses.[19] Without performance, however, Middleton's dramatic technique is significantly compromised.

Dutton's description of Robert Osborne's 1978 production at Lancaster University makes manifest the ways in which performance itself functions as a form of criticism. 'Set in a modern Italy' with 'nudity and Mafia-style hit-men',[20] Osborne's view of Bianca and Leantio's marriage is influenced by the final frame of

> Mike Nichol's touchstone 1960s movie, *The Graduate*. In the movie Dustin Hoffman improbably snatches Katherine Ross from the altar of a conventional marriage, and the lovers head for the future in a passing bus. But in the closing shot [...] the exhilaration slowly drains from their faces, they register confusion, doubt, and perhaps resignation as the reality of the moment takes over from the romance. This seemed to apply perfectly to the elopement of Leantio and Bianca, a fairy-tale romantic impulse which Middleton's play subjects to the sobering realities of money, sexuality, and power.[21]

For Dutton, Osborne's perspective illuminates *Women Beware Women*'s 'disorientating duality'. The play is clearly a product of seventeenth-century England, yet '*some* of the issues [...] chime urgently with modern sensibilities',[22] and an effective means of allowing students to grasp the critical possibilities of Middleton's playtext for themselves is to ask them to read through and block the short scene that they chose before the session. The most recent cohort opted for the dialogue between Livia and Isabella in which the aunt's artfulness is exposed (2.1.73–179). Alert to Middleton's use of 'generic social labels', the students explore Livia's fractured relationships with her female relatives, living and dead. They notice that the 'solemn vow [she] made / To [Isabella's] dead mother, [her] most loving sister' (2.1.98–100) seems at odds with Livia's eagerness to assist her brother's incestuous desires. Likening the plot to those of current soap operas, the students consider the ways in which voice, tone and blocking might dramatize the aunt's duplicitous designs.

Stagecraft

In this way, the students observe that Livia's relationship with Isabella is concerned with sexual rather than emotional bonds. They also discern how the widowed aunt's function as an intermediary extends to the unification of the narrative strands involving Bianca and Isabella. At this point, their understanding of 'the playwright's three-dimensional imagination'[23] can be increased by examining the inaugural moment when the female inhabitants of the Florentine household encounter the male constituents of the court. The episode begins with the sound of the impending parade:

> Music
> Mother: I hear 'em near us now. Do you stand easily?
> Bianca: Exceeding well, good Mother.
> Mother: Take this stool.
> Bianca: I need it not, I thank you.
> Mother: Use your will, then. (1.3.99–101)

If, as Mulryne argues, 'value is associated by the play's people with possessions, not with morality',[24] Bianca's dismissal of the stool, a utilitarian object at odds with the luxuries of the court, is emblematic of her eventual rejection of her husband's lifestyle. This apparently slight exchange between wife and mother-in-law deftly betrays the drama's exploration of social schism while drawing attention to the Venetian woman's 'will': one of the play's decisive themes. In response to the Mother's concerns about Leantio's inability to keep Bianca financially satiated, the son implores 'I pray do not you teach her to rebel / When she's in a good way to obedience' (1.1.74–75). Defined at the outset as Leantio's 'most unvaluedest purchase' (1.1.12), the house is supposed to keep the young wife from the outside world. Bianca's back-story, however, reveals a predisposition for contravening patriarchal codes of conduct.

As Bianca looks out of the window at the passing spectacle, Middleton deploys the stage set in a striking fashion.[25] In 4.1.43–45 the audience hear that Bianca and Leantio eloped through a window,[26] and the following passage from Henry Smith's *A Preparative To Marriage* (1591) provides a seventeenth-century commentary on the play's repeated trope of woman and window:

> [...] we call the wife *housewife*, that is, house wife, not a street wife like Tamar (Gen. xxxviii. 14), nor a field wife like Dinah (Gen. xxxiv. 1), but a house wife, to show that a good wife keeps her house. And therefore Paul biddeth Titus to exhort women that they be chaste and keeping at home (Tit. ii. 5); presently after *chaste* he saith *keeping at home*, as though *home* were chastity's keeper. And therefore Solomon, depainting the whore, setteth her at the door, now sitting upon her stalls, now walking in the streets (Prov. vii. 12), now looking out of the windows, like curled Jezebel (II Kgs. ix. 30), as if she held forth the glass of temptation for vanity to gaze upon.[27]

In seeming alignment with such didactic tracts, windows in *Women Beware Women* are configured as dangerous, sensual spaces. This particular example of Middleton's 'harping on location'[28] is developed as 1.3 concludes:

> *Enter in great solemnity six knights bare-headed, then two cardinals, and then the Lord Cardinal, then the Duke; after him the states of Florence by two and two; with variety of music and song. [...] exeunt.*
> Mother: How like you, daughter?
> Bianca: 'Tis a noble State.
>   Methinks my soul could dwell upon the reverence
>   Of such a solemn and most worthy custom.
>   Did not the Duke look up? Methought he saw us.
>   (1.3.102–5)

Simultaneously depicting the bourgeois and the courtly domains, the playwright's inclination to 'exploit the visual potential of a scene in support of thematic concerns'[29] is clearly on show. R. V. Holdsworth reminds us that just before the arrival of the state procession, Bianca has been bidding a reluctant farewell to her husband. The vignette alludes to the 'balcony and aubade scenes in *Romeo and Juliet*, which Leantio's parting from Bianca invariably recalls', while the exchange of glances between the Duke and the married woman draws upon 'the Petrarchan tradition of the earth-bound lover and his elevated mistress'.[30] Utilizing the semiotic range of the performance space, and paradigmatic of *Women Beware Women*'s overarching narrative, Act 1's closing episode encapsulates Middleton's exploration of the complex dynamics of legitimate and illegitimate desires.[31]

While the words on the page delineate Bianca's objectification, it is rather more difficult to envision costume's influence upon audience reaction.[32] In order to augment an awareness of the visual aspects of the play, I find it helpful to provide students with early modern images such as Giuliano Bugiardini's *Portrait of a Woman, called 'The Nun'* (c. 1510)[33] and Paolo Veronese's *Figures behind the Parapet* (c. 1560).[34] Dressed in black, Bugiardini's lone figure stands in front of a casement which acts as an interface between her body and the outside world; accompanied by an older chaperone, Veronese's elaborately clothed young woman stands on a balcony in front of an open window. Lisa Hopkins has discussed *Women Beware Women*'s portrayal of gender. She writes that:

> the first time we see [Bianca] after her initial appearance she is presented to us very much as a work of art: framed in the window, she is seen by the duke as being as much a market commodity as the wares in a shopfront; framed as a painting is, she is an object for the eye;[35]

Hopkins's analysis elucidates the intricate ways in which images and words conjoin to construct, and perhaps to contest, the early modern period's representation of women. In performance, Bianca's reification can be exaggerated. G. B. Shand describes how Denyse Lynde's 1982 production at Hart House in Toronto portrayed Leantio 'unveiling Bianca like a statue' as he pronounces 'And here's my masterpiece; do you now behold her!' (1.1.41).[36]

Women Beware Women has been described as dramatizing 'a "proppy" world, one where in the modern theatre a stage-director and stage-designer need to be alert to the cascade of stage properties which are indicated not just in stage directions but in the dialogue'.[37] In their respective readings of Middleton's drama, Hopkins and Shand implicitly show how women in this 'proppy' play are treated as 'props' themselves. This is clearly evident in the Ward and Sordido's explicit examination of Isabella (3.4). Dawson argues that this scene 'parodies the Petrarchan mode' and exemplifies *Women Beware Women*'s scopophilic tendencies.[38] This 'eroticism of looking'[39] takes on a greater significance when Guardiano escorts Bianca into Livia's gallery of erotic art (2.2.403–4) as a prelude to her encounter with the Duke.

Architectural details such as windows and galleries are further examples of a distinctly Middletonian dramatic method. Alongside a 'degree of historical realism',[40] stage-set and narrative combine to offer a veracious socio-cultural critique. However, with 'no clear mention of the Florentine location until the end of the first scene',[41] students observe that *Women Beware Women*'s propensity to conceal information about geographical setting and characters' names undermines its realist qualities. Dutton suggests that 'There is much about it that is surprisingly modern in its self-referential awareness of its own artifice.'[42] Structured by way of props, verbal patterns and spatial repetitions, Middleton's drama makes expert use of the genre's varied systems of signification to convey its tale of sexual and social unease. Consequently, students find the play's subtle shift from the court's marital celebrations to the dramatic space of the masque in 5.2 an extension of *Women Beware Women*'s overarching concerns about drama and verisimilitude.

Mapping Spaces

Once the students have grasped some ways of handling Middleton's dramaturgy, and with a view to developing a wider conceptual framework, the seminar moves on to consider *Women Beware Women*'s exploration of topographical and geographical boundaries, and the fashioning of identities. Bianca's ultimately fatal translation from Venice to Florence and from house to court to masque suggests that there is something dangerous about early modern border crossings.[43] In terms of foreign travel, Roger Ascham's *The Scholemaster* (1570) famously discussed the perils for an Englishman journeying to Italy where 'Some *Circes* shall make him, of a plaine Englishman, a right *Italian*.'[44] When the 'English man Italianiated' returns home,[45] there are further problems to face:

> Our Italians bring home with them other faultes from Italie, though not so great as this of Religion, yet a great deale greater, tha[n] many good men can well beare. For commonlie they cum home, common contemners of mariage and readie persuaders of all other to the same: not because they love virginitie [...] but, being free in Italie, to go whither so ever lust will cary them, they do not like, that lawe and honestie should be soch a barre to their like libertie at home in England.[46]

Early modern England's orthodox view of Catholic Italy as dissolute is upheld in Ascham's text. As we have seen above, Middleton's drama bears traces of notorious Italian events. Published in Celio Malespini's *Ducento Nouelle* (Venice, 1609), the 'high scandal'[47] concerning the Florentine Grand Duke and his Venetian mistress is arguably an account of 'contemners of mariage', but it cannot be said with any certainty that *Women Beware Women* takes a pejorative view of Italianate culture. For example, the Lord Cardinal might seem a familiar example of Catholic otherness or 'a schemer',[48] yet his speech at 4.1.187–90 'would not disgrace a Calvinist pulpit'.[49] Furthermore, if travelling to Italy is deemed treacherous in the late sixteenth century, then London is perceived as an increasingly hazardous environment. In 1642, Henry Peacham discussed *The Art of Living in London* in the following way:

> Now the Citie being like a vast Sea (full of gusts) fearfull dangerous shelves and rocks, ready at every storme to sinke and cast away, the weake and unexperienced Barke (with her fresh-water souldiers) as wanting her compasse and her skilfull Pilot; my selfe, like another *Columbus* or *Drake*, acquainted with her rough entertainment and stormes, have drawn you this chart or map for your guide, as well out of mine owne, as my many friends experience.[50]

Ascham's and Peacham's extracts help to initiate a seminar discussion of early modern boundaries, and the ways in which 'others' and 'selves' are textually constructed. While students are interested in Ascham's representation of Catholic alterity, they keenly observe the gender politics of Peacham's narrative. Allying himself with notable travellers of the period,[51] the seventeenth-century author declares himself 'the skilfull Pilot' who can 'chart or map' the precarious feminized surroundings.

Mapping Bodies

Like the textual contours of national and urban spaces, corporeal identities are fashioned by patriarchal discourses. Following a brief consideration of the critically neglected topic of *Women Beware Women*'s re-presentation of masculine bodies,[52] the seminar's focus returns to the ironic nature of the play's title and its depiction of women. Coppélia Kahn argues that 'Whatever their vocation, social role, or temperament, [women] are conceived within the framework of one social institution: marriage'.[53] Famously, Middleton's drama explores a taxonomy of women alongside 'a vigorous dialogue [...] between misogynist literature and defences of women [which] may be traced back to the Middle Ages'.[54] Joseph Swetnam's *The Araignment of Lewd, Idle, Froward and Unconstant Women* (1615), as its title suggests, is one of the most strident participants in the debate:

> [...] the best time for a young man to marry, is at the age of twenty and five, and then to take a wife of the age of seventeene yeares, or thereabout, rather a maid then a widdow; for a widdow is framed to the conditions of another man, and can hardly be altered, so that thy pains will be double: for thou must unlearne a widdow, and make her forget and forgoe her former corrupt and disordered behaviour, the which is hardly to be done: but a young

woman of tender yeares is flexible and bending, obedient and subject to doe any thing, according to the will and pleasure of her husband.[55]

There is much that could be said about the ways in which neither Bianca nor Isabella conforms to Swetnam's notions of 'obedient' young women, but the line instructing the reader that 'thou must unlearne a widdow, and make her forget and forgoe her former corrupt and disordered behaviour' seems particularly resonant in Middleton's Livia. Garrulity opposes the period's association of chastity and silence, and as the character who speaks the most lines in the play,[56] Livia is a stereotypical representation of the 'the lusty widow'; an early modern woman deemed 'other in [her] independence and wordliness'.[57] Livia's archetypal tendency for sexual unruliness is exacerbated by the fact that she has 'buried [...] two husbands' but 'never mean more to marry (1.2.50–51). Swetnam's address 'To the Reader' states that the author 'will follow my own vein in unfolding every pleat, and shewing every wrinckle of a womans disposition'.[58] Like Swetnam's pamphlet, Middleton's play scrutinizes Livia's body,[59] but with rather different effects.

Towards the end of *Women Beware Women* the audience is encouraged to focus on the widow as she *'descends like Juno'* (5.2.98 s.d.), the goddess of marriage: a dramatic gesture that suspends one of the play's central concerns above the stage. Comparable with the Ward's survey of Isabella, this climactic scene also puts a woman's body on display. However, it is Middleton's treatment of Bianca in 2.2 which emphasizes the drama's inscrutable attitude toward women.[60] As Livia and the Mother move chess pieces on board, Bianca moves from Guardiano's side to the Duke's grasp on the upper level of the stage:

[A] lustful male and a resistant female meet onstage, grapple a moment, exit from stage, and return some three minutes and one ejaculation later, leaving unspoken either the word 'rape' or the word 'seduction,' letting the audience, or at least the reader, guess.[61]

Indicative of Middleton's ludic, yet troubling, representation of social and sexual interactions,[62] the disturbing encounter dramatizes the insidious politics of power.[63] Lacking resolution, moreover, it is an episode which invites its spectators to enter the debate.

Conclusion: Reading Middleton

The play interrogates the transparency of meaning in many ways. However, the figure of irony often defines Middleton's mode of dramatic address. As Jowett explains, 'Irony is dialogic, for it happens when the hearer is made to hold two (or more) perspectives at once'.[64] Arguably, it is this bifurcated quality that contributes to *Women Beware Women*'s delineation as a 'puzzle', and which permits it to be critically appropriated in numerous ways.[65] In this context, Gary Taylor's assessment of the portrait which accompanies the play's 1657 publication offers a useful gloss on reading Middleton:

With a finely shaded face, shoulder-length curls, and a trim beard, the Calvinist Middleton [...] looks sexier and more stylish than any authenticated likeness of any other early playwright. His dark gown could be legal or academic, classical or modish, masculine or effeminate, warm or swank. His left arm propped akimbo on his hip, he wears his crown of laurel as casually as one might a low-slung feathered hat.[66]

Here, Taylor shows how the author's image challenges its onlooker's notions of seventeenth-century religious, intellectual, sexual and social sensibilities. Similarly, *Women Beware Women* is a discursive site for the fashioning of textual, spatial and corporeal identities. In Taylor's opinion, the writer 'yokes opposites'.[67] As this seminar has shown, however, it is the audience (or the critic) who is responsible for making sense out of Middleton's exceptionally dialogic dramaturgy.

Resources

Select Individual Editions
Carroll, William C. (ed.), *Women Beware Women*, New Mermaids, second edition (London: A. & C. Black, 1994).
Counsell, Colin and Trevor R. Griffiths (eds), *Women Beware Women*, Drama Classics (London: Nick Hern Books, 2005).
Mulryne, J. R. (ed.), *Women Beware Women*, Revels Student Editions (Manchester: Manchester University Press, 2007).

Select Anthologies which include *Women Beware Women*
Dutton, Richard (ed.), '*Women Beware Women*', in *Thomas Middleton: Women Beware Women and Other Plays*, Oxford World's Classics (Oxford: Oxford University Press, 1999), pp. 73–163. Other plays: *A Chaste Maid in Cheapside*, *The Changeling* and *A Game at Chess*.
Gill, Roma (ed.), '*Thomas Middleton: Women Beware Women*', in Brian Gibbons (gen. ed.), *Six Elizabethan and Jacobean Tragedies*, New Mermaids (London: A & C Black, 1994), pp. 375–486. Other plays: J. R. Mulryne (ed.), 'Thomas Kyd: *The Spanish Tragedy*'; Roma Gill (ed.), 'Christopher Marlowe: *Doctor Faustus*'; W. F. Bolton (ed.), 'Ben Jonson: *Sejanus His Fall*'; Elizabeth M. Brennan (ed.), 'John Webster: *The White Devil*'; Brian Morris (ed.), 'John Ford: '*Tis Pity She's a Whore*'.
Jowett, John (ed.), '*Women Beware Women*: A Tragedy', in Gary Taylor and John Lavagnino (gen. eds), *Thomas Middleton: The Collected Works* (Oxford: Clarendon Press, 2007), pp. 1488–541.
Loughrey, Bryan and Neil Taylor (eds), '*Women Beware Women*', in *Thomas Middleton: Five Plays*, Penguin Classics (London: Penguin, 1988), pp. 239–344. Other plays: *A Trick to Catch the Old One*, *The Revenger's Tragedy*, *A Chaste Maid in Cheapside*, *The Changeling*.

Select Secondary Resources

Introduction
Carroll, William C., 'Introduction', *Women Beware Women*, New Mermaids, second edition (London: A & C Black, 1994), pp. xi–xxxviii.
Dawson, Anthony B., '*Women Beware Women* and the Economy of Rape', *Studies in English Literature*, 27 (1987), 303–20.
Dutton, Richard (ed.), 'Introduction', *Thomas Middleton: Women Beware Women and Other Plays* (Oxford: Oxford University Press, 1999), pp. vii–xxxvii.
Jowett, John, 'Mapping the Text', in *Shakespeare and Text*, Oxford Shakespeare Topics (Oxford: Oxford University Press, 2007), pp. 93–114.

Jowett, John, 'Women, Beware Women', in Gary Taylor and John Lavagnino (gen. eds), *Thomas Middleton and Early Modern Textual Culture: A Companion to The Collected Works* (Oxford: Clarendon Press, 2007), pp. 414–16.
Levin, Richard A., 'The Dark Color of a Cardinal's Discontentment: The Political Plot of *Women Beware Women*', *Medieval and Renaissance Drama in England*, 10 (1998), 201–17.
Mulryne, J. R. (ed.), 'Introduction', *Women Beware Women*, Revels Student Editions (Manchester: Manchester University Press, 2007), pp. 1–30.
O'Callaghan, Michelle, *Thomas Middleton, Renaissance Dramatist* (Edinburgh: Edinburgh University Press, 2009).
Sullivan, Ceri, 'Thomas Middleton', in Andrew Hiscock and Lisa Hopkins (eds), *Teaching Shakespeare and Early Modern Dramatists* (Basingstoke: Palgrave Macmillan, 2007), pp. 146–57.

The Playtext

Batchelor, J. B., 'The Pattern of *Women Beware Women*', *Yearbook of English Studies* (1972), 79–88. Reprinted in R. V. Holdsworth (ed.), *Three Jacobean Revenge Tragedies*, Casebook Series (Basingstoke: Macmillan, 1990), pp. 207–21.
Dawson, Anthony B., '*Women Beware Women* and the Economy of Rape', *Studies in English Literature*, 27 (1987), 303–20.
Jowett, John (ed.), 'Introduction: *Women Beware Women*: A Tragedy', in Gary Taylor and John Lavagnino (gen. eds), *Thomas Middleton: The Collected Works* (Oxford: Clarendon Press, 2007), pp. 1488–92.
Jowett, John, 'Thomas Middleton', in Arthur Kinney (ed.), *A Companion to Renaissance Drama* (Oxford: Blackwell, 2004), pp. 507–23.
Ricks, Christopher, 'Word-Play in *Women Beware Women*', *Review of English Studies*, 12 (1961), 238–50. Reprinted in R. V. Holdsworth (ed.), *Three Jacobean Revenge Tragedies*, Casebook Series (Basingstoke: Macmillan, 1990), pp. 172–85.
Shakespeare, William, '*Romeo and Juliet*', in Stephen Greenblatt, Walter Cohen, Jean E. Howard and Katherine Eisaman Maus (eds), *The Norton Shakespeare*, second edition (New York: W. W. Norton, 2008), pp. 897–972.
Taylor, Gary, 'How to use this book', in Gary Taylor and John Lavagnino (gen. eds), *Thomas Middleton and Early Modern Textual Culture: A Companion to The Collected Works* (Oxford: Clarendon Press, 2007), pp. 19–22.
Taylor, Gary, 'No Holds Barred', The Guardian, 21 February 2006 < http://www.guardian.co.uk/stage/2006/feb/21/theatre >.
Wigler, Stephen, 'Parent and Child: the Pattern of Love in *Women Beware Women*', in Kenneth Friedenreich (ed.), '*Accompaninge the Players*': *Essays Celebrating Thomas Middleton, 1580-1990* (New York: AMS Press, 1983), pp. 183–201.

Stagecraft

Bromham, A. A., 'The Tragedy of Peace: Political Meaning in *Women Beware Women*', *Studies in English Literature*, 26 (1986), 309–29.
Holdsworth, R. V., '*Women Beware Women* and *The Changeling* on the Stage', in R. V. Holdsworth (ed.), *Three Jacobean Revenge Tragedies*, Casebook Series (Basingstoke: Macmillan, 1990), pp. 247–74.
Keeble, N. H. (ed.), *The Cultural Identity of Seventeenth-Century Woman: A Reader* (London: Routledge, 1994).
Potter, John, '"In Time of Sports": Masques and Masking in Middleton's *Women Beware Women*', *Papers on Language and Literature*, 18.4 (1982), 368–83.
Roberts, Marilyn, 'A Preliminary Checklist of Productions of Thomas Middleton's Plays', *Research Opportunities in Renaissance Drama*, 28 (1986), 37–61.
Shand, G. B., 'The Stagecraft of *Women Beware Women*', *Research Opportunities in Renaissance Drama*, 28 (1986), 29–36.
Shewring, Margaret and J. R. Mulryne, 'Dancing Towards Death: Masques and Entertainments in London and Florence as Precedents for Thomas Middleton's *Women Beware Women*', *Dance Research* 25.2 (2007), 134–43.

Sutherland, Sarah, 'Middleton's *Women Beware Women*', in *Masques in Jacobean Tragedy* (New York: AMS Press, 1983), pp. 87–100.
Taylor, Neil and Bryan Loughrey, 'Middleton's Chess Strategies in *Women Beware Women*', *Studies in English Literature*, 24 (1984), 341–54.
Thomson, Leslie, '"*Enter Above*": The Staging of *Women Beware Women*', *Studies in English Literature*, 26 (1986), 331–43.
Tricomi, Albert H., *Anticourt Drama in England 1603–1642* (Virginia: University Press of Virginia, 1989).
Web Gallery of Art. < http://www.wga.hu/ > [accessed 30 September 2010].

Mapping Spaces

Ascham, Roger, *The Scholemaster* (London, 1570), *Early English Books Online*. Cambridge University Library.
  < http://gateway.proquest.com/openurl?ctx_ver = Z39.88-2003&res_id = xri:eebo&rft_id = xri:eebo:image:4597:2 > [accessed 1 October 2008].
Betteridge, Thomas (ed.), *Borders and Travellers in Early Modern Europe* (Aldershot: Ashgate, 2007).
Bromham, A. A., 'The Tragedy of Peace: Political Meaning in *Women Beware Women*', *Studies in English Literature*, 26 (1986), 309–29.
Bruzzi, Zara and A. A. Bromham, 'The soil alters: Y'are in another country': Multiple perspectives and political resonances in Middleton's *Women Beware Women*', in Michelle Marrapodi, A. J. Hoenselaars, Marcello Cappuzzo and L. Falzon Santucci (eds), *Shakespeare's Italy: Functions of Italian Locations in Renaissance Drama*, revised edition (Manchester: Manchester University Press, 1997), pp. 251–71.
Chakravorty, Swapan, *Society and Politics in the Plays of Thomas Middleton* (Oxford: Clarendon Press, 1996).
Findlay, Alison, *Playing Spaces in Early Modern Women's Drama* (Cambridge: Cambridge University Press, 2006).
Howard, Jean E., *Theater of a City: The Places of London Comedy, 1598-1642* (Philadelphia: University of Pennsylvania Press, 2007).
Peacham, Henry, *The Art of Living in London* (London, 1642), *Early English Books Online*. Cambridge University Library < http://gateway.proquest.com/openurl?ctx_ver = Z39.88-2003&res_id = xri:eebo&rft_id = xri:eebo:image:64533 > [accessed 1 October 2008].
Rye, William Benchley, *England as Seen by Foreigners in the Days of Elizabeth and James I* (1865), facsimile (Boston: Adamant Media, 2005).

Mapping Bodies

Biggs, Murray, 'Does the Duke rape Bianca in Middleton's *Women Beware Women?*', *Notes and Queries*, 44 (242) (1997), 97–100.
Blamires, Alcuin (ed.), *Woman Defamed and Woman Defended: An Anthology of Medieval Texts* (Oxford: Clarendon Press, 1992).
Bromham, A. A., '"A Plague Will Come": Art, Rape and Venereal Disease in Middleton's *Women Beware Women*', *EnterText*, 3.1 (2003), 145–60.
  < http://www.brunel.ac.uk/about/acad/sa/artresearch/entertext/issues/entertext3_1 > [accessed 9 November 2008].
Bromham, A. A., '*Women Beware Women*, Danae, and Iconographic Tradition', *Notes and Queries*, 50 (2003), 74–76.
Calbi, Maurizio, *Approximate Bodies: Gender and Power in Early Modern Drama and Anatomy* (London: Routledge, 2005).
Daileader, Celia R., *Eroticism on the Renaissance Stage: Transcendence, Desire, and the Limits of the Visible*, Cambridge Studies in Renaissance Literature and Culture 30 (Cambridge: Cambridge University Press, 1998).
Dawson, Anthony B., '*Women Beware Women* and the Economy of Rape', *Studies in English Literature*, 27 (1987), 303–20.
Detmer-Goebel, Emily, 'What More Could Woman Do?: Dramatizing Consent in

LEARNING AND TEACHING RESOURCES 183

Heywood's *Rape of Lucrece* and Middleton's *Women Beware Women*', *Women's Studies*, 36 (2007), 141–59.
Goldberg, Jonathan, 'Fatherly Authority: The Politics of Stuart Family Images', in Margaret W. Ferguson, Maureen Quilligan and Nancy J. Vickers (eds), *Rewriting the Renaissance: The Discourses of Sexual Difference in Early Modern Europe* (Chicago: University of Chicago Press, 1987), pp. 3–32.
Heller, Jennifer L., 'Space, Violence, and Bodies in Middleton and Cary', *Studies in English Literature*, 45.2 (2005), 425–41.
Hopkins, Lisa, 'Art and Nature in *Women Beware Women*', *Renaissance Forum* 1.2 (1996) < http://web.archive.org/web/20050915004430re_/www.hull.ac.uk/Hull/EL_Web/renforum/v1no2/hopkins.htm > [accessed 7 October 2010].
Hopkins, Lisa, 'Middleton's *Women Beware Women* and the Mothering Principle', *Journal of Gender Studies*, 7.1 (1998), 63–72.
Hutchings, Mark, 'Middleton's *Women Beware Women*: Rape, Seduction – or Power, Simply?', *Notes and Queries*, 45 (243) (1998), 366–67.
Kahn, Coppélia, 'Whores and Wives in Jacobean Drama', in Dorothea Kehler and Susan Baker (eds), *In Another Country: Feminist Perspectives on Renaissance Drama* (Metuchen, NJ: Scarecrow Press, 1991), pp. 246–60.
Kehler, Dorothea, '"That Ravenous Tiger Tamora": *Titus Andronicus*'s Lusty Widow, Wife, and M/Other', in Philip C. Kolin (ed.), *Titus Andronicus: Critical Essays* (New York: Garland, 1995), pp. 317–32.
Levin, Richard A., 'If Women Should Beware Women, Bianca Should Beware Mother', *Studies in English Literature*, 37 (1997), 371–89.
Swetnam, Joseph, *The Araignment of Lewd, Idle, Froward and Unconstant Women* [...] (London, 1615), *Early English Books Online*. Cambridge University Library < http://gateway.proquest.com/openurl?ctx_ver=Z39.88-2003&res_id=xri:eebo&rft_id=xri:eebo:image:25624 > [accessed 1 October 2008]

Reading Middleton
Bate, Jonathan, 'The mad worlds of Thomas Middleton', *The Times Literary Supplement* 23 (April 2008) < http://entertainment.timesonline.co.uk/tol/arts_and_entertainment/the_tls/tls_selections/literature_and_criticism/article3801281.ece > [accessed 5 May 2008].
Chakravorty, Swapan, *Society and Politics in the Plays of Thomas Middleton* (Oxford: Clarendon Press, 1996).
Ewbank, Inga-Stina, 'Realism and Morality in *Women Beware Women*', *Essays and Studies*, 22 (1969), 57–70. Reprinted in R. V. Holdsworth (ed.), *Three Jacobean Revenge Tragedies*, Casebook Series (Basingstoke: Macmillan, 1990), pp. 196–207.
Heinemann, Margot, *Puritanism and Theatre: Thomas Middleton and Oppositional Drama under the Early Stuarts* (Cambridge: Cambridge University Press, 1980).
Holmes, David M., *The Art of Thomas Middleton: A Critical Study* (Oxford: Clarendon Press, 1970).
Hutchings, Mark and A. A. Bromham, *Middleton and his Collaborators*, Writers and Their Work (Northcote: Devon, 2008).
Martin, Matthew, 'Introduction', *Early Modern Literary Studies* 8.3 (2003) < http://purl.oclc.org/emls/08-3/intro.htm > [accessed 5 May 2008].
McElroy, John, '*The White Devil*, *Women Beware Women*, and the Limitations of Rationalist Criticism', *Studies in English Literature*, 19 (1979), 295–312.
Stachniewski, John, 'Calvinist Psychology in Middleton's Tragedies', in R. V. Holdsworth (ed.), *Three Jacobean Revenge Tragedies*, Casebook Series (Basingstoke: Macmillan, 1990), pp. 226–47.
Taylor, Gary, 'Middleton, Thomas', *Oxford Dictionary of National Biography*, Oxford University Press, Sept 2004; online edn, May 2008 < http://www.oxforddnb.com/view/article/18682 > [accessed 10 Nov 2008].
Taylor, Gary, 'Thomas Middleton: Lives and Afterlives', in Gary Taylor and John Lavagnino (gen. eds), *Thomas Middleton: The Collected Works* (Oxford: Clarendon Press, 2007), pp. 25–58.

Taylor, Gary and Trish Thomas Henley (eds), *The Oxford Handbook of Middleton Studies* (Oxford: Oxford University Press, forthcoming).

Select Electronic Resources: Public Access
'The Early Seventeenth-Century', *Norton Topics Online*.
< http://www.wwnorton.com/college/english/nael/17century/topic_1/welcome.htm > [accessed 16 November 2008].
This site provides a general introduction to gender, the family and the household, and encourages students' active engagement with primary and secondary material.
Lexicons of Early Modern English (LEME).
< http://leme.library.utoronto.ca/ > [accessed 1 January 2009].
Edited by Ian Lancashire, this database has replaced *The Early Modern English Dictionaries Database* (EMEDD). Although some features require subscription, 'public users can query all 500,000 word-entries' to explore how words were variously defined in seventeenth-century England.
Thomas Middleton
< http://www.thomasmiddleton.org > [accessed 5 May 2008].
The companion website to *The Oxford Middleton* is a work in progress. Alongside material which relates directly to Gary Taylor and John Lavagnino's *Thomas Middleton: The Collected Works* and *Thomas Middleton and Early Modern Textual Culture: A Companion to The Collected Works*, it also contains information about 'Middleton's Life' and 'Selected Middleton Publications'.
'Thomas Middleton (1580–1627)', *The Centre for the Study of the Renaissance*, University of Warwick.
< http://www2.warwick.ac.uk/fac/arts/ren/elizabethan_jacobean_drama/middleton/ > [accessed 30 November 2008].
Part of Nicoleta Cinpoes' webpages on 'the Jacobethans', this site describes itself as an 'open access resource for education'. Though a work in progress, it already contains a useful catalogue of *Women Beware Women*'s performance history and '313 entries on editions, criticism and production reviews on *Women Beware Women* and [...] *The Changeling*'.
'Thomas Middleton (c. 1580–1627)', *Luminarium*.
< http://www.luminarium.org/sevenlit/middleton/index.html > [accessed 3 June 2008]. Annina Jokinen's site offers a basic introduction to the playwright and links to some secondary criticism.
Taylor, Gary, 'Our Other Shakespeare: Thomas Middleton's Boys (and Girls) Able to Ravish a Man', *Globelink*.
< http://www.globelink.org/research/thomasmiddleton/thecollectedworks/ > [accessed 29 November 2008].
Primarily a recording of Taylor's 33-minute lecture introducing *Thomas Middleton: The Collected Works*, this podcast makes some significant comparisons between Shakespearean and Middletonian dramaturgies.

Electronic Resources: Subscription Required
Early English Book Online (EEBO).
Thomas Middleton, '*Women Beware Women*', in *Two New Playes... written by Tho. Middleton, Gent.* (London, 1657), *Early English Books Online*, Cambridge University Library.
< http://gateway.proquest.com/openurl?ctx_ver=Z39.88-2003&res_id=xri:eebo&rft_id=xri:eebo:image:55290 > [accessed 5 May 2008].
EEBO provides a searchable transcription and an electronic image of the 1657 edition.
Literature On Line (LION).
Thomas Middleton, '*Women Beware Women*', in *Two New Playes... written by Tho. Middleton, Gent.* (London, 1657) *Literature Online*, Cambridge, Chadwyck-Healey, 1994 < http://gateway.proquest.com/openurl?ctx_ver=Z39.88-2003&xri:pqil:res_ver=0.2&res_id=xri:lion&rft_id=xri:lion:ft:dr:Z000102745:0 > [accessed 28 May 2008]. LION offers a searchable transcription of the 1657 edition.

LEARNING AND TEACHING RESOURCES 185

Notes

* I am extremely grateful to Alison Findlay for sharing her experiences of teaching early modern drama with me. I should also like to thank the students taking 'Renaissance to Restoration: English Literature 1580–1688' for their comments.
1 My title is indebted to John Jowett, 'Mapping the Text', in *Shakespeare and Text*, Oxford Shakespeare Topics (Oxford: Oxford University Press, 2007), pp. 93–114.
2 Ceri Sullivan usefully identifies 'five concerns in approaching Middleton: the staging, the language, key items or images, the social use of drama, and the physical text', and she discusses *Women Beware Women* in these terms. Ceri Sullivan, 'Thomas Middleton', in *Teaching Shakespeare and Early Modern Dramatists*, ed. by Andrew Hiscock and Lisa Hopkins (Basingstoke: Palgrave Macmillan, 2007), pp. 146–57 (pp. 149, 155–56). Another helpful resource is provided by Michelle O'Callaghan, *Thomas Middleton, Renaissance Dramatist* (Edinburgh: Edinburgh University Press, 2009).
3 Richard A. Levin, 'The Dark Color of a Cardinal's Discontentment: The Political Plot of *Women Beware Women*', *Medieval and Renaissance Drama in England*, 10 (1998), 201–17 (p. 201).
4 John Jowett, '*Women, Beware Women*', in *Thomas Middleton and Early Modern Textual Culture: A Companion to The Collected Works*, gen. ed. by Gary Taylor and John Lavagnino (Oxford: Oxford University Press, 2007), pp. 414–16 (p. 414).
5 J. R. Mulryne has 'hesitatingly suggested in an essay published elsewhere that the text we have of *Women Beware Women*, dated by scholars to around 1621, in part due to an allusion to the age of King James (see 1.3.91 and note), may in fact represent a revision of a play first written in 1613 or so, at the height of Middleton's interest in citizen comedy'. J. R. Mulryne, 'Introduction', in Thomas Middleton, *Women Beware Women*, ed. by J. R. Mulryne, Revels Student Editions (Manchester: Manchester University Press, 2007), pp. 1–30 (p. 5).
6 Richard Dutton, 'Introduction', in Thomas Middleton, *Women Beware Women and Other Plays*, ed. by Richard Dutton (Oxford: Oxford University Press, 1999), pp. vii–xxxvii (p. xxi).
7 William C. Carroll, 'Introduction', in Thomas Middleton, *Women Beware Women*, New Mermaids, 2nd edn (London: A & C Black, 1994), pp. xi–xxxviii (p. xvi). As cited in Carroll, these respective descriptions are by Samuel Schoenbaum, *Middleton's Tragedies: A Critical Study* (New York: Columbia University Press, 1955), p. 130; Robert Ornstein, *The Moral Vision of Jacobean Tragedy* (Madison: University of Wisconsin Press, 1960), p. 192; Margot Heinemann, *Puritanism and Theatre: Thomas Middleton and Opposition Drama under the Early Stuarts* (Cambridge: Cambridge University Press, 1980), p. 172; Albert H. Tricomi, *Anticourt Drama in England 1603-1642* (Charlottesville, VA: University of Virginia Press, 1989), p. 128; Tricomi, *Anticourt Drama*, p. 121; Robert N. Watson, in *The Cambridge Companion to English Renaissance Drama*, ed. by A. R. Braunmuller and Michael Hattaway (Cambridge: Cambridge University Press, 1990), p. 313; Alexander Leggatt, *English Drama: Shakespeare to the Restoration, 1590–1660* (London: Longman, 1988), p. 147; Inga-Stina Ewbank, 'The Middle of Middleton', in *The Arts of Performance in Elizabethan and Early Stuart Drama*, ed. by Murray Biggs et al. (Edinburgh: Edinburgh University Press, 1991), pp. 156–72 (p. 169); and Nicholas Brooke, *Horrid Laughter in Jacobean Tragedy* (London: Open Books, 1979), p. 110. Carroll, 'Introduction', p. xvi, fns 13–16.
8 Mulryne, 'Introduction', p. 7.
9 Anthony B. Dawson, '*Women Beware Women* and the Economy of Rape', *Studies in English Literature*, 27 (1987), 303–20 (p. 311). Cited in Carroll, 'Introduction', p. xvii. Richard Dutton also asks 'just how ironic, or otherwise, is the title?' ('Introduction', p. xxii).
10 For a discussion of 'ambivalence' in relation to the play, see Carroll, 'Introduction', p. xvii.
11 Thomas Middleton, *Two New Plays [...] written by Tho. Middleton, Gent.* (London, 1657), *Early English Books Online*, Cambridge University Library < http://

gateway.proquest.com/openurl?ctx_ver = Z39.88-2003&res_id = xri:eebo&rft_id = xri:eebo:image:55290> [accessed 5 May 2008], sig. A. 3ʳ.
12 See further Alison Findlay, *Departmental Webpage, Lancaster University* <http://www.lancs.ac.uk/fass/english/profiles/Alison-Findlay/> [accessed 25 November 2008].
13 Gary Taylor, 'No Holds Barred', The Guardian, 21 February 2006 <http://www.guardian.co.uk/stage/2006/feb/21/theatre/ [accessed 5 October 2008], paras 1–2.
14 All quotations are from '*Romeo and Juliet*', in *The Norton Shakespeare*, ed. by Stephen Greenblatt, Walter Cohen, Jean E. Howard and Katherine Eisaman Maus, 2nd edn (New York: W. W. Norton, 2008), pp. 897–972.
15 All quotations are from Mulryne's edition.
16 John Jowett, 'Thomas Middleton', in *A Companion to Renaissance Drama*, ed. by Arthur Kinney (Oxford: Blackwell, 2004), pp. 507–23 (p. 516).
17 In his discussion of character names in Middleton's dramatic corpus, Gary Taylor makes the point that 'In the original texts, many characters are not given personal names, but identified by generic social labels'. Gary Taylor, 'How to use this book', in *Thomas Middleton and Early Modern Textual Culture: A Companion to The Collected Works*, gen. ed. by Gary Taylor and John Lavagnino (Oxford: Oxford University Press, 2007), pp. 19–23 (p. 19).
18 John Jowett (ed.), 'Introduction: *Women Beware Women*: A Tragedy', in *Thomas Middleton: The Collected Works*, gen. ed. by Gary Taylor and John Lavagnino (Oxford: Oxford University Press, 2007), pp. 1488–92 (p. 1491). R. V. Holdsworth also discusses the play's 'namelessness' in '*Women Beware Women* and *The Changeling* on the Stage', in *Three Jacobean Revenge Tragedies*, ed. by R. V. Holdsworth, Casebook Series (Basingstoke: Macmillan, 1990), pp. 247–74 (p. 253).
19 Christopher Ricks, 'Word-Play in *Women Beware Women*', *Review of English Studies*, 12 (1961), 238–50. Reprinted in *Three Jacobean Revenge Tragedies*, ed. by Holdsworth, pp. 172–85.
20 Dutton, 'Introduction', pp. viii–ix.
21 Dutton, 'Introduction', pp. viii–ix.
22 Dutton, 'Introduction', p. viii.
23 Mulryne, 'Introduction', p. 9.
24 Mulryne, 'Introduction', p. 10.
25 R. V. Holdsworth comments that 'locations as well as gestures are subject to ironic patterning', in '*Women Beware Women* and *The Changeling*', p. 251.
26 For a further discussion of windows and 'scenic patterning', see A. A. Bromham, 'The Tragedy of Peace: Political Meaning in *Women Beware Women*', *Studies in English Literature*, 26 (1986), 309–29 (pp. 318–19).
27 Cited in *The Cultural Identity of Seventeenth Century Woman*, ed. by N. H. Keeble (London: Routledge, 1994), pp. 148–49.
28 Holdsworth, '*Women Beware Women* and *The Changeling*', p. 251.
29 Leslie Thomson, '"*Enter Above*": The Staging of *Women Beware Women*', *Studies in English Literature*, 26 (1986), 331–43 (p. 332).
30 Holdsworth, '*Women Beware Women* and *The Changeling*', p. 251.
31 Holdsworth states that 'Middleton fixes on this image because it evokes contradictory associations of romantic fidelity and prostitution', in '*Women Beware Women* and *The Changeling*', p. 251.
32 Mulryne notes that 'Costume played a considerable part on the Jacobean stage', 'Introduction', p. 10.
33 *Web Gallery of Art* <http://www.wga.hu/html/b/bugiardi/the_nun.html> [accessed 25 October 2008].
34 *Web Gallery of Art* <http://www.wga.hu/html/v/veronese/07/2loggia.html> [accessed 7 October 2010].
35 Lisa Hopkins, 'Art and Nature in *Women Beware Women*', *Renaissance Forum* 1.2 (1996) <http://web.archive.org/web/20050915004430re_/www.hull.ac.uk/Hull/EL_Web/renforum/v1no2/hopkins.htm> [accessed 7 October 2010] para 5. See also Neil Taylor and Bryan Loughrey, 'Middleton's Chess Strategies in *Women Beware Women*', *Studies in English Literature*, 24 (1984), 341–54 (p. 348).
36 G. B. Shand, 'The Stagecraft of *Women Beware Women*', *Research Opportunities in*

LEARNING AND TEACHING RESOURCES   187

   Renaissance Drama, 28 (1985), 29–36 (p. 30). Details of this production are from
   Marilyn Roberts, 'A Preliminary Checklist of Productions of Thomas Middleton's
   Plays', *Research Opportunities in Renaissance Drama*, 28 (1986), 37–61 (p. 56).
37 Mulryne, 'Introduction', p. 10.
38 Dawson, 'Economy of Rape', p. 307.
39 Dawson, 'Economy of Rape', p. 306.
40 Mulryne, 'Introduction', p. 8.
41 Zara Bruzzi and A. A. Bromham, ' "The soil alters; Y'are in another country" ':
   multiple perspectives and political resonances in Middleton's *Women Beware
   Women*', in *Shakespeare's Italy: Functions of Italian Locations in Renaissance
   Drama*, ed. by Michelle Marrapodi, A. J. Hoenselaars, Marcello Cappuzzo and L.
   Falzon Santucci, rev. edn (Manchester: Manchester University Press, 1997), pp. 251–
   71 (p. 256).
42 Dutton, 'Introduction, p. x.
43 See further *Borders and Travellers in Early Modern Europe*, ed. by Thomas
   Betteridge (Aldershot: Ashgate, 2007) and Swapan Chakravorty, *Society and Politics
   in the Plays of Thomas Middleton* (Oxford: Clarendon Press, 1996), p. 128 ff.
44 Roger Ascham, *The Scholemaster* (London, 1570), *Early English Books Online*,
   Cambridge University Library < http://gateway.proquest.com/openurl?ctx_
   ver = Z39.88-2003&res_id = xri:eebo&rft_id = xri:eebo:image:4597:2 > [accessed 1
   October 2008], sigs. H.iiii^r–H.iiii^v. I have modernized i/j and u/v.
45 Ascham, *The Scholemaster*, sig. J.i^v.
46 Ascham, *The Scholemaster*, sig. K.i^v.
47 Mulryne, 'Introduction', p. 6.
48 Levin, 'The Dark Color of a Cardinal's Discontentment', p. 214.
49 Dutton, 'Introduction', p. x.
50 Henry Peacham, *The Art of Living in London* (London, 1642), *Early English Books
   Online*, Cambridge University Library. < http://gateway.proquest.com/open-
   url?ctx_ver = Z39.88-2003&res_id = xri:eebo&rft_id = xri:eebo:image:
   64533 > [accessed 1 October 2008], sig. A1^v. I was alerted to the significance of this
   extract by Jean E. Howard's analysis in *Theater of a City: The Places of London
   Comedy, 1598-1642* (Philadelphia: University of Pennsylvania Press, 2007), pp. 11–12.
51 See Howard, *Theater of a City*, p. 11.
52 For an examination of *Women Beware Women* and homosocial desire, see Maurizio
   Calbi, *Approximate Bodies: Gender and Power in Early Modern Drama and
   Anatomy* (London: Routledge, 2005), pp. 86–91.
53 Coppélia Kahn, 'Whores and Wives in Jacobean Drama', in *In Another Country:
   Feminist Perspectives on Renaissance Drama*, ed. by Dorothea Kehler and Susan
   Baker (Metuchen, NJ: Scarecrow Press, 1991), pp. 246–60 (p. 246).
54 Carroll, 'Introduction', p. xvii, and Mark Hutchings and A. A. Bromham, *Middleton
   and his Collaborators*, Writers and Their Work (Northcote: Devon, 2008), p. 21. For
   those interested in exploring the medieval tradition that Carroll alludes to, I
   recommend *Woman Defamed and Woman Defended: An Anthology of Medieval
   Texts*, ed. by Alcuin Blamires (Oxford: Clarendon Press, 1992).
55 Joseph Swetnam, *The Araignment of Lewd, Idle, Froward and Unconstant Women
   [...]* (London, 1615), *Early English Books Online*, Cambridge University Library
   < http://gateway.proquest.com/openurl?ctx_ver = Z39.88-2003&res_id = xri:
   eebo&rft_id = xri:eebo:image:25624 > [accessed 1 October 2008], sig. G3^v. I have
   modernized i/j and u/v.
56 John Jowett records that Livia has 581 lines. Jowett, '*Women Beware Women*: A
   Tragedy', p. 1541.
57 Dorothea Kehler, ' "That Ravenous Tiger Tamora": *Titus Andronicus*'s Lusty
   Widow, Wife, and M/Other', in *Titus Andronicus: Critical Essays*, ed. by Philip C.
   Kolin (New York: Garland, 1995), pp. 317–32 (p. 318).
58 Swetnam, *Araignment*, sig A.3^r.
59 John Jowett considers the way in which Middleton's writing is characterized by 'the
   interweaving of abstraction and concrete physical detail relating to the human body'
   ('Thomas Middleton', p. 512).

60 For an extended discussion of this scene see Taylor and Loughrey, 'Middleton's Chess Strategies', pp. 341–54.
61 Ceila R. Daileader, *Eroticism on the Renaissance Stage: Transcendence, Desire, and the Limits of the Visible*, Cambridge Studies in Renaissance Literature and Culture 30 (Cambridge: Cambridge University Press, 1998), p. 1.
62 Christopher Ricks states that 'sensual pleasure is itself a *game* or a *sport*', 'Word-Play', p. 179.
63 Mark Hutchings argues that 'More rape than seduction [...] II.ii surely affirms patriarchal power'. Mark Hutchings, 'Middleton's *Women Beware Women*: Rape, Seduction – or Power, Simply?', *Notes and Queries*, 45 (243) (1998), 366–67 (p. 367). This scene has prompted much critical debate. See further: Murray Biggs, 'Does the Duke rape Bianca in Middleton's *Women Beware Women?*', *Notes and Queries*, 44 (242) (1997), 97–100; Dawson, 'Economy of Rape', 303–20; Emily Detmer-Goebel, 'What More Could Woman Do?: Dramatizing Consent in Heywood's *Rape of Lucrece* and Middleton's *Women Beware Women*', *Women's Studies*, 36 (2007), 141–59; Jennifer Heller, 'Space, Violence, and Bodies in Middleton and Cary', *Studies in English Literature*, 45.2 (2005), 425–41.
64 Jowett, 'Thomas Middleton', p. 513.
65 For an overview of Middletonian criticism, see Matthew Martin, 'Introduction', *Early Modern Literary Studies*, 8.3 (2003) < http://purl.oclc.org/emls/08-3/intro.htm > [accessed 5 May 2008].
66 Gary Taylor, 'Middleton, Thomas', *Oxford Dictionary of National Biography*, Oxford University Press, Sept 2004; online edn, May 2008 < [http://www.oxforddnb.com/view/article/18682 > [accessed 10 Nov 2008], para 43. See also Gary Taylor, 'Thomas Middleton: Lives and Afterlives', in *Thomas Middleton: The Collected Works*, pp. 25–58, p. 47.
67 Gary Taylor, 'Middleton, Thomas', para. 42.

Bibliography

A *select collection of old plays, in twelve volumes. The second edition, corrected and collated with the old copies, with notes critical and explanatory* (London, 1780), V.
Alwes, Derek B., 'The Secular Morality of Middleton's City Comedies', *Comparative Drama*, 42.2 (2008), 101–19.
Amussen, Susan Dwyer, *An Ordered Society: Gender and Class in Early Modern England* (Columbia: Columbia University Press, 1988).
Andrews, Michael Cameron, *This Action of Our Death: The Performance of Death in English Renaissance Drama* (Newark: University of Delaware Press, 1989).
Aristotle, *The Poetics*, in *Classical Literary Criticism*, trans. by T. S. Dorsch (London: Penguin Books, 1965).
Ascham, Roger, *The Scholemaster* (London, 1570), *Early English Books Online*, Cambridge University Library < http://gateway.proquest.com/openurl?ctx_ver = Z39.88-2003&res_id = xri:eebo&rft_id = xri:eebo:image:4597:2 > [accessed 1 October 2008].
Baines, Barbara Joan, *The Lust Motif in the Plays of Thomas Middleton* (Salzburg: Institut für Englische Sprache und Literatur, 1973).
Bakhtin, M. M., 'Forms of time and the chronotope in the novel: Notes towards a historical poetics' in *The Dialogical Imagination: Four Essays* (Austin: University of Texas Press, 1981).
Bakhtin, M. M., *Speech Genres and Other Late Essays* (Austin: University of Texas Press, 1986).
Barker, Howard, 'The redemptive power of desire', *The Times*, 6 February 1986.
Barker, Richard Hindry, *Thomas Middleton* (New York: Columbia University Press, 1958).
Barroll, Leeds, *Politics, Plague and Shakespeare's Theater: The Stuart Years* (Ithaca: Cornell University Press, 1991).
Batchelor, J. B., 'The Pattern of *Women Beware Women*', *Yearbook of English Studies*, 2 (1972), 78–88.
Bate, Jonathan, 'The mad worlds of Thomas Middleton', *Times Literary Supplement*, 23 April 2008.
Bawcutt, N. W., 'Was Thomas Middleton a Puritan Dramatist?', *Modern Language Review*, 94.4 (1999), 925–39.
Bentley, Gerald Eades, *The Jacobean and Caroline Stage*, 5 vols (Oxford: Oxford University Press, 1956), IV.
Berggren, Paula S., '"Womanish Mankind": Four Jacobean Heroines', *International Journal of Women's Studies*, 1 (1978), 349–62.
Betteridge, Thomas, ed., *Borders and Travellers in Early Modern Europe* (Aldershot: Ashgate, 2007).
Biggs, Murray, 'Does the Duke Rape Bianca in Middleton's *Women Beware Women*?', *Notes and Queries*, 44.1 (1997), 97–100.
Blamires, Alcuin, ed., *Woman Defamed and Woman Defended: An Anthology of Medieval Texts* (Oxford: Clarendon Press, 1992).
Blow, John, *Venus and Adonis: A Masque for the entertainment of the King*, ed. by Bruce Wood, Purcell Society Edition Companion Series, II (London: Stainer and Bell, 2008).
Boas, Frederick S., *An Introduction to Stuart Drama* (London: Oxford University Press, 1946).

Boehrer, Bruce, *Monarchy and Incest in Renaissance England: Literature, Culture, Kinship, and Kingship* (Philadelphia: University of Pennsylvania Press, 1992).
Boose, Lynda, 'The 1599 Bishop's Ban, Elizabethan Pornography, and the Sexualization of the Jacobean Stage', in *Enclosure Acts*, ed. by Richard Burt and John Michael Archer (Ithaca: Cornell University Press, 1994), pp. 185–200.
Born-Lechleitner, Ilse, *The Motif of Adultery in Elizabethan, Jacobean, and Caroline Tragedy* (Lewiston: Mellen, 1995).
Bourcier, Elisabeth, ed., *The Diary of Sir Simonds d'Ewes 1622–1624* (Paris: Didier, 1974).
Bourdieu, Pierre, *Invitation to Reflexive Sociology*, trans. by L. J. D. Wacquandt (Cambridge: Polity, 1992).
Bourdieu, Pierre, *The Rules of Art* (Palo Alto: Stanford University Press, 1996).
Bradbrook, M. C., *Themes and Conventions of Elizabethan Tragedy* (Cambridge: Cambridge University Press, 1935).
Bradford, Gamaliel, *Elizabethan Women* (Boston: Houghton Mifflin, 1936).
Bradford, Gamaliel, 'The Women of Middleton and Webster', *Sewanee Review*, 29 (1921), 14–29.
Braunmuller, A. R., and Michael Hattaway, eds, *The Cambridge Companion to English Renaissance Drama* (Cambridge: Cambridge University Press, 1990).
Breitenberg, Mark, *Anxious Masculinity in Early Modern England* (Cambridge: Cambridge University Press, 1996).
Brittin, Norman A., *Thomas Middleton* (New York: Twayne, 1972).
Brodwin, Leonora Leet, *Elizabethan Love Tragedy 1587–1625* (New York: New York University Press, 1971).
Bromham, A. A., ' " A Plague Will Come": Art, Rape, and Venereal Disease in Middleton's *Women Beware Women*', *EnterText*, 3.1 (2003).
Bromham, A. A., 'The Tragedy of Peace: Political Meaning in *Women Beware Women*', *Studies in English Literature*, 26 (1986), 309–29.
Bromley, Laura, 'Men and Women Beware: Social, Political, and Sexual Anarchy in *Women Beware Women*', *Iowa State Journal of Research*, 61.3 (1987), 311–21.
Brooke, Nicholas, *Horrid Laughter in Jacobean Tragedy* (London: Open Books; New York: Barnes & Noble, 1979).
Brundage, James A., *Law, Sex, and Christian Society in Medieval Europe* (Chicago: University of Chicago Press, 1987).
Bruster, Douglas, *Shakespeare and the Question of Culture* (New York: Palgrave, 2003).
Bruzzi, Zara, 'A Device to Fit the Times: Intertextual Allusion in Thomas Middleton's *Women Beware Women*', in *The Italian World of English Renaissance Drama: Cultural Exchange and Intertextuality*, ed. by Michele Marapodi and A. J. Hoenselaars (Newark: University of Delaware Press; London: Associated University Presses, 1998), pp. 302–17.
Bruzzi, Zara, and A. A. Bromham, 'The soil alters; Y'are in another country': multiple perspectives and political resonances in Middleton's *Women Beware Women*', in *Shakespeare's Italy: Functions of Italian locations in Renaissance drama*, ed. by Michele Marrapodi et al. (Manchester: Manchester University Press, 1993; rev. edn 1997), pp. 251–71.
Buland, Mable, *The Presentation of Time in the Elizabethan Drama* (New York: Holt, 1912).
Bullinger, Heinrich, *The Christen State of Matrimony, wherein husbands and wyves may learne to keepe house together, with love* (London, 1575).
Buonomo, Leonardo, 'Domestic Themes in Thomas Middleton's *Women Beware Women*', *Prospero* 7 (2000), 21–33.
Bushnell, Rebecca W., *Tragedies of Tyrants: Political Thought and Theater in the English Renaissance* (Ithaca, NY: Cornell University Press, 1990).
Butler, Judith, *Gender Trouble: Feminism and the Subversion of Identity* (New York: Routledge, 1999).
Calbi, Maurizio, *Approximate Bodies: Gender and Power in Early Modern Drama and Anatomy* (London: Routledge, 2005).
Calvin, Jean, *A commentarie vpon S. Paules epistles to the Corinthians. Written by M. Iohn Caluin: and translated out of Latine into Englishe by Thomas Timme* (London, 1577), fol. 130r.

Camoin, Francois Andre, *The Revenge Convention in Tourneur, Webster, and Middleton* (Salzburg: Institut für Englische Sprache und Literatur, 1972).
Carroll, William C., 'Introduction', in Thomas Middleton, *Women Beware Women*, New Mermaids, 2nd edn (London: A & C Black, 1994), pp. xi–xxxviii.
Chakravorty, Swapan, *Society and Politics in the Plays of Thomas Middleton* (Oxford: Clarendon Press, 1996).
Champion, Larry S. *Tragic Patterns in Jacobean and Caroline Drama* (Knoxville: University of Tennessee Press, 1977).
Cherry, Caroline Lockett, *The Most Unvaluedst Purchase: Women in the Plays of Thomas Middleton* (Salzburg: Institut für Englische Sprache und Literatur, 1973).
Choyce drollery, songs & sonnets being a collection of divers excellent pieces of poetry, of severall eminent authors, never before printed (London, 1656).
Christensen, Ann C., 'Settling House in Middleton's *Women Beware Women*', *Comparative Drama*, 29.4 (1995–96), 493–518.
Cogswell, Thomas, 'Middleton and the Court 1624: *A Game at Chess* in Context', *Huntington Library Quarterly*, 47 (1984), 237–88.
Cole, J. A., 'Sunday dinners and Thursday suppers: Social and moral contexts of the food imagery in *Women Beware Women*', in *Jacobean Drama Studies: Jacobean Miscellany 4*, ed. by James Hogg (Salzburg: Institut für Englische Sprache und Literatur, 1984), pp. 86–98.
Coleridge, Samuel Taylor, *The Collected Works of Samuel Taylor Coleridge*, ed. by R. A. Foakes (London: Routledge & Kegan Paul; Princeton: Princeton University Press, 1987), II.
Colie, Rosalie, *The Resources of Kind: Genre Theory in the Renaissance*, ed. by Barbara Lewalski (Berkeley: University of California Press, 1973).
Collinson, Patrick, *The Elizabethan Puritan Movement* (Oxford: Clarendon Press, 1967).
Core, George, 'The Canker and the Muse: Imagery in *Women Beware Women*', *Renaissance Papers* (1968), 65–76.
Corneille, Pierre, *Nicomede a tragi-comedy translated out of the French of Monsieur Corneille by John Dancer as it was acted as the Theatre-Royal, Dublin; together with an exact catalogue of all the English stage plays printed till this present year 1671* (London, 1671).
Cox, Nicholas (attr. Gerard Langbaine), *An exact catalogue of all the comedies, tragedies, tragi-comedies, opera's, masks, pastorals and interludes that were ever yet printed and published till this present year 1680* (Oxford, 1680).
Cronin, Lisa, 'A Checklist of Professional Productions in the British Isles since 1880 of plays by Tudor and Stuart Dramatists (excluding Shakespeare)', *Renaissance Drama Newsletter*, Supplement Seven (University of Warwick: Graduate School of Renaissance Studies, 1987).
Daileader, Ceila R., *Eroticism on the Renaissance Stage: Transcendence, Desire, and the Limits of the Visible*, Cambridge Studies in Renaissance Literature and Culture 30 (Cambridge: Cambridge University Press, 1998), pp. 25–34.
Dawson, Anthony B., '*Women Beware Women* and the Economy of Rape', *Studies in English Literature. 1500–1900*, 27.2, Elizabethan and Jacobean Drama (1987), 303–20.
de Grazia, Margreta, *Hamlet Without Hamlet* (Cambridge: Cambridge University Press, 2007).
Dessen, Alan C., and Leslie Thomson, *A Dictionary of Stage Directions in English Drama, 1580-1642* (Cambridge: Cambridge University Press, 1999).
Detmer-Goebel, Emily, 'What More Could Woman Do?: Dramatizing Consent in Heywood's *Rape of Lucrece* and Middleton's *Women Beware Women*', *Women's Studies*, 36 (2007), 141–59.
Dilke, C. W. (ed.), *Old English Plays; being a Selection from the Early Dramatic Writers*, 6 vols (London: Whittingham and Rowland, 1815).
Dod, John, and Robert Cleaver, *A Godlie Forme of Household Government* (London: Thomas Man, 1598); rpt. William St Clair and Irmgaard Maasen, *Conduct Literature for Women*, 6 vols (London: Pickering and Chatto, 2000), III, pp. 25–412.
Dodson, Daniel, 'Middleton's Livia', *Philological Quarterly*, 27 (1948), 376–81.

Doelman, James, '"A King of Thine Own Heart": The English Reception of King James VI and I's *Basilikon Doron*', *Seventeenth Century*, 9 (1994), 1–9.
Dollimore, Jonathan, and Alan Sinfield, *Political Shakespeare: New Essays in Cultural Materialism* (Manchester: Manchester University Press, 1985).
Dowland, John, 'In Darkness Let Me Dwell', in Robert Dowland, *A Musical Banquet* (London, 1610).
Dusinberre, Juliet, *Shakespeare and the Nature of Women* (Basingstoke and London: Macmillan, 1975).
Durston, Christopher, and Jacqueline Eales, eds, *The Culture of English Puritanism, 1560–1700* (New York: St Martin's Press, 1996).
Dutton, Richard, ed., *'Women Beware Women' and Other Plays* (Oxford: Oxford University Press, 1999; repr. 2009).
Eccles, Mark, 'Thomas Middleton A Poett', *Studies in Philology*, 54 (1957), 516–36.
Eliot, T. S., *Elizabethan Essays* (London: Faber & Faber, 1934).
Eliot, T. S., *Essays on Elizabethan Drama* (New York: Harcourt, Brace and World, 1956).
Ellis-Fermor, U. M., *The Jacobean Drama: An Interpretation* (London: Methuen, 1936).
Else, Gerard, *Aristotle's 'Poetics': The Argument* (Cambridge, MA: Harvard University Press, 1957).
Engelberg, Edward, 'Tragic Blindness in *The Changeling* and *Women Beware Women*', *Modern Language Quarterly*, 23 (1962), 20–28.
Erasmus, Desiderius, *A Book Called in Latin Enchiridion Militis Christiani and in English The Manual of the Christian Knight, replenished with the most wholesome precepts made by the famous clerk Erasmus of Rotterdam, to which is added a new and marvellous profitable Preface* (London: Methuen, 1905). Chapter: *Of the outward and inward man: Chap. iv.* Accessed from http://oll.libertyfund.org/title/191/5516 on 20 February 2009.
Erasmus, Desiderius, *The Education of a Christian Prince*, ed. by Lisa Jardine, Neil M. Cheshire, Michael John Heath (Cambridge: Cambridge University Press, 1997).
Ewbank, Inga-Stina, 'The Middle of Middleton', in *The Arts of Performance in Elizabethan and Early Stuart Drama*, ed. by Murray Biggs et al. (Edinburgh: Edinburgh University Press, 1991), pp. 156–72.
Ewbank, Inga-Stina, 'Realism and Morality in "Women Beware Women"', *Essays and Studies* (1969), 57–70.
Ewbank, Inga-Stina, 'Realism and Morality in *Women Beware Women*', *Essays and Studies*, 22 (1969), 57–70.
Farley-Hills, David, *Jacobean Drama: A Critical Study of the Professional Drama, 1600–25* (London: Macmillan, 1988).
Farmer, John, *Madrigals a 4* (1599).
Farr, Dorothy M., *Thomas Middleton and the Drama of Realism: A Study of Some Representative Plays* (New York: Barnes & Noble, 1973).
Feldman, A. Bronson, 'The Yellow Malady: Short studies of five tragedies of jealousy', *Literature and Psychology*, 6 (1956), 38–52.
Findlay, Alison, *Departmental Webpage, Lancaster University* < http://www.lancs.ac.uk/fass/english/profiles/Alison-Findlay/ > [accessed 25 November 2008].
Foster, Verna Ann, 'The Deed's Creature: The Tragedy of Bianca in *Women Beware Women*', *Journal of English and Germanic Philology*, 78 (1979), 508–21.
Friedenreich, Kenneth, ed., *'Accompaninge the players': Essays Celebrating Thomas Middleton, 1580–1980* (New York: AMS Press, 1983).
Fumerton, Patricia, *Cultural Aesthetics: Renaissance Literature and the Practice of Social Ornament* (Chicago: University of Chicago Press, 1991).
Gasper, Julia, *The Dragon and the Dove: The Plays of Thomas Dekker* (Oxford: Oxford University Press, 1990).
Given-Wilson, Chris, and Alice Curteis, *The Royal Bastards of Medieval England* (London: Routledge & Kegan Paul, 1984).
Goldsworthy, Jeffrey, *The Sovereignty of Parliament: History and Philosophy* (Oxford: Oxford University Press, 1999).
Gouge, William, *Eight Treatises of Domesticall Duties. Workes*, 2 vols (London, 1627).
Greenblatt, Stephen J., *Renaissance Self-Fashioning from More to Shakespeare* (Chicago: University of Chicago Press, 1980).

Greenblatt, Stephen J., *Shakespearean Negotiations: The Circulation of Social Energy in Renaissance England* (Oxford: Clarendon Press, 1988).
Gurr, Andrew, *Playgoing in Shakespeare's Londonu*, 2nd edn (Cambridge: Cambridge University Press, 1996).
Hakewill, George, *King Davids Vow for Reformation of Himselfe. His Family. His Kingdome*. Delivered in twelve sermons before the Prince his Highness upon Psalm 101 (London, 1621).
Hall, Joan Lord, *The Dynamics of Role-Playing in Jacobean Tragedy* (New York: St Martin's Press, 1991).
Hallahan, Huston D., 'The Thematic Juxtaposition of the Representational and the Sensational in Middleton's *Women Beware Women*', *Studies in Iconography*, 2 (1976), 66–84.
Hallett, Charles A., 'The Psychological Drama of *Women Beware Women*', *Studies in English Literature, 1500–1900*, 12.2 (1972), 375–89.
Haselkorn, Anne M., 'Sin and the Politics of Penitence: Three Jacobean Adultresses', in *The Renaissance Englishwoman in Print: Counterbalancing the Canon*, ed. by Anne Haselkorn and Betty Travitsky (Amherst, MA: University of Massachusetts Press, 1990), pp. 119–36.
Hazlitt, William, *The Complete Works of William Hazlitt*, ed. by P. P. Howe after edition of A. R. Waller and Arnold Glover (London and Toronto: J. M. Dent & Sons, 1931).
Heinemann, Margot, *Puritanism and Theatre: Thomas Middleton and Opposition Drama under the Early Stuarts* (Cambridge: Cambridge University Press, 1980).
Heller, Jennifer, 'Space, Violence, and Bodies in Middleton and Cary', *Studies in English Literature*, 45.2 (2005), 425–41.
Helm, Paul, *Calvin and the Calvinists* (Edinburgh: The Banner of Truth Trust, 1982).
Herbert, George, *The English Poems*, ed. by Helen Wilcox (Cambridge: Cambridge University Press, 2007).
Herrup, Cynthia, 'The King's Two Genders', *Journal of British Studies*, 45 (2006), 493–510.
Heywood, Thomas, *The hierarchie of the blessed angells Their names and offices the fall of Lucifer with his angells* (London, 1635).
Hibbard, G. R., 'The tragedies of Thomas Middleton and the decadence of the drama', *Renaissance and Modern Studies*, 1 (1957), 35–64.
Hill, Christopher, *The English Revolution 1640* (London: Lawrence and Wishart, 1940).
Hill, Christopher, *Society and Puritanism in Pre-revolutionary England* (London: Secker & Warburg, 1964).
Hirst, Derek, *England in Conflict 1603-1660: Kingdom, Community, Commonwealth* (London: Arnold, 1999).
Hiscock, Andrew, and Lisa Hopkins, eds, *Teaching Shakespeare and Early Modern Dramatists* (London: Palgrave, 2007).
Holdsworth, R. V., '*Women Beware Women* and *The Changeling* on the Stage', in *Three Jacobean Revenge Tragedies*, ed. by R. V. Holdsworth, Casebook Series (Basingstoke: Macmillan, 1990), pp. 247–74.
Holdsworth, R. V., ed., *Three Jacobean Revenge Tragedies* (Basingstoke: Macmillan, 1990).
Holmes, David M., *The Art of Thomas Middleton* (Oxford: Clarendon Press, 1970).
Holmes, Jonathan, and Adrian Streete, eds, *Refiguring Mimesis: Representation in Early Modern Literature* (Hatfield: University of Hertfordshire Press, 2005).
Hopkins, Lisa, 'Art and Nature in *Women Beware Women*', *Renaissance Forum* 1.2 (1996) < http://web.archive.org/web/20050915004430re_/www.hull.ac.uk/Hull/EL_Web/renforum/v1no2/hopkins.htm > [accessed 7 October 2010] para 5.
Hopkins, Lisa, *The Female Hero in English Renaissance Tragedy* (Basingstoke: Palgrave Macmillan, 2002).
Hopkins, Lisa, 'City Tragedy: Middleton, Shakespeare and Ford', *Compar(a)ison*, 1 (1994), 71–76.
Hotz-Davies, Ingrid, 'A *Chaste Maid in Cheapside* and *Women Beware Women*: Feminism, Anti-Feminism and the Limitations of Satire', *Cahiers Elisabethains*, 39 (1991), 29–39.
Howard, Jean E., *Theater of a City: The Places of London Comedy, 1598–1642* (Philadelphia: University of Pennsylvania Press, 2007).

Howard-Hill, T. H., *Middleton's 'Vulgar Pasquin': Essays on A Game at Chess* (Newark, NJ: University of Delaware Press, 1995).
Howard-Hill, T. H., 'Political Interpretations of Middleton's *A Game at Chess*', *Yearbook of English Studies*, 21 (1991), 274–85.
Huebert, Ronald, *The Performance of Pleasure in English Renaissance Drama* (Basingstoke: Palgrave Macmillan, 2003).
Hughes, Ann, 'Local history and the origins of the civil war', in *Reformation to Revolution: Politics and Religion in Early Modern England*, ed. by Margo Todd (London: Routledge, 1995), pp. 252–71.
Hutchings, Mark, 'Middleton's *Women Beware Women*: Rape, Seduction – or Power, Simply?', *Notes and Queries*, n.s. 45.3 (September 1998), 366–67.
Hutchings, Mark, and A. A. Bromham, *Middleton and his Collaborators*, Writers and Their Work (Northcote: Devon, 2008).
Hutchings, William, '"Creative Vandalism" Or, A Tragedy Transformed: Howard Barker's "Collaboration" with Thomas Middleton on the 1986 Version of *Women Beware Women*', in *Text and Presentation: The University of Florida, Department of Classics, Comparative Drama Conference Papers*, VIII, ed. by Karelisa Hartigan (Lanham, MD: University Press of America, 1988), pp. 93–101.
Hutera, Donald J., 'Women Beware Women and Les Liaisons Dangereuses', *Theatre Journal*, 38.3 (October 1986), 366–67.
Innes, Paul, '"*Pluck but his name out of his heart*": A Caesarean Cross-section', in *Refiguring Mimesis: Representation in Early Modern Literature*, ed. by Jonathan Holmes and Adrian Streete (Hatfield: University of Hertfordshire Press, 2005), pp. 79–98.
James VI and I, 'A Speech to the Lords and Commons of the Parliament at White-Hall, on Wednesday the XXI of March. Anno 1609', in *King James VI and I: Political Writings*, ed. by Johann P. Sommerville (Cambridge: Cambridge University Press, 1994), pp. 179–203.
James VI and I, *The True Law of Free Monarchies; And, Basilikon Doron*, ed. by Daniel Fischlin and Mark Fortier (Toronto: Centre for Reformation and Renaissance Studies, 1996).
Jameson, Fredric, 'Magical narratives: Romance as genre', *New Literary History*, 7.2 (1975), 135–63.
Jones, Norman, *The English Reformation: Religion and Cultural* (Oxford: Blackwell, 2002).
Jonson, Ben, *Ben Jonson*, ed. by C. H. Herford and Percy Simpson (Oxford: Clarendon Press, 1925), I.
Jonson, Ben, *Ben Jonson*, ed. by C. H. Herford and Percy and Evelyn Simpson (Oxford: Clarendon Press, 1938), VI.
Jowett, John, ed., 'Introduction: *Women Beware Women*: A Tragedy', in *Thomas Middleton: The Collected Works*, gen. ed. by Gary Taylor and John Lavagnino (Oxford: Clarendon Press, 2007), pp. 1488–92.
Jowett, John, 'Mapping the Text', in *Shakespeare and Text*, Oxford Shakespeare Topics (Oxford: Oxford University Press, 2007), pp. 93–114.
Jowett, John, 'Thomas Middleton', in *A Companion to Renaissance Drama*, ed. by Arthur Kinney (Oxford: Blackwell, 2004), pp. 507–23.
Jowett, John, '*Women, Beware Women*', in *Thomas Middleton and Early Modern Textual Culture: A Companion to The Collected Works*, gen. ed. by Gary Taylor and John Lavagnino (Oxford: Clarendon Press, 2007), pp. 414–16.
Kahn, Coppélia, 'Whores and Wives in Jacobean Drama', in *In Another Country: Feminist Perspectives on Renaissance Drama*, ed. by Dorothea Kehler and Susan Baker (Metuchen, NJ and London: Scarecrow Press, 1991), pp. 246–60.
Keeble, N. H., ed., *The Cultural Identity of Seventeenth Century Woman* (London: Routledge, 1994).
Kehler, Dorothea, '"That Ravenous Tiger Tamora": *Titus Andronicus*'s Lusty Widow, Wife, and M/Other', in *Titus Andronicus: Critical Essays*, ed. by Philip C. Kolin (New York: Garland, 1995), pp. 317–32.
Kendall, R. T., *Calvin and English Calvinism to 1649* (Oxford: Oxford University Press, 1979).

Kiernan, Pauline, *Shakespeare's Theory of Drama* (Cambridge: Cambridge University Press, 1998).
King, Laura Severt, 'Violence and the masque: A ritual sabotaged in Middleton's *Women Beware Women*', *Pacific Coast Philology*, 21.1–2 (1986), 42–47.
Kipling, Gordon, *Enter the King: Theatre, Liturgy, and Ritual in the Medieval Civic Triumph* (Oxford: Clarendon Press, 1997).
Kistner, A. L., and M. K. Kistner, 'Will, fate, and the social order in *Women Beware Women*', *Essays in Literature*, 3 (1976), 17–31.
Knights, L. C., *Drama and Society in the Age of Jonson* (London: Chatto and Windus, 1937).
Knoppers, Laura Lunger, *Puritanism and Its Discontents* (Newark: University of Delaware Press; London: Associated University Presses, 2003).
Krook, Dorothea, *Elements of Tragedy* (New Haven: Yale University Press, 1969).
Lamb, Charles, *Specimens of English Dramatic Poets who lived about the Time of Shakespeare. With Notes, A new edition in two volumes* (London: Edward Moxon, 1835, 1st pub. 1808).
Lancaster, Marjorie S., 'Middleton's use of the upper stage in *Women Beware Women*', *Tulane Studies in English*, 22 (1977), 69–85.
Langbaine, Gerard, 'Thomas Middleton', in G. Langbaine, *An Account of the English Dramatick Poets, or, Some observations and Remarks on the Lives and Writings of all those that have publish'd either comedies, tragedies, tragi-comedies, pastorals, masques, interludes, farces or opera's in the English tongue* (Oxford, 1691), p. 374.
Laqueur, Thomas, *Making Sex: Body and Gender from the Greeks to Freud* (Cambridge, MA: Harvard University Press, 1990).
Leggatt, Alexander, *English Drama: Shakespeare to the Restoration, 1590–1660* (London: Longman, 1988).
Levin, Richard A., 'The Dark Color of a Cardinal's Discontentment: The Political Plot of *Women Beware Women*', *Medieval and Renaissance Drama in England*, 10 (1998), 201–17.
Levin, Richard A., 'If Women Should Beware Women, Bianca Should Beware Mother', *Studies in English Literature*, 37.2 (1997), 371–89.
Limon, Jerzy, *Dangerous Matter: English Drama and Politics in 1623/4* (Cambridge: Cambridge University Press, 1986).
Lockyer, Roger, *Buckingham: The Life and Political Career of George Villiers, First Duke of Buckingham: 1592–1628* (London: Longmans, 1981).
Macewan, Ian, *The Renaissance Notion of Woman: A Study in the Fortunes of Scholasticism and Medical Science in European Intellectual Life* (Cambridge: Cambridge University Press, 1983).
MacGregor, Catherine, 'Undoing the Body Politic: Representing Rape in *Women Beware Women*', *Theatre Research International*, 23.1 (1998), 14–23.
Marcus, Leah, *Unediting the Renaissance: Shakespeare, Marlowe, Milton* (London: Routledge, 1966).
Marsh, David, 'Erasmus on the Antithesis of Body and Soul', *Journal of the History of Ideas*, 37 (1976), 673–88.
Martin, Matthew, 'Introduction', *Early Modern Literary Studies*, 8.3 (2003) < http://purl.oclc.org/emls/08-3/intro.htm > [accessed 5 May 2008].
McAlindon, T., *English Renaissance Tragedy* (Vancouver: University of British Columbia Press, 1986).
McCabe, Richard A., *Incest, Drama and Nature's Law 1550–1700* (Cambridge: Cambridge University Press, 1993).
McCanles, Michael, 'The Moral Dialectic of Middleton's *Women Beware Women*', in *'Accompaninge the players': Essays Celebrating Thomas Middleton, 1580–1980*, ed. by Kenneth Friedenreich (New York: AMS Press, 1983), pp. 203–18.
McEachern, Claire, *The Poetics of English Nationhood, 1590–1612* (Cambridge: Cambridge University Press, 1996).
McElroy, John F., '*The White Devil*, *Women Beware Women*, and the Limitations of Rationalist Criticism', *Studies in English Literature, 1500–1900*, 19 (1979), 295–312.
McLuskie, Kathleen, *Renaissance Dramatists* (Hemel Hempstead: Harvester Wheatsheaf, 1989).

Middleton, Thomas, *The Collected Works*, gen. ed. by Gary Taylor and John Lavagnino (Oxford: Clarendon Press, 2007).
Middleton, Thomas, *Five Plays*, ed. by Bryan Loughrey and Neil Taylor (London: Penguin, 1988).
Middleton, Thomas, *A Game at Chess* (London, 1625).
Middleton, Thomas, *The Selected Plays of Thomas Middleton*, ed. by David L. Frost (Cambridge: Cambridge University Press, 1978).
Middleton, Thomas, *Two New Playes. Viz. More DISSEMBLERS besides WOMEN. VIZ. WOMEN beware WOMEN* (London, 1657).
Middleton, Thomas, *Two Newe Playes ... written by Tho. Middleton, Gent.* (London, 1657), Early English Books Online, Cambridge University Library < http://gateway.proquest.com/openurl?ctx_ver = Z39.88-2003&res_id = xri:eebo&rft_id = xri:eebo:image:55290 > [accessed 5 May 2008], sig. A. 3ʳ.
Middleton, Thomas, *Women Beware Women*, ed. by Charles Barber (Berkeley: University of California Press, 1969).
Middleton, Thomas, *Women Beware Women*, ed. by William C. Carroll (London: A. & C. Black and New York: W. W. Norton, 1994).
Middleton, Thomas, *Women Beware Women*, ed. by Roma Gill (London: Ernest Benn, 1968).
Middleton, Thomas, *Women Beware Women*, ed. by John Jowett, in *Thomas Middleton: The Collected Works*, gen. ed. by Gary Taylor and John Lavagnino (Oxford: Clarendon Press, 2007).
Middleton, Thomas, *Women Beware Women*, ed. by J. R. Mulryne, The Revels Plays (London: Methuen, 1975; reprinted Manchester: Manchester University Press, 1975).
Middleton, Thomas, *Women Beware Women*, ed. by J. R. Mulryne, Revels Student Editions (Manchester: Manchester University Press, 2007).
Middleton, Thomas, *The Works of Thomas Middleton*, ed. by A. H. Bullen (London: J. C. Nimmo, 1885–86).
Middleton, Thomas, *Works of Thomas Middleton. Now first collected with some account of the Author and Notes [...] in five volumes*, ed. by Rev. A. Dyce (London: Edward Lumley, 1840).
Middleton, Thomas, and Howard Barker, *Women Beware Women* (London: John Calder, 1986).
Milton, John, *Eikonoklastes*, in *Complete Prose Works*, ed. by Merritt Y. Hughes, 8 vols (New Haven: Yale University Press, 1962), III, pp. 337–601.
Miola, Robert S., 'Othello *Furens*', *Shakespeare Quarterly*, 41 (1990), 49–64.
Mocket, Richard, *God and the King* (London, 1615).
Montrose, Louis, *The Purpose of Playing: Shakespeare and the Cultural Politics of the Elizabethan Theatre* (Chicago and London: University of Chicago Press, 1996).
Moody, William Vaughan, and Robert Morss Lovett, *A History of English Literature* (New York: Scribner's, 1902).
Muir, Kenneth, 'The Role of Livia in "Women Beware Women"', in *Poetry and Drama 1570–1700*, ed. by Antony Coleman and Antony Hammond (London: Methuen, 1981), pp. 76–89.
Mullaney, Steven, *The Place of the Stage: License, Play, and Power in Renaissance England* (Chicago and London: University of Chicago Press, 1988).
Muller, Richard A., *Post-Reformation Reformed Dogmatics: The Rise and Development of Reformed Orthodoxy, ca. 1520 to ca. 1725* (Grand Rapids, MI: Baker Academics, 2003).
Mulryne, J. R., 'Annotations in some copies of *Two New Playes by Thomas Middleton*, 1657', *The Library*, 5th series, 30 (1975), 217–21.
Mulryne, J. R., 'Introduction', in Thomas Middleton, *Women Beware Women*, ed. by J. R. Mulryne, Revels Student Editions (Manchester: Manchester University Press, 2007), pp. 1–30.
Mulryne, J. R., 'Introduction', in *Women Beware Women*, ed. by J. R. Mulryne (Manchester and New York: University of Manchester Press, 2007).
Mulryne, J. R., 'Thomas Middleton, *Women Beware Women*, and the Myth of Florence', in *The Italian World of English Renaissance Drama: Cultural Exchange and*

Intertextuality, ed. by Michele Marapodi and A. J. Hoenselaars (Newark: University of Delaware Press; London: Associated University Presses, 1998), pp. 141–64.
Nauer, Bruno, *Thomas Middleton: A Study of the Narrative Structures* (Zürich: Juris Druck & Verlag Zürich, 1977), pp. 51–67.
Ng, Su Fang, *Literature and the Politics of Family in Seventeenth-Century England* (Cambridge: Cambridge University Press, 2007).
O'Callaghan, Michelle, *Thomas Middleton, Renaissance Dramatist* (Edinburgh: Edinburgh University Press, 2009).
Orlin, Lena Cowen, *Private Matters and Public Culture in Post-Reformation England* (Ithaca and London: Cornell University Press, 1994).
Ornstein, Robert, *The Moral Vision of Jacobean Tragedy* (Madison: University of Wisconsin Press, 1960).
Parker, R. B., 'Middleton's Experiments with Comedy and Judgement', in *Jacobean Theatre*, ed. by John Russell Brown and Bernard Harris (London: Edward Arnold, 1960), pp. 178–99.
Patterson, William Brown, *King James VI and I and the Reunion of Christendom* (Cambridge: Cambridge University Press, 1997).
Peacham, Henry, *The Art of Living in London* (London, 1642), Early English Books Online, Cambridge University Library. < http://gateway.proquest.com/openurl?ctx_ver = Z39.88-2003&res_id = xri:eebo&rft_id = xri:eebo:image:64533 > [accessed 1 October 2008].
Phillips, Edward, *Theatrum Poetarum, or, A compleat collection of the poets especially the most eminent, of all ages [...] together with a prefatory discourse of the poets and poetry in generall* (London, 1675).
Playford, John, *The English Dancing Master* (London, 1651).
Porter, Bertha, 'Mocket, Richard (1577–1618)', rev. Glenn Burgess, *Oxford Dictionary of National Biography*, ed. by H. C. G. Matthew and Brian Harrison (Oxford: Oxford University Press, 2004). Accessed 21 February 2009 < http://www.oxforddnb.com/view/article/18866 > .
Potter, John, ' "In Time of Sports": Masques and Masking in Middleton's *Women Beware Women*', *Papers on Language and Literature*, 18.4 (1982), 368–83.
Ravelhofer, Barbara, *The Early Stuart Masque: Dance, Costume, and Music* (Oxford: Oxford University Press, 2006).
Ribner, Irving, *Jacobean Tragedy: The Quest for Moral Order* (London: Methuen, 1962).
Ricks, Christopher, 'Word-Play in *Women Beware Women*', *Review of English Studies*, 12 (1961), 238–50. Reprinted in *Three Jacobean Revenge Tragedies*, ed. by R. V. Holdsworth (London: Macmillan, 1990), pp. 172–85.
Roberts, Marilyn, 'A Preliminary Checklist of Productions of Thomas Middleton's Plays', *Research Opportunities in Renaissance Drama*, 28 (1986), 37–61.
Rollenhagen, Gabriel, *Nucleus Emblematum* (Cologne, 1611).
Roper, Lyndal, ' "The Common Man", "the Common Good", "Common Women": Gender and Meaning in the German Reformation Commune', *Social History*, 12 (1987), 1–21.
Rowe, George E., *Thomas Middleton and the New Comedy Tradition* (Lincoln: University of Nebraska Press, 1977).
Russell, Conrad, *The Origins of the English Civil War* (London: Macmillan, 1973).
Russell, Conrad, *Parliaments and English Politics 1621–1629* (Oxford: Clarendon Press, 1979).
Russell, Conrad, *Unrevolutionary England, 1603–42* (London: Hambledon, 1990).
Saintsbury, George, *A History of Elizabethan Literature* (London: Macmillan, 1887).
Salisbury, Joyce, 'Gendered Sexuality', in *Handbook of Medieval Sexuality*, ed. by Vern L. Bullough and James A. Brundage (New York: Taylor & Francis, 2000), pp. 88–131.
Schafer, Elizabeth, *Research Opportunities in Renaissance Drama*, 34 (1995).
Schama, Simon, *The Embarrassment of Riches: An Interpretation of Dutch Culture in the Golden Age* (London: Collins, 1987).
Schoenbaum, Samuel, *Middleton's Tragedies: A Critical Study* (New York: Columbia University Press, 1955).
[Scott, Thomas]?, *Tom Tell-Troath: or, a free Discourse touching the Manners of the*

Time. Directed to his Maj by waye of humble advertisement, in John Somers, *A Collection of Scarce and Valuable Tracts, Chiefly Such as Relate to the History and Constitution of These Kingdoms*, ed. by Walter Scott, 2nd edn, 10 vols (London: James Ballantyre, 1809–1815), II, pp. 470–92.
Scott, Thomas, *Vox Populi Or Newes From Spayne* (London, 1620).
Scott, Sir Walter, *The Journal of Sir Walter Scott*, ed. by W. E. K. Anderson (Oxford: Clarendon Press, 1972).
Shakespeare, William, *The Riverside Shakespeare*, ed. by G. Blakemore Evans et al. (Boston: Houghton Mifflin, 1974).
Shakespeare, William, 'Romeo and Juliet', in *The Norton Shakespeare*, ed. by Stephen Greenblatt, Walter Cohen, Jean E. Howard and Katherine Eisaman Maus, 2nd edn (New York: W. W. Norton, 2008), pp. 897–972.
Shand, G. B., 'The Elizabethan Aim of *The Wisdom of Solomon Paraphrased*', in '*Accompaninge the Players': Essays Celebrating Thomas Middleton, 1580–1980* , ed. by Kenneth Friedenreich (New York: AMS Press, 1983), pp. 67–78.
Shand, G. B., 'The stagecraft of *Women Beware Women*', *Research Opportunities in Renaissance Drama*, 28 (1985), 29–36.
Shelley, Mary, *The Novels and Selected Works of Mary Shelley*, ed. by Fiona Stafford (London: William Pickering, 1996).
Shephard, Robert, 'Sexual Rumours in English Politics: The Cases of Elizabeth I and James I', in *Desire and Discipline: Sex and Sexuality in the Premodern West*, ed. by Jacqueline Murray and Konrad Eisenbichler (Toronto: University of Toronto Press, 1996), pp. 101–22.
Shiells, Robert, *The Lives of the Poets of Great Britain and Ireland, to the time of Dean Swift. Compiled from ample materials scattered in a variety of books [...]*, 5 vols (London, 1753), I.
Sidney, Sir Philip, *A Defence of Poetry*, ed. by J. A. Van Dorsten (Oxford: Oxford University Press, 1996).
Siemon, James R., *Word Against Word: Shakespearean utterance* (Amherst: University of Massachusetts Press, c.2002).
Skura, Meredith Anne, *Shakespeare the Actor and the Purposes of Playing* (Chicago and London: University of Chicago Press, 1993).
Smith, Bruce, *The Acoustic World of Early Modern England: Attending to the O-Factor* (Chicago: University of Chicago Press, 1999).
Smith, Logan Pearsall, *Life and Letters of Sir Henry Wotton*, 2 vols (Oxford: Clarendon Press, 1907, rep. 1966), I.
Smith, Peter, '*Women Beware Women*', *Cahiers Elisabéthains*, 36 (1989), 90–91.
Sommerville, J. P., *Politics and Ideology in England 1603-1640* (London: Longman, 1986).
Spens, Janet, *Elizabethan Drama* (London: Methuen, 1922).
Spivack, Charlotte, 'Marriage and Masque in Middleton's *Women Beware Women*', *Cahiers Elisabethains*, 42 (1992), 49–55.
Stachniewski, John, 'Calvinist Psychology in Middleton's Tragedies', in *Three Jacobean Revenge Tragedies: A Selection of Critical Essays*, ed. by R. V. Holdsworth (Basingstoke: Macmillan, 1990), pp. 226–47.
Steen, Sara Jayne, *Ambrosia in an Earthern Vessel: Three Centuries of Audience and Reader Response to the Works of Thomas Middleton* (New York: AMS Press, 1991).
Steen, Sara Jayne, *Thomas Middleton: A Reference Guide* (Boxton: G. K. Hall, 1984).
Sternhold, Thomas, *The whole booke of Psalmes, collected into English meter* (London, 1565).
Stilling, Roger, *Love and Death in Renaissance Tragedy* (Baton Rouge: Louisiana State University Press, 1976).
Stodder, Joseph Henry, *Satire in Jacobean Tragedy* (Salzburg: Institut für Englische Sprache und Literatur, 1974).
Stone, Lawrence, *The Family, Sex and Marriage in England, 1550-1800* (New York: Harper and Row, 1977).
Strauss, Jennifer, 'Dance in Thomas Middleton's *Women Beware Women*', *Parergon*, 29 (1981), 37–43.
Streete, Adrian, ' "An old quarrel between us that will never be at an end": Middleton's

BIBLIOGRAPHY 199

Women Beware Women and Late Jacobean Religious Politics', *Review of English Studies* (2008), published online at http://res.oxfordjournals.org/cgi/content/full/hgm167v1.
Streete, Adrian, '"An old quarrel between us that will never be at an end": Middleton's Women Beware Women and Late Jacobean Religious Politics', *Review of English Studies*, 60.244 (2009), 230–54.
Styan, J. L., *The English Stage: A History of Drama and Performance* (Cambridge: Cambridge University Press, 1996), pp. 228–29.
Sullivan, Ceri, 'Thomas Middleton', in *Teaching Shakespeare and Early Modern Dramatists*, ed. by Andrew Hiscock and Lisa Hopkins (Basingstoke: Palgrave Macmillan, 2007), pp. 146–58.
Swetnam, Joseph, *The Araignment of Lewd, Idle, Froward and Unconstant Women* ... (London, 1615), *Early English Books Online*, Cambridge University Library < http://gateway.proquest.com/openurl?ctx_ver = Z39.88-2003&res_id = xri:eebo&rft_id = xri:eebo:image:25624 > [accessed 1 October 2008].
Swinburne, Algernon Charles, *The Complete Works of Algernon Charles Swinburne*, ed. by Edmund Gosse and Thomas James Wise, 20 vols (London: William Heinemann; New York: Gabriel Wells, 1926).
Swinburne, Algernon Charles, 'Introduction' to *The Best Plays of the Old Dramatists. Thomas Middleton*, ed. by Havelock Ellis, Mermaid series, vol. 1 (London, 1894).
Swinburne, Algernon Charles, 'Thomas Middleton', *The Nineteenth Century*, 19.107 (January 1886), 138–53.
Symons, Arthur, *Studies in the Elizabethan Drama* (New York: Dutton, 1919).
Taylor, Gary, 'Divine [ ]sences', *Shakespeare Survey* 54 (2001), 13–30.
Taylor, Gary, 'Forms of Opposition: Shakespeare and Middleton', *English Literary Renaissance*, 24.2 (1994), 283–314.
Taylor, Gary, 'How to use this book', in *Thomas Middleton and Early Modern Textual Culture: A Companion to The Collected Works*, gen. ed. by Gary Taylor and John Lavagnino (Oxford: Clarendon Press, 2007), pp. 19–22.
Taylor, Gary, 'Middleton, Thomas', *Oxford Dictionary of National Biography*, Oxford University Press, Sept 2004; online edn, May 2008 < [http://www.oxforddnb.com/view/article/18682 > [accessed 10 Nov 2008], para 43.
Taylor, Gary, 'No Holds Barred', The Guardian, 21 February 2006 < http://www.guardian.co.uk/stage/2006/feb/21/theatrehistory-byline > [accessed 5 October 2008], pars. 1–2.
Taylor, Gary, 'Thomas Middleton: Lives and Afterlives', in *Thomas Middleton: The Collected Works*, gen. ed. by Gary Taylor and John Lavagnino (Oxford: Clarendon Press, 2007), pp. 25–58.
Taylor, Gary, and John Lavagnino, eds, *Thomas Middleton and Early Modern Textual Culture: A Companion to the Collected Works* (Oxford: Clarendon Press, 2007).
Taylor, John, *The praise of hemp-seed With the voyage of Mr. Roger Bird and the writer hereof in a boat of brown-paper, from London to Quinborough in Kent. As also, a farewell to the matchlesse deceased Mr. Thomas Coriat. Concluding with the commendations of the famous riuer of Thames* (London, 1623).
Taylor, Neil, and Bryan Loughrey, 'Middleton's Chess Strategies in *Women Beware Women*', *Studies in English Literature, 1500–1900*, 24 (1984), 341–54.
Thompson, William Irwin, *The Time Falling Bodies Take to Light: Mythology, Sexuality, and the Origins of Culture*, 2nd edn (Basingstoke: Palgrave Macmillan, 1996).
Thomson, Leslie, '"Enter Above": The Staging of *Women Beware Women*', *Studies in English Literature*, 26 (1986), 331–43.
Tilley, Arthur, ed., *A Dictionary of Proverbs in England in the Sixteenth and Seventeenth Centuries* (Ann Arbor: University of Michigan Press, 1950).
Todd, Margo, *Christian Humanism and the Puritan Social Order* (Cambridge: Cambridge University Press, 2003).
Todd, Margo, 'Humanists, Puritans and the Spiritualized Household', *Church History*, 49 (1980), 18–34.
Tomlinson, T. B., *A Study of Elizabethan and Jacobean Tragedy* (Cambridge: Cambridge University Press, 1964).

Trexler, Richard, *Sex and Conquest: Gendered Violence, Political Order, and the European Conquest of the Americas* (Ithaca, NY: Cornell University Press, 1995).
Tricomi, Albert H., *Anticourt Drama in England 1603-1642* (Charlottesville: University of Virginia Press, 1989).
Tricomi, Albert H., 'Middleton's *Women Beware Women* as Anticourt Drama', *Modern Language Studies*, 19.2 (1989), 65–77.
Trotter, David, 'An end to pageantry', *Times Literary Supplement*, 21 February 1986, p. 194.
Tyacke, Nicholas, *Anti-Calvinists: The Rise of English Arminianism c. 1590–1640* (Oxford: Clarendon Press, 1987; rev. pb. edn, 1990).
Tyacke, Nicholas, 'Puritanism, Arminianism and Counter-Revolution', in *The Origins of the English Civil War*, ed. by Conrad Russell (London: Macmillan, 1973), pp. 119–43.
van 't Spijker, Willem, *Calvin: A Brief Guide to His Life and Thought*, trans. by Lyle D. Bierma (Louisville, KY: Westminster John Knox Press, 2009).
Web Gallery of Art <http://www.wga.hu/frames-e.html?/html/b/bugiardi/the_nun.html> [accessed 25 October 2008].
Weimann, Robert, *Authority and Representation in Early Modern Discourse*, ed. by David Hillman (Baltimore and London: Johns Hopkins University Press, 1996).
Weimann, Robert, *Author's Pen and Actor's Voice: Playing and Writing in Shakespeare's Theatre*, ed. by Helen Higbee and William West (Cambridge: Cambridge University Press, 2000).
Weimann, Robert, *Shakespeare and the Popular Tradition in the Theater: Studies in the Social Dimension of Dramatic Form and Fiction*, ed. by Robert Schwartz (Baltimore and London: Johns Hopkins University Press, 1978).
Wells, Henry W., *Elizabethan and Jacobean Playwrights* (New York: Columbia University Press, 1939).
Welu, James A., and Pieter Biesboer, eds, *Judith Leyster: Schilderes in een mannenwereld* (Zwolle: Waanders Uitgevers, 1993).
Whately, William, *A bride-bush, or A wedding sermon: compendiously describing the duties of married persons* (London, 1617).
White, Martin, *Middleton and Tourneur* (Basingstoke and London: Macmillan, 1992).
Whythorne, Thomas, *The Autobiography*, ed. by James M. Osborn (Oxford: Clarendon Press, 1961).
Wigler, Stephen, 'Parent and Child: The Pattern of Love in *Women Beware Women*', in *'Accompaninge the players': Essays Celebrating Thomas Middleton, 1580–1980*, ed. by Kenneth Friedenreich (New York: AMS Press, 1983), pp. 183–201.
Wilson, Arthur, *The History of Great Britain, Being the Life and Reign of King James the First* (London, 1653).
Worthen, W. B., *Shakespeare and the Authority of Performance* (Cambridge: Cambridge University Press, 1997).
Wymer, Rowland, 'Jacobean Tragedy', in Michael Hattaway, ed., *A Companion to English Renaissance Literature* (Oxford: Blackwell, 2000), pp. 545–55.
Wymer, Rowland, *Suicide and Despair in the Jacobean Drama* (New York: St Martin's Press, 1986).
Yachnin, Paul, 'Reversal of Fortune: Shakespeare, Middleton, and the Puritans', *English Literary History*, 70.3 (2003), 757–86.
Young, Michael, *King James and the History of Homosexuality* (New York: New York University Press, 2000).
Ziraldo, Cristiana, 'Thomas Middleton's *Women Beware Women*: A Portrayal of Feminism or Misogyny?', *Rivista di Letterature Moderne e Comparate*, 17.1 (2004), 1–28.

Notes on Contributors

Annaliese Connolly is Senior Lecturer in English at Sheffield Hallam University. Her publications include 'Peele's *David and Bethsabe*: Reconsidering the Drama of the Long 1590s', *Early Modern Literary Studies* Special Issue 16 (October, 2007) and 'Evaluating Virginity: A Midsummer Night's Dream and the iconography of marriage', in *Goddesses and Queens: The Iconography of Elizabeth I* (Manchester University Press, 2007). She is also managing editor of *Early Modern Literary Studies*.

Joost Daalder is a Professor of English at Flinders University. He published his edition of *The Changeling* for New Mermaids in 1990, which became his best-known book and was reprinted many times. It has continued to attract interest because of its innovative introduction and illuminating annotation. He has also published many papers on *The Changeling*, and one on *A Yorkshire Tragedy*.

Robert C. Evans, who has taught at Auburn University Montgomery since 1982, received his PhD from Princeton University in 1984. At AUM he has been selected Distinguished Research Professor, Distinguished Teaching Professor, and University Alumni Professor. The recipient of grants from the ACLS, the NEH, the Mellon Foundation, and the UCLA Center for Renaissance Studies and from the Beinecke, Folger, Huntington, and Newberry Libraries, he has also won various teaching awards. He is the author of numerous articles and the author or editor of over twenty books.

Edward Gieskes is Associate Professor of English at the University of South Carolina. He is the author of *Representing the Professions* (2006), co-editor (with Kirk Melnikoff) of *Writing Robert Greene: New Essays on England's First Notorious Professional Writer* (2008). He contributed an essay on legal texts to the *Companion* to the Oxford Works of Middleton, and has published essays on Shakespeare and Jonson. He is working on a book-length study of generic change in early modern drama.

Andrew Hiscock is Professor of English at Bangor University, Wales. He has published widely on early modern literature and his most recent monograph is entitled *The Uses of this World: Thinking Space in Shakespeare, Marlowe, Cary and Jonson*. He is series co-editor for the *Continuum Renaissance Drama*, edited the MHRA's *2008 Yearbook of English Studies* devoted to Tudor literature, and co-edited Palgrave's *Teaching Shakespeare and Early Modern Dramatists*. He is co-editor of the academic journal *English* (Oxford University Press) and his forthcoming monograph is entitled *Reading Memory in Early Modern Literature* (Cambridge University Press).

Paul Innes was born in Glasgow and studied at the universities of Glasgow and Stirling; his PhD was on Shakespeare's sonnets. He has worked as a lecturer at the universities of Warsaw, Edinburgh and Strathclyde, and is currently a Senior Lecturer at the University of Glasgow. He specializes in Critical Theory and English Renaissance Literature and Drama. His publications include the *Dictionary of Class and Society in Shakespeare* (London and New York: Continuum Books, 2007) and *Shakespeare and the English Renaissance Sonnet: Verses of Feigning Love* (London and New York: Macmillan and St Martin's Press, 1997). His current research interests are on the culture of Renaissance performance and the forms and functions of the epic.

Coppélia Kahn is Professor of English at Brown University, and author of *Man's Estate: Masculine Identity in Shakespeare* (1981) and *Roman Shakespeare: Warriors, Wounds and Women* (1997). She has also co-edited several anthologies, among them *Representing Shakespeare: New Psychoanalytic Essays* (1980) and *Making A Difference: Feminist Literary Criticism* (1985). Her current research interest is Shakespeare as cultural capital in nineteenth- and twentieth-century America.

Anne McLaren is Senior Lecturer in the School of History, University of Liverpool. Her research tracks the effects of religious reformation on early modern political thought and culture. Her book, *Political Culture in the Reign of Elizabeth I: Queen and Commonwealth 1558-1585* (Cambridge, 1999), appeared in paperback in 2006. Recent and forthcoming publications include 'Contesting the Monarchical Republic: Jacobean Conceptions of Kingship', in *The Monarchical Republic of Early Modern England: Essays in Response to Patrick Collinson*, ed. John McDiarmid (Ashgate, 2007), 'Memorializing Regnant Queens in Tudor and Jacobean England', in *Tudor Queenship: The Reigns of Mary and Elizabeth*, ed. Anna Whitelock and Alice Hunt (Palgrave MacMillan, 2010) and a chapter on 'Political Thought' in *The Elizabethan World*, ed. Susan Doran and Norman Jones (Routledge, 2010). Her forthcoming monograph, *Embodied Kingship: Regicide and Republicanism in England, 1553-1650*, investigates the relationship between the regicidal politics of Elizabeth's reign and the English revolution.

Liz Oakley-Brown is a Lecturer in Renaissance writing at Lancaster University. Her recent publications include the monograph *Ovid and the Cultural Politics of Translation in Early Modern England* (Ashgate 2006) and the edited collection *Shakespeare and the Translation of Identity in Early Modern England* (Continuum, forthcoming).

Helen Wilcox is Professor of English at Bangor University, Wales. Her research interests range widely across early modern literature, and include drama, devotional poetry, autobiography, literature and related arts, and women's writing. She has published over a hundred articles and chapters, and books such as *Women and Literature in Britain, 1500–1700* (1996), *Betraying Our Selves: Forms of Self-Representation in Early Modern English Texts* (2000) and the Cambridge annotated edition of *The English Poems of George Herbert* (2007). Among her forthcoming works are the Arden 3 edition of *All's Well That Ends Well*, and a monograph on the textual cultures of the year 1611.

Index

Adams, John 66
Alwes, Derek B. 92
Andrews, Michael Cameron 36
Anouilh, Jean 61
Aristotle 99, 142
Ascham, Roger 177–8

Baines, Barbara Joan 30
Bakhtin, M.M. 144–6, 148
Ban on satire (1599) 146
Barber, Charles 28
Barker, Howard 55, 62–6
Barker, Richard Hindry 24, 25–6
Bassett, Kate 69, 72
Batchelor, J.B. 30
Bawcutt, N.W. 80–1
Berger, Jesse 71
Berggren, Paula S. 32
Biggs, Murray 88
Billington, Michael 65, 68, 69, 70, 71, 72–3, 74
Birmingham Repertory Company 66–7
Boas, Frederick S. 24
body
  mapping bodies 178–9
  mind, soul and 108–9, 110
Boehrer, Bruce 37
Boose, Lynda 146
Born-Lechleitner, Ilse 38
Boswell, Laurence 70
Bourdieu, Pierre 145, 146, 146–7, 150
Bradbrook, M.C. 23
Bradford, Gamaliel 22
Brittin, Norman A. 29–30
Brodwin, Leonora Leet 29
Bromham, A.A. 35–6, 38, 91
Bromley, Laura 36
Brooke, Nicholas 32, 172
Brown, Paul 66
Bruster, Douglas 147
Bruzzi, Zara 38, 91
Bryden, Ronald 61–2
Buckingham, Duke of (George Villiers) 91, 114–15
Bugiardini, Giuliano, *Portrait of a Woman*,

called *'The Nun'* 176
Buland, Mable 22
Bullen, Arthur Henry 2, 13–14, 20
Bullinger, Heinrich 157–8
Bullough, Geoffrey 147
Buonomo, Leonard 90–1
Bushnell, Rebecca 109
Buttonhole Theatre Company 67

Calvin, John 101
Calvinism 82–4
  see also Puritanism
Capello, Bianca 150, 172, 178
Caravaggio (Michel Angelo Merisi) 128
Carroll, William C. 38, 79, 85
Catholicism 112
Chakravorty, Swapan 161
Champion, Larry S. 32
Chapman, George 8
characterization 49–53
Charles I 112, 114, 115, 116, 117
chastity 167
Chaucer, Geoffrey 9
Cherry, Caroline Lockett 30–1
Christensen, Ann C. 38, 90
city comedy 149, 150, 153
city tragedy 93
Cleaver, Robert 158
Cole, J.A. 35
Coleridge, Samuel Taylor 7
Colie, Rosalie 141, 143, 149
comedy 149–53
companionate marriage 157
Cook, Kandis 64
Core, George 27–8
costumes 61, 68, 69, 71–2, 176
Coveney, Michael 68, 72, 73, 74
cultural materialism 62–3

Daileader, Celia R. 84–5
dances 131–2, 134
Dawson, Anthony B. 36, 85, 167, 172
De Jongh, Nicholas 62
De la Tour, Georges 128
Dekker, Thomas 8, 13–14

204 WOMEN BEWARE WOMEN

Dench, Judi 61–2
Detmer-Goebel, Emily 88
D'Ewes, Sir Simonds 113, 116
Dilke, Charles Wentworth 6–7
Dod, John 158
Dodsley, Robert 6
Dodson, Daniel 24
Dollimore, Jonathan 62–3
Dowland, John 129
dramaturgy of *Women Beware Women* 45–9
Drummond, William 3
Dryden, John 4
Dutton, Richard 79, 80, 81, 83, 171, 174, 177
Dyce, Alexander 2, 8, 19

Eccles, Mark 3
editions 1–2, 28, 31, 38, 77–9
effeminacy 106–11, 113–16, 117
Eliot, T.S. 2, 3, 6, 10–11, 14, 22–3
Elizabeth, Princess 112
Elizabethan Settlement 1562 82
Elliott, Marianne 71, 74
Ellis-Fermor, Una 23
Engelberg, Edward 27
Erasmus, Desiderius 97, 105, 106–7, 108, 109
Ewbank, Inga-Stina 29

Farley-Hills, David 36
Farr, Dorothy 30
fatherhood 99, 102, 111
Feldman, A. Branson 25
Felton, John 115
figurenposition 46, 51
Findlay, Alison 173
Fishburne, Richard 81
Fletcher, John 13
Florence 61, 73, 91–2
Fludd, Robert 110
Ford, John 13
Foster, Verna Ann 32–3
Frederick V of Bohemia 112

Game at Chess, A (Middleton) 80
Gaskill, William 64
Gasper, Julia 81
gender issues 84–90, 92
genre
 mixing 140–2
 theory 12–13, 139–55
Genesis 157
Gibbons, Orlando 129
Gill, Roma 28, 77, 84, 85
Glasgow Citizens' Company 67–8
Gosse, Edmund 21
Gouge, William 157

Graduate, The 174
Greenblatt, Stephen 44, 158

Hakewill, George 99
Hall, Joan Lord 37
Hallahan, Huston D. 31–2
Hallam, Henry 19
Hallett, Charles A. 30
Hamlet (Shakespeare) 44, 45, 139
Hals, Frans 128
Hands, Terry 61
Haselkorn, Anne M. 88
Hazlitt, William 2, 7, 19
Heinemann, Margot 33, 50, 79–82, 114
Heminges, William 4, 81
Herbert, George 132
Herford, Charles Harold 21
Herrup, Cynthia 102
Heywood, Thomas 4, 8, 13
Hibbard, G.R. 25
history 149–53
 genre, theory and 146–9
Holdsworth, R.V. 37, 176
Holmes, David M. 29
Hooker, Richard 101
Hope-Wallace, Philip 60, 61
Hopkins, Lisa 89–90, 92, 93, 176, 177
Hotz-Davies, Ingrid 37
household
 crisis of paternal authority 102–5
 issues of location 90–1
 phallocentric social order 99–100
Howard, Frances 38
Hudson, Richard 69
Huebert, Ronald 167
humanism 107–8
Hutchings, William 65
Hutera, Donald J. 65–6

Italian setting 91–2, 177–8

Jacobean cultural narratives 12, 97–120
James I 35–6, 81, 100, 106, 111–17
 kingship, effeminacy and tyranny 111–16
 speech to Parliament in 1623 116–17
Jameson, Fredric 143–4, 153
Johnson, Robert 129
Jonson, Ben 3–4, 38, 145, 171
 Volpone 151
Jowett, John 1, 55, 77–9, 173–4, 179

Kahn, Coppélia 178
Keats, John 2
King, Laura Severt 35
kingship *see* monarchy
Kistner, A.L. 32
Kistner, M.K. 32

INDEX 205

Knox, John 99
Krook, Dorothea 29

Lamb, Charles 1–2, 6, 9, 18–19
Lancaster, Marjorie S. 32
Lancaster University 174
Langbaine, Gerard 5
Lavagnino, John 1, 78
Leggatt, Alexander 36, 93
Levin, Richard A. 79, 89, 171
Lewalski, Barbara 143
listening 12, 122–3, 128–36
London 178
looking 12, 122–8, 133–6
Loughrey, Bryan 34–5, 36
Lovett, R.M. 22
lust 63, 81, 86, 106
  love, marriage and 13, 156–70
  reason vs 97, 98–9
Lyly, John 140, 141–2

Malespini, Celio 159, 178
Marlowe, Christopher 35
marriage 178–9
  Bianca and Isabella 164–9
  Leantio 159–64
  lust, love and 13, 156–70
  'one flesh' 157–9
  tracts 98, 99–101, 158–9
Marston, John 8, 146
masque 133, 134, 168–9
Massinger, Philip 13, 150
McAlindon, T. 36
McCabe, Richard A. 37–8
McCanles, Michael 34
McDougall, Gordon 62
McEachern, Clare 99
McElroy, John F. 33
McLuskie, Kathleen 66
Medici, Grand Duke Francesco de 150, 172, 178
Medici family 71
Meisle, Kathryn 71
Middleton, Thomas
  portrait 14, 15, 179–80
  reputation 3–11
Miola, Robert 147
Mocket, Richard 111
monarch 101, 102, 105–6
  effeminate kings and tyrants 106–11
  see also Charles I; James I
Moody, W.V. 22
Moseley, Humphrey 18, 59
Muir, Kenneth 33–4
Mulryne, J.R. 18, 31, 38, 77, 78–9, 84, 91–2, 134, 172, 175
Murdoch, Iris 61
music 128–33, 133–4, 136

National Theatre 60, 71–4
New Criticism 27, 33
Ng, Su Fang 102
Nightingale, Benedict 72

opposition drama 80–1
Orlin, Lena Cowen 162
Ornstein, Robert 26
Osborne, Robert 174
Oxford Middleton 70, 77–9
Oxford Playhouse Company 62

Palazza Signoria, Florence 61, 73
Pall Mall Gazette 13–14
Parker, R.B. 26–7
Parliament 101, 100, 114, 116–17
'Parliamentary Puritan Opposition' 80–1
patriarchy, early modern 102–6
Peacham, Henry 178
Pembroke, Earl of 80
performance history 11, 43–76
  challenges posed for acting companies 11, 59–76
  neglect of *Women Beware Women* 11, 43–58
performance techniques 45–9
Peyton, Edward 115
Phillips, Edward 5
play-within-the-play 54
playtext see text
poetics 143
politics
  allusions to English politics 91
  Jacobean 111–16
  religio-political issues 79–84, 92
Potter, John 34
Protestantism 100–1, 112, 113
  see also Puritanism
Prowse, Philip 67–8
Puritanism 79–84
  see also Protestantism

rape/seduction 36, 49, 63, 65–6, 66–7, 84–9, 151–2, 179
Ratcliffe, Michael 65
reason
  body, soul and spirit (reason) 108–9, 110
  vs lust 97, 98–9
Red Bull Theater, New York 55–6, 71
religion
  Jacobean politics and 111–13, 115–16
  and marriage 157–8
  phallocentric social order 99
  religio-political issues 79–84, 92
Ribner, Irving 27
Richards, Nathanael 4, 18, 59, 149
Ricks, Christopher 27, 174

206 WOMEN BEWARE WOMEN

Romeo and Juliet (Shakespeare) 32, 173
Roper, Lyndal 99
Rowe, George E. 32
Rowley, William 8, 25
Royal Court Theatre 55, 62–6
Royal Shakespeare Company (RSC)
  1962 production 60–1
  1969 production 61–2
  2006 production 68–71

Sabol, Andrew J. 134
Saintsbury, George 9–10, 21
Scarborough, Victoria 68
Schafer, Elizabeth 67
Schoenbaum, Samuel 24–5, 149–50, 153, 172
Scott, Thomas 113
Scott, Sir Walter 7–8
seduction/rape 36, 49, 63, 65–6, 66–7, 84–9, 151–2, 179
senses 12, 121–38
  hearing 12, 122–3, 128–36
  seeing 12, 122–8, 133–6
  smell 122
  taste 121–2
  touch 122
set design 61, 62, 64, 66, 69, 71
setting
  genre and 148–9
  Italian setting 91–2, 177–8
Shakespeare, William 10, 21, 31, 43, 44, 150
  Hamlet 44, 45, 139
  A Midsummer Night's Dream 70
  Romeo and Juliet 32, 173
  Twelfth Night 126–7
  The Winter's Tale 126
Shand, G.B. 35, 82, 176, 177
Shelley, Mary 2
Shiells, Robert 5–6
Sidney, Sir Philip 140, 141–2
sight/seeing 12, 122–8, 133–6
Simpson, Wallis (later Duchess of Windsor) 73–4
Sinfield, Alan 62–3
smell, sense of 122
Smith, Henry 175
Smith, Peter 66, 67
sodomy 115–16
songs 130–1, 133, 136
soul 107–9, 110
Spens, Janet 22
Spivack, Charlotte 37
Stachniewski, John 82
stagecraft 35, 175–7
  stage culture, early modern 43–5
  stage properties 177
Steen, Sara Jayne 18
Stilling, Roger 31

Strauss, Jennifer 34
Streete, Adrian 82–3
Sullivan, Ceri 132
Swetnam, Joseph 178–9
Swinburne, Algernon Charles 1, 8–9, 13, 20, 128
Symons, Arthur 22

taste, sense of 121–2
Taylor, Gary 1, 3, 12, 78, 128, 134, 173, 179–80
Taylor, John 4
Taylor, Neil 34–5, 36
Taylor, Paul 69
Tennyson, Alfred, Lord 103
text
  learning and teaching resources 172–5
  and performance 44–5
theatrical productions 55–6, 59–76, 174
Thirty Nine Articles 82
Thirty Years War 112, 116
Tom Tell-Troath 114
Tompkins, Thomas 129
Tomlinson, T.B. 27
touch, sense of 122
tragedy 142, 149–53
Trick to Catch the Old One, A (Middleton) 140, 150
Tricomi, Albert H. 36–7
Trollope, Anthony 19
Twelfth Night (Shakespeare) 126–7
twentieth-century critical response 21–38
  1900–45 21–4
  1945–60 24–6
  1960–70 26–9
  1970–80 29–33
  1980–85 33–5
  1985–95 35–8
Tyacke, Nicholas 81–2
Tynan, Kenneth 60
Tyndale, William 109, 114
tyranny 106–11, 114–16

Veronese, Paulo, *Giustiniana Barbara and Nurse* 176
Villiers, George, Duke of Buckingham 91, 114–15
Volpone (Jonson) 151

Walter, Harriet 73
Ward, Adolphus William 19–20
Ward, John 129
Wardle, Irving 60–1, 65
Webster, John 13
Weimann, Robert 11, 44–5, 45–6, 54
Wells, Henry W. 23–4
Whately, William 98, 99, 100, 104, 158–9, 167

Wigler, Stephen 34
Williamson, Nicol 60
Wilson, Arthur 117
Wilton, Penelope 69–70
Winstanley, William 5

Winter's Tale, The (Shakespeare) 126
Wordsworth, William 2
Wymer, Rowland 35

Yachnin, Paul 84

www.ingramcontent.com/pod-product-compliance
Lightning Source LLC
Chambersburg PA
CBHW061444300426
44114CB00014B/1825